PENGUIN BOOKS

OPEN ICE: THE TIM HORTON STORY

Douglas Hunter is a freelance writer, editor and graphic designer. He is the author of two books on yacht racing, *Against the Odds* and *Trials* (with co-author Jeff Boyd), as well as *A Breed Apart: An Illustrated History of Goaltending*. He lives in Burlington, Ontario with his wife Debbie and their three children.

OPEN ICE

THE
TIM HORTON STORY

DOUGLAS HUNTER

Penguin Books

PENGUIN BOOKS
Published by the Penguin Group
Penguin Books Canada Ltd, 10 Alcorn Avenue, Toronto,
Ontario, Canada M4V 3B2
Penguin Books Ltd, 27 Wrights Lane, London W8 5TZ, England
Penguin Books USA Inc., 375 Hudson Street, New York,
New York 10014, U.S.A.
Penguin Books Australia Ltd, Ringwood, Victoria, Australia
Penguin Books (NZ) Ltd, 182-190 Wairau Road, Auckland 10,
New Zealand

Penguin Books Ltd, Registered Offices: Harmondsworth,
Middlesex, England

First published in Viking by Penguin Books Canada Limited,
1994

Published in Penguin Books, 1995

10 9 8 7 6 5 4 3 2 1

Copyright © Douglas Hunter, 1994
All rights reserved

Manufactured in Canada

Canadian Cataloguing in Publication Data

Hunter, Doug, 1959-
    Open ice

ISBN 0-14-023511-6

1. Horton, Tim, 1930-1974. 2. Hockey players - Canada -
Biography. 3. Businessmen - Canada - Biography. I. Title.
GV848.5.H67H8 1995   796.962'092   C94-931417-X

For my father, who came along for the ride.

"There is comfort in certainty.
It is simpler to sound off than it
is to find out."

Harry Evans

Acknowledgments

I would like to acknowledge the co-operation of the following people (in alphabetical order) who were interviewed for this work: Andy Barbe, Bob Baun, Jean Beliveau, Sam Bettio, Johnny Bower, Spencer Brown, Dr. John Butsch, Ted Carlton, Charlie Cerre, Jim Charade, George Collins, Pete Conacher, Joe Crozier, Brian Cullen, Bob Davidson, Dave Dryden, Dick Duff, Bill Gadsby, Cal Gardner, Russ Gioffrey, Dennis Griggs, Rev. Gordon Griggs, Anne Hannigan, Mark Hannigan, Pat Hannigan, Father Ray Hannigan, Billy Harris, Bob Hassard, Gord Heale, Larry Hillman, Gerry Horton, Jeri-Lynn Horton, Lori Horton, Traci Horton, Ron Hurst, Ron Joyce, Larry Keenan, Stan Kemp, Ted Kennedy, Dave Keon, Seymour Knox III, Leo Labine, Dan Lewicki, Frank Mahovlich, Frank Mathers, Red McCarthy, Gus Mortson, Bob Nevin, Brian O'Neill, Sam Pollock, Hughie Phillips, Jim Primeau, Joe Primeau, Jr., Don Rope, Mel Rothwell, Phil Samis, Jim Schoenfeld, Cathy Siekierko, Ed Siekierko, Tod Sloan, Dr. Hugh Smythe, Allan Stanley, Frank Sullivan, Paul Terbenche, Ray Timgren, Jerry Toppazzini, Zellio Toppazzini, Dick Trainor and Harry Watson.

Unfortunately, a number of people who were vital figures in Tim Horton's life—people such as Jim Dewey, Gentleman Joe Primeau, Gord

Hannigan, Punch Imlach, Pete Backor, Stafford Smythe, Harold Ballard, and Ken Gariepy—are no longer among us to lend their own perspectives, but I feel fortunate to have received such broad co-operation in this project from those who were available. It was a particular privilege to meet and interview Tim's only sibling, his brother Gerry, a matter of weeks before his untimely death. Gerry contributed immeasurably to my understanding of the family history and Tim's early days, and I regret that I will never be able to thank him personally for his contribution.

A special note of thanks is due to Father William O'Brien of St. Michael's College School for his tireless and prompt assistance and his provision of generous access to the school archives. For pointing me in the right direction and toward the right people, I thank Larry Playfair of the Buffalo Sabres, Father Les Costello, Larry Rubic, Jack Riley, John McCormack and Larry Regan, as well as Bob Baun. For their assistance in reviewing Leaf game films of the 1960s, I thank Carl Creighton and Murray McDonald at CBC Sports; I am similarly indebted to numerous staff members at the National Film Board in Montreal for helping me unearth vintage hockey footage from the NFB vaults; and to the archivists at the Ontario Public Archives for their assistance with the Conn Smythe Papers and other resources that they were good enough to reveal to me. Sam Bettio went above and beyond the call of duty in chauffeuring me around greater Sudbury, taking me home for dinner and providing me with a wealth of primary material from his basement archives, which included the exceedingly rare "Red Book" statistical records of the American Hockey

League for 47/48, 48/49 and 51/52, and a pristine copy of *Hendy's 1950 Official Who's Who in Hockey*. Jeff Davis and Craig Campbell at the Hockey Hall of Fame archives provided terrific help, in person and over the phone, and Helen Schoeder of the American Hockey League faithfully tracked down individual player records and shipped them my way via fax.

Particular thanks must be extended to Lori Horton and Ron Joyce, who granted repeated interviews and were willing to explore with me more than the basic facts. Ron Joyce was particularly helpful in pointing me toward people other than himself who were critical in Tim Horton's first forays into business, and deserves high marks (as does Jim Charade) for allowing introspection to be part of the research agenda. Lori Horton was bracingly forthcoming about her life with Tim. Her own life has seen more than its share of troubles, as the public has come to know. She is a smart, very likable lady, and anyone who spends time with her can understand the relief expressed by friends and relatives that she has been so forthrightly in charge of her life in recent years. I am grateful to have had the opportunity to explore the world of her late husband with her. In addition, Tim and Lori's eldest daughter, Jeri-Lynn, brought a welcome perspective to my understanding of her father's public and private lives.

Additional thanks go to the former teammates of Tim Horton who put in the right word for me when it was needed and opened doors that otherwise would have remained closed. They know who they are, even if I don't.

A number of books and publications were turned

to in the course of writing this book. The early history of northern Ontario drew upon *Ontario Since 1867* (Ontario Historical Studies Series) by Joseph Schull; *The Cochrane Northland Post: The Story of the Town of Cochrane*, by Alice Marwick; *History of Clute, Cochrane Districts* (Tweedsmuir Histories); *Arrow North: The Story of Temiskaming*, by Brigadier General George Cassidy; *The Town That Stands On Gold*, by Michael Barnes; *L'Abitibi, Pays de l'Or*, by Emile Benoist; and *L'Abitibi, d'autrefois d'hier et d'aujour-d'hui*, by Pierre Trudelle.

For a basic record of Tim Horton's Sudbury days, I followed the reportage of the *Sudbury Daily Star.* George Grace, sports editor at the time, wrote with great insight on amateur sport and its relationship to the professional game, and deserves to be better known for it. Books useful in filling in the Nickel Belt's history were *At the End of the Shift: Mines and Single Industry Towns in Northern Ontario*, edited by Matt Bray and Ashley Thomson; *Sudbury Basin: The Story of Nickel*, by Donat Marc Le Bourdais; and *Sudbury: Rail Town to Regional Capital*, edited by C.M. Wallace and Ashley Thomson.

On the hockey front, in addition to periodical publications cited in the work, I have culled information from (or made comment upon) the following: *Hockey Night in Canada*, by Foster Hewitt; Conn Smythe's autobiography, *If You Can't Beat 'Em in the Alley* (with Scott Young); Punch Imlach's autobiographies, *Hockey Is a Battle* and *Heaven and Hell in the NHL* (both with Scott Young); *The Glory Years*, by Billy Harris; *The Defense Never Rests*, by Bruce Dowbiggin; King Clancy's autobiography, *The King's Story* (as told to Brian McFarlane); *Net Worth*, by David Cruise and Alison Griffiths; *The Stanley Cup,* by D'Arcy Jenish; and *Inside Maple Leaf Gardens: The Rise and Fall of the Toronto Maple Leafs,* by William Houston. Contemporary accounts of events and issues were provided by daily newspapers and articles in Toronto Maple Leaf programs. For player records and basic histories of the game, I have relied upon the *NHL Official Guide & Record Book; The Complete Encyclopedia of Hockey,* edited by Zander Hollander; and the *American Hockey League Official Guide and Record Book;* as well as the treasure trove loaned to me by Sam Bettio, the archival records of the Hockey Hall of Fame and the facts-by-fax service of the AHL's Helen Schoeder.

I must thank Cynthia Good of Penguin for giving this book a green light based on my rather flimsy proposal. Two supportive editors made the project actually bear fruit. Meg Masters has been a tireless champion of my work, and deftly steered this book through the conceptual stage. Barb Berson rolled up her shirtsleeves and helped shape a story that was at times overwhelming in its sheer mass of raw material.

Finally, my thanks are extended to The Tragically Hip for "Fifty Mission Cap," a great song that kept me company on many long and empty roads.

Introduction

He is a logo now, a maroon signature, and there is a subtle importance in the way his name is written on the signage. On most shops it is Tim Hortons, plural, not Tim Horton's, possessive. The chain is not his, nor is it of him. "Tim Horton" is a thing of seemingly endless replication, a coffee-and-donut phenomenon moving into sandwiches and soups, a brand name bearing no more subtext than McDonald's or Arby's or Harvey's.

It is not ignorance or indifference that makes Tim Horton a trivia item in the restaurants that bear his name. His memory is respected within the organization that now has more than 1,000 franchises, and counting. The franchisees vigorously support four summer camps for underprivileged children under the auspices of the non-profit Tim Horton Children's Foundation. Many franchisees and head office staff, including owner Ron Joyce, who was Horton's partner, can claim to have known him personally.

But while old friends and associates maintain that the restaurant chain could not have reached the heights it has without a figure of popularity and integrity like Tim Horton having been its original focal point, his affiliation with the business as it stands today is more a quirk of history than a logical correlation. There were thirty-five Tim Hortons

Donuts restaurants when Horton was killed in a single-vehicle car crash on February 21, 1974. The business, formally incorporated as Tim Donut Ltd. in 1965, was less than a decade old, and Horton, at age forty-four, was still playing in the National Hockey League eight months of the year. In the two decades that have followed his death, the business has expanded more than thirtyfold, with no growth horizon in sight. Tim has been gone too long now for his personal reputation to convince people to buy the coffee, or desire a franchise. It may have his name as signage, but the business has acquired its own momentum.

The success of the chain has not come without controversy. In 1987, Tim Horton's widow Lori sued Joyce, his numbered company, Tim Donut Ltd., and her lawyer at the time of the sale, Jim Blaney, claiming that she had been improperly counselled by Blaney, and taken advantage of by Joyce when she sold her inherited half of the company to Joyce in December, 1975 for a million dollars and the company car she was driving, a Cadillac. She wanted her piece of the company back, or $10 million. Lori's quest to turn back the clock reached judgment day on February 1, 1993, when Justice Patricia German of the Ontario Court of Justice handed down her ruling, in favour of the defendants. Lori began preparing an appeal, but soon decided to drop the portion of her action against Blaney, concentrating on Joyce alone. On March 9, 1995, Lori again got her day in court. It was brief in the extreme as the three appeal court judges quickly dismissed her case, describing Justice German's factual findings as "careful and detailed," and that the grounds of appeal were without merit.

Lori soon moved to wield the last weapon at her disposal. She wanted the portrait of her late husband by Canadian artist Ken Danby taken down from the restaurant walls. She had originally given her permission for the painting to be made as a poster supporting the children's camps, but she had come to view the camps as more of a promotional tool for the chain than as a charitable extension of the good works of her late husband. And his legacy, she maintained, was enshrined in the Hockey Hall of Fame, not in a restaurant chain. Maintaining that it didn't legally require Lori's permission to display Horton's image, Tim Donut Ltd., nevertheless acquiesced. When the pictures came down, the final tangible link between the restaurants and the man who had given them his name was symbolically broken.

If it were within his means, Horton probably would have marched into every restaurant himself and yanked the pictures—which carried the label "The Legend"—from the wall. The act would have had nothing to do with whether or not the painting looked like him or whether it was promoting camps or coffee sales. Tim Horton simply never liked his own likeness. There was a corner in his house where he displayed trophies and photos, but the photos were always of himself with another teammate, never of himself alone. Lori once made the mistake of having a photo of him framed and hung. When she came downstairs the next morning, she found it smashed on the floor, and Tim in the basement rec room, sourly nursing a drink. He had scrawled across the back of the picture, *What do you know?*

What do we know? We know much, sometimes too much, about Lori. The original trial for her suits was a nasty affair, anchored as it was in Lori's fundamental argument that she was mentally incompetent at the time of the sale of her half of the chain. To make her case, Lori and the witnesses her defense called had to table her medical records and expose her as a former drug addict who for fifteen years was allegedly incapable of making a sensible financial decision. She also had to deal with the legal novelty that she was incompetent no longer— in case law precedents, the plaintiff entered a state of incompetence and generally stayed there. To thwart the suit, the defendants built a countercase of reckless spending on Lori's behalf in the years following the sale, a scenario of fiscal irresponsibility, independent of any alleged incompetence, which led her to file suit only after all the money had run out and she had sold such assets as the family home in Toronto and the cottage in the Lake of Bays region.

A longstanding friend of the Hortons, observing the traumatic turn for the worse Lori's life took after Tim's death, voices the opinion that Tim "would never have let this happen to Lori." But exactly what Tim would or would not have let happen could be answered any number of ways, and every one of those answers, no matter how contradictory, could be delivered with the firm conviction that it was the right thing, and it would be the right thing because it was Tim Horton who did it. Remarkable for a suit of this nature, Tim Horton's reputation or behaviour was never a factor in its proceedings. He was, ultimately, above it all; removed from it by virtue of his death, but also by virtue of his character. He is a person with whom people readily seek alliance: it is important to them that in the final analysis they are seen to be on Tim Horton's side of the equation, and that he be seen on theirs. There is an unwavering constancy in people's admiration for him. He is someone about whom people want to be able to say: I was his friend. Larry Hillman, who was his friend as well as a teammate, avows: "Nobody was perfect, but he was 99.9 per cent pure. You *had* to like him."

To the people who knew him, Tim Horton remains a profoundly affective presence, a person whose memory can still evince tears. To the public, he is little more than a trademark, a synonym for a double-double and a cruller to go, and an error-ridden footnote in a clash between a widow and her late husband's former business partner. Yet he is also that compellingly complex individual holed up in his basement after smashing his own image like some false idol, chafing at any effort to transform him from a person into a persona. Determined to the end to be nothing more than an ordinary man, he could not insulate himself from the consequences of his own extraordinary life. He is, finally, the story that begs to be told.

Chapter 1

Natural Resources

In Ontario at the turn of the century, the threshold of the north was described by the rolling stock of the Canadian Pacific's Canada Central Line of 1881. It stretched from Mattawa, the lumber town on the Ottawa River that predated the coming of the train, westward to North Bay, over Lake Nipissing to Sudbury, and (by 1888) along the north shore of Georgian Bay's North Channel through Espanola, Massey, Algoma Mills, Thessalon and Bruce Mines, until Sault Ste. Marie was reached and Lake Superior sprawled. Above that line of steel rail was Ontario's *terra incognita*, a bald geographic fact that beckoned with no particular promise other than its vast, vague potential.

When George Ross was elected Premier in 1899, he was in need of initiatives. He later wrote that "the only striking policy offering itself was the development of the district between the CPR and Hudson Bay." The summer of his first year in office, Ross sent forth ten large survey parties to see what was up there, north of North Bay.

To no one's surprise, they found farmers around Lake Temiskaming, the headwaters of the Ottawa River, but they also found a big chunk of arable land, a million acres in all, to the west and northwest of the lake. This clay belt would be the perfect spot for veterans of the South African War, who had

received 160-acre land grants and were interested in
settling up there. And so, on May 12, 1902, the first
sod for the new Temiskaming and Northern
Ontario Railway was turned at Trout Lake, east of
North Bay.

The plan was to push ahead to Lake
Temiskaming, and to proceed from there as time
and money allowed. The federal government was
working on a plan to run an east-west line above the
Canadian Pacific trans-Canada line, a co-operative
effort between the Grand Trunk Pacific and the
Canadian National Railway to be called the National
Transcontinental. The TNO[1] would meet up with
this line somewhere north of Iroquois Falls, in the
heart of the clay belt.

Following groundbreaking at Trout Lake, the
TNO forged about eighty miles northward and
reached the far end of Lake Temiskaming by the
end of 1904, in the process triggering the first of
what would be several mining booms when silver was
discovered. All the way up to the new transcontinental line, the TNO set off boom towns primed with
lumber, silver and gold like firecrackers tied along a
single fuse. And these boom towns, without exception, produced a natural resource of their own: professional hockey players.

There is a splendid photograph of the 1963
Stanley Cup champions, of nineteen Maple Leafs
(Ed Litzenberger is not present) in jackets, dress
shirts, slacks and spit-and-polished shoes, sitting on
or leaning against the boards of Maple Leaf
Gardens. They are a mix of veterans and emerging
stars, Dave Keon (rookie season 60/61) next to Red
Kelly (47/48). Tim Horton, wearing glasses so thick
his eyes aren't discernible, is perched on the

boards, sixth from right, between Kelly and Frank Mahovlich.

Of the team's twenty players, eleven were born and raised in the natural resources belt that stretches across northern Ontario and into Quebec, between about latitudes 46 and 50, longitudes 79 and 82. Between 1926 and the opening years of the Second World War, the north had sired this remarkable crop of talent, in dots-on-the-map mining, forestry and railway towns, and they had come to represent Toronto in the National Hockey League in numbers out of all proportion to their hometown populations. The Toronto area, by comparison, had given the Leafs only four players in that photo— Billy Harris, Carl Brewer and Bob Baun[2] (Toronto), and Bob Pulford (Newton Robinson)—with a fifth and sixth, Don Simmons (Port Colborne) and Red Kelly (Simcoe), born along southern Ontario's Lake Erie shore. The three remaining players— Johnny Bower, Ed Litzenberger and Ron Stewart— were westerners.

Three of the northern Ontario players were from the Sudbury area. Eddie Shack was from Sudbury proper, while Jim Pappin was from the Inco company town of Copper Cliff. George Armstrong was born in Bowland's Bay, a hamlet carved out of the sand cliffs on the shore of Lake Wanapitei, just down the road from the Falconbridge company town of Skead.

The Leafs held their training camp up north in Sudbury in 1956 and 1957, but by Leaf roster standards the mining centre was far from "north." Eight of the eleven northerners on the 62/63 team were favourite sons of the towns arranged along an axis reaching halfway from North Bay to James Bay.

These towns—virtually all northern Ontario towns, 85 per cent of which were founded between 1880 and 1920—owed their existence to the railway, and in their case the railway was the TNO.

The birthplace of the Leafs' rookie defenceman Kent Douglas was Haileybury, the centre of activity for the Temiskaming region, which included the towns of New Liskeard and Cobalt (altogether known as Tri-Town). The silver boom before the First World War made the Temiskaming region a wild capitalist frontier, with all the diversionary amenities that entailed.

When Babe Pratt, Billy Taylor and Don Gallinger scandalized the NHL by gambling on games in the late 1940s, they were only being true to the roots of the sport and the league. Hockey was huge in Temiskaming before the First World War because wagering was huge. There were teams in Cobalt, New Liskeard and Haileybury playing in the Temiskaming League that encouraged shameless ringers brought in by rail and outrageous wagering that topped $4,000. As Brigadier General George Cassidy relates in *Arrow North: The Story of Temiskaming*, "Special trains would start from Englehart, taking on bettors, money and liquor in accumulating quantity, and arrive for a fateful meeting between, say, Haileybury and Cobalt. By night's end one town would be poorer by literally thousands of dollars."[3]

Fifty-five miles north of Tri-Town on the TNO is the whistle-stop of Swastika. Gold was discovered just east of here, at Kirkland Lake, in 1911, and by 1938, at the peak of gold production, seven major mines employing more than 4,000 miners were producing 30 million ounces annually along the vein known as the Mile of Gold. In the 1930s and 1940s, one future NHLer after another, nearly all quality players who would enjoy long careers, was born in Kirkland Lake, including the 62/63 Maple Leafs Dick Duff and Larry Hillman.

About fifty-five miles east of Kirkland Lake, just across the Ontario–Quebec border, a search for copper came up with gold at Rouyn, which soon became the fiefdom of resources giant Noranda. It took until 1927 for the TNO to throw off a spur line to Noranda, as Quebec politicians didn't like the idea of an Ontario railroad (even though Toronto money was behind the mines) linking the town with the rest of the world. This was the launching point for Dave Keon, Maple Leaf star and rookie sensation of 60/61.

Fifty-five miles up the track from Kirkland Lake, the TNO threw off another spur line at Porquis Junction; twenty-five miles southwest this spur met the gold-mining bonanza of 1911 that made one Noah Timmins a wealthy man. More important to the future of professional hockey, the bonanza also made a wealthy man of J.P. Bickell. With the profits from the McIntyre and Dome mines, Bickell would become a shareholder in the St. Patricks, Toronto's franchise in the fledgling National Hockey League.

Greater Timmins, known as the Porcupine, has been one of the NHL's steadiest sources of players. It provided the 62/63 Maple Leafs with Tim Horton's veteran defence partner, Allan Stanley, its celebrated new scorer, Frank Mahovlich, and its young right-winger, Bob Nevin, in his third full season with the team. Nevin was from the Timmins mining centre of South Porcupine, once the highest-yield gold operation in the province. Just down the road is

Schumacher, home to the McIntyre Arena, built by
J.P. Bickell, ground zero of the Porcupine League,
the Gold Belt League, and any other local hockey
enterprise one cares to name. It was one of those
rare places in Canada that could boast an artificial
ice rink in the days after the Second World War.

Timmins and its mining centres encapsulated the
full breadth of the northern Ontario hockey dream.
Two dozen Timmins natives born between 1904 and
1946 played in the NHL, but more than half had
league careers of thirty-three games or less. They
were players who couldn't quite avoid the final cut,
whose careers were cut short by injury, or who were
platooned in from the minors to fill in for injured
players and then dispatched back to the profession's second tier—or, as Timmins' Bill Barilko put
it, back to the arena with the leaky roof. For countless others, hockey put bread on the table exclusively through tier-two professional leagues and the
grey-area amateurism of mine leagues and Senior
leagues near and far, where payment might come in
the form of a guaranteed job in the neighbourhood
mine or a discreet fold of bills.

These brief NHL careers were testament to the
realities of hockey as a profession. Opportunities to
play at the game's highest level were minimal. With
a six-team circuit, only about a hundred steady NHL
jobs were available, and talents who today would
have no trouble playing with one of the NHL's two-
dozen plus teams had to be satisfied with careers
just beyond the limelight. Timmins' climate of
hockey riches and rags seems a perfect starting
place for Bill Barilko, the bruising defenceman who
cracked the Leaf lineup in 1947. His career
appeared overwhelmingly charmed: in five seasons

he had his name stamped on the Stanley Cup four times, the last time after scoring the overtime goal in the deciding fifth game. And after scoring that goal, he boarded a floatplane in Timmins, headed north for a fishing trip, and was never seen alive again. Barilko's death was certainly a tragedy—the Leafs retired his number—but it was also a job opportunity. As it turned out, one of the players pegged to fill his skates was from a town just up the TNO line.

It took six years for the TNO to make the link with the National Transcontinental line, twenty-five miles north of Porquis Junction. A settlement sprang up, called Cochrane, which was incorporated as a town in 1910. It became the marshalling point for the continuing construction of the transcontinental line, with work crews dispatched east and west from the TNO terminus for the next three years.

Even with the subsequent rail extension to Moosonee (known to modern tourists as the Polar Bear Express), Cochrane remains one of the province's northernmost communities. Tim Horton was born here on January 12, 1930.

In the years following the founding of Cochrane, there was much enthusiasm for the future of the north, dubbed New Ontario. The silver boom was well under way at the head of Lake Temiskaming, gold had been discovered in the Porcupine and at Kirkland Lake, agriculture in the clay belt showed great promise and there seemed no end to the region's timber resources. Cochrane in particular was being touted as the future Winnipeg of New Ontario. Not even the great Porcupine Fire of 1911, which burned over 864 square miles of land, killed

seventy-three people and levelled Cochrane, was
capable of damping enthusiasm.

The following March, Cochrane's streets were
still blemished by charred stumps and trees when a
seventeen-year-old Torontonian named Conn
Smythe came to town, bent on homesteading in this
promised land. Smythe lay claim to 150 acres of
bush and water at Lot 13 in Concession 4 of Clute
Township, immediately to the north and west of
Cochrane. Both Conn Smythe's father, editor of the
Toronto World, and S.J. Dempsay, the Crown lands
agent in Cochrane, were Protestants from County
Antrim in Northern Ireland. Whether young Conn
and Mr. Dempsay had occasion to reflect on this
coincidence isn't known.

How Smythe foresaw making his fortune he never
did explain. His homesteading adventure appears in
his memoirs as little more than a few paragraphs of
youthful wanderlust, adolescent defiance of
parental authority, and character building. He had
gone as far past the new gold fields as one could in
the spring of 1912 without leaving the service of the
railway. If he had fancied himself a farmer, he had
chosen an odd site. The main settlement pattern in
Clute Township followed the east side of Frederick
House River, where there was rich, well-drained
land, and the pattern anticipated the extension of
the TNO north to Moosonee and the construction
of the north–south Boundary Road. Smythe, by
comparison, had chosen a lot deeply veined by the
Frederick House and two of its tributaries, a good
eight miles from what would be Boundary Road.

But the lot was in one respect a prized site. It was
a very short walk north of Frederick station, the first
stop west of Cochrane on the new transcontinental

line, about ten miles from town. It was, in fact, the
first lot available north of the lot that would
become the settlement of Frederick House. Perhaps
he saw himself enjoying the outdoor pursuits of
hunting and fishing while working for the railway,
because the following summer he was employed by
the CNR as a timekeeper during the construction of
Toronto's Brock Avenue rail underpass.

He cleared his land and built his cabin, then
went back home to Toronto that summer to visit
family. In his absence, he would write, fire tore
through his homestead, destroying what he had
accomplished. Conn Smythe decided the pioneer
life was not, after all, for him. A fire was possible—
fires were used, sometimes recklessly, to clear
land—but not necessarily probable. Perhaps his
ambition died clearing bush in a cloud of black
flies, but if it did die, it must not have succumbed
easily. Smythe had an iron will and a ramrod fearlessness, and was by nature a gambler, but he knew
better than to play long odds with his own life
where king and country were not in peril. He
missed the city, and headed for the University of
Toronto, as his father had prescribed, in pursuit of
a civil engineering degree. The following spring he
found a carpenter's son willing to buy his stake, and
later that summer, he contended, fire again swept
through the area, killing the new homesteader.
Smythe wrote that the man boiled to death in a
small stream.

Fire absolved Conn Smythe; fire was an absolute
judgment, as firm as the hand of God. More a
rebuttal than a punishment, it released him from
failure. The earth had been scorched, not once, but
twice, and that was an irrefutable statement that did

not warrant repeating. Conn Smythe had gone to the extreme of the new north, and had been beaten back by smoke and flame.

Yet Smythe's own diary casts doubt on his tale. It says nothing about fires, fatal or otherwise. It does relate that on August 31, he departed for Cochrane again, on a trip that surfaces briefly in his memoirs. Accompanied by his school pal Harvey "Wreck" Aggett, he headed for the Frederick House and a two-week vacation with his old neighbours before classes started at the University of Toronto. When the vacation was over, he and Aggett arose at 4 a.m. and walked into Cochrane to catch the train home.

Smythe slept all the way to North Bay as the train retraced the TNO's progress through bush and rock and muskeg. Where Smythe retreated, others found toeholds. The moderation in the north's acceptance of newcomers was exquisite: it rejected Smythe, yet accommodated those who would some-day allow him to realize his true fortune. Around Smythe as his train pressed homeward, his percep-tion wrapped in sleep, his very future was igniting.

Fifteen years after failing to establish himself in the province's northern hinterlands, Conn Smythe would lever a purchase of the St. Pats and turn them into the Maple Leafs. Old J.P. Bickell of Timmins would stay on board as a minority share-holder, making Smythe's future, and that of dozens of players who hailed from TNO towns, possible.

"To Mr. and Mrs. A.O. Horton, at the Lady Minto Hospital, on Sunday, January 12, a son." The birth notice for Miles Gilbert "Tim" Horton, who had yet to be named, appeared on page four of the January 17, 1930, edition of Cochrane's *Northland Post*. The lead story on page one related how the Canadiens beat the Wolves 1-0 in Town League hockey action.

When Tim was born, Cochrane was no wild frontier town—at least not any more. There were three lawyers, two physician-surgeons and two dentists. The Eugine Theatre offered the latest Hollywood releases. Cochrane township was counting its agricultural output (22,170 bushels of potatoes, 17,890 tons of hay, 10,174 bushels of oats, 1,600 bushels of turnips, 2,400 bushels of wheat, 150 bushels of barley), its livestock (4,370 horses, 1,700 cattle) and its people (4,800). The CNR was urging residents in its newspaper advertising to visit California and "Let the Summer Last Year Round," but that would have meant no hockey, and the sport was the focal point of town life in the winter.

The Town League featured play by the Canadiens, Wolves and Rails; the Commercial League pitted merchants against TNO and CNR employees and yard office workers; Cochrane was playing Smooth Rock Falls and Kapuskasing in the Mattagami League; and there was even a women's hockey team, on the road to a game in Kapuskasing the week of Tim Horton's birth. The town's open-air rink was next to the rail yard. "A cold southwest wind was blowing," reported the *Northland Post* on a 4-2 victory for Cochrane over Smooth Rock Falls, "and with each puff of the CNR yard engine quantities of cinders deposited themselves on the ice along the south boards."

Naturally Tim came to play the game in earnest. "There wasn't much you could do in Cochrane other than play hockey," says Tim's younger brother Gerry, his only sibling and the last surviving member of the family in 1993.[4] "If you didn't play on the rink, you played on the road."

Like many parents of this era, the Hortons were hardly the stereotypic mom and dad of the modern suburban arena, clutching coffees while screaming at the officials, the coaches, other parents, the players, their own kids. "I don't think my mother or father saw either of us play until we were sixteen, because they were not very adept at standing in five feet of snow in forty below zero," says Gerry. But their Uncle Mel, who was married to their dad's sister, managed the local rink. "He saw Tim play regularly. My dad was down in Sault Ste. Marie all the time."

Even the sketchiest biographies of Tim Horton repeat two truisms: that he was of Irish stock and that his father, Aaron Oakley Horton, better known as "Oak," was a CNR mechanic. The first is half true. His mother, Ethel, Canadian-born, was of Irish ancestry—her maiden name appropriately was "Irish." Tim's father, who is usually considered the Irishman, was also Canadian-born, but of English stock.

The second truism is also a half-truth. Oak Horton never worked for the CNR. While he did work as a railway mechanic, it was not the only thing he did for a living. Although Cochrane was a railway town, it was not work with the railway that brought Oak Horton to Cochrane. Ethel Irish had moved from North Bay, where she was born, to Cochrane with her family in the 1920s. Oak Horton, who had been born near Belleville, came north to Cochrane about the same time looking for work—Cochrane was enjoying a boom with construction of the TNO's extension to Moosonee. His sister Mabel had preceded him, and had married there. Ethel and Oak met and wed, back in Belleville, in 1928, returned to Cochrane, and then came Miles Gilbert.

"His mother told me that she used to crochet while she was pregnant," says Tim's widow, Lori. "She was making little booties and things, and called it Timmy's Trousseau. Then she had toxemia when Tim was born and his father took him to his christening and named him after his two grandfathers, Miles and Gilbert." When Ethel's mother heard "Miles," says Gerry, she wanted nothing to do with it. Although nothing could be done about his christening, she promptly renamed the infant Tim, as Ethel had originally wished. Tim would share his grandmother's disdain for his Christian name; no one ever dared refer to him by it.

Tim's birth fell between two great calamities—one general, one specific. The stock market crash of October 1929, which ushered the world into the Great Depression, had occurred only a few months earlier. And in the fall of 1931, while Conn Smythe was opening his Maple Leaf Gardens, Cochrane was dealt a punishing blow when the CNR decided to reroute its transcontinental service. No longer would it pass through Cochrane on the line that was being built when Conn Smythe dabbled in homesteading. Henceforth, the CNR service would be carried by the Canadian Northern Transcontinental Line, completed in 1914, which ran from Capreol just east of Sudbury northwest to Nakina, some 250 miles west of Cochrane along the National Transcontinental tracks. The route was chosen because it was shorter, and because it was said that the Canadian Northern track was in better shape. In time, the National Transcontinental track west of

Kapuskasing would atrophy; the Algoma Central, running north from the Soo, would service Hearst.

The rerouting made a mockery of the vision of Cochrane as a new Winnipeg, but by then New Ontario itself had long failed to materialise. In 1911, Premier Whitney predicted a population of one million for the province's north; by 1921, when the TNO extension from Cochrane to Moosonee was approved, only about one-quarter of that goal had been reached. Kapuskasing, seventy miles west of Cochrane along the National Transcontinental, was a washout as a bold new agricultural centre. Cochrane, devastated again by fire in 1916, had five local townships set aside for settlement by war veterans the following year, but the town's population stalled at about five thousand. As a veteran, Conn Smythe, ironically, could have been one of those settlers, but he had plainly seen enough of Cochrane. After returning home from the war,[5] he completed his civil engineering degree and entered the contracting business in Toronto.

The cancellation of the transcontinental service deepened the Depression in Cochrane, putting more people out of work and swelling the social assistance rolls. A long and ultimately fruitless dalliance with the potential exploitation of local lignite deposits as locomotive fuel, which dragged on through the Second World War, underscored the town's desperation. Oak found what work he could. There was a stint distributing pop with a beverage company, and spells in the lumber business. Gerry was born in 1933, and when he was about three the family left Cochrane to relocate in the Quebec mining town of Duparquet, twenty miles across the provincial border, and twenty miles north of

Noranda–Rouyn. It was a boom time for mining in the Abitibi region, and for two years, Oak Horton worked at Duparquet's Beattie mine, the largest gold operation in Quebec; in 1937, $2.3 million in ore was removed from the ground by this town of fifteen hundred.

"Duparquet was actually where Tim started playing hockey," says Gerry. "Tim would have been about five when we went over there and about eight when we came back." Coincidentally, Tim's future Leaf teammate Dave Keon would also spend part of his childhood in Duparquet. When the family returned to Cochrane, Oak began work with the provincial highway department. Gerry says a provincial election cost Oak his job as a wave of patronage appointments swept in a new workforce; Gerry thought the job ended in 1938, but if its loss was tied to a change of electoral fortune, it would have to have been in 1943, when premier Mitchell Hepburn's Liberals were defeated.

Oak then turned his attentions to the railway. The Algoma Central, which had taken over the servicing of Hearst from the National Transcontinental, hired him as a mechanic. Unfortunately for the Hortons, the job was based in Sault Ste. Marie. Oak travelled to the Soo, returning home to visit his family every second or third weekend. Finally, in 1945, Oak had had enough; he quit the Algoma Central and signed on with the CPR's Sudbury district. The job would still mean regular travel throughout the district, but he could at least be close to his family. In the summer of 1945, the Hortons, with fifteen-year-old Tim and twelve-year-old Gerry, moved to a two-storey home on McLeod Street in the community of Gatchell, in the southwest section of Sudbury.

Tim would be a full-time resident of Sudbury for only two years, but those years were the most critical of his youth, overshadowing the previous fifteen in Cochrane and Duparquet. His strongest, most lasting friendships were made here, and he would be exposed to some of the finest hockey in northern Ontario.

"The only thing I remember about him playing hockey in Cochrane was that he was probably the best hockey player they ever had," says Gerry, who was a pretty fair hockey player himself.[6] "The last game he played there, his team won 8-1 or 8-3, and he scored all eight goals. At the end of the year they wouldn't give him the Most Valuable Player award because he wouldn't pass the puck. Of course, he didn't really have to."

Although it was assuredly the furthest consideration from the minds of Oak and Ethel Horton, outside of Timmins they could not have picked a better place in northern Ontario than Sudbury for a promising hockey player to come of age in the years immediately following the Second World War. Cochrane was too far off the beaten path to permit Tim's development during his critical Junior years, and he would not have come to the attention of scouts so readily had he stayed at the furthest reaches of the railway.

No one else has ever come out of Cochrane to play in the NHL, although the area did, in its own brief and vivid way, produce Conn Smythe. For professional hockey, Cochrane was truly the end of the TNO line. And for both of these men, Cochrane was a departure point.

Chapter 2

Copper Cliff

Sudbury could not have been more different from Cochrane and still be part of the province's north. The town had more than eight times Cochrane's population. Cochrane was a rail town with failing aspirations to become a new Winnipeg; Sudbury was a rail town that had been overrun by a surrounding mining collosus known as the Nickel Belt. While both places were steeped in the northern enthusiasm for hockey, Sudbury had a far greater heritage in the sport, and the ways and means to produce fresh talent for the professional game.

Tim Horton turned sixteen during his first year in Sudbury, and that put him in the pipeline of aspiring hockey stars hoping to attract the offers of the scouts and talent spotters combing the rosters of northern Ontario teams. All he had to do was get himself on a contending team and make an impression. Those who made such a team found their futures mapped out with startling speed. From their first tryout practice in the fall to the moment a professional scout offered them a form to sign, a matter of months would pass. Their career paths would be on track, and they could only hope that they had affixed their signature to the right form, that somewhere down that track their careers would not derail. Signed at sixteen or seventeen, they could be left by the wayside by twenty. Across the country, there were thousands of boys aspiring to careers in a league that offered about a hundred jobs. A top Junior team would be fortunate to see even one of its players from any given year move on to an NHL career. Very few teams could expect to send even a handful of players from one season to the professional ranks. Against all expectations, the 46/47 Copper Cliff Redmen of the Nickel District league proved to be one of those rare teams. On October 25, 1946, Tim Horton came out for their first practice.

Jim Dewey stood on the ice of Stanley Stadium in the mining town of Copper Cliff, watching two dozen teenagers try to impress him with their hockey skills. He wasn't that impressed. "They didn't look too good," he told a writer from the *Sudbury Daily Star* after that first tryout practice. "There were some good boys on the ice but not enough of them."

As the coach of the Copper Cliff Junior Redmen, the thirty-four-year-old Dewey was facing the discouraging task of trying to repeat the team's success of 45/46. That squad had surprised even themselves by winning the Junior A title of the Northern Ontario Hockey Association, needing only four games to defeat the favoured Porcupine Combines in a best-of-five series. When the Redmen advanced to the all-Ontario Junior A final to decide who would represent the province in the Memorial Cup, the nation's Junior championship, Toronto's St. Michael's College Majors shellacked them 13-2 and 8-1 to sweep the best-of-three series. But then, managing any kind of offence against St. Mike's was something of a moral victory. A key component of the Toronto Maple Leaf farm system, the college was ridiculously powerful as it drew its players from across the country through scholarships paid for by Conn Smythe's Maple Leaf Gardens Ltd. The Majors had won the Memorial Cup in 1945, and it had taken the Winnipeg Monarchs all seven games of the 1946 finals to deny the Majors, whose lineup included future NHL greats Red Kelly and Tod Sloan, a repeat title.

Sloan was a Nickel Belt boy—he had played for the Falconbridge Juniors, and the Sudbury Junior B Macabees of 44/45, coached by Jim Dewey—and was now with the Leafs' American League farm team, the Pittsburgh Hornets. Conn Smythe would shortly pronounce him "the greatest Junior prospect I have ever seen." But Smythe's St. Michael's squad seemed a bottomless cornucopia of quality prospects. He hadn't even bothered to sign Red Kelly, one of his scouts unwisely concluding the kid from southern Ontario's tobacco country wouldn't last twenty games in the National league. And if the Majors of 45/46 were strong, then the 46/47 version were Herculean. They would open their latest campaign in the OHA Junior A circuit on November 3 by beating the Windsor Spitfires 15-0. By mid-December, five St. Mike's players—Fleming MacKell, Ed Sandford, Fran Harrison, Rudy Migay and Les Costello, all of whom would play in the NHL—occupied the top five spots in the OHA scoring race.

Jim Dewey's biggest concern in October wasn't getting past the latest version of the all-powerful Majors in the spring of '47—it was assembling a team that could even hold its head up in local competition. Hockey in the Sudbury area, as in many centres across the country, was just getting back on its feet following the disruption of the Second World War, which had limited resources at home and robbed communities of young men who could either play or organise the competition. It was noted that of some forty kids who were playing Junior B hockey around Sudbury at the beginning of the war, only five were still active locally. (Thirty-two recent graduates of Sudbury High alone had been killed in the war.) Sudbury's Midget "NHL" league for six-teen-and-unders had only been organised the previous season. In the local mining town of Capreol, the rink had burned down in 1943 and still hadn't been replaced. While the Nickel District league used to be capable of icing three or four Junior A teams, for the second season in a row there was only one such team in the league; for the second season in a row, it was the Copper Cliff Redmen.

The Nickel District league officials' choice of the Redmen as the area's lone Junior A team was so obvious as to be beyond the point of debate. Copper Cliff was where the nickel giant Inco had its main mines, smelting operation and headquarters. Although there were fewer than 5,000 people in Copper Cliff (compared to 42,000 in Sudbury and 71,000 in the entire Nickel Belt, according to the 1951 census), its status as the dominant company town gave it a sociocultural weight out of all propor-tion to its size. Most important in hockey matters, Copper Cliff had Stanley Stadium.

The Nickel Belt had at first been touched by the Depression like most of the rest of the country, but in the mid-Thirties, with metals prices rebounding, it experienced its own economic boom, and that boom benefited Copper Cliff above all other communities.

Flush with earnings, Inco had set out to make Copper Cliff a more desirable address than Sudbury, so as to lure employees closer to their jobs, in company-owned homes that gave Inco a prescribed minimum 6 per cent annual return on its investment. Inco built a curling rink, and in 1935 an artificial ice arena, dubbed Stanley Stadium in honour of R.C. Stanley, the company's president and CEO.

Built on a bed of slag in two months at a cost of $41,000, the arena was an extraordinary luxury—Sudbury didn't have one, but neither did North Bay or a lot of other Canadian communities, including Winnipeg. Stanley Stadium wasn't NHL size, but it was enclosed, and heated, with enough seating (and standing room) for about fifteen hundred spectators, and the ice was even resurfaced between periods. Kids playing high-school hockey could not have found a greater contrast than that between Stanley Stadium and the natural outdoor rink in Sudbury at College du Sacré-Coeur, the Jesuit boarding school for French Canadian kids in northern Ontario. Sacré-Coeur—known to anglophone residents as Sacred Heart—was where you kept the game moving because it was fifteen below and the wind was tearing at your face, where the game had to be stopped every five minutes so the ice could be shovelled clean when it was snowing, where the shovelled snow banked against the four-foot-high boards swallowed the puck. The only hardship at Stanley Stadium was that it didn't have a dehumidifier, which meant fog on warmer days. Players were issued blankets and dispatched to skate around with them stretched out to break it up, which in retrospect was good training for playing in places like Hershey and Boston.

Thanks to Stanley Stadium, hockey could be played year-round in this tiny, scorched-earth mining town. There was no waiting for outdoor rinks to freeze, the fate of hockey players in the rest of the Nickel Belt, and much of the rest of the country. Not surprisingly, the Copper Cliff High School Senior hockey team began its 46/47 season as the reigning champion in local scholastic play for eight years running, and had won the 1946 northern Ontario school title by acclamation because nobody was keen to take them on.

The construction of Stanley Stadium also gave rise to the phenomenon of the Midget NHL League, a Copper Cliff invention in 1937 that soon spread throughout the province. Midget-age players—that is, fourteen to sixteen-year-olds—played on teams named after NHL clubs, and champions of local leagues advanced to an all-Ontario final to contest the Calder Cup. But that was not all. The Midget NHL teams had farm systems. The twelve to fourteen-year-olds in Bantam competition played for teams named after Senior teams that had won the Allan Cup, such as the Ottawa Flyers and the Quebec Aces. Below them was yet another level of "farm team": the Minor Bantams, who played on teams named after great Junior teams such as the Oshawa Generals and Copper Cliff's own Redmen. While Midget NHL had been conceived as a way to keep teenagers off the street and out of trouble, it also indoctrinated kids in a hierarchical hockey system, with the NHL as the ultimate goal of every player.

In the Porcupine, hockey organizers facing the same postwar pressures as the Nickel District league

had opted for a pooled Junior team called the
Combines, rather than select one existing team and
allow it all the glory. By choosing the Redmen,
Nickel District league officials automatically made a
prospect from Sudbury like Tim Horton an outsider. He would have to come to Copper Cliff and
prove himself worthy of wearing the celebrated
Redmen uniform. Jim Dewey was the man who,
through the process of sorting through and sizing
up his swirling rink of prospects, could provide Tim
with his first important step toward a professional
career. And if Dewey didn't feel he deserved that
first step, or slotted him into a position that didn't
suit him, there wasn't much Tim could do about it.
The Redmen were the only Junior game in town,
and Tim's parents were hardly sufficiently committed to the idea of their son having a professional
hockey career to up stakes and move to another
community for his benefit.

Being in the position of making—and breaking—budding hockey careers was not something
Dewey particularly relished. His coaching spell with
the Redmen was a rare turn for him, a result of a
sense of community duty. He much preferred to
play the game rather than to organise it, and he was
not one of those former professionals who came to
coach in their home towns and helped feed a fresh
crop of prospects into the system.

Dewey himself had been able to resist the ferocious pull of the NHL felt by the youngsters he
coached. He hadn't been raised in the Nickel Belt:
the only reason he was even there was because the
Nickel Belt was on the Canadian Pacific transcontinental line and because a train he was aboard
stopped there a few days shy of Christmas, 1933. A

student at the University of Saskatchewan, the pride of Moose Jaw was a star centre with the Saskatoon Quakers, who had won the Allan Cup, the national Senior hockey title, in 1933. The Quakers were on their way to Europe to represent Canada at the world championship in Milan when they disembarked at Sudbury to play an exhibition game against a local Junior team, the Sudbury Cub Wolves. The visitors had an easy go of it, winning 4-0.

The Quakers players had found themselves in a town that, by the measure of the day, was thriving, as if isolated in a nurturing greenhouse while the rest of the country was turning into a literal and figurative dustbowl. (Between 1932 and 1938, nickel production at Inco increased eightfold.) They discovered that the Nickel Belt was a fine place for skilled players like themselves, for whom jobs could always be found while they brought honour to Senior clubs in the local mining towns. The Quakers got back on their train, proceeded to Italy, won their world championship and when the train passed through Sudbury that spring on the way back to the hardscrabble prairies, a significant proportion of the team, led by Jim Dewey, as good as defected. They became Nickel Belters, with Inco jobs in Inco towns like Copper Cliff, Frood and Creighton.

With Dewey as his departure point, Harry Towns, the paid athletic director of Frood Mine, began methodically assembling a hockey powerhouse, the Frood Tigers. Scouring the Junior and Senior hockey teams of Canada for recruits, by 1937 Towns at last had a serious contender for the Allan Cup. The Frood Tigers made it to the Senior finals in Calgary: it took all five games for Jim Dewey and the Tigers to overcome the North Battleford Beavers and put the Allan Cup that Dewey had won for Saskatoon four years earlier on the train back to Sudbury. (That same year, the Redmen reached the Memorial Cup finals, but lost.) Harry Towns quit his post of athletic director of Frood Mine, and the following year rode the public delirium over the Tigers victory to a seat on Sudbury city council.

Some "amateurs" didn't stay long in their Inco positions, but others, like Dewey, had recognised employment with Inco as a genuine opportunity, and made careers with the mining giant. Dewey never did complete his university studies. After spending the winter of 40/41 playing hockey in Glace Bay, Nova Scotia, in April 1941 he formally became an Inco employee proper, and was promoted to superintendent of diamond drilling. His interest in athletics did not wane, and Dewey was one of those athletes who mastered virtually any sport he turned his mind to. He'd been a football star at the University of Saskatchewan, and in 1942 was in the backfield of the Sudbury Grads of the Northern Ontario league. He'd also been the men's springboard diving champion of Saskatchewan in 1934; in 1946 he won the event at a regatta on Sudbury's Ramsey Lake. He joined the Copper Cliff Curling Club and skipped and curled on several bonspiel winners. His attention turned to racquet sports, and he became active in badminton and tennis. He also played softball and continued to compete in Senior hockey.

Dewey was assuredly of NHL quality. He is remembered above all as a mesmerising stickhandler, a skill valued by the game during the inter-war years, when offside and passing rules helped shape players who had the finesse to go end-to-end alone.

But in those days unless you were a star, the league
didn't pay any better than you could make in a
good white-collar job, and certainly didn't offer
long-term career opportunities or job security.
While four members of the Frood Tigers of 1937—
Don Grosso, Mel Hill, Murph Chamberlain and
Bingo Kampman—went on to play in the NHL,
Dewey was satisfied with his job at Inco, his home in
the new Inco community of Lively, his wife and four
daughters, and his many sporting diversions.

Meanwhile, the power centres of amateur hockey
in the province continued to shift. Before the war,
northern mining centres like Sudbury, Timmins
and Kirkland Lake had been a talent drain for
southern Ontario, as gifted players headed north to
play profitably for Junior and Senior teams. But the
war, and the repercussions of the Dominion Labour
Relations Act of 1944, had made the northern
teams poorer cousins to the south. The Act had
paved the way for Inco's labour force to be
unionised, and there was nothing in the collective
agreement of the mine, mill and smelter workers
that accommodated jobs being handed out to pseu-
do-amateur athletes. In Junior hockey, the Majors
and the rest of the OHA Junior A reigned supreme
over their northern counterparts. And in the north,
the Porcupine had become the greater force. If a
revival were to come in Nickel District Junior hockey, it would have to come out of Copper Cliff.

In the late forties, Copper Cliff was as bleak a settlement as it ever would be. Inco had improved its
smelting operations throughout the 1930s, but sulphur dioxide fumes continued to scar the landscape—not only in Copper Cliff, but around the
region as well. Donat Marc Le Bourdais, in his 1953

book *Sudbury: The Story of Nickel,* made this grim observation: "The entrance [to Sudbury] from the southeast is through gaunt, bare hills where fire and sulphur have destroyed nearly every vestige of vegetation, leaving the countryside as devoid of living matter as the dark side of the moon, an aspect which only a Dante in his worst moments might envisage." Indeed, during the 1950s, Sudbury Wolves backer Max Silverman was always careful to introduce Wolves recruits from southern Ontario to Sudbury in the dark of night, so as not to have the blasted landscape panic them before they even made it into town.

Copper Cliff was a classic northern company town in that it was completely controlled by the company. Inco picked the mayor and the rest of the town council, routinely elected by acclamation. All were White Anglo-Saxon Protestant: Inco ran the town with policies grounded in ethnic privilege. Only WASPs were eligible for company housing. The rest of the population—about half of it, comprising Italians, Poles, Ukrainians, Finns and French Canadians—lived in homes built on land leased from Inco. Most of them were in the neighbourhood on the wrong side of the Inco railway line, next to the smelter, known as Shantytown, but the Italians, being the largest non-WASP segment with 20 per cent of the population, had their own subsection of Shantytown appropriately known as Little Italy, with streets named Milan, Florence, Venice, Basilio, Pietro, Genoa and Dominico. Much of Copper Cliff life was segregated along ethnic lines, with a notable exception: Stanley Stadium and its sports programs were open to all Inco employees, even those not living in Copper Cliff.

Through that loophole, Little Italy would make its
mark on hockey.

Following the Second World War, the most
promising hockey players in Copper Cliff were three
members of the mining town's Italian community:
Silvio "Sam" Bettio, Zellio Toppazzini and his
younger brother Jerry. Their parents had a long
association. When Sam Bettio's father had first come
to Copper Cliff in 1926 from Treviso, a town north
of Venice, he had boarded with Zellio and Jerry's
mother. After enough of a spell in Copper Cliff to
convince him that there was a future for him in the
Nickel Belt, he returned to Treviso, married and
came back to live and work in Coniston for a year.
Sam was born there on December 1, 1928; within a
year the family relocated to Copper Cliff for good,
and Sam's father found work in the converter building. Zellio Toppazzini was born in 1930, his brother
Jerry in 1931.

The Bettios lived on Florence Street, on the highest section of the dome of rock that was Little Italy.
To the north of the house, in a valley devoid of vegetation, was the tailing line, which carried away
waste from the flotation cells where raw ore was separated from the crushed rock. To the north of the
tailing line was the shaft for Mine 2, better known
as North Mine. The drifts for North Mine reached
under Little Italy; within the Bettio house, workers
could be heard toiling far beneath them.

While he was a teenager during the war, Sam
Bettio found work at Inco during the summer, as
well as on weekends and on holidays. Inco arranged
the job for him because he was playing baseball for
a company-sponsored team. He landed one of the
better jobs the nickel giant could offer: out of

doors, in a gang working the tailing line behind his house. He never worked in the mine that reached beneath his home. He never went down it and never had any desire to do so.

Little Italy was a microcosm of the country that had spawned its population. Different dialects were spoken on different streets, and politics was equally varied. The residents were uniform, however, in their second-class status as citizens, a condition exacerbated by the Second World War, when they were registered as enemy aliens. Sam Bettio can remember days when to get to school he had to fight his way past the English kids who lived in the better part of Copper Cliff.

To an outsider, life in Copper Cliff might have seemed bleak, with its denuded landscape and overtones of Johannesburg North. And today Zellio Toppazzini will acknowledge that the segregation of the town may have been felt more by his parents' generation than his own, particularly during the war. But for a kid from Little Italy fanatical about sports, Copper Cliff was just fine. "We were always playing hockey indoors. It was very nice. Copper Cliff was the nicest place to grow up because we had our own public school, our own high school, all the facilities you wanted there, and it was only a small town of about five thousand. And there was a lot of competition between Sudbury High and Copper Cliff High, Sudbury High and Sudbury Tech." And it was hard to argue with a first-class hospital, a horse-drawn milk wagon, paved streets, and sidewalks that were plowed in the winter, when the company town of Falconbridge to the east of Sudbury had dirt roads and wood-slat sidewalks to keep your feet out of the muck.

Hockey was a sport that they took to readily. After school Bettio and his chums would lace on their skates and walk down the hill behind Bettio's house to the ponds dotting the Inco railway line. To resurface the ice, they would chop a hole in it and let fresh water well up and coat it. And of course they had Stanley Stadium, the Midget NHL and school-league hockey to sate their enthusiasm. By the time Bettio was fifteen, he was playing on five different teams.

As a member of the Copper Cliff team, Bettio had participated in the Ontario Midget NHL tournament for the first time in 1944. Tod Sloan, added from the Falconbridge league, had been part of the team. "It was my first trip to Toronto," says Bettio. "We walked into the Gardens, and we were going, 'Where's the ice?' " At little Stanley Stadium, you came in the door and there it was. At Maple Leaf Gardens, getting in the door was only the beginning. "There wasn't a building this big anywhere, never mind a rink," Bettio had decided. Once you'd found that ice, you never wanted to leave it.

Five players from the championship 45/46 Redmen team came out for that first practice on October 25, 1946. There was Bill Organ, who had been the team's backup goalie, defenceman Ronald "Specs" Telford and forwards Sam Bettio and John "Yacker" Flynn.[1] But Dewey's top line—centre Gordie Heale and wingers Roland "Hickory" Cooney and Stanton "Tatter" McClellan—was no more. Heale was with the Barrie Flyers of the Junior A OHA, a team trying to find respectability by filling ten of fifteen starting positions with talent from the north. Hickory Cooney had tried out with the Detroit Red

Wings, then settled with its farm team, the Galt Red
Wings of the Junior A OHA. Only McClellan was
back from that potent line. Dewey would shortly put
his veterans—McClellan, Bettio and Flynn—together on his top line, which became known as the Kid
Line, in part because they were the older players, in
part because McClellan and Flynn were fairly compact players. Organ got the starting goalie's job.
Dewey had to find at least three new defencemen
and two more forward lines in the crowd of kids
dashing around the Stanley Stadium ice.

Dewey had a tough time putting names to faces
and skills to bodies, but after one practice he'd
identified several promising newcomers—in particular a big, rangy, impressive sixteen-year-old named
George Armstrong. George's mother was part
Ojibway, part French Canadian (his father was of
Irish stock), and George wouldn't be long picking
up the nickname "Chief." Still, there were a couple
more candidates who hadn't turned out that Dewey
said he wanted to see in action: Gord Byers and
Zellio Toppazzini of Copper Cliff and Red
McCarthy of Sudbury.·

Remarkably absent from this list of young nota-
bles is Tim Horton. As a new arrival to Sudbury, in
45/46 he had played defence for Sudbury High
School's junior-level team and for the Holy Trinity
Midget team in Nickel District competition. The
presence of Horton, a churchgoing Protestant, on
the Holy Trinity team wasn't as irregular as it might
seem. Only two Midget teams in Sudbury in 45/46
were playing in the Nickel District league, and the
other one was sponsored by the Catholic Youth
Organization. Either way, Tim was going to be
coached by a priest and surrounded by Catholics.

Holy Trinity had won the 1946 Nickel District Midget championship; Tim had even scored a goal in the deciding game against Falconbridge, whose lineup had included George Armstrong.

But Tim was well out of Dewey's loop. The coach's hockey savvy was limited largely to Copper Cliff—to the players who lived there and the players who had come from other communities to play there. Dewey was keeping an eye out for Red McCarthy, the son of a Sudbury butcher, because back in 44/45 McCarthy had played on Dewey's Sudbury Junior B Macabees, along with Gordie Heale and Yacker Flynn.

Actually, Tim wasn't as far flung as George Armstrong, who came from Skead, in Falconbridge Nickel country on the eastern extreme of the Nickel Belt. Tim lived in Gatchell, halfway between Copper Cliff and Sudbury proper. The Horton household was only a block away from Lorne Street, which connected Copper Cliff and Sudbury, and the electric streetcar service that ran between the two communities made Stanley Stadium a short ride from home. But Tim was beginning only his second season of hockey in the Sudbury area. While he had played high-school hockey, it wasn't considered as serious as the other leagues. And his Holy Trinity team had been overlooked by the 1946 Ontario Midget championship tournament, hosted by Conn Smythe at Maple Leaf Gardens: only teams representing Midget NHL leagues were invited. Tim Horton and the rest of the talented Holy Trinity team had stayed home while local players from Copper Cliff, Sudbury and Falconbridge like Sam Bettio, Zellio Toppazzini, Red McCarthy and George Armstrong had been able to showcase their talents.

Zellio Toppazzini and George Armstrong were the two most promising young recruits as a new Junior Redmen team took shape, and by the time the 46/47 Redmen began practising both players were known to Tim Horton. In September 1946, Tim began his second year at Sudbury High; now in grade 11, he would play on the school's senior hockey team with Armstrong, who had just transferred to Sudbury High from Falconbridge Continuation for grade 11. And Tim knew all about Zellio Toppazzini. In the opening game of the junior interscholastic playoffs in the spring of 1946, Tim had scored once for High; Zellio had responded with five for Copper Cliff as the Cliffs captured both the junior and senior high-school titles. Zellio, now also in grade 11, would play against both Horton and Armstrong in senior high-school competition in 46/47.

The Copper Cliff High senior hockey team proved to be practically a scholastic-league version of the new Junior Redmen. And the Cliff High hockey team, when not forming the core of the Junior Redmen, were starring in the Cliff High football team. (Though called rugby at the time, the game they played was three-down Canadian football.) The boys played sports incessantly. When they weren't playing hockey or football, some of them were playing basketball, or baseball, which was a huge sport in the Nickel Belt area.[2] Sam Bettio, for example, was a devastating hitter. George Armstrong was a good pitcher and an even better hitter, and Red McCarthy was starring on the diamond for Garson. But Zellio Toppazzini and Tim Horton stuck to football as they awaited the start of hockey season. Seven of the boys who would become Redmen hockey players that fall were also on the Copper Cliff Senior football team, but Copper Cliff wasn't as strong on the gridiron as it was on the rink. Its standout player was Bettio, a triple threat who could run, pass and kick. He was good enough to attract a scholarship offer in football from St. Michael's College, arranged for him by Copper Cliff's Father O'Leary, but Bettio turned it down, eager to put his education behind him with minimal fuss and get on with being a hockey star. In the final game of the 1946 football season, on October 17, Tim Horton's Sudbury High beat Sam Bettio's Copper Cliff High 15-0, then lost a wild championship game 13-12 to Tech in the near-dark on October 23. Two days later, the bats and balls and cleats were put away and the skates and sticks and pucks unpacked: tryouts for the Junior Redmen hockey team began at Stanley Stadium, and so did Jim Dewey's task of shaping a winning team.

Red McCarthy had decided not to try out for the 46/47 Redmen; as a sixteen-year-old McCarthy felt he would be out of his league. But Jim Dewey, McCarthy recalls, asked Tim where Red was, and encouraged him to get Red to come and try out. Despite the fact that Dewey passed no judgment on Tim in the press, from the first practice, it would seem, Dewey knew who Tim Horton was. Tim had not wasted time making an impression. Sam Bettio agrees that Tim's reputation, despite his play in high school and in Nickel District Midget competition, did not precede him, but that he made up for it in person. "Tim," says Bettio, "came out of nowhere. All of a sudden, it was: Who the hell's this guy? He didn't live in Copper Cliff, and most of the guys on our team were from Copper Cliff."

By then, Red McCarthy had formed a very firm opinion of Tim. They had known each other for a year, having met on the playing field of Sudbury High the previous September, when tryouts were held for the school's junior football team. Both were starting grade 10, and Tim was brand new to Sudbury. It was everybody's first year at Sudbury High, because in grade 9 students were required to attend Sudbury Tech next door, before choosing their particular educational stream. Because Tim had been in Cochrane in grade 9, he was even more of an unknown to the kids who had been together at Tech.

They lined up in practice. "There's this guy across from me I don't know at all, that none of the guys knew," says McCarthy. "He didn't look big and I thought, no problem. But he was so strong. He ran all over me for the first couple practices. I made sure I moved to another position so I wouldn't be opposite him from then on. I think he could have ended up being a great halfback somewhere."

Dick Trainor was another fifteen-year-old who encountered Tim for the first time on a football field in the fall of 1945. "I will never forget Tim. I don't think he'd ever played organised football before. He was wearing a pair of Oxfords during the game where the rest of us had full equipment, and he was still probably the best football player on the field."

In addition to football, Trainor, McCarthy and Horton had all played hockey together that first year at Sudbury High. Red and Dick had also played in the Sudbury Midget NHL league and attended the Midget tournament at Maple Leaf Gardens together. Trainor notes that there were "always some sour grapes because the better team [Holy Trinity] didn't get to the tournament in Toronto. Holy Trinity had an exceptionally talented hockey team, and there's no doubt in my mind that the quality of the Nickel District league and of Holy Trinity itself was much higher than the Midget NHL. I know Tim was a star hockey player with them. He was a star hockey player on every team he ever played on."

McCarthy and Trainor, along with anybody else encountering Tim Horton for the first time, marvelled at his strength, which was only made more remarkable by his modest dimensions. "He was very athletic and very muscular," says Trainor. "Those were days when hockey players did not stress weight training, but Tim had his own way of muscle building. He had chin-up bars in his basement. He could do hundreds without stopping, pushups with one hand...He was probably the strongest kid in the neighbourhood and one of the strongest kids in high school. We used to wrestle with him. Two of us could not hold him down."

Tim was not a case of a ninety-eight-pound weakling turning himself into a daunting physical specimen. "Even when we were living in Cochrane, before he was fifteen, he was always muscular," says his brother Gerry, who feels Tim's conditioning had as much to do with the regimen of his life as any concerted training system. During the construction of Sudbury General Hospital, Tim had a job running up ladders carrying bricks in a hod—a V-shaped carrier on the top of a pole. "When fall came along," says Gerry, "he was in pretty fair shape."

There were other jobs, all far from white collar. "He worked at Copper Cliff in the converter room," says Gerry. "He was laughing at me because he was working at Inco, making $1.10 an hour, and I was working at Fraser Brace Engineering at Copper Cliff in construction, making 85 cents. Tim's attitude was, well, all the dumb guys were working in construction, and I'm making $1.10. He wasn't there more than two weeks in the converter room shovelling hot coals in a pit. He had gloves on, but the hot coals would go down the cuffs, burn his wrists, drop down the back of his pants. For $1.10. A month after that he was working at Fraser Brace making 85 cents."

Tim was a quiet kid, and George Armstrong wasn't much different. "Both Tim and George were basically very shy in those days," says Dick Trainor. "A lot of us loved to dance then. The big bands were important, and there was jitterbugging." Tim and George stuck to their athletics. Dating was almost unheard of.

Tim was also a different kind of kid from his younger brother; Gerry was more inclined to let you know how good a hockey player he was. If you didn't know they were brothers, it would be hard to imagine they were related. Tim was three years older than Gerry, and exceptionally well built, and without resorting to violence he wasn't above using his strength to remind Gerry who was the older brother. Gerry was more outgoing—"bubbly" is how Red McCarthy describes him—and more inclined to walk up to a complete stranger and strike up a conversation. There was the sense that Gerry had to compensate for the daunting presence and reputation of his brother by being the more forceful personality. "This is my personal opinion," says McCarthy, "but Gerry sort of lived in the shadow of

Tim, played a little hockey, never got really as good.
And I don't know if there was always a little jeal-
ousy." Whether there was or not, as the only siblings
in the family they remained close. Tim named his
first daughter, Jeri-Lynn, after his brother; Gerry in
turn named his son after Tim.

During the mid-1960s, when a business dispute
left Tim and Gerry estranged for several months,
Tim would complain to a friend that Gerry had
more hockey talent than he did, and that he could
have made it to the big leagues if only he'd applied
himself. But it was a harsh judgment to pass on a
younger brother who was never as big or as strong
as Tim and who didn't start out with the same package of talent. "Tim had skills a lot of people didn't,"
says McCarthy. "And he had explosive strength."

The community's hearts were still with the valiant
Redmen of 45/46, but as practices progressed in
the fall of 1946 expectations rose to modest for the
new Copper Cliff Juniors. They would compete in
Nickel District competition against three Senior
teams: the Sudbury Wolves, the Creighton Mines
Eagles and a Canadian Legion team composed
entirely of returning war veterans.

The unique nature of Junior hockey in the Nickel
Belt following the Second World War proved to be
an effective crucible for developing outstanding talent. Rather than being spread among three or four
Junior teams in Copper Cliff, Sudbury and
Falconbridge, the kids who made the cut with the
46/47 Redmen were an elite who would grow as
players as a potent unit, rather than as opponents on
teams with diluted talent. And their skills would be
hardened by competing against bigger, older, more

experienced players on the three Senior teams.

Surveying the four Nickel District league teams, the November 13 *Daily Star* observed: "There are a few new faces with the Senior teams, but most of the newcomers will be with the Redmen—not new-comers to the district, but graduates from the juve-nile ranks who will be making their bow in the 'big leagues.' Coach Jim Dewey sounded none too hope-ful in the early practices, but with the squad gradu-ally whittled down he's sounding a brighter tune of late."

Dewey had seen enough of Tim to be intrigued by his possibilities. In two days, a preseason series between the four Nickel District teams would begin, and Dewey made known his intention to play Tim up on right wing, on a line centred by George Armstrong. There is no record of where Tim actual-ly played the opening game of the series. After that first game, the *Daily Star* reported that the Redmen "could probably stand a little more beef to go with the speed, but in Tug Parri, Zellio Toppazzini, Tim Horton, Specs Telford and Sambo Bettio (when he returns to the lineup) [he was sidelined by a sore throat], they have a nucleus of players who can do some bouncing."

In practice, Dewey must have been impressed with Tim's speed and the scoring touch he had already demonstrated in Midget competition with Holy Trinity in 45/46. But ultimately more impres-sive to Dewey was Tim's ability to keep the opposi-tion well away from the Redmen net. He was paired back on the blueline with Specs Telford for the rest of his Redmen days.

The Redmen would play a nine-game regular-sea-son schedule through to the end of January, when

Nickel District playoffs began. Once that was over, the Redmen would enter the NOHA playoffs, the first step toward any Memorial Cup appearance. This nine-game schedule, spread over more than two months, was deceptively leisurely; the players' commitment to hockey was absolute. Between games for the Redmen and their high-school teams, practices with both teams and Redmen exhibition games at home and on the road to hone them for the NOHA playoffs, these players were on the ice as many as five or six days a week. They were seeing as much ice time as many professionals, and were having to go to school on top of it. It was no surprise when school rapidly took a back seat.

Until the 46/47 season, students in northern Ontario wishing to play high-school hockey were required to maintain minimum grades on final and term exams. When the Northern Ontario Secondary School Association had its first sports meeting in five years on December 9, 1946, in North Bay, the standards went by the board. Henceforth, a player's eligibility would be determined by the school principal, who would judge him on the quality of his schoolwork and "attitude."

By abandoning empirical standards for eligibility, the school system was conceding that athletes—above all hockey players—were a breed apart. In the embryonic postwar era, the player-student was both tolerated in his scholastic dedication and appreciated for his revenue-generating capability. Nowhere was this more true than in the Nickel Belt, where hockey was a potential career path and a means by which the schools could pay their bills. In an arena like Stanley Stadium, the schools could charge admission to high-school games—fifty cents for adults, twenty-five cents for students—and the profits from hockey (and football) were used to underwrite less popular athletic programs. These admissions were not small change: a Northern Ontario miner made about forty dollars a week then. The educational system thus could be said to be the first line of exploitation the budding hockey star crossed.

"For most hockey players in my day, school wasn't a big deal," says Bettio. "Not to brag, but I didn't find school that hard. I never took the books home. I got the marks I needed to get. I went to school to play hockey and football. I turned down the scholarship to go to St. Michael's College to play football because I didn't want to go to school anymore. I wanted to go to work, and I didn't want to go in the smelter like my dad. I turned St. Michael's down for hockey."

"I knew when I was six years old that I wanted to play professional hockey," recalls Zellio Toppazzini. "And I remember my history teacher Bessie Kennedy always saying to me: What if you go blind? What are you going to remember if you don't study? Then she'd ask me who was leading the National league in scoring and I'd rattle it right off."

Chapter 3

"Just Sign Here"

In October 1947, Roy Conacher was sitting at home in Toronto, refusing to play hockey for the Detroit Red Wings until they paid him more money. Butch Bouchard and Maurice Richard had also been holdouts in Montreal, but had signed their contracts and returned to the Canadiens lineup before the season started. Conacher, who had come back to hockey after four years of soldiering to finish second to Richard in the 46/47 scoring race, wasn't budging. Three games into the regular season, with no Conacher in sight, Detroit dealt him to the Rangers. Conacher refused to go, choosing instead to announce his retirement from professional hockey. "It's time I settled down and got a real job," said one of the game's great stars.

If you were a parent at the end of the Second World War with a young boy who could pass and shoot, and if you didn't believe that professional hockey was the most wholesome or promising career for your offspring, Conacher's words were worth framing above the living-room chesterfield. Conacher undercut its message by promptly coming out of retirement to play for the Blackhawks, but it was the thought that counted. For such parents, the hockey scout was their child's greatest enemy, an amalgam of the worst aspects of the Pied Piper, Fagin and P.T. Barnum. The professional hockey system was a good rough draft for *Pinocchio,* with the paid ruffians Foulfellow and Gideon luring away impressionable lads for the proprietor of Pleasure Island, a devil-may-care amusement park that turns its guests into braying donkeys enslaved in a salt mine.

Well, that was the case for the prosecution. The case for the defence was that hockey gave a talented kid a chance to see the world, or at least some interesting bits of North America, be a hero to his friends and fans and the next generation of youngsters, and make more money working three hours a day (at the most) for six months a year doing something he loved than he could by hacking ore out of a mine on shiftwork for the whole twelve months.

But in the minds of many parents, even people dedicated to hockey, the prosecution's case was looking pretty persuasive in the years immediately following the war.

The scout of Tim Horton's teenage years was a very different creature from the scout of today. True, then as now, they were generally former players. But today the scout's recruiting job is fairly narrow: find and assess talent so that the general manager can decide who is worth drafting or trading for. In Tim's day, there was no universal amateur draft, so the scout's job was to find young talent and tie it up by whatever means necessary. The less scrupulous ones preyed on dewy-eyed ambition, and all of them rolled into town by auto or rail with a sheaf of documents that would give Doctor Faustus pause. These pertained to the NHL's reserve list, the means by which league teams secured rights to young amateurs.

There was the A-form, the most benign scrap of

paper to which a kid could affix his signature. It complimented the prospect as much as anything, committing him to nothing more than showing up for a tryout at an NHL team's training camp the next fall. The A-form brought the prospect onto the team's own turf with no strings attached. An NHL club held its training camps in conjunction with that of its main minor professional affiliate. In St. Catharines, Ontario, for example, the Toronto Maple Leafs would hold a combined training camp with its American league affiliate, the Pittsburgh Hornets (later the Rochester Americans). The prospect could be offered a contract after that tryout, but there was nothing in the A-form that obligated him to accept it. It would be rare for an A-form prospect to make the NHL team's cut after such a tryout. More likely, the player—if he showed promise—would be offered a contract with the affiliated minor-professional team, or encouraged to enter the team's amateur feeder system at Junior or Senior level.

The B-form granted the club an option on a player's future services for an agreed term. The option was secured with a minimum fee of fifty dollars, although the fee was often much higher— upwards of $1,000. (The B-form usually paid substantially more on the first signing because, unlike the C-form, there was no signing payment when it was renewed.) It was generally used in conjunction with assisting the kid in continuing his education or getting a job while he played for an amateur team, often one with which the NHL team had a sponsorship agreement. This let the NHL team bring the player along through his Junior years while giving it the exclusive right to sign him if and when he decided to turn pro.

Teams much preferred to tie up talent with the C-form. This was the Faustian pact realized, according to its critics. Often called a professional contract, technically it was an agreement between the player and the team that the team could call upon him within one year to sign a standard contract and play professionally. There was a minimum fifty-dollar signing payment—a hundred dollars was almost standard with the Leafs at the time—and an option to renew annually. If the club decided not to exercise the C-form's renewal option, then the player automatically became a free agent. (Technically the player, too, could opt not to renew, although in practice this proved difficult, particularly if the club was determined to sign him.) A bonus to be paid when the player finally signed a professional contract was spelled out, and it could run anywhere from a few hundred to a few thousand dollars. The form also outlined how much the player would earn in which league while under contract with the parent club: the NHL, the American league, the U.S. league, the Pacific Coast league or even a so-called amateur Canadian Senior league. (The minor pro loops with territorial agreements with the NHL also had their own reserve lists and corresponding forms.) A pro rata formula also sketched out how much he'd make if he split his season between the farm and parent team. (In rare instances, a player was able to negotiate a "one-way" contract, which specified that he be paid the same salary, no matter where in the parent club's system he played.) Players were signing a commitment of professional service when they were old enough to drive but not old enough to drink, vote or serve on a jury.

Often the C-form was signed by a minor, and in those instances it also required the signature of a parent or guardian, though this didn't necessarily make the agreement any less onerous to the player. There is evidence that a team sometimes simply received verbal assent over the telephone from a player's father, suggesting the C-form was never properly scrutinised. Even when parents did see the form, there was no guarantee it would receive the scrutiny it deserved. Parents could be as excited as their offspring about the promise of a professional hockey career the C-form held out, and could be blinded to the implications of the document. And many parents working in mines in small northern towns were ill-equipped to fathom the legal and tactical implications of the form. Perhaps the greatest danger the C-form posed to youngsters was that the Fagins proffering it were sometimes loath to explain its fine print or possible consequences. There are plenty of tales of outright fraud being practised in small-town rinks across the country as players as young as sixteen, their senses dulled by an envelope of money, scribbled their names on C-forms when they thought they were signing something on the commitment level of an A-form. Often the C-form was the only form a player would see, so he wouldn't know the difference between the three forms. When it came to securing a player's professional rights, the Leafs, for example, overwhelmingly preferred to deal in C-forms rather than B-forms, because of the control it delivered them.

Certainly there were cases where a player who pleaded ignorance after signing a C-form had been ignorant only about how much money his services were actually worth. When the professional club tried to call him up with the C-form, the player would cry foul, claiming he had misunderstood the implications of the form, when what he was really upset about was the amount of money he would be making. But in hindsight, the benefit of the doubt in cases where a player said he was shanghaied should generally go to the player. He was invariably below the age of majority when he signed the C-form, there were no agents, and the relationship between the amateur and professional hockey systems was at once so confusing and so incestuous that a player might be forgiven for feeling that his rights were entirely secondary to the cause of developing players for the professional system.[1]

Even a player who understood perfectly well what he was signing had little choice in which team he signed with. His rights had been tied up well in advance of any Fagin from a professional team sidling up to him at a practice and complimenting him on his back-checking. The device that accomplished this was the negotiating list. Rather than having to go to the unseemly length of bidding against each other for a player's services, the teams in the NHL and the leagues with which it had territorial agreements came to a collusive agreement to stay out of each other's way. Each team was permitted a limited number of parking spaces for potential signees on their negotiating list. Without the consent of the player, his parent or guardian, or even the knowledge of any of the above, the day the prospect turned sixteen a scout could give the nod to his employer, say, the Maple Leafs, and the Leafs would notify the NHL head office in Montreal that they had first dibs on the professional services of Mikey La Flamme, that sharp-shooting kid from

Flin Flon. Now that Mikey was on the Leafs' negotiating list, no other professional team could go near
him with forms A, B or C, or a playing contract.
This in turn meant that Mikey could go near no
franchise but the Maple Leafs if he was interested in
playing hockey for serious money. He could say no
to signing a Maple Leaf C-form, but that didn't
mean he was free to sign one offered by someone
else. If a team was stubborn enough, it could keep
the uncooperative player parked on its negotiating
list for as long as three years, hoping to wear him
down.

A player could move from one negotiating list to
another without ever knowing he was ever on any
negotiating list at all. If Mikey wasn't shaping up the
way they'd hoped, the Leafs could quietly drop him
from their list and the Rangers, who were more
optimistic about his future development or more
desperate for recruits, could put him on theirs. It
would take a scout, wanting him to take the first
step toward indentured hockey servitude by signing
form A, B or C, to reveal to him that an NHL team
(or a club in an associated professional league) had
essentially owned his backside since the day he
turned sixteen.

Getting an outstanding prospect's name on a
club's negotiating list was a race against the clock.
Scouts would literally be poised in their local tele-
graph office at midnight, waiting for the first second to tick by on the prospect's sixteenth birthday,
hoping to beat each other to the player's rights with
their respective missives to the NHL head office,
which acted as the central record office for the professional leagues with territorial agreements. Often
players were implicitly pledged to a particular NHL

club well before they turned sixteen, through sponsorship agreements forged between their local amateur hockey operation and the professional team. These weren't always large-scale sponsorship agreements like the one between the Leafs and St. Mike's. Leaf chief scout Squib Walker was well known for making a donation to some small-town hockey program—a hundred dollars would do it—and receiving in return an unofficial pledge from its organizers that the tykes on their rink were now his and no one else's. If a player grew up in the greater Toronto area, for example, he was the property of the Maple Leafs. Conn Smythe's team automatically had right of first refusal for amateurs playing within its territory who were not already signed by another team. A prospect from Kirkland Lake who had signed a C-form with Detroit could come to Toronto and play for St. Michael's College, and would still remain the property of Detroit.

The negotiating list could act as a powerful lever for a scout trying to get a kid to sign a C-form. The argument went like this: "Look, Mikey, we've got your rights tied up anyway with the negotiating list, and if you don't sign the C-form we'll still keep you on the list. Either way, you belong to us. So what will it be: sit on the negotiating list and make nothing, or sign the C-form and pick up a hundred bucks?"

Scouts were eager to convert players on negotiating lists into C-form signees because a team was extremely limited in the number of players it could keep on a negotiating list at any one time. According to Bob Davidson, who became the Leafs' chief scout in 1951, NHL teams had four spots on their negotiating list, American league teams three, and teams like Tulsa in a lower-tier professional

loop had two. "The way to make room," says Davidson, "was for a player to sign a C-form." And while
the team could still keep him on the negotiating list
if he refused to sign, the team would have to be particularly confident of one day signing him, since the
player was taking up a spot on the negotiating list
that could be put to better use securing the rights to
a prospect more willing to sign on. In their pursuit
of Jean Beliveau, the Montreal Canadiens kept him
on their negotiating list for the full three years while
his father refused to let him sign a C-form. Beliveau
finally agreed to sign a B-form.

The NHL clubs controlled a large pool of talent
through a pyramid scheme of sponsorships.
According to Bob Davidson, each NHL club was
permitted to sponsor two professional clubs, and
those clubs in turn could sponsor two clubs. "We
had a lot of players tied up," says Davidson. In addition, a team like the Leafs could come to informal
sponsorship agreements with still more teams. It
would supply an unofficially sponsored professional
club with contracted players in return for having
access to spaces on that club's reserve and negotiating lists. It was through such an arrangement with
Eddie Shore's Springfield Indians of the American
league that Toronto defenceman Larry Hillman was
"loaned" to Springfield as he recuperated from a
shoulder injury rather than being sent to the Leafs'
officially sponsored American league club, the
Rochester Americans.

The player's signature on a C-form gave the club
power over him; it gave the club the right to decide
precisely when he would turn pro, where he would
turn pro and how much he would get paid for turning pro. On every one of these items—when, where

and how much—there was potential for acrimony. All too often, the club would tap the player on the shoulder and, like the Grim Reaper, intone: It's time. And all too often, an eighteen-year-old who thought he'd end up renewing the C-form after the year went by, who thought he'd be getting another season or two of Junior experience, another year or two of education, would protest: But I'm not ready! If he was absolutely serious about playing hockey professionally, he had no choice but to report, and a kid who'd never been away from home, who'd never learned how to cook, who had the hots for some hometown sweetheart, was being stuck on a train and pointed in the direction of Tulsa. And as the train rattled southward and westward, the unreality of the salary figures on that C-form became glaringly real. He'd never really thought much about the salary on the bottom rung of the agreement, because he'd always pictured the pot at the end of the rainbow—being in the NHL. But now he could only shake his head and mutter: I can't believe I'm going to Oklahoma for $2,200 a season, and I didn't even finish high school.

The C-form was your ticket on the train to the big cities of the NHL, but that train very often dumped your car on a siding in a tier-two league, where you could still make a fair buck, but it wasn't the Leafs or the Canadiens. The fact is, once a team had called you up with the C-form and had you affix your scrawl to a contract, you became the chattel of whatever team held that contract, and that contract could be bought, sold and traded with impunity. So, for that matter, could your negotiating rights. You might have been playing happily for some Senior club when, unbeknown to you, your

negotiating rights were tossed into a multi-player
trade between two NHL teams to sweeten the pot
for one of the parties. Then you got a phone call
from the general manager of the Red Wings, say,
who informed you that their star defenceman Biff
Smith had just been shipped to the Rangers in
exchange for Killer Kowalski and Shaky Muldoon,
and that the Rangers had been moved to toss in
your rights to make the deal, and would you be
interested in coming to the Red Wings training
camp in September? And all you could think was:
The Rangers had me on their negotiating list?

Once you were signed to a professional contract,
that contract could act like a bill of lading as you
were shipped from team to team, from one corner
of the continent to the other, without so much as an
okay-with-you from the team's general manager.
Your contract could be auctioned off for a solid five
figures when you were only being paid a handful of
four figures. If you were really bounced around, you
couldn't put down roots, your wife got fed up, your
kids were as good as army brats. Even if you stayed
in the same organization, it could move you back
and forth between the majors and the minors.
Former Leaf Billy Harris has recounted the financial consequences of bruised pride in this situation.
You had a house in the big-league town and you
couldn't admit to yourself when you got sent down
to Rochester that the demotion might not be temporary, so you ended up hanging onto the big-
league abode and renting a place in Rochester and
now you were carrying twice the domestic overhead
you should be.

Players could balk at being traded, but this might
only get them sent down to the minors; players

might balk at being sent down to the minors, but this might only get them traded. The leading professional leagues stuck together on matters of player discipline. When Clarence Campbell banned Billy Taylor and Don Gallinger from hockey for life for gambling in the late 1940s, the other leading leagues agreed to honour the ban. You could not walk out on an NHL team and find employment with one in, say, the American league. (In baseball, players would revolt by bolting for the Mexican league, which only got them blackballed by the American and National leagues.) For that matter, you could not dodge a C-form call-up by deciding to play for money with an amateur Senior team, because the Senior leagues were part of the Canadian Amateur Hockey Association, and the CAHA's master agreement with the NHL and its affiliated leagues would rule out a player defying a C-form call-up by bolting to one of the teams under CAHA jurisdiction. After all, the professional leagues were paying the CAHA annual lump-sum payments for the rights to the amateurs its teams were taking into inventory on their reserve lists.

Not even outright retirement from playing professionally could free a player from the control of a team, because "voluntary retirees" could also be placed on a separate reserve list. It often happened that NHL players quit to play Senior hockey in Canada, applied to the CAHA to have their "amateur" status reinstated, and then drew a salary from the amateur club (or received an arranged job) to do so. But the existence of the retiree reserve list meant that if you chose to play or coach at the amateur level, you needed your former team's permission, which translated into an amateur team having to compensate the professional team. And whereas a team's regular reserve list was limited,[2] the retiree reserve list was bottomless.

Searching out prospects was just what it sounded like: prospecting, wherein the kids were the lodes of ore and their rights were stakes to be claimed.[3] And a kid could no more choose to join a specific team's negotiating list than a vein of silver could walk into the nearest town and pick his favourite prospector from the crowd at the local watering hole. Both scenarios were not only impossible: they were unthinkable.

Sixteen-year-old grade 11 students like Zellio Toppazzini, Tim Horton and George Armstrong were surrounded by the temptations of a professional hockey career. Recruiters and scouts for all manner of leagues and teams passed through town, serving up compliments, making promises, offering pieces of paper to sign, sometimes off-the-books bonuses. "The territory between Sudbury and Timmins," proclaimed Boston Bruins scout Hal Cotton, "is one of the best breeding grounds in Canada—bar none."

In Sudbury in the fall of 1946, the pages of the *Daily Star* and the talk around the rinks was a constant hum of where-are-they-now and where-are-they-going stories, updates on the budding hockey careers of local kids making (or hoping to make) good as the training camps of professional teams opened and sorted prospects. There were three main professional leagues with understood territorial rights—the National Hockey League in eastern North America, the American Hockey League in the eastern U.S., and the United States Hockey League

in the American Midwest. As well, there was a new
circuit out west, the Pacific Coast Hockey League (at
first a so-called amateur league, but by 1948 an
above-board professional operation), and a slew of
minor professional loops as well as the Senior and
Junior Canadian amateur leagues and quasi-profes-
sional U.S. amateur teams. The scuttlebutt on who
was bound for where was intoxicating and inspira-
tional. George Blake, a Coniston outfielder, is heading for the Detroit Red Wings camp in the middle of
the Nickel Belt Senior League finals. Andy Barbe,
Gariston Buzzers outfielder and league batting
champion, is heading to Port Arthur for a tryout
with the St. Louis Flyers of the United States league.
His first baseman, Lem Lemieux, is leaving town for
a tryout with the Maple Leafs. This just in: Nick
Evenshen is heading for the Pacific Coast league,
where he played last year. Louis Prete, that flashy forward with the Legion team, the Senior Wolves and
the Junior Redmen last winter, is going with him.
Connie Smythe is moving our boys around: Armand
Lemieux of Coniston—remember, he played with
Providence of the American league last year—and
Tod Sloan of Falconbridge are being sent to the
Pittsburgh Hornets of the AHL. And Toronto's sending Ray Powell to Tulsa of the USHL. Powell update:
scratch Tulsa. Ray's been dealt to Detroit with Billy
Taylor of the Leafs and Doug Baldwin of the
Hornets. Ray was originally with Fort Worth, but
then the Leafs bought his rights for $5,000 and now
that Detroit has him, Detroit is sending him to
Omaha. Maurice Vaillancourt is off to Minneapolis,
Lino Gasperini is bound for Cleveland, and it turns
out Andy Barbe and the St. Louis Flyers couldn't
agree on money, so he's come to play baseball for

Coniston against Kirkland Lake in the Northern
Ontario Senior championship, and then he's expecting to be lacing skates with the L.A. franchise of the
PCHL. And now we hear that Dick Halverson, who
played goal with the Wolves last season, is heading
overseas with Mauno Kauppi to become a Wembley
Lion in the British ice hockey league.

And on and on. Just as loud was the hum of the
National Hockey League beginning its first proper
postwar season, a season two weeks longer than
before, with ten more games per team. The arrival
of a new league president, Clarence Campbell—a
former NHL referee and a lawyer who had just finished contributing to the prosecution of Nazi war
criminals at the Nuremburg trials—added to the
atmosphere of anticipation.

The NHL was becoming an ever more forceful
presence on the amateur scene. On September 5,
Conn Smythe shrewdly responded to the Memorial
Cup loss of his St. Mike's Majors to the Winnipeg
Monarchs by signing a sponsorship deal with the
Monarchs as well. The Chicago Blackhawks then
dumped the Moose Jaw Canucks and inked a three-
year deal with the Winnipeg Rangers, which included Juniors, Juveniles, Midgets and Bantams—in
other words, every player in the Ranger system
down to the age of twelve. By mid-October the
Sudbury Midget League had decided to drop the
"NHL" label from its name, in part to remove what
was seen as the taint of professionalism. Explained
Sudbury's Max Silverman, vice-president of the
Northern Ontario Hockey Association, the name-
doffing would serve "to break that professional link
in the minds of the boys. There is too much of the
professional angle being instilled in young players

today anyway. And after all very few of them make the grade…"

In mid-December, relations between the CAHA and the NHL were at their most rocky. *Daily Star* sports columnist George Grace lit into Clarence Campbell's league on December 17. Grace was a writer with a healthy scepticism of the amateurism of the amateur sport system and the morality of the top professional league. "You may not know it," he proposed, railing against the insidious negotiating and reserve lists, "but the NHL controls, heart, soul and pocketbook, the destinies of every young hockey hopeful from one end of the Dominion to the other. No matter what hopes and aspirations might be beating in the youthful hockey breast, unless they are in line with what the NHL plans for the Senior or Junior—or even the Juvenile or Midget player—they don't mean a thing.

"Most hockey players," Grace observed, "the younger they are, have high hopes of going places in the game and no matter what unglamorous angles there might be to the NHL, that's the 'big time'—what the kids are shooting for. In their haste to get there it's not hard, sometimes, for old experienced hands to get them to sign their lives away with a handful of folded money dangling before their eyes."

The secretive, manipulative system was aptly illustrated by the circumstances of former Redman Gordie Heale when he returned to Sudbury from the Barrie Flyers for the Christmas holiday in 1946. Heale had heard from Bob Wilson, the Leafs' northern Ontario scout, that he was on the Leafs' negotiating list. But it turned out that the Leafs had dropped him, and his rights were scooped up by the

Red Wings. "All I know," Heale confessed, "is what I read in the papers."

That is not to say the Canadian amateur hockey system was lily white. It was a farce of amateurism, a set up that gave rise to the widely applied label "shamateurism." When players, particularly Seniors, weren't having jobs arranged for them in the communities in which they starred, they were being paid outright to play. In October, Hugh Vallant, chairman of the Fort Frances recreational committee, had made a tepid denial of accusations that Senior players in his town were being paid. He preferred to call it "remuneration" from the recreational council funds. "But that is merely to reimburse the player for time lost at his occupation," he explained lamely.

Gordie Heale left no doubt that he was earning a living playing for the Barrie Flyers of the OHA Junior A, and he would go on to play profitably for the Quebec Aces of the Quebec Senior league, a team with which Jean Beliveau earned an estimated $25,000 a season before joining the Montreal Canadiens in 1953. Indeed, Grace understood that a player could earn about fifty dollars a week in this black-market professional hockey business. That was ten dollars a week more than a miner, and miners were already the highest-paid labour group in Ontario. But Grace had underestimated just how lucrative the amateur game could be. Today Gordie Heale says he was getting one hundred dollars a week, plus room and board, to play in Barrie, a fairly standard remuneration package in the Junior OHA at the time. The talent drain south is understandable, given that playing for the Redmen didn't earn you any money at all.

The Junior clubs were also working outside the CAHA's own code by selling their players to each other, albeit with the tacit approval of the CAHA. CAHA regulations only addressed transfer of player rights from amateur to professional clubs—the NHL was paying the CAHA $20,000 for the right to sign Junior players, and that sum would soon more than double. But there were no guidelines for its "amateur" clubs selling player rights to each other. Needless to say, it went on all the time.

It was no big secret in Sudbury that the Barrie Flyers had "bought" Gordie Heale from the Redmen for an undisclosed sum. It was also no big secret that NOHA clubs in general were demanding payment for releases allowing their players to go to other leagues, in particular the OHA. Critics of the player-sale practice were wont to make it sound like white slavery, but in truth the practice was prima facie evidence of the remarkable freedom Junior players enjoyed. For the more talented teenage prospects, their Junior years, generally from age sixteen to twenty, were the first, and often the only, time they had reasonable control over where they played for money. They shopped their services from team to team, from one Junior league to another, offering their talents to the highest bidder, or to the team that presented the best prospect for improving their game and bringing them a Memorial Cup.

Much of the flow of Junior players was toward southern Ontario, which had the most affluent Junior A teams. These teams would make mid-season tours of northern Ontario hockey centres, playing exhibition games and recruiting new players for the following season in the process. The attraction of the OHA teams was such that few northern

Ontario centres could hold on to enough of their
own young players to ice A-level Junior teams, and
those that could were hard-pressed to retain their
best players much past the age of seventeen.

Talent flowed through northern Ontario Junior
rosters like water through a sieve as the better players heeded the call of the OHA. It was inevitable,
and for all practical purposes it was unstoppable.
The clubs being denuded of players reacted by
charging money for granting releases, the logic
being that the compensation would permit them to
recoup the costs of developing these players for the
wealthier teams, many of which had ties to the NHL
and other professional clubs.

While some officials in the amateur system like
Max Silverman felt the amateur clubs, not the professional leagues, should be the ones controlling the
players, that day would never dawn. Professional
sponsorship of amateur teams increased and the C-
form reigned supreme. It was only in 1966, with
expansion from six to twelve teams imminent, that
the NHL did away with sponsored amateur teams,
negotiating lists and the C-form in favour of a universal draft, first held in 1969—although a grandfa-
thering clause upheld C-forms already signed by
kids, and there were still players entering the league
in 1972 who had been indentured by the notorious
form. And even though the NHL clubs no longer
controlled amateur teams through a club farm system, by the time the C-form was dead the very existence of Junior hockey had become defined by the
NHL's need for fresh talent.

Although they would take another decade to blossom into an outright movement, the players at the

NHL level in 1946 were starting to think seriously about getting themselves properly organised. A formal players' association proved to be two full decades away, but the players who took to the ice in the first season of Clarence Campbell's reign did take an important step toward treating their trade as more of a profession than a calling. That step arose from the game's rapid escalation of brutality in the short period since the end of the war. Rock-'em, sock-'em hockey was in the ascendant. On September 28, 1946, Campbell set the tone for the coming season by defining hockey as "a game of speed and fierce bodily contact. If these go out, hockey will vanish." Conn Smythe had begun the season by addressing his Leafs at training camp on the merits of playing it rough. According to an October 1 news report, Smythe "let his Leaf charges know that he doesn't want to feel proud of the team's record last year—the least penalised. He said he wanted a squad which carried shoulder chips, took the ice that way and fought all the way."

In 46/47 the physical punishment of the new postwar game took its predictable toll. At one point nine members of the starting lineup of the Rangers were injured, and by early February Smythe's chips-on-shoulders Leafs had had those chips knocked off so many times that injuries caused a nine-point lead in the standings to melt away. The league's players took notice of all this career-threatening carnage and the influx of fresh recruits and decided that what they needed was a pension plan.

By March 5 the league had appointed a committee to discuss the plan proposed by players; the plan would go into effect the next season. That March, the league also introduced bonus pay for playoff performance. Players on the team finishing first in the standings got $1,000; on the second-place team, $500; the third-place team, $350; and the fourth-place team, $150. Being on a semifinal winner netted a player another $1,000 and winning the Stanley Cup still another $1,000, as did an All Star team appearance.

For the kids who were playing Junior hockey in 46/47, professional hockey as played by the NHL was now even more appealing. Despite all the wailing from the adults about professional dominance of the amateur game and those horrible C-forms, the NHL offered them more money than it ever had, and now it was going to have a pension to take care of them (or so they imagined) in their old age, or if Maurice Richard ever caused permanent injury when he next whacked someone on the head with his stick.

There was even the possibility of more job openings. New NHL franchises were being considered for Philadelphia, Los Angeles and San Francisco. All three franchise bids were turned aside in 47/48: the cities (San Francisco in the form of Oakland) wouldn't get teams until 1967, when the "Original Six" of 42/43 finally expanded to twelve. But the atmosphere in 46/47 was one of growth, and while the NHL was the ultimate goal of young players, circuits like the American league (which had a record eleven franchises in 47/48), the U.S. league and the Pacific Coast league all offered gainful employment. While some of these leagues held NHL farm teams, the leagues were less subordinate to the NHL then. In the late forties (and for nearly twenty more years), Campbell's circuit was only a six-team enterprise and didn't dominate every corner of the market. Its territorial agreements with the American, U.S. and Pacific Coast leagues helped prevent it from doing so. It was possible for a player who might be marginal in the NHL actually to make more money as a star in one of these competing leagues.

For the teenagers dreaming of glory, their chances of playing in the NHL were heightened by the fact that the league was on a youth kick. The two-line offside, introduced in the 43/44 season, encouraged the notion that this new wrinkle in the game demanded a new breed of player, and the demand for that new breed was heightened by the fact that the war had interrupted the flow of recruits, making the first Junior graduates of the postwar years a rare and valued commodity. One needed only to ask Chicago general manager Bill Tobin. Desperate for talent, Tobin had been dangling $100,000 in bait before his fellow NHL owners. According to a Canadian Press story, his overtures for "ready-made players to strengthen his last-place team fell on deaf ears. In effect, the other five clubs told him that players were too hard to find these days—they had to be caught young and weaned carefully."

A kid playing hockey in northern Ontario in the late 1940s experienced the temptation of the professional game like no kid before him. Professional leagues were clamouring for new players at the same time that the local mine could no longer give you a job simply because you had a mean wrist shot. The chance of going to university was remote, there was no such thing as community college, and prosperity in the natural resources game was ephemeral. "Mining is a wasting industry and the inevitability of ending as a ghost town is the skeleton in the closet of every mining community." So wrote Donat Marc Le Bourdais in 1953.

The latest kids to wear the uniform of the Copper Cliff Junior Redmen had an enormous opportunity before them. All they had to do was live up to the new NHL president's standards of "speed and fierce bodily contact," and fame and relative fortune were theirs. As to who had first dibs on their services and how much the Redmen could sell them for if they moved elsewhere, they were as much in the dark as ever.

Chapter 4

The Redmen

In the first days of January 1947, one of the Fagins came to Copper Cliff. This one was entirely benign. Ralph "Cooney" Weiland, a Boston Bruins scout, had been a fireplug of a centre for ten seasons from 1928 to 1939, most of them with the Bruins.[1] In 28/29, when the Bruins won the Stanley Cup, Weiland had centred the Dynamite Line, teamed with Dutch Gainor and Dit Clapper. He'd coached the Bruins for two seasons, winning the Stanley Cup in 40/41. Art Ross had taken over coaching the Bruins for the rest of the war while Weiland moved behind the bench of the Bruins' AHL farm team, the Hershey Bears. He had been coaching the New Haven Ramblers in 45/46, and would go on to coach Ivy League hockey at Harvard.

Weiland was in town to put the finishing touches on the scouting work already done by the Bruins' local bird dog, Normie Mann. Scouts like Weiland relied on talent spotters like Mann, who were an eclectic breed of fans and local boosters. Mann was a hockey enthusiast and a well-liked gentleman who frequented the stands of Stanley Stadium when he wasn't operating Sudbury Paint and Wallpaper. In the Copper Cliff Redmen of 46/47, he appeared to have an exceptionally talented crop of professional prospects. Jim Dewey's Juniors had managed to reach the season's Christmas break in second place in the Nickel District league with a 3-2 record.

Mann drew Weiland's attention to at least three solid professional prospects: Sam Bettio, Zellio Toppazzini and Specs Telford. While the Boston Bruins were only faintly recognised by the youth of the Nickel Belt, before departing for points west Weiland had convinced Bettio, who had turned eighteen at the beginning of December, and Toppazzini, who turned seventeen the week of Cooney's visit, to sign A-forms committing them to attend the training camp of the Hershey Bears in St. Catharines the following fall. St. Catharines was also home to the Tee-Pees of the OHA, with which Boston had informal ties. Weiland had words with George Armstrong, but the big, lanky centre, who was seven long months away from his seventeenth birthday, made no commitment.

"Didn't get a cent," Bettio told the *Daily Star.* "We just had a talk with him and agreed to try out with the team." Before the month was out, Specs Telford also committed himself to the Hershey tryout by putting his signature to an A-form. For Telford and Bettio, it was the beginning of a wild ride with the conniving forces of professional and amateur hockey.

If Tim Horton attracted any attention, it wasn't reflected in the incessant press coverage given the Redmen players. He had gone away over the holidays with his family, and Weiland simply may have missed crossing paths with him. But Horton, who turned seventeen on January 12, didn't appear to be attracting the stares of the scouts the way some of his teammates were.

Tim was certainly capable of scoring and play-making—his Midget and high-school performances provide evidence of that. And before the season had started, Dewey had considered playing Tim on right wing on a line with George Armstrong. But paired for good with sophomore Junior Specs Telford, Tim was a classic stay-at-home defenceman, clearing the zone and running into anybody who tried to approach Bill Organ's goal. He wouldn't log a single point over the entire regular season. He played the style of defensive game the team required, and this team, averaging six goals per game, didn't need any help on offence. Dewey had the experienced players of the Flynn–McClellan–Bettio line producing half the Redmen scoring during the season. And his second line of Armstrong, Toppazzini and Smrke was a godsend. The newcomers, in particular Armstrong and Toppazzini, had exceptional talent. The right-winger Toppazzini was a born marksman, and the centre Armstrong had it all: speed, size, playmaking and a scoring touch. While Armstrong would never be mistaken for a physical player, he was tough, and willing to stand his ground.

Tim's teammates knew he was a special talent. "You don't forget Tim," says Bettio. "He could skate as good as any forward we had on the team. He might have been an even better skater. He had an explosive style.. He started, and he was going. He always took the shortest route, and if you got in his way, he ran right over you." Horton was young, solid, dependable, workmanlike. But his "bouncing" game also had an Achilles' heel, which had been glimpsed in the final game of the first half of the season against the Sudbury Wolves that decided who should be at the top of the standings. The Redmen were nursing a 1-0 lead when Horton drew a boarding penalty halfway through the second period. The Wolves tied the game on the power play and then moved ahead to win 2-1 and take sole possession of first place. If Horton wasn't scoring goals or setting them up for the Redmen, then he couldn't afford to be sitting in the penalty box while the other team scored.

A few days before the Redmen had met the Wolves, A. D. Dutton, chairman of the board of the Canadian Broadcasting Corporation, announced that his board "has decided that studies should be made of the possibilities of establishing publicly owned television facilities in Montreal and Toronto." Until that statement, the "B" in CBC had stood for nothing but radio broadcasting.

Tim Horton's generation was the last to come of age with no picture of the game they would play professionally. Many of them lived in northern mining towns or remote prairie communities. There was no NHL team to sell them a ticket, and no television broadcast to relay them a facsimile of the game. Today, several networks, local and national, in Canada and in the United States, carry game telecasts into our homes several nights a week. The isolation of the emerging prospects from their chosen profession in the years surrounding the Second World War would strike the modern aspiring young player as sensory deprivation. There was no way in which to study the finesse of the era's equivalents of Gretzky, Lemieux, Coffey and Roy. Without television, the stars could provide only ephemeral role models for the new players who filled their skates. They were models of success itself, of heroism and notoriety. They could not be models of the perfect drop pass or wrist shot or body check.

The game had the most tenuous feedback with its roots, which is to say that the game as played by the NHL could not be *the* game without television. If it could not be witnessed and worshipped by the multitudes, then it could not be the image of the game. Although the NHL before television could be coveted and adored, the sport had a reality that was divorced from what transpired on the ice at Conn Smythe's rink. As children grew, they were indoctrinated in its rituals by mentors like Jim Dewey, and developed rituals of their own, all in the most basic ignorance of how the young Maurice Richard scored any of his fifty remarkable goals in 44/45. There was no channel changer with which to summon the highlights of Richard's feat on an all-sports-channel recap. The game was understood by playing it, not by watching it, and it was perhaps this isolation that made the new generation such a potent addition to the postwar league. Many of them graduated ready-made to the NHL straight out of Junior hockey, their character and style established independent of the major league. And while the game as played by the major league had changed so profoundly with the two-line offside of 1943/44, the new game was the only game they had played, and they were inventing it as they mastered it.

Television came to the NHL during the 1949/50 season, when Detroit's Channel 4 began broadcasting the last half of Red Wings games to a local audience.[2] The CBC began experimental broadcasts in 1952, and with the appearance of bulky television cameras in league arenas, no longer would the professional game be a privileged experience to the 12,000 to 20,000 spectators in a particular arena.

Soon the game would be experienced by millions in a way that it could not when Foster Hewitt related the action over the radio waves. (It was no coincidence that hockey trading cards began to be issued by Toronto's Parkhurst gum company in 1952, as soon as hockey was embraced by the new medium.) Until television arrived, the game was not simply described to the radio audience: the game *was* description, an aural imagining, a distant and ghostly thing, electrifying through the implied action. It was Hewitt's voice: dramatic, excited, forewarning. The players were invisible muses to Hewitt's performances—they shaped his delivery, they were his cues. They were not flesh-and-blood heroes or villains. Their game had no nuance, which only the physical presence of the players could hope to deliver. The game, as passionately as it was followed by Hewitt's radio audience, was as remote as the Normandy invasion.

Television would change many things in the life of the nation, and hockey was one of them. It would change it in superficial ways—the ice would be painted white to eliminate the dull glaze transmitted by the cameras, and the use of home and away uniforms would be formalised to provide contrast for the monochromatic electronic eye. Much later, names would be stitched on players' backs to help the audience at home figure out who was playing when it seemed a player was with a different team every time he pulled on his game jersey. But most important, television would change the role the NHL played in the public's perception of the game.

The absence of television gave Tim Horton's generation an unclouded ambition. A game that could not be seen, that could only be imagined, was more approachable, more possible, to an aspiring young player, than one that had indisputable dimensions. In the absence of television the players were not so much bigger than the young would-be professionals, nor did they shoot or hit so much harder or pass so much better. The stars were only as marvellous as the kids' minds would allow, and the kids' minds would allow themselves to be just like the stars—someday, even today.

Despite differences in age, differences in communities—Copper Cliff kids versus Sudbury kids, Copper Cliff High versus Sudbury High—the Redmen managed to unite as a team. But for the kids from Sudbury, playing hockey professionally was not an avowed ambition, a focal point of their youth. While their parents weren't necessarily any better off—few families had cars, and the Sudbury kids would make their way to Stanley Stadium by the streetcar—they weren't growing up in the shadow of Inco the way their teammates from the company town of Copper Cliff were, and they weren't so entranced by the idea that hockey could allow them to avoid living the lives of their parents. The Sudbury kids were aware of the possibilities hockey held out—they couldn't help but be aware of them, with the scouts floating through the Nickel Belt and the examples set by older boys like Tod Sloan. But the idea of making it in the NHL was more of a "what if" than an "I will" for them.

The adults sometimes sent them mixed signals about their professional prospects. At Sudbury High, the really big sport was basketball, and some Nickel Belt hoopsters made money playing on shamateur American teams. But the school's athletic director, Charlie Cerre, would sometimes send the students outside to shoot pucks against the wall, telling them that pro hockey was where their real athletic futures were. The school principal would take them aside and tell them that not everyone could make it to the big leagues, and in particular would tell Red McCarthy that he didn't have the size to play the game for big money. Tim could see the possibility of playing hockey professionally as well as any other student, but his commitment to schoolwork showed that he hadn't allowed his love for the game to blind him to the need to prepare for the sort of life that Jim Dewey found completely satisfying: a good white-collar job with Senior hockey on the side.

The Esquire pool room in downtown Sudbury was a favourite hangout, particularly for the Sudbury players, and Dick Trainor would join them there as they shot stick and hustled a bit of money off each other. Tim was pretty good with a cue—Gerry Horton says it was how his brother picked up his pocket money. Tim was a notorious skinflint: his nickname on the team, says Red McCarthy, was Thrifty. Gerry says his brother kept a book in which he tallied his IOUs. "If he lent you a quarter, a dollar, two dollars, he had it tallied, boy," says Gerry. "He knew exactly what was coming to him and what wasn't. If he was owed two bucks for a pool game, by God he collected it."

When the games at the Esquire were over, Tim would step out to wait for the streetcar back to Gatchell. There was a large clock on the post office tower, and he would ask Red McCarthy or anyone else who was available to tell him what time it was. Tim was terribly nearsighted, and wore coke-bottle glasses when he wasn't on the ice. During a house league game in grade 10 at Sudbury High, he had crashed into the goalpost, fracturing his cheekbone. The bone was in danger of puncturing his eye, and he had to be flown to Toronto to have the bone reset. Some friends would wonder whether that accident had exacerbated his sight problems, but Tim's eyesight had never been 20/20. He had 20/100 vision in his right eye and 20/400 (nearly blind) in his left eye. His vision would always be factored into discussions of the nature of his game.

The second half of the 46/47 Nickel Belt season got off to a fine start for the Redmen on January 10, with a 10-7 victory over the Legion and hat tricks for Bettio and Armstrong. The next day, two games all too typical of the high-school Seniors' season were played: Copper Cliff High flattened Sudbury Tech 12-1 and Sacred Heart beat Sudbury High 8-2.

At the beginning of the high-school season, it was suggested that Sudbury High might challenge Copper Cliff High for the Senior championship that the Inco town school had held so long, but despite the presence of Horton and Armstrong (who missed a few games) the High team was dreadful. After winning their season opener, they lost nine straight games and missed the playoffs; the season's so-called highlights included drubbings of 8-1, 17-3 and 12-3 by Copper Cliff High, which was loaded with Redmen players and went on to win the provincial high-school championship.

By defeating the Creighton Eagles 7-3, the Redmen moved back into a first-place tie with the Wolves. But it was a poor game for Horton, who drew three penalties, two of which resulted in Creighton goals. In the second period he got into a fight with a new member of the Eagles, Elio Flora, which resulted in a roughing minor, during which Creighton scored. Tim had just stepped back onto the ice after serving the first of his two third-period penalties when Creighton scored again.

"One feature of the Juniors' play that has become more noticeable with passing games," lamented the *Daily Star,* "is their chippy style of play, with plenty of illegal tactics thrown in—tactics that have not drawn as much official ire as they should have locally and which could get them into a mess of trouble when they get into Junior competition away from the home stomping grounds."

An exhibition trip to the American Soo was reassuring for Redmen supporters looking forward to a trip to the NOHA Junior finals. They easily handled the local Juniors 7-3 in their exhibition match. January 18 found them in North Bay for an exhibition game against the town's Senior all-stars. On the bus ride there, says Trainor, George Armstrong and Tim Horton stood Red McCarthy on his head, trying to make him say "fuck." McCarthy, who was notably well mannered, refused. He stayed on his head the whole way to North Bay.

Bettio scored twice as the more experienced North Bay players prevailed, 5-3. Tim continued to have his problems with the rule book, landing in the penalty box with minors in the first and third periods.

The Winter Carnival was coming to Stanley Stadium, and this being Copper Cliff, it meant hockey games on tap three nights out of four. The Redmen and the Wolves provided the show on January 23, a Wednesday night. The Juniors had yet to beat the top Senior team in the Nickel District,

but both previous games had been close, with scores
of 4-3 and 2-1. In their last meeting, just before
Christmas, the Redmen had been leading 1-0 when
Tim's boarding penalty started the Wolves' comeback. On this Wednesday carnival night, it happened again. The Copper Cliff Juniors were leading
2-0 on a pair of Tatter McClellan goals with five minutes clocked in the second period when Tim was
sent off for tripping. Just before the power play
ended, a minute of scrambling around Bill Organ
produced the Wolves' first goal, and the Seniors
were off and running. McClellan scored again but it
wasn't enough; the Wolves won 4-3. The next night
Zellio Toppazzini took out his frustrations by pot-
ting four goals to Armstrong's two as Cliff High
buried Sud High 12-3.

By then, the news of George Armstrong's success
had hit the papers. It was no wonder the young
Falconbridge prospect had been so noncommittal
with Boston scout Cooney Weiland about something as simple as a tryout promise—Armstrong
had just signed a C-form with the Toronto Maple
Leafs, and by the sounds of it he would be heading
to Toronto's vaunted St. Michael's College in the
fall to study grade 12 and play for the Majors.

Armstrong was an important signing for Toronto,
and an important addition to the student body for
St. Mike's. The Majors might have seemed unstoppable in January, but they would be very stoppable
come fall if the school didn't do something about
the talent leak created by its graduating class. All
five of its top scorers—Fleming MacKell, Ed
Sandford, Fran Harrison, Rudy Migay and Les
Costello—wouldn't be available. A stellar prospect
like Armstrong, even if on hand only for a year, was

critical to the Majors making a respectable finish in
the 47/48 OHA Junior standings.

That Saturday, Armstrong, Toppazzini and
McClellan each scored a pair of goals as the
Redmen thrilled the Carnival audience at Stanley
Stadium with a 7-3 win over the North Bay Senior
all-stars in an exhibition rematch. Tim was in familiar circumstances, occupying the penalty box twice
in the third period, but his misbehaviour didn't
affect the outcome.

Over his next three games, Tim managed to steer
clear of the penalty box. He made it four games
when the Redmen met the Legion in the opener of
their best-of-three playoffs to decide who would
meet the first-placed Sudbury Wolves in the finals.
This was no small feat for Tim. It was one of the
wildest games ever played in the Nickel Belt.

The rhythm of the game was set in the first period
when Bill Organ's calf was sliced open by a skate in a
goalmouth scramble. The Redmen goaltender was
sent off for eight stitches and was lost for the rest of
the game. Terry Powell was dressed in his place and
the momentum shifted in the Legion's favour. At
one point the Redmen trailed 3-1 and the Juniors
had one goal disallowed by a high stick, but before
the second period was over the gap had been closed
to a goal.

In the third period, the Redmen began an all-too-
familar comeback against the Legion, scoring two
unanswered goals to put the Juniors ahead 4-3.
Then Sam Bettio loosed a shot that hit the Legion
goalie, Wes Edwards, in the mouth. "He went down,"
Bettio remembers, "like a ton of bricks." Of course,
there was no such thing as a face mask in February
1947, and Edwards' lip was too badly cut for him to

continue playing. This seemed like a good time for all hell at last to break loose between these two unlikely opponents—a band of overachieving teenagers and a group of veterans who had recently finished battling the international forces of tyranny. The brawl was on when Don McNabb of the Legion team, who would become the president of the local mine union, slugged George Armstrong in front of the Legion net. Dick Trainor was in the rink that night as the crowd erupted. "McNabb suckerpunched George. George wasn't a fighter. He fought when he had to. We were outraged because of the age difference between McNabb and George. It started a riot. I remember the bench clearing."

Armstrong had taken only four penalty minutes during the entire Nickel Belt season, but in highschool play he'd racked up fourteen minutes. Armstrong was a big kid who didn't go looking for trouble, but who also didn't back down. On this night his obstinacy cost him a five-minute major and several front teeth. At sixteen he had acquired the smile of a true hockey star, which nicely complemented that of Jim Dewey, who had lost two teeth in the third game of the 1937 Allan Cup final.

As Armstrong was sent off, the fighting continued in and around the penalty box, around the ice, and even over the boards. McNabb, who had been sent off as well, was swatted at by an irate Copper Cliff supporter; McNabb excused himself from the box to chase his assailant down the stadium corridor. The referee brought the festivities to an end by sending both teams to their dressing rooms while the Legion suited up a new goalie. When play resumed, Tatter McClellan scored twice to put the Redmen ahead 6-3. The Legion scored just as the buzzer sounded to make it a 6-4 final for the Juniors.

As tumultuous as the Legion game was for the Redmen, it was not their biggest game of the week. On Wednesday night they had an exhibition match, and although it would make no difference to their Nickel Belt playoffs or their bid to win the NOHA Junior title, it would sum up their very character for the people of greater Sudbury. The Barrie Flyers were coming to town: a team from the celebrated OHA packed with northern Ontario players carefully picked and purchased by Hap Emms, including Copper Cliff's own hero of the 45/46 Redmen season, Gordie Heale. The assuredly bigger, stronger, faster cousins were suiting up in Stanley Stadium, and 1,400 paying customers—the biggest crowd to watch a hockey game in the arena that season— were turning out to see once and for all what the new version of the Redmen was made of. But the night and the ice belonged to the new Redmen, a mix of holdovers from 45/46 and new recruits. Four of them would make it to the biggest big league, and two of them would one day win four Stanley Cups and have their careers honoured in the Hockey Hall of Fame. No one who moved on from the Redmen of 45/46, not even Gordie Heale, would ever play an NHL game.

The Bettio–McClellan–Flynn line was all the offence the Redmen needed that joyous night as the Cliff Juniors defeated the Flyers 6–5. And for once the boys behind the blueline were saluted. The Redmen attack, the *Daily Star* cheered, had been "backed up by a hard-hitting defence that sent many a Flyer for a flyer...Coach Jim Dewey's defense was in its most rambunctious mood of the season. Specs Telford and Tim Horton in particular were laying about incoming Barrie players with vim, vigour and enthusiasm to burn. It was a rousing blueline display."

It should have ended there. All that needed to be proved by the 46/47 Redmen was proven on that night in Stanley Stadium, the stands packed to the rafters, the score in their favour. It was the highlight of Tim Horton's first Junior season. But there was an ill omen for Horton when the *Sudbury Daily Star* ran a picture of the celebrating Redmen on February 11, 1947. They had just soundly beaten the Legion (soundly enough to earn George Armstrong a fighting major) 9-5 in the third and final game of the NDHL semi-finals, having lost game two in overtime. Horton is the only player missing from the picture, although he had been on the ice.

The best-of-three finals against the Wolves opened with a 4-1 loss. The next night Horton showed up without Armstrong to submit to a 14-1 thrashing of Sudbury High by Sacred Heart in high-school action. Three days later Tim endured a nightmarish second game between the Redmen and the Wolves. The Redmen had been able to keep the Wolves off the scoreboard until Tim, trying to keep the Wolves bottled up inside their blueline, had the puck snap off the blade of his stick—the Seniors jumped on the opportunity and got their first goal. Later, Copper Cliff was hanging on to a 4-3 lead when Tim again found himself with a broken stick, this time in his own end. The Wolves promptly tied the game. To add insult to injury, Jack Gladstone, a Legion player who had come over to the Wolves, then started out alone from his own blueline, stepped around Tim and scored the game- and series-winner for the Wolves. The Redmen had come up short, and Horton had been the game's unfortunate goat.

Tim promptly came down with the flu, missing practices as the Redmen put the Nickel District behind them and turned their attention to the NOHA Junior championship. When the team boarded a bus for the Soo to begin their best-of-five semifinal series, Tim was too sick to join them. The team had also lost Jim Dewey, who had to commit himself to the Wolves as they entered the Senior NOHA semifinals against the Soo Atomics.

Dewey's influence on his players varied. "Jim Dewey is the fellow I would give credit to for getting me into hockey," says Bettio. "He was my first hockey coach of any sort that knew a hockey stick from a canoe paddle." In the case of Red McCarthy (whose future wife would have Dewey as her boss), Dewey's influence was limited. "Jim always treated me well. I liked him and had no complaints. But Jim was a very busy person. He didn't spend a lot of time with us. Lots of times he couldn't get out. He was playing Senior hockey, he curled, he had a big job at Inco. It ended up that Jack Newell [father of NHL referee Dave Newell], who was our trainer, took over as coach in the playoffs, and did a great job. Jack worked at it. I don't know how much influence Jim could have had on anybody because he just wasn't around a lot."

It's generally felt that Tim respected Dewey, and recognised him for the star he was. A year after he played his last game as a Copper Cliff Redman, Tim participated in an exhibition game between

Redmen alumni and Jim Dewey's Senior Wolves. Tim devoted part of his night to trying to live up to his reputation as a physical presence by taking aim at Dewey. There was no malice intended—it was more a case of the Young Turk having a mischievous go at the old guard. "Before the game," says Dick Trainor, "there was a big writeup in the paper, and it was Horton and Dewey. Stanley Stadium was jammed. Tim took a run at Jim, and Jim deked him right out of the rink. I remember kidding Tim for years afterwards. I only saw Tim get shifted that badly on one other occasion, and that was by Gordie Howe."

As the NOHA playoffs began, neither Tim nor Dewey were missed—not yet, anyway. The Redmen beat the Soo team 11-3, with pretty well everybody getting in on the scoring. The Cliff team had spent almost half of the second period cruising around inside the Soo blueline, and the Soo squad immediately conceded the series.

When the Wolves eliminated the Atomics, it meant that Sudbury and Timmins would be meeting in both the Junior and Senior NOHA finals. The Wolves were playing the Hollinger Greenshirts, while the Redmen were matched with the Porcupine Combines.

When the NOHA Junior finals opened at Stanley Stadium on March 10, Tim had emerged as a player of importance and promise. The northern Ontario Leaf scout, Bob Wilson, lived in Cobalt, but he was no stranger to the Nickel Belt: he had organised the Falconbridge Midget NHL and was keeping tabs on the local Juniors. He came to Copper Cliff for the Redmen–Combines final, revealing that he had already procured A-forms from several northern

Juniors, committing them to an appearance at the Leafs training camp in the fall. He'd also had the sense to place Tim on the Leafs' negotiating list.

Thus, Wilson was on hand when a Combines forward, Berle Small, bore down on Tim in the opening minutes of the game. Tim stepped out of his way and watched Small crash into the boards. Small had to be carried off the ice but eventually returned.

Late in the second period, the ill omen of Tim's absence from the team picture was fully realized. Tim was notoriously superstitious throughout his life, and had he connected his absence from the photo with his misfortune in the playoff game, he would have made sure he was front and centre in every team picture ever taken for the rest of his career. After he hit the boards heavily, Tim had to be helped off the ice, but unlike Small he didn't return. At first an old ligament complaint was suspected, but a trip to the hospital revealed a broken ankle. Tim's season with the Redmen was over.

His friends on the team feared that he had missed his big chance to demonstrate his skills to Wilson, and the Redmen weren't the same without him. They had entered the best-of-seven NOHA finals against the Porcupine Combines as the favourites—the Combines had finished last in the Gold Belt League, like the Redmen playing against Senior teams. But the Redmen came up flat in the opening game, losing 4-2, and dropped the rematch the next day 3-1.

"The club will feel the loss of Tim Horton on defence," the *Daily Star* concluded after the second loss, referring to him as their "stellar defenceman." The paper opined that one Redmen weakness "was the inability of the defencemen to launch successful rushes." It is the first public recognition that Tim can do more than patrol a blueline and knock people down. Within him was a player with rushing capability. Dewey had recognised that at the beginning of the season, when he considered making him a forward. As it happened, Tim had picked up his first (and only) point as a Redman in the second game of the Nickel Belt semifinal against the Legion, contributing to a nice three-way play with Bettio and Flynn. But his way with the body check was also missed. The Combines defence was big—three of the players were 175, 185 and 200 pounds—and they were knocking around the Redmen wingers.

Toppazzini, plagued by a recurring leg injury, got full marks for effort. George Armstrong was wonderful. "He uncorked plenty of speed and appears to be headed for the bigger time," Grace wrote after the first game. "He still has lots to learn but he has what it takes in pinches and didn't back down once last night."

The Redmen got back in the series with a 5-4 win in which Toppazzini collected a hat trick, but the fourth game of the series was brutally decisive. The Redmen got the first two goals and the Combines got the next nine. Down three games to one, the Cliff kids made a last-ditch effort to get back in the series, but Bettio got the only goal on a Toppazzini pass as the Combines won 2-1 and advanced to the all-Ontario Junior finals.

Things weren't going much better for Jim Dewey and the Wolves in Senior play. They had won the opening game, but the Hollinger Greenshirts roared back with four straight wins to advance to the

Ontario Senior finals against the Hamilton Tigers. The Porcupine was sticking it to the Nickel Belt without mercy. In the Northern Ontario Juvenile championship, the South Porcupine Red Wings overwhelmed the Sudbury Grads 18-0 and 14-4.

While the season was over for Horton and Armstrong, other Redmen carried on. The NOHA Junior champions were allowed to add three players from the rest of the northern region to their lineup for the Memorial Cup playdowns, and they chose the top line of the Redmen: Tatter McClellan, Sam Bettio and Yacker Flynn. Flynn and McClellan were off helping Copper Cliff High win the provincial high-school championship when the playdowns began. Only Bettio was on hand at Maple Leaf Gardens as the double-blue of St. Mike's gave the Porcupine Combines a 16-2 hockey lesson. With the McClellan–Bettio–Flynn line reunited for game two, St. Mike's was held to a 1-0 win. Back in Schumacher for game three, both McClellan and Bettio scored—to no avail, as the Majors swept the series with a 7-3 decision.

Events shortly proved that there was no shame in losing to the Majors. While the Maple Leafs and the Canadiens met in the Stanley Cup, their farm teams, the Majors and the Junior Canadiens, were squaring off in the eastern Memorial Cup play-downs. Like fathers, like sons: the Leafs won the cup and St. Mike's swept their series 11-3 and 21-0, the final rout partly due to injuries that reduced the Montreal Juniors to ten skaters.

Then it was on to the Memorial Cup finals for the St. Mike's juggernaut. The Moose Jaw Canucks, beaten by the Majors in the '45 finals, wilted under the St. Mike's attack. They went down four straight games: 6-1, 12-3, 8-1 and 3-2.

It was possibly the most potent Junior team ever assembled in this country. It would be a hard act to follow.

The ice in Stanley Stadium that summer of '47 was put to use. Jim Dewey made up for his absence behind the bench during the Redmen's ill-fated playoff drive by putting together a pick-up team to play some Labour Day exhibition games in the Michigan Soo. Tim joined him, and so did Bettio, Flynn, McClellan, Toppazzini, Telford and others. There was baseball, too, and on the Garson Juniors squad two future Leaf greats could be found as George Armstrong pitched to catcher Tod Sloan.

The 46/47 Redmen were breaking up, even though many of them were still young enough to play another season or two in Copper Cliff. The south and the professional leagues were exerting their inexorable pull.

Come September, the professional training camps opened. Yacker Flynn and Tatter McClellan headed to Guelph to try out with the New York Rangers. They couldn't crack the pro ranks, but they were still eligible to play Junior hockey and signed on with the Guelph Biltmores of the OHA. Zellio Toppazzini, Sam Bettio and Specs Telford honoured their A-forms and attended the Bruins camp in St. Catharines. Toppazzini had just finished grade 11 and was offered a spot with the Tee-Pees of the OHA, which he accepted.

Bettio and Telford got themselves into one fine mess. In mid-September they were reported to have signed professional contracts with the Bruins, which meant they would play no lower than the Hershey

Bears of the AHL. It's not known what Telford signed, but Bettio had actually signed a B-form with the Bruins, which paid him a $1,000 bonus. By Christmas they were hockey outlaws. It had been a busy autumn for the Copper Cliff pair. It was reported that they had also tried out—and signed registration cards—with Guelph (where Flynn and McClellan were), but Bettio doesn't remember this. He agrees they went to the Oshawa Generals of the Junior OHA, but they didn't show up to play after signing registration cards and accepting the standard registration signing fee, which was around $300. Then they were spotted in the lineup of the Boston Olympics, a Bruins farm team in the Quebec Senior league. Guelph and Oshawa protested to the CAHA, which suspended the pair for jumping teams. They were ordered to pay back their registration money to Oshawa, and told that if they ever wanted to play under the auspices of the CAHA again they had better report to Guelph.

Bettio says his troubles began when he listened to the Bruins, principally general manager (and former Nickel Belter) Art Ross. The Bruins wanted him with the Olympics, even though he had agreed to play in Oshawa. "Art Ross from day one said, 'Don't worry about the Junior A card. We'll take care of everything. We want you to be a hockey player.'" The Boston Olympics were actually two teams. "The black shirts were the good guys. They were in the Quebec Senior league." The other squad played in the Eastern U.S. amateur league. The Bruins wanted him in a black shirt.

"I thought, 'I've got to play hockey. What difference is it if I wear a white sweater or a green sweater or a red sweater? The name of the game is money."

When it came to money, the Olympics won hands down. They were paying $200 a week. His dad was making $32 a week at Inco. It meant he wouldn't have to work at all when he was off the ice. "I wanted to be a hockey player, and I wanted to get there as fast as I could. The Boston Bruins were right there. I went down for three months. Then I got suspended by the CAHA.

"I got railroaded into the Boston Olympics," says Bettio. "It was embarrassing. Hugo Harrington, the coach of the Olympics, came to me and said, 'I can't use you any more.' 'What's going on?' I said. 'You've been suspended,' he told me. It was devastating to me at the time.

"You're a youngster, you believe people. What reason did I have to doubt the manager of the Copper Cliff Redmen, who said, 'Don't worry, son, you just go out and do what you want.' Why shouldn't I trust Art Ross, who was the manager of the Boston Bruins?"[3]

Telford and Bettio were summoned to Toronto for a hearing. Telford, says Bettio, "was a victim of circumstance. He was just tagging along with me."

Guelph, meanwhile, was negotiating their releases from the Redmen, which was said to be seeking about $500 for the pair. Specs Telford came home at Christmas and decided to play out the remainder of the 47/48 season with the Redmen. Bettio waved goodbye to the CAHA and turned professional, joining Boston's American league farm team, the Hershey Bears. Zellio Toppazzini found Bettio there when he moved up from Junior hockey in 1948. The two became roommates.

Zellio Toppazzini was called up by the Bruins for five regular-season and two playoff games in 48/49, then divided the 49/50 season between the Bears and the Bruins. In November 1950, the Bruins dealt him, along with Fran Harrison of the Memorial Cup-winning Majors of '47, to the Rangers for Dunc Fisher. The Rangers played him for sixteen games, then moved him down to Cincinnati of the AHL, which in turn dealt him to Providence—all in the same season.

In Providence, Zellio became a star of the AHL in an era when the AHL had stars, when it wasn't simply a collection of farm teams owned by NHL clubs. With the exception of seven games with the Blackhawks in 56/57, he played ten and a half seasons with Providence, setting regular-season and playoff scoring records in 55/56. In 1964 he turned to coaching with Providence College; he still lives in Providence today.

Sam Bettio also got the call-up to the Bruins with Zellio in 49/50 when a check by Bill Barilko severed former St. Mike's star Ed Sandford's Achilles tendon. The Bruins were going to pay him a salary of $8,400. He rushed to a phone booth in a drugstore in downtown Boston, called his mother (collect) in Copper Cliff, and crowed, "Ma, I'm going to make more money than anybody's got in this whole wide world. I'll never be able to spend it all." He gave it his best shot.

Bettio's performance as a Bruin garnered generally positive reviews, but he couldn't stick with the NHL. Though his nickname was "Chunky," he was on the small side and took a pounding. "I got a lot of bad injuries. For the first five or six years I either came home to Copper Cliff with crutches or a sling. If I came home with nothing, my mom didn't know me."

The Bruins sent him back to Hershey after forty-four games; he stayed with the Bears for four seasons, collecting along the way a badly separated shoulder and a stick in the mouth that cost him fourteen teeth. After a season with Victoria of the Western league in 53/54, he hooked up with the Buffalo Bisons of the American league from 1954 to 1958. He played a partial season of Senior hockey with the Sudbury Wolves, then squeezed out three more seasons of professional service as the Wolves joined the short-lived Eastern professional league. Finally he settled into a thirty-year career as a salesman at Carrington Lumber and Builder's Supply, which supplied the local construction trade. His manager was none other than Wes Edwards, the Legion goaltender whose lip had been split open by Bettio's shot—the incident that had led to the brawl that cost George Armstrong three teeth. ("Needless to say," says Bettio, "we became good friends.")

Increasingly serious arthritis finally forced Bettio's retirement from Carrington's. At one point he was expected to spend the rest of his life in a wheelchair. There was no doubt that the punishment he had sustained in his first choice of career was the culprit. When he began treatment for his arthritis, he underwent a full skeletal X-ray. The nurse who examined it asked him with alarm: "What *happened* to you?" "I was a professional hockey player," Bettio replied. That explained everything.

Specs Telford tried his luck with different teams in different leagues. After a half-season with the 47/48 Redmen, he played OHA Junior hockey with the Tee-Pees. Tulsa of the U.S. league took him for two seasons, then he managed eight games with Syracuse of the American league before dropping

out of professional hockey for a year. Springfield of
the Quebec league and Syracuse of the American
league gave him another season each, then the
game stopped paying its way for him. His last known
address was in the Soo. His present whereabouts are
unknown.

Yacker Flynn and Tatter McClellan were insepara-
ble. Too small to have a shot at the NHL, the pair
went from the Guelph Biltmores to the New York
Rovers to the St. Paul Saints to the Atlantic City
Seagulls before they, too, gave up the dream. Both
have since died.

The two members of the 46/47 Copper Cliff
Redmen who would realize the hockey dream of
the northern Ontario kid to its fullest were Tim
Horton and George Armstrong, neither of whom
were from Copper Cliff and both of whom were
property of the Toronto Maple Leafs. Their careers
had become linked with the Nickel Belt's Midget
league of 45/46, when they played each other for
the league title. They had been brought together by
Sudbury High, by the Redmen and by Leaf scout
Bob Wilson, and now fate and circumstance were
going to wind their futures even more tightly
together.

The Leafs had intended to place Armstrong in
St. Michael's College as part of his development,
but in the spring of 1947 the hot young prospect
from Falconbridge put schooling behind him and
quit Sudbury High without completing grade 11.
With grade 12 at St. Mike's out of the picture,
Armstrong, still the property of the Leafs, joined
the Stratford Kroehlers of the Junior OHA.

The number of boys abandoning their education
in the belief that their future lay entirely in hockey

was raising concerns. At the National Council on Physical Fitness Conference in Ottawa in January 1949, J.L. Murray, principal of Kingston Collegiate, presented a survey of fifty Ontario schools taken since 1947 which revealed that 117 boys between sixteen and eighteen had left school to play hockey. "I think this is an evil which has grown without the governing bodies realising the result," Murray fumed, calling for "drastic and immediate action." He noted that the boys have been "taken away from home to another centre and away from parental control for tryout periods with NHL and OHA teams. These are held in October [actually September] and if the youngsters don't make the grade, they return to school late in the term and their studies are retarded." Put on the spot, NHL president Clarence Campbell offered that there had been "a frightful scarcity of hockey players the last two or three years. Some of the boys who had gone to professional leagues would not ordinarily be called up."

George Armstrong's decision to quit school left St. Mike's at least one scholarship short of a rebuilding program for the Majors. They needed a kid who could play hockey who was also still interested in going to school. He didn't even have to be Catholic—when it came to the Majors, the Basilian fathers who ran the college and suited up the Majors with Conn Smythe's support put their faith in playmaking. This flexibility was fortunate, for in Tim Horton they had a perfect candidate—maybe not a sparkling forward like Armstrong, but a solid defenceman who could move the puck and was on the Leaf reserve list, a kid who would give his homework the old college try and, if not a Catholic, then at least someone with Irish blood in his veins who went to church every Sunday.

Even though Tim had broken his ankle in the playoff game that Leaf scout Bob Wilson had attended, he had made enough of an impression to compel Wilson to offer him a C-form, which he accepted. But his immediate future was far from firm. He might well have ended up playing another season with the Copper Cliff Redmen (although he might have been considering the Toronto Marlboros) had his high-school coach, Charlie Cerre, not launched a persuasive lobby on his behalf at St. Michael's College.

Cerre was a St. Mike's alumnus who had grown up playing hockey on the same outdoor rinks as Bob Davidson at Withrow Park near Pape and the Danforth in Toronto. A fine player, he starred with the Majors in 26/27 and 27/28. After completing grade 12 in 1929, he entered the Basilian congregation and began his undergraduate studies. In 1935 he was teaching grade 9 French; soon after that he left his studies for the priesthood, opting for the secular life. But Cerre never lost touch with his alma mater and would return in the 1950s to coach the Majors.

He came to Sudbury High as its athletic director after the war, and impressed everyone with his abilities and enthusiasm. He coached hockey and football, and ran an impressive number of in-house sports leagues. He made them something special: for baseball, he brought the principal out to throw the first pitch of the season, and posted batting averages every morning.

In Tim Horton, Cerre appeared convinced he had a future star. While Cerre himself cannot remember exactly what role he might have played in Tim's arrival at St. Mike's ("That was a hundred years ago," he says), Tim's high-school friends, like Dick Trainor and Red McCarthy, credit Cerre with engineering Tim's placement at the school.

Gerry Horton agrees. "Tim didn't really get invited to St. Mike's. I'm sure Charlie Cerre wrote letters down there and coaxed them and begged them to put him on the team. It wasn't Bob Wilson or the Leafs that brought him down. The Leafs never made plans for him to go anywhere. Charlie Cerre was the one who talked the school into putting Tim on the hockey team."

And it was a career path that Red McCarthy is sure Cerre would have advocated for Tim. "Charlie would be the kind of guy that would say, 'Still play hockey, but try to get your education.'" The best way to do that in 1947 was a hockey scholarship with St. Michael's College. However much influence Charlie Cerre had in its ultimate bestowal, Tim Horton got one.

The great NHL left-winger Dick Duff, who came to St. Michael's College in 1951 and was coached there by Cerre, and who himself became a professional hockey scout, refutes the notion that any player owes his career to being "discovered." "Who sent Mahovlich down to St. Mike's beside Mahovlich? Or Dave Keon? The credit mostly lies with the players. Those people, like Cerre, to their credit, probably encouraged guys to go with something they were half decent at, and knowing the kid was interested in being a player, would know some of the channels that young guys in the north might not. But it wasn't going to be long before there were ten guys up there looking for the player to come down."

It was back to square one for the St. Michael's
Majors in the fall of 1947, and Tim Horton, not
George Armstrong, became that square.

Chapter 5

St. Mike's

The Wall of Fame begins with Joe Primeau and ends 127 players later with Joe Day: row after row of framed portraits of National Hockey League players arranged in chronological order, with little room left for the ones who will follow them—already several frames overlap a doorway. Scan the portraits and you scan a kaleidoscope of professional hockey careers, some measured in decades, others measured in single games. But every player here is a measure of accomplishment for the priests who tutored them in Latin composition and penalty killing, guided by the motto *Doce me bonitatem et disciplinam et scientiam*: Teach me goodness, discipline and knowledge. The order is important—goodness and discipline first, knowledge later. The school seal consists of a church belfry, a chalice and an open book. The seal is circular, but you could also say that it's puckular.

This is the Old Boys' Room of Toronto's St. Michael's College School, done up in early Canadian rec room on the second floor of an add-on to the school's quonset-hut hockey arena. A sign above the Wall of Fame proclaims: ST. MICHAEL'S IN THE NHL. THE TRADITION LIVES ON. The tradition certainly does, even though the team that did the most to bring St. Mike's its enduring fame, the Majors of the Ontario Hockey Association's

Major Junior A league, hasn't existed for more than
thirty years. The mystique of that wall has insured
that kids from across North America continue to be
drawn to the enigmatic high school run by Basilian
fathers, most to study but some mainly to skate and
score on the same rink that gave the sport so many
marquee players. On the end wall is a window that
provides a pretty good view of the rink, and beside
that window are two large framed colour portraits
of Eric and Brett Lindros. Brett played with the
school's 1991/92 Junior B Buzzers, while his older,
more famous brother Eric amassed 24 goals, 33
assists and 193 penalty minutes in thirty-seven
games with the 88/89 Buzzers.

"There's Tim," says Father William O'Brien, and
he points to a photo eight from the left in the second row from the top. Tim Horton, Class of '49, is
between Rudy Migay, Class of '47, a Maple Leaf centre throughout the 1950s, and Benny Woit, Class of
'48, a defenceman who logged six full seasons in
the 1950s with Detroit and Chicago. Tim is just
below Nick Metz, Class of '34, one of the greatest
classes of all. And kitty-corner below Tim is Frank
Mahovlich, Class of '57, and the class of the classic
Maple Leaf teams of the 1960s.

For at least three decades, St. Mike's was one of
the most productive, and most unusual, finishing
schools for prospective professional hockey players.
With the financial support of an Irish Protestant
named Conn Smythe, an Irish Catholic institution
run by a French order of priests served as one of
hockey's most productive centres of excellence.

Father O'Brien has been with St. Mike's since
1935. His six decades of teaching and his responsibilities as the school's archivist give him a casual

familiarity with many of the faces arrayed along the Wall. He points to three favourites, well-known to fans of the sixties Leafs: Dave Keon, Class of '60, Dick Duff, Class of '55, and Frank Mahovlich. "Wonderful guys," he says. "They didn't use their hockey clout at school as some I've known, swaggering down the corridors. Even as schoolboys, they were gentlemen, quiet. Not scholastic stars, but they became everything we could hope they would be."

Some turned out less than St. Mike's could hope they would. Billy "the Kid" Taylor, Class of '36, led the NHL in assists in 46/47, then was expelled for life the following season after placing a $500 bet on a league game.

Back in Father O'Brien's office in the priests' residence wing of the school, a steel-door closet conceals what he calls the school's "holy of holies": a cast-iron safe containing the microfiche records of the students who have attended St. Mike's over nearly a century and a half. Beside the safe is a stack of framed sporting photos. On top is a picture of Frank Mahovlich and younger brother Peter in their Team Canada uniforms, preparing to do battle with the Soviet red machine in the momentous 1972 series.

The picture is autographed and addressed personally to Father O'Brien. He doesn't like to hang it up—that would be self-aggrandizing—but he does treasure it. It was Peter who indirectly caused Father O'Brien to grasp the essence of the St. Michael's hockey program, after watching it churn out stars for nearly thirty years. Peter attended the school from 1961 to 1963, playing with the Buzzers and not doing very well in French, which Father O'Brien was teaching. Father O'Brien took his complaint to

Father David Bauer, who had coached the final
Majors squad to the 1961 Memorial Cup win and
was the school's assistant principal at the time. "He
had to give me the facts of life," Father O'Brien
recalls. "He said, you have to go easy on these kids.
It's not their fault. They're in a terribly competitive
situation. They had to make a career decision in
grade 10, these striplings at the age of fourteen, to
become professional hockey players, and they're
here to get what education they can and what education we can give them."

Which raises the subject of Tim Horton. "This
I'm sure explains why Tim's scholastic record is not
that of a top-flight student," Father O'Brien says.
"But it is that of a student taking every course he
can, suiting up for every exam, passing some and
flunking some."

The school newspaper called him Tim the
Terrible.

Tim Horton and about forty other St. Mike's alumni whose portraits hang in the Wall of Fame never
walked the corridors of the two-storey yellow-brick
structure now synonymous with the glory of St.
Mike's. The school was founded in 1852 by the
French order of St. Basil; they came to Toronto to
educate the city's underclass of Irish Catholics, who
at the time comprised fully one-third of its population. In 1902 a new St. Michael's College was built
at the corner of Bay and Bloor; part of the
University of Toronto, it continued to be known as
an Irish Catholic institution, attracting students of
this extraction from across North America. The college offered education at the prep school (grade 7
and 8), high school and university level. It also

became famous for its athletic programs, particularly football, and picked up the monicker "the Fighting Irish of Bay Street."

About three hundred students attended the high-school portion of St. Mike's when Father O'Brien began teaching there in 1935 (he had also been a student). By the late 1940s the enrolment was up to 450, and they were crammed into every corner of a tired building. In 1950 a new facility—the present school—was opened at Bathurst and St. Clair just for the high-school program, with a sports field and hockey arena. (The present arena was opened in 1961.) Where the high-school instruction had been part and parcel of St. Michael's College, in its new location it became St. Michael's College School, independent of, though affiliated with, the University of Toronto school.

St. Mike's' reputation as a sporting school was well established on the gridiron when the open-air rink at the rear of the property began to bring it acclaim in the 1920s. "Gentleman Joe" Primeau was the first major star to emerge from the school, playing with the Maple Leafs from 1927 to 1936. He was exceptionally good-tempered, winning the Lady Byng award for gentlemanly play in 1932 and finishing runner-up to Frank Boucher in 1933 and 1934, which didn't diminish his stature in the eyes of Conn Smythe, who had brought Primeau aboard the first season he owned the Toronto franchise. A prototypic defensive forward, he centred the great Leaf Kid Line of the 1930s between Harvey (Busher) Jackson and Charlie Conacher.[1]

Another Jackson with the thirties Leafs, named Art, was part of the St. Mike's Junior team of 1934, which won the school its first Memorial Cup by beating the Edmonton Superiors. Three other members of that team—Nick Metz, Reg Hamilton and Pep Kelly—also graduated to the NHL, and it was this foursome that made the hockey reputation of the Fighting Irish.

In the 1930s, a dozen St. Mike's graduates showed up on NHL teams; more followed through the war years, and in 1944 St. Mike's graduated a superstar for the next decade in Ted Lindsay. Although Lindsay became a Red Wing, many of these players ended up as Maple Leafs. The Leaf connection was the handiwork of Conn Smythe, whose Maple Leaf Gardens Ltd. became a sponsor of the school hockey program, and his prominence in the history of the Majors is such that it must be emphasized that the "Majors" name came from the fact that the team played OHA Major Junior A, not because Connie Smythe was a major in the Second World War.

When some Leaf players pursued university degrees part-time in the 1960s, Conn Smythe did not hesitate to publicly pooh-pooh the value of higher education, even though he had attended university himself. He certainly never pooh-poohed the value of the collegiate hockey system, having both played and coached at the University of Toronto, and found some of his best professional prospects—like Joe Primeau—while they were still in school. Nor did his ingrained ill-feelings toward Catholics, as the son of an Irish Protestant, stand in the way of tapping a good source of players or hiring Catholic managers (such as King Clancy), although he retained a basic suspicion of them, and religion could be the final litmus test of friendship with him. In March 1943, Smythe was overseas with the Canadian army, exchanging correspondence with his longstanding friend and Leaf scout, George "Squib" Walker. Walker felt he was getting a raw deal in salary negotiations with Frank Selke, another old friend and associate of both men.[2] Smythe stood by Walker in a letter to him: "I have not said anything about it but when I get back you can be sure they will do right by our George or else. FJS [Selke] is not the strongest friend in the world when the chips get down as is probably due to the RC in him."

Smythe, in fact, would link Catholicism in general and St. Mike's in particular in some of his most terrifying childhood memories. In 1900 the five-year-old Smythe had to make his way past St. Mike's, at Bay and Bloor, on his way to and from Wellesley School, at Bay and Wellesley. "The route to and from kindergarten," he wrote in his memoirs, "was full of fear, because we had to pass St. Michael's College. Religion was very bitter in those days. The Knights of Columbus, Catholic, celebrated St. Patrick's Day; the Orangemen, Protestant, July 12. But those were just the *big* fighting days. All year when Protestant and Catholic kids came together there would be fights. Sometimes coming out of school we little kids would run east all the way over to Yonge before cutting back toward home on Czar Street [which no longer exists]; we were scared to death of being attacked by the Catholics if we went the short route past St. Michael's…In our ignorance, we sincerely believed that if we were captured by the priests, we'd never be seen alive again."

His support for the St. Mike's Junior program continued until 1961, when St. Mike's itself pulled the plug on the grounds that the sixty-game OHA schedule and the increasing commercialisation of the Junior game made it impossible for the school to run a hockey program and educate the players at the same time. Father David Bauer led the Majors to their fourth Memorial Cup in the spring of 1961, then stunned Smythe by unilaterally ending the Majors program. "In the minds of some of the older alumni," says Father O'Brien, "the dream of St. Michael's returning to the Junior A is a dream that will not go away."

Smythe readily confessed to his suspicion of Catholics in a frank letter to the principal of St. Michael's College School on June 6, 1961, the day the school announced the end of the Majors: "I myself, with a father born a few miles from Belfast, had always a wary eye turned toward the Catholics,[3] but in my association with your school through your Sports Directors, and knowing the way you have treated the Protestants who have attended your school, I have gained a knowledge of your Religion, which at least has made me respect your whole organization very much."

Gaining a knowledge of that religion did not necessarily make him more welcoming of it. Billy Harris, who played for Conn's son Stafford as a Junior Marlie and as a Maple Leaf, says Conn wasn't happy when Stafford married Dorothy, a Catholic. And when Conn's granddaughter Candy married both a player and a Catholic, Mike Walton—and became a Catholic in the process—the Major was seen at the wedding reception, hammering out a financial agreement with the mother of the bride to ensure that any children issuing from this union would be educated in a Protestant school. Smythe himself had attended Upper Canada College, a High Anglican institution, and so had his sons. He may have valued St. Mike's for its hockey savvy, but no great-grandson of his was going to be taught by Basilians.

While Tim was honing his hockey skills in Sudbury, the St. Mike's Majors were ruling the Canadian Junior hockey system, their successes masterminded by alumnus Joe Primeau. Gentleman Joe had retired from the NHL at the end of the 35/36 Leaf season, thirty years of age, already well established in business. In his early twenties he'd become a partner in Dundas Block Co., and then struck out on his own with Primeau Block. The construction trade was a common experience in Leaf circles—Conn Smythe owned a sand and gravel operation, which Hap Day as his minority partner ran for him even while coaching the Leafs in the forties and serving as their general manager in the fifties, and Joe Primeau bought sand from Smythe's operation.[4]

During the war Primeau coached the RCAF Flyers. The armed forces teams attracted top-quality players who enlisted, were exempted from overseas service and were put to use entertaining on the home front.[5] Primeau's Flyers could have terrorised any NHL club: their lineup included the Bruins' "Kraut" line of Milt Schmidt, Woody Dumart and Eddie Bauer, all Kitchener-Waterloo natives. In the fall of 1944, Primeau returned to his alma mater to coach the Majors. He got them a Memorial Cup the following spring, took them to a seven-game final in 1946, and in 1947 made amends for the previous season's heartbreaking shortfall by marshalling a rout of the Canadian Junior hockey system that ended in the four-straight defeat of the Moose Jaw Canucks.

Primeau would go on to coach the Leafs for three seasons, winning the Stanley Cup on his first try in 1951. No other coach has ever won an Allan, Memorial and Stanley Cup. Despite his sterling coaching record, Primeau was never enthusiastic about the Leaf job. He loved the players more than the occupation, and tradition has it that he walked away from coaching the Leafs because he couldn't stand having Smythe second-guessing him.

"He was a player's coach," says Cal Gardner, who played for Primeau for the first two of the three seasons Primeau spent behind the Leaf bench. "If we lost the last game, he didn't rant and rave. He'd come down the next day at practice and all he would say is, 'Boys, I got it up to here'—and he'd put his hand across his neck—'from the Old Man. And if that's not enough for you, I don't want to see anybody going down to Pittsburgh.' That was enough to scare everybody, because at that time they sent you down if you made one or two mistakes. You were gone."

In contrast, Hap Day, another former Leaf player who successfully turned to coaching, "wasn't someone you could get close to," says Harry Watson, who spent eight seasons as a Leaf. Being neither a drinker nor a smoker limited his carousing potential, had he been so inclined. "He had determination and he wanted to win," says Gardner, "and that's the way he was brought up." He was wont to lead by example. At training camp, Day, pushing fifty, would be out front of the whole team, leading them in their running sessions. "Making an example of you," says Gardner. "If you can't keep up, there's something wrong."

Don Rope, who played at St. Mike's with Tim Horton, was deeply impressed with Primeau. "Joe took an interest in you personally. He made you feel good about yourself. Joe was very good because he gave a young person a feeling of being wanted, and to go out and do his thing to the best of his ability, and if he didn't quite do it, it wasn't the end of the world. You had the feeling that Joe was behind you. He created a feeling of respect." When Primeau died in 1989, Rope wrote to the surviving members of the family, telling them that there are many people in Canada who are proud to say they were coached by Gentleman Joe.

"He knew everything there was to know about the game," Tim said in 1969. "We listened to every word he had to say, even though he never raised his voice. He got a great deal out of us because of his attitude. Actually it would have been embarrassing for him to start shouting at us because we would have thought he had suddenly been taken ill. It was just the opposite with Punch [Imlach]. If he had stopped screaming we would have gone looking for a doctor."[6]

Yet as gifted a coach as Primeau was, during his St. Michael's days he wouldn't have been able to strategize his way out of an OHA final if he hadn't been blessed with the talent the school was attracting. Part of it was reputation. The great 33/34 Majors team had started it, and the persistent flow of graduates into NHL uniforms in the 1930s and early 1940s had helped make St. Mike's a finishing school of choice for Catholic kids who dreamed of NHL careers. But prospects had to identified, and the best of them courted. The kids and their families might have to be convinced that going to school and playing for the Majors in exchange for

an education and some pocket money was a better
option than playing Junior hockey elsewhere in
exchange for a lot of money. The Toronto Maple
Leaf scouting system lent a big hand. Alumni and
current Majors players would keep an eye out for
talent in their home towns. Pep Kelly, for example,
coaching kids' hockey back in North Bay, could be
counted on to direct prospects the school's way, and
of course, in Sudbury, Charlie Cerre had his eye
peeled for talent. And like other OHA clubs, the
Majors would make an annual exhibition tour of
northern Ontario hockey centres, bagging recruits
as they went.

Perhaps St. Mike's' biggest recruitment asset was
the world's greatest talent-spotting system: the
Roman Catholic clergy, located in small towns all
across the country. Parish priests kept tabs on the
local rinks and passed along intelligence to the
Basilians in Toronto. Sometimes, to secure the
player they wanted, the Basilians had to be as proac-
tive as the dignity of the cloth allowed. To get Frank
Mahovlich before Jack Adams' Red Wings did,
Father Ted Flanagan, who was in charge of the
school's hockey program, drove to the Porcupine
with a translator so that he could convince Frank's
Ruthenian parents that St. Mike's was where their
boy belonged. It may be apocryphal, but St. Mike's
tradition has it that Jack Adams was not moved to
charity in the presence of Basilians from that day
forward.

And sometimes, to get the player they wanted,
the Basilians had to adopt a flexible approach to
their educational mandate. With the right prospect,
there was no sense letting something like the precise configuration of his personal faith get in the

way of a hockey scholarship that would benefit both the school and the player.

Generally, the non-Catholics came to St. Mike's through the Leaf talent system. For out-of-town kids signed to Leaf C-forms who were coming to Toronto to play Junior hockey, those serious about continuing their education were directed toward St. Mike's, regardless of their faith, while the others played for the Marlboros or the Junior Rangers. Tim Horton was certainly not the first or the last non-Catholic in the St. Mike's hockey program. Phil Samis, for example, came to St. Mike's for the 44/45 season with two other Albertans, Bobby Gray and John Arundel. All three of them were Protestant, and all three played on the Junior B Buzzers, who won the provincial title. (Samis then moved up to the Majors for the Memorial Cup at the end of the season, and won that, too.) At any rate, playing in a Catholic hockey program was old hat to Tim, having already been a Holy Trinity defenceman in the Nickel Belt Midget league. His Irish blood was at least consistent with the school's traditions.

Regardless of faith, Tim came to St. Mike's as the strength of its hockey program was plunging from sky-high to rock-bottom. The depopulation of virtually the entire Majors team after the 1947 Memorial Cup, when players either graduated, took their services to other Junior teams (with payrolls) or became too old for Junior hockey, left Gentlemen Joe and the fathers with some imposing skates to fill for the next season. Ed Sandford and Ed (Fran) Harrison, two cousins from Mimico, had signed with the Bruins and started playing in the NHL that fall. Red Kelly had also cracked the Detroit Red Wings lineup, straight out of Juniors. Les Costello and Fleming MacKell, both Leaf properties, were playing with the Pittsburgh Hornets, the club's American league farm team. Benny Woit and Rudy Migay began the 47/48 season with the Brandon Wheat Kings of the Manitoba Junior league, but in November transferred to the Port Arthur West End Bruins of the Thunder Bay league—both were born in Fort William—and would win a Memorial Cup with them. Migay was two seasons away from becoming a Maple Leaf, while Woit was three seasons away from his first game as a Red Wing. The Majors' goaltender, Howie Harvey (brother of Montreal Canadien Doug Harvey, the dominant NHL defenceman of the next decade and a half), as well as Bob Paul, Harry Psutka and Ray Hannigan, had moved up to the Toronto Marlboros senior team.

The Marlies had returned to play after the Second World War, serving as a potent farm system for the Maple Leafs. While the hockey teams were officially the property of the Marlboro Athletic Club, the Marlboro system was the de facto property of the Leafs. The club president was Harold Ballard. The Senior team was also coached by Joe Primeau, while the Juniors were at first handled by Stafford Smythe, who wanted nothing more than to follow in his father's footsteps. (While Conn was heading up his own artillery battery in the Second World War, Stafford was in the navy. Like his father, he acquired an engineering degree.) Stafford soon took over as the team's general manager, and also managed the club's Junior B team, the Weston Dukes.

The only player returning to the Majors from the champion 46/47 team was the backup goaltender, Joe Williams, and he wouldn't make the cut. St.

Mike's had searched near and far for more skaters. In Schumacher they found Gord Hannigan, younger brother of Ray from the 46/47 Majors, who had played with the South Porcupine Red Wings the previous season when they dumped the Sudbury Grads in the northern Ontario Juvenile finals. From the lineup of the Edmonton Capitals they plucked Ray Barry, who was in his final year of Junior eligibility and began university studies when he joined the Majors. Joe Primeau's son, Joe Jr., donned his dad's number 10 and took to the ice as a forward. As a defenceman they suited up Bill McNamara, the third of three McNamara brothers to come to St. Mike's, who hadn't played the game in two years. Up from the Buzzers was Joe DeCourcy, one of three DeCourcy brothers to wear the Majors uniform. (Their dad ran the band at the Old Mill Inn, and its harmonies could be heard from the Primeau family home, on the opposite side of the Humber River on Orchardcrest Road.)

Before the season could start, the new Majors watched two of their starters, Don Oberholtzer and Murray Valliquette, crash into each other at a practice. Oberholtzer had a broken collarbone and Valliquette a broken nose and fractured skull. They wouldn't be lacing up for a while.

When Guelph (with Tatter McClellan in the line-up) beat the Majors 9-3 in an exhibition game in Waterloo on October 15, a long season was plainly ahead of the pride of St. Mike's.

But Tim's play quickly turned heads. He was big, "bouncing" and aggressive, and while he would collect points a little more frequently than he did as a Redmen, he would collect penalty minutes at an impressive clip. It was a run-of-the-mill game when

Tim left the ice with two minor penalties to his name. The Toronto *Globe and Mail* ran his picture and fingered him as a player to watch in an upcoming game against the Young Rangers. Those who did watch saw him pick up an assist and three minors as St. Mike's won 6-2.

He was "rock-ribbed," he "dished out heavy body-work," he was in the penalty box a lot, and he was playing for a team that over the course of the summer had gone from being the terror of Canadian Junior hockey to being the whipping-boy of the OHA Junior A. The season was slipping beyond reach when St. Mike's hooked up with Galt for a game on December 13. The body checks were in abundance and tempers flaring when Gord Hannigan was cross-checked into the boards by Pete Tkachuk. The gloves came off and the fight was on. Tim skated in with Galt defenceman Bobby Robertson to keep the peace while officials tried to break up Hannigan and Tkachuk, but before order could be restored Tim and Robertson were whaling away at each other. The fights carried on for several minutes, and the game was still no more winnable for St. Mike's when the bleeding was staunched and the gloves and sticks retrieved. Tim, who already had a minor from the first period, collected his first OHA fighting major, and Galt won 4-1.

The slide became sickeningly steep. Oshawa won 4-0 (two minors for Tim); Barrie won 9-3 (two minors for Tim); Barrie won 2-0 (one minor for Tim). At the Christmas holiday break, St. Mike's had a 4-14 record, George Armstrong of the Stratford Kroehlers was fourth in the scoring race, and Tim Horton was belting his way toward a National Hockey League career.

In his penalty-laden approach to the game, Tim brought to mind Maple Leaf defenceman Bill Barilko, the twenty-year-old Timmins native who had been called up by the injury-plagued Leafs from the Hollywood Wolves of the Pacific Coast league the preceding February. Barilko had played only eighteen games in 46/47, which made 47/48 his official rookie season. Barilko described himself as someone who couldn't skate, shoot or pass, who made a place for himself on the team with his body check, and in this first full season he would rack up a league-leading 147 penalty minutes in fifty-seven games while scoring five goals and assisting on nine. Tim was just about on pace with him, and while he had more innate offensive ability than a grinder like Barilko, he was playing his physical game to the hilt. As a Redman he had been a stay-at-home defenceman on a team that poured in goals. On the Majors he was the last line of defence on a team that lacked offensive power, and he was slowing down the opposition by throwing at them everything he had. The important difference with the Majors was that the lack of offensive power gave Tim a new role in which to shine. His statistics didn't reflect it, but he was winning critical approval as a rushing defenceman. Someone had to jump-start the anaemic Majors offence, and if the role was there to be played, Tim would play it. Tim had stepped into the new game created by the two-line offside, the punishing game presided over by Clarence Campbell, and had begun to master both those games.

Ted Carlton was a St. Mike's rarity: a boarding student who came from the city of Toronto. His family's "housing situation had collapsed around our ears," so his parents enrolled him and his brother in St. Mike's while they worked on securing a new home, which took a year. He came to St. Mike's in the fall of '47 for grade 12 and scarcely left, as there was nowhere for him to go, living there even on holidays while the other boys headed home. Far from being a traumatic, if temporary, dislocation (Carlton returned as a day student the next year, when the family was back in one house together), he and his brother appreciated and enjoyed the hospitality of the Basilian priests. "They were wonderful," he says today.

He was a student proper, not a hockey player, although he had been attending St. Mike's Majors games at the Gardens long before he became a St. Mike's student. For the first half of the year, he was assigned to the dormitory, a great room that could hold upwards of fifty boys and was normally reserved for the younger students. Around Christmas, a bed became available in a room on the top floor of the building, and Carlton, one of the oldest students in the dorm, was asked if he was interested in moving into it. Tim Horton of the Majors would be his roommate. He said that was fine.

Tim had had a roommate, a fellow hockey player, but something had happened to him—as Carlton recalls, the player had either been cut from the team or kicked off it for some transgression. Carlton already knew Tim casually from class, and while the Majors' star defenceman became more familiar to him through their living arrangements, he couldn't say they ever became close. It was an amicable relationship, and nothing more. He found Tim quiet, shy, not outwardly impressed with himself. "He was never the big blowhard type of guy."

But Tim was *big*. It was impossible not to be impressed by Tim's physical conditioning, and he shared his fitness mania with a number of other players, above all Gord Hannigan and Jean-Paul Belisle. Belisle was an old friend of Tim's from Cochrane. He had come down to North Bay to study and play hockey at Scollard Hall, and from there had moved on to St. Mike's and its Junior B Buzzers. Belisle had always been into fitness, and while they were in Cochrane together Tim would go over to Belisle's house to try out his barbells.

"These guys used to gather and do pushups, sixty or a hundred," says Carlton. "They'd be going up and down like machines. They were awesome physical specimens. Timmy was just amazing. He was as wide as he was high. He'd be at the side of the bed in the morning, doing a hundred or two hundred pushups, in the bathroom doing chinups on the stalls."

The top floor of St. Mike's, which contained rooms housing two to three students, was known as the Jew's Flat; one floor below it was the dorm, and the floor below the dorm was another block of rooms, called the Irish Flat. The name "Jew's Flat" has vague origins. The best, if apocryphal, story Ted Carlton can offer is that a Jewish clothes pedlar supposedly once infiltrated the floor while the boys were in class and stole all their clothes. Tim and Ted shared a small room with a low, sloping roof overlooking Bay Street. (This section of St. Mike's has long since been torn down.) There were two beds and two desks opposite each other. In the evenings, Tim and Ted would sit three feet apart, bashing at their homework.

Ted saw Tim as someone "consumed by hockey." In addition to regular games and tours of the province, players had 7 a.m. practices, and 2 p.m. practices from which they'd return, inquiring about what homework had been assigned in the classes they'd missed. Some never bothered to inquire. While Tim was not alone on the hockey team in making a serious effort at schoolwork, it did make him stand out. "For a hockey player," says Carlton, "he tried hard. He was not a dummy. Tim never impressed me as other than someone who was capable of being a student. I met a lot of hockey players during my years at St. Mike's, and he was not one of those airheads. Some of them just did not give a damn about school and went through the motions."

Carlton developed a unique perspective on athletes and academics by rooming with a first-class St. Mike's hockey player and then later instructing his kind, when he spent two of his thirty-five years in the teaching profession at St. Mike's in the mid-1950s. "I ended up teaching a lot of Junior A players from the Frank Mahovlich era on, and some of them were just not interested in school. They were nice guys, they'd cause you no trouble, but they never let an academic thought penetrate their brain. But guys like Tim Horton and others—not just him but others—who were serious about school had a tough row to hoe." In addition to studying between all their practices and games, says Carlton, the players had to cope with the fact that "it's hard to keep your mind on grade 12 when you're playing in Maple Leaf Gardens in front of 14,000 people."

Tim did not dash off his scholastic assignments. Carlton distinctly remembers him hunched over his desk in their room, executing fastidious diagrams

for geometry. "But his eyesight was so terrible. His
face was about three inches from the paper, right
over the top of the page, peering down at his work. I
often thought that was what dictated his hockey
style. He used to say he couldn't see anybody else
out there. We used to accuse him of being a puck
hog. He'd wind up behind his own net with the
puck and race through everybody with his head way
up in the air—he was trying to *see*."

The Majors had a long layoff over the Christmas holidays, and they were a long way from making the
playoffs. The top six teams in the ten-team league
advanced, and at year-end the Majors were eighth,
with only four wins in eighteen starts. In the new
year things didn't go any better. In a Saturday afternoon game at Maple Leaf Gardens in January, Tim
recorded two minors in a fight-filled second period
as the Majors went down 3-2 to the Oshawa
Generals. The next day, Tee-Pees coach Art Jackson
led his players over the boards in an assault on the
referee when their tying goal against the Guelph
Biltmores was nullified by the game's final buzzer.
Zellio Toppazzini's three-goal night was for nought
as the score stood 7-6. The referee needed a police
escort to get out of the arena. It suddenly seemed
that hockey, at every level of the game, had never
been more brutal.

A week later, the Maple Leafs' Bill Ezinicki was
brawling with Montreal's Butch Bouchard when
linesman Joe Springer made the mistake of trying
to intervene. Montreal defenceman Ken Reardon
watched Springer approach and flattened him with
a punch in the face. For this insolence, Reardon
was tapped on the wrist by a ten-minute misconduct

dispensed by referee King Clancy.

The next night, in Boston, Maurice Richard was sent off for slashing. He tossed two sticks in the direction of referee Bill Chadwick from the penalty box, then decided to leave the penalty box altogether and resume his protest of the penalty from the ice. The performance earned him a game misconduct and a police escort to the dressing room. Clarence Campbell's response to this assault on his officials was a seventy-five-dollar fine. That same night, Tim Horton was recording a fighting major in the first period of a game against the Tee-Pees.

Two nights later, referee Frank Elliott was brutally assaulted while officiating a game between the Owen Sound and Brantford Senior teams. Elliott had ordered Brantford defenceman Lloyd Mohns to the penalty box for roughing. Mohns, who had played one game for the New York Rangers in 43/44, responded by butt-ending Elliott three times in the head. When that encouraged Elliott to issue a game misconduct, Mohns cross-checked Elliott in the head, cutting him open near the eye. Mohns received an indefinite suspension from the OHA for his performance.

The next day, six players and the coach of the St. Paul Saints of the U.S. league were fined for leaving the bench in a January 10 game against Minneapolis. A St. Paul player in the penalty box had been slugged by a Minneapolis fan, and St. Paul coach Murray Patrick (a New York Ranger during the war years) had definitely put too many men on the ice in their quest to participate in the fracas. Patrick got a twenty-five-dollar fine, the players who joined him ten dollars.

Four days later McGill beat Queen's 4-2 in an

intercollegiate game that generated twenty minor and three major penalties. "Most of the trouble came in the second period," the *Globe and Mail* dryly noted, "when the teams abandoned hockey in favour of wrestling."

This was not going to go away. The tone of hockey, as set by the NHL under the guidance of Clarence Campbell,[7] was becoming increasingly physical. When Maurice Richard played his first NHL game in 1942, the war-years stars were managing better than a point per game in scoring and logging only three-tenths of a minute per game in infractions. Richard scored his record fifty goals in fifty games in 44/45 with only forty-six minutes in penalties. But by 49/50 his minutes had steadily increased to 114. In eighteen seasons with the Canadiens, Richard averaged slightly less than a point per game, and complemented it with 1.3 penalty minutes per game.

The players that blossomed in this new game were more like the pre-thirties stars in their predilection for infractions. Gordie Howe, who had made his league debut in 46/47, would join that circle of elite players who scored plenty and collected penalty minutes. Howe was no goon, but he did know how to use his elbows and there would be seasons in which he topped one hundred minutes in infractions in a seventy-game season. He and Ted Lindsay (whose rookie season was 44/45) were an intimidating combination in Detroit, just as Richard, Elmer Lach and Hector "Toe" Blake (and soon Bernie "Boom Boom" Geoffrion and Bert Olmstead) were forceful arguments for winning in Montreal. Lindsay won the scoring title in 49/50 with 141 penalty minutes, better than two minutes a

game. Even Jean Beliveau, widely acknowledged to
be one of the classiest players ever to grace the
NHL, could get the referee's whistling blowing: he
won the 55/56 scoring title with 143 minutes in the
penalty box, 43 more than Howe, who was second.

The fifties came to favour teams that could score
goals and rattle teeth. In 52/53, Richard had more
penalty minutes than anyone in the league; in
58/59, Lindsay managed the same feat in a
Blackhawks sweater. The new stars were aggressive
and driven and not afraid to push the rules; they
bounced the opposition off the boards and
dropped the gloves as readily as they split the
defence, and their style became so much the style of
the game that the game changed to accommodate
them. A minor penalty then had to be served in its
entirety: a team with a potent power play could pot
goal after goal while the two minutes ticked away.
After Jean Beliveau scored three times on one
power play, the league decided that, rather than
crack down on rule infractions, it should crack
down on the power plays. Beginning in 56/57, the
penalised player could return to the ice once the
opposition scored. And there the modern game was
born, as surely as it had been in 43/44 with the new
neutral zone, for the league had decided that the
power and speed and passion that the new stars
embodied were not to be tampered with, and that if
the typical new star was being caught flouting the
rules on average every other game (rather than
once every six games by the typical wartime star),
then the rules would have to change.

At the same time, the new game as it was played,
and not just as it was governed, was adjusting to the
presence and the talents of the stars. Disciplined

defensive styles emerged, along with a superb new generation of goaltenders, like Jacques Plante, Terry Sawchuk, Glenn Hall and Gump Worsley, who were perfectly capable of preventing fewer than three pucks from getting by them in a game. Total goals per game, which during the war years had soared from 5.0 in 39/40 to 8.2 in 43/44,[8] retreated steadily to 5.4 in 48/49, and in 52/53 and 53/54 they reached their modern low of 4.8. In 46/47 the top ten scorers had averaged one point in scoring and 0.38 minutes in penalties every game. By 53/54 the stars' points-per-game were down to 0.8 and their penalty minutes were up to 1.0. An exciting, explosive offensive game had emerged from wartime, a strong defensive game had risen in response, tempers were flaring and the league was nodding enthusiastically.

No one in the 47/48 OHA Junior A league had more penalty minutes than Tim Horton. By January 30, after playing twenty-six games (and losing twenty-one of them), Tim had amassed 119 minutes. That was 4.57 minutes per game: Tim was out-Barilkoing even Bill Barilko, who would top the NHL's penalty collectors in 47/48 with 2.57 minutes per game. Tim would end the season with 137 minutes, an average of 4.28 minutes per game. To put it in modern perspective, Tim's season average has been exceeded on a career basis in the NHL only by the likes of Bob Probert of Detroit, who in seven seasons through 91/92 averaged 4.64 minutes per game.

But not all penalty minutes are equal. To amass ten minutes' worth, you can interfere with another player five times or spear them twice. While the minutes are the same, the infractions speak volumes about the character of the player. Tim was attracting the odd roughing or fighting penalty, but he was not a mean player; he never was and never would be. In the NHL he would become known as a peacekeeper, the player who broke up fights rather than started them. His exceptional strength allowed him to pull apart combatants or tie up in a bone-crunching bear-hug anyone who got out of line: Tim would simply wrap his opponents in his arms and squeeze until the fight and the breath went out of them. As a St. Mike's Major, he played like a runaway train, dishing out body checks as he went, and not all of them met with the referee's approval. He may not have been playing any more aggressively than he did as a Redman, when observers felt the local Nickel Belt officiating was letting the boys get away with a little too much. In the OHA, Tim wasn't getting away with much at all, except that he was playing the game his way, regardless of what the rulebook said.

His robust work at the blueline was probably enough to keep him in good favour with the Maple Leafs, but Tim sweetened the pot in the new year by turning into a clear offensive threat. It started in a January 18 game against the Tee-Pees, in which he went off for fighting in the first period. The Majors were trailing 5-1 with less than a minute to play in the game when Tim got himself a goal. It didn't change the outcome, but it did accentuate his profile. Six days later, Tim opened the scoring for St. Mike's in a game against Armstrong's Stratford Kroehlers and helped shore up a 2-0 lead through two periods before the dam burst, as it always seemed to do against Stratford, and three unanswered goals stole away the game.

Tim endured several more losing games with his usual collection of minor penalties before turning in a signature performance on February 11 in a Wednesday-night game at the Gardens. The 5-23 Majors downed the Guelph Biltmores 4-1. Noted the *Globe and Mail:* "The Irish victory was highlighted by burly Tim Horton, who took time out from his blueline bashing to fire one goal and assist on another." Horton's goal, the Majors' third, which came late in the second period, "was the neatest of the night. He climaxed a rink-long dash by rapping the puck home as he fell to the ice with the Guelph defence pair draped over his shoulders." Late goals seemed to be Tim's trademark: he would let his forwards do what they could, but as the clock ran down on the period he would take matters into his own hands and get the job done.

Three nights later, Tim opened the scoring for St. Mike's late in the first period against Galt, then emerged from a brawl-filled second period with four minors. With the game tied at the end of regular play, Galt assured itself of fifth overall by winning 6-4 in overtime, three points ahead of the St. Catharines Tee-Pees, who had secured the sixth and final playoff spot. With that overtime loss, the Majors ended the season with a 6-26 record—an astonishing about-face from the juggernaut season of 46/47. They finished a miserable ninth overall, the poverty of their performance exceeded only by the Young Rangers team from Toronto, which won only two games, scored 63 goals while allowing 259, and would not reappear for the 48/49 OHA season. St. Mike's' offence had been only slightly better, amassing 76 goals. That was little more than two goals per game, a big change for Tim, who as a

Redman had played behind an offence that pumped out six goals per game. There was small consolation in the fact that none of the three Toronto-based teams had made it to the playoffs, although this was of little cheer for Conn Smythe: the Junior Marlies, his other source of future Maple Leafs, had missed the final playoff spot by eight gaping points.

On a positive note for Smythe, two of the most impressive players in the league that season, Tim Horton and George Armstrong, were his property. Armstrong edged out Gil St. Pierre of the Barrie Flyers by one point to win the league scoring title, and was named the league's most valuable player, an honour held by St. Mike's players—Tod Sloan and then Ed Sandford—the previous two seasons. That March, Squib Walker was photographed with Armstrong as the Falconbridge youngster renewed his C-form.

Tim, who was on the Leaf reserve list via his C-form, had made his own impression by leading the league in penalties. St. Mike's' alumni voted Ray Barry the Majors' most valuable player, a deserved honour for an effective defensive forward who was called upon time and again to kill the penalties Tim was serving. But in the voting for MVP by Majors players, Tim won out. Barry would be too old to play Junior hockey the following season, and everyone was looking forward to the return of Tim the Terrible.

The failure of the Majors to make the playoffs meant that its players could turn their attention back to their schoolwork. In Tim's case, the scholastic side of his efforts at St. Michael's were a lost cause. He would not be able to complete grade 12 that year.

Hockey players across the country weren't supposed to do well in school; they weren't even supposed to be smart. But grades were no reliable measure of brainpower. A kid making a serious commitment to hockey by the age of sixteen was hardpressed to maintain decent grades. A good student could muddle through. A borderline student wouldn't be able to make practices and games and still master a course load. Some of the talented Redmen of 46/47 hung in. Zellio Toppazzini completed his grade 12 while playing for the Tee-Pees in St. Catharines. Others, like George Armstrong, gave up on school altogether, their futures cast unconditionally with hockey.

Tim gave it his best shot. He was intrinsically a good student—bright above all. His marks in grades 9 and 10 had been those of a solid "B" student with some moments of brilliance—he got a ninety-three in geography in grade 9 while still in Cochrane. In grade 11, when he began playing for the Redmen and the Sudbury High senior team, the marks had started to slip. He scored Cs in physics and algebra, scraped by in English with fifty-seven, and failed Latin with thirty-one. But it was good enough to get him into grade 12 at St. Mike's.

There, he passed English composition and English literature, elected not to take ancient history, passed modern history and just passed chemistry with fifty-one. But he failed geometry and Latin composition (no surprise, given his thirty-one in grade 11), and while he scored sixty-five in French composition for term work, he didn't write the final exam and so received no mark. His roommate, Ted

Carlton, correctly recalls that Tim "didn't finish the year. I don't think he stayed around for exams. What struck me was him just leaving."

It's possible Tim deliberately tanked several courses—French above all—so that he would have an excuse to return the next season, carry a minimal course load, and play for the Majors again. As it happened, when he reappeared at St. Mike's in the fall of '48, his course load consisted of only the three grade 12 subjects he had missed; he made no apparent effort to pick up any grade 13 courses. (Gord Hannigan, it is believed, returned to St. Mike's to take only one class, a grade 13 subject, in 48/49.)

St. Mike's was happy to let Tim come back in the fall to have another go. He was one of the few shining stars of the St. Mike's Majors, and for Tim, staying made a lot of sense. He was only eighteen, and if he quit school he would just end up playing Junior hockey somewhere else. The Leafs had first dibs on his services and were in the midst of winning four Stanley Cups. They were not hurting for talent on defence, especially with a fresh young bruiser like Barilko in the lineup. The best he could hope for was a professional contract that shipped him to the Pittsburgh Hornets, the Leaf farm club in the AHL. He was better off staying at St. Mike's, polishing his game and finishing school. That is what he chose to do.

Chapter 6

Looting the Ranks

When Don Rope's mother died during the opening years of the Second World War, his father headed for Vancouver, leaving Don behind in Winnipeg in the care of a cousin. Though his family was Protestant, one of the last wishes of Rope's mother was that her son go to St. Paul's College, a local Jesuit boarding school. The cousin, who had married a Catholic, looked into it, and Rope was found a place in the school as a young high-school student.

St. Paul's changed Rope. "It was a turning point in my life, because until then I lived on the ball diamond and the hockey rink and didn't have much time for school." Father Jobin, a math teacher and hockey coach, turned him around in the classroom while at the same time making him a much better hockey player. He was a speedy centre, and his play earned him a place on the 47/48 Winnipeg Monarchs, the Junior team that had faced down Joe Primeau's stellar St. Mike's Majors in the seven-game Memorial Cup final of 1946. Denied the Memorial Cup, the Majors' sponsor, Conn Smythe, had signed a sponsorship agreement with the victorious Monarchs as well; thus it happened that when Don Rope joined the Monarchs he was destined to be Leaf property. Acceding to Squib Walker's overture, Rope signed a C-form, and the Leafs made plans to bring Rope east.

Smythe wanted Rope for his Junior Marlies, but Father Jobin insisted that the young man have the chance to complete a proper education. The Old Man relented, and agreed to have Rope assigned to St. Mike's where he could play for the Majors and study grade 13. Rope was headed for the hallowed halls only recently walked by Tod Sloan and Fleming MacKell, whose names by virtue of their Memorial Cup heroics were magic among the young players of Winnipeg. Rope had already spent three years of high school in a Catholic institution, so it's no surprise that his Protestantism was (and is) overlooked by those who assert that Tim Horton was the only Protestant playing for the Majors at the time.

Father Jobin's intervention on Don Rope's behalf in the name of higher learning did not dissuade Conn Smythe from attempting to have the last word. Rope admits that "I had no idea what grade 13 was all about," and the fact that he was attempting to find out, with a full load of nine subjects, while playing for the Majors, "was of a little consternation to Conn Smythe. I met him in his office, and he complained that some kids spent more time on education than on hockey." This encounter disturbed Rope, but did not compel him to shelve the books. There were many kids who came out of Winnipeg with little more than a grade 9 education, who committed themselves to hockey without any fallback, and did so because they weren't good enough students, or because they didn't have teachers that cared, or because they didn't have a sports scholarship to pay for their education. Even if you managed to play professionally, an injury or a poor training camp could put you back on the street, and it had been drummed into Rope that without an education he had very little foundation to a professional life. By sticking with school, he at least would have the luxury of choosing between hockey and a more workaday profession. Not every kid with his talent had that choice. Ultimately, Rope would turn down the chance to play professionally with the Leaf organization in 1950 in favour of a teaching career. As an amateur playing Senior hockey, he would win silver and bronze medals at the Olympics and a silver at the 1962 world championship.

The combination of schooling and hockey made St. Mike's an anomaly in the Junior hockey system, but within St. Mike's Don Rope was something of an anomaly in his own right. "The thing was, the guys on the team knew they were there for hockey. Education was secondary. But those who wanted it could get it. I wouldn't have recommended taking the nine subjects because it kept me up every night until 11:00, 11:30, midnight." His roommate, who was carrying only three grade 12 courses while playing for the Majors, was turning in at 10:30 or 11:00.

Rope was paired with the only other Protestant at St. Mike's when he arrived in the fall of 1948, in the largest room on the upper floor, the Jew's Flat. His first night as Tim Horton's roommate remains vivid. Tim, wearing only his underwear, jumped up and grabbed the door sill with his fingertips, and began doing chin-ups. "He kept going, and going, and going, and then there were the push-ups. I was into fitness, but not to that extent. I was more into running and having my oxygen intake up. But I was impressed that night. His muscle definition would have done the Greek sculptor Phidias proud. His build and strength stood out. Everyone was in awe. Yet he didn't lift weights, to my knowledge. Weight-training was a no-no with the Leafs. The feeling was that it made you musclebound. Bill Ezinicki was one of the first to use weights, and he helped change that."

Gord Hannigan, who had become a close friend of Tim's, was two floors below, rooming with Peter Whelan in the Irish Flat. Rope and Horton had begun the year with a third roommate, a non-hockey student from British Columbia. But the prompt transformation of their spacious room into the social hub of the Majors soon altered the living arrangements. When team members converged on the room after dinner, hockey games would break out, with the closet serving as the goal and a roll of tape as the puck. Father Crowley, the flat master, took pity on the hapless third roommate and moved him out, leaving Rope and Horton to live like comparative kings.

They were well matched in that they were serious about hockey and conditioning. Neither had a steady girlfriend during this period. Both were studious in their own way. When the team hi-jinks were through for the night, Rope would settle in at his desk and chip away at his course load. With only three courses, Tim could have filled much of the rest of the night with more hi-jinks, but instead he would seat himself at his own desk, turn on his small light and study the Bible. "He was always quoting from it, making references to it in a joking way," says Rope. "It was a factor in his life and in his advice to others, without ever evangelising. He was guided by it considerably."

This was a significant change from his first year at

St. Mike's, when his roommate Ted Carlton recalls Tim filling his spare time in the room by thumbing through a magazine. He cannot recall Tim ever devoting study time to the Bible, though Tim was firm in his faith. All students went to mass every morning, and Carlton does remember Tim making a regular Sunday pilgrimage to a church of his own. The Hortons were members of the United Church congregation in whatever town they happened to be living. During Tim's second year at St. Mike's, Don Rope remembers his church of choice being Metropolitan United Church, and on at least one occasion Tim brought Rope along with him. Surrounded by Catholics and the teachings of Rome, Tim had become even more committed to his religious roots.

Elbow room was not the only reason for Rope's and Horton's room becoming the Majors' social hub. Beginning his second year at St. Mike's, Tim was one of the most popular figures on campus. "Tim was very modest, very laid back, with the occasional burst of laughter," says Rope. "He always had a ready smile. He loved the camaraderie of the team, but there were other people at St. Mike's who weren't into hockey, who were up from the States to go to university, and he enjoyed talking to them all. He seemed to have friends coming in from all different avenues. And he was our big star. We didn't have that much going for us at the time. Willie Marshall had not yet come into his own; he was still a young kid. Tim was unquestionably the leader."

At the first opportunity, Tim led a half-dozen newly minted Majors, including Rope, on a sightseeing excursion to Maple Leaf Gardens. For Rope, entering this shrine of hockey, known to him only

through the radio broadcasts of Foster Hewitt, was a
momentous occasion. Tim led them in through the
back door, introducing them to virtually everyone
they encountered. He was very much in his element. In fact, the short stretch of city between St.
Mike's and the Gardens had become Tim's casual
haunt. He would stop at the fruit stands on Yonge
Street, chatting to the vendors. A Japanese restaurant was the site of late-night dinners. Yet Tim's
familiarity with the neighbourhood went beyond
the local knowledge almost every boarding-school
student acquires. It spoke of a larger confidence of
his future: that this was where he would be, where
he belonged. "As laid back as he was," says Rope,
"he seemed to be aware of his destiny, to know that
he was going to be with the Leafs some day. It was as
if somebody had said to him, 'Look, do this and
you're going to be with us in a certain number of
years.' He knew that, but not in a conceited, arro-
gant way. He was very modest, and very confident."

In 1948, Babe Pratt, who had spent a few seasons
with Conn Smythe's Maple Leafs before winding up
his NHL career in Boston after the 46/47 season,[1]
was credited by *Globe and Mail* columnist Jim
Coleman with observing that NHL teams "are grab-
bing players so young that only recently he saw two
scouts crashing their way into the maternity ward at
General Hospital." In the same vein, Coleman predicted that "Squib Walker, chief scout for the Maple
Leafs, will sign a 3-year-old Eskimo boy at Atavik."
    Conn Smythe wouldn't be happy simply scouring
maternity wards and signing young Eskimos. He
was building a development system that would be
the envy of any professional team. His gallant,

teetotalling Leaf captain, Syl Apps, had just retired, and Smythe had immediately assigned him the task of coaching his woeful Junior Marlboros, bumping his own son Stafford upstairs to develop the overall Marlies system. The Leaf-supported Marlboro operation was turning into a talent octopus, its tentacles entwining the Junior A and B clubs, the Senior club, and reaching all the way down to pee-wee level in the Toronto minor-hockey system. While Apps would only coach the Junior Marlies for a few months before deciding the job was not for him, other former Leaf greats were coaching clubs with Maple Leaf ties. Joe Primeau was behind the bench of the St. Mike's Majors and the Senior Marlies. Bob Davidson, whose eleven-season Leaf career ended in 1946, was handling the Pittsburgh Hornets in the American league. And the new Leaf captain, Ted Kennedy, was dishing out strategy to the Upper Canada College team.

Now that Smythe had a regional talent empire, he needed winning efforts from the teams within it. The St. Mike's Majors had had a disastrous season in 47/48, but Smythe didn't exert direct control over the playing lineup. His sponsorship agreement called for him to provide a flat fee that the college could use to offset scholarship costs, and he split the Maple Leaf Gardens gate for Majors games with the school. The kids who played for the Majors didn't necessarily have any contractual ties to the Leaf organization.

The Junior Marlies had experienced an only modestly less disastrous season than the Majors, and Smythe intervened directly to improve its depth of talent. He had three bright young Junior prospects with their signatures on C-forms, and he wanted

them in Junior Marlie uniforms for the 48/49 season. One, Don Rope, had already eluded him when
the priorities of education had steered him into St.
Mike's. The other two were Dan Lewicki and George
Armstrong.

The seventeen-year-old Lewicki was a swift, compact, high-scoring left-winger with the Fort William
Columbus Club of the Thunder Bay league. When
the league's Port Arthur West End Bruins advanced
to Memorial Cup playdowns with western Canadian
teams in the spring of 1948, they added three players, including Lewicki, who helped them win the
national Junior title. Lewicki's professional rights
were held by the Providence Reds of the American
league; more than a year before the Memorial Cup
win, Lewicki's coach in Fort William, Leo Barbini,
who worked as a Reds scout on the side, had placed
Lewicki on the Reds negotiating list practically the
second that the prospect turned sixteen. This was
quite a coup for Barbini, as Fort William was also
home base for Squib Walker. Barbini's prescience
cost Walker's employer, Conn Smythe, an estimated
$20,000—$10,000 in cash plus the rights to Jackie
Hamilton. That was the tithe Providence owner Lou
Pieri demanded for handing over Lewicki's professional rights to the Leafs in August 1948. It was one
of the largest financial deals the Major had ever
made.[2]

That done, Smythe just had to get Lewicki to
Toronto, and here Smythe hit a profound and
unsettling snag, one that taught the hockey tycoon
that not even $20,000 would let him move a teenag-
er around like a piece of freight. The C-form that
committed Lewicki's professional services to
Smythe did not erase the amateur rights to Lewicki,

and those rights were held by the Fort William Columbus Club. Ed Romano, president of said club, informed the Major that Dan Lewicki wouldn't be allowed to leave Fort William. As far as Mr. Romano was concerned, Mr. Smythe might have Dan Lewicki's signature on a C-form, and Mr. Pieri might have Mr. Smythe's $10,000 and the rights to Jackie Hamilton, but the Junior hockey operation of Fort William still had Dan Lewicki for at least the upcoming 48/49 season. Under the NHL's master agreement with the CAHA, a player could not be called up by a C-form to play professionally before the age of eighteen unless permission was granted by his amateur club. For that matter, the club holding the player's C-form could not order him to switch amateur clubs.

As for Dan Lewicki, in the fall of 1948 he wanted to continue playing Junior hockey, but with the Stratford Kroehlers of the OHA. More than four decades after he'd become a five-star example of the machinations of the hockey system, Dan Lewicki maintains he'd been bamboozled by Squib Walker. He had no idea that signing the C-form implied anything more than coming down to the Leaf training camp in September for a tryout. He only got $100 for signing the C-form, and had already turned down an offer from the Rangers with an $800 signing bonus, in all likelihood for a B-form. "The NHL scouts would do anything they had to do—lie, cheat—to get a player," he says. "That's just the way it was, the way they operated. As far as the welfare of the kid, they couldn't care less. The C-form was a form of slavery. No one was ever tutored on it. Most cases, people signed it and didn't have a clue what they were signing."

After signing a promise of his professional services, Dan Lewicki was busy shopping himself around the Canadian Junior hockey scene. In the end, he wanted to play with the Stratford Kroehlers. They offered less money than the Brandon Wheat Kings, but Stratford had just hired Barbini as their coach. "I was only seventeen," he explains, "when you're scared to death of leaving home." Barbini was a familiar face, and another Thunder Bay player, Joe Beda, had come down to Stratford the previous year.

Lewicki's determination to play in Stratford raised another sore point with Connie Smythe. The Kroehlers had George Armstrong, who was on a Leaf C-form but not playing in its system. There was a bit of miscalculating there: the Leafs paradoxically didn't seem to realize just what a hot prospect young George was, but after he had won the OHA scoring race and the league's MVP award, Connie Smythe wanted him back, at the very least in a Toronto Marlies uniform. The eighteen-year-old right-winger looked so good that he had been invited to the Maple Leaf training camp in St. Catharines in September, and after most of the rest of the amateur hopefuls had come and gone, George Armstrong was still there, scrimmaging with the Maple Leafs and the Pittsburgh Hornets, the Leafs' AHL farm team.

Armstrong was making it clear that the only place he wanted to play that season was Stratford, but Conn Smythe had decided Armstrong belonged in a Junior Marlies uniform. To get him in one, he was prepared to use professional hockey's form of blackmail, a contractual squeeze play. Smythe had no legal claim on Armstrong's services as a Junior-level amateur, but he did have Armstrong's signature on a C-form. And unlike Lewicki, Armstrong had turned eighteen in July, which meant that Smythe could call him up to play professionally without either Armstrong's or his amateur club's okay. It didn't matter that Smythe didn't actually want Armstrong to become a professional at that moment: he could use the threat of forcing him to turn pro to make him accept switching Junior teams as an alternative. He declared that Armstrong "will either play in the Maple Leaf organization or not at all."

George Armstrong went home to Falconbridge.

By mid-October, Armstrong was in Conn Smythe's office, working out an agreement to come over to the Junior Marlies. According to Dick Trainor, Smythe agreed to provide Armstrong with an extra-ordinary package: free room and board, plus a salary of $175 a week, paid to him in Maple Leaf Gardens stock. But David Pinkney, manager of the Stratford Kroehlers, announced that he wouldn't grant the release necessary to allow Armstrong to move to the Marlies. With the Fort William Columbus Club seemingly steadfast in its unwillingness to let Dan Lewicki go anywhere, it was time for the Leaf organization to find out what it would take these amateur outfits to change their minds.

In the case of the Fort William organization, it was cash, pure and simple. The Leafs got into a bidding war with Stratford, and actually lost. For $3,500, the Kroehlers secured the services of Lewicki for one season. And the Kroehlers agreed to let George Armstrong go to the Marlies....in exchange for two Marlies and $2,000.

"ARMSTRONG UNSHACKLED" read the *Globe and Mail* caption to a photo of Armstrong signing on as a Marlie beside a joyful Stafford Smythe. Two days later, the OHA's hottest professional prospect scored one goal, assisted on another, and drew a minor penalty in a Saturday afternoon game at Maple Leaf Gardens as the Junior Marlies lost 4-3 in overtime to the Barrie Flyers.

Tim Horton was spared all of this stress and nonsense. He didn't attend the Maple Leaf training camp, even though Majors goalie Tommy Shea was there, as was Denis Mooney of the Buzzers, and even though the Leafs were inspecting Junior prospects as they mulled over who to drop into the skates of defenceman Wally Stanowski, who'd been dealt to the Rangers over the summer. While the forces of amateur and professional hockey were treating George Armstrong and Danny Lewicki precisely like the chattel Junior players were, Tim was snapping the ball to quarterback Gord Hannigan on the St. Mike's senior football team.

Playing for St. Mike's was a good way to be insulated from the chicanery and avarice of the Junior hockey system. Tim was a student on a sports scholarship; St. Mike's was not going to trade him or sell him to some other team. St. Mike's might have been in the same league as the Marlies and the Kroehlers, but the Majors occupied a different universe. While top players in Canadian Junior hockey could command a salary of about $150 a week at the time, players on the Majors were compensated through a free education, room and board at the school, and a weekly stipend of ten dollars. The Majors stood out in the 48/49 season schedule for having only thirty-two game dates, so that players might actually be able to study and attend classes.

The Junior A circuit's seven other teams were playing a forty-eight-game schedule. For their last sixteen games of the season, the Majors or their opponents would score four points for a win, to give the schedule some balance. There would be almost three weeks in November when the Majors didn't play a single OHA game.

The Majors' lineup was far from settled. Don Oberholtzer, who had missed most of the previous season after that horrific preseason collision in practice, had been lured away by the Guelph Biltmores. Team star Ray Barry was too old for Junior play, and had moved on to play in the Quebec Senior league. Apart from Tim, the Majors' most potent players were Don Rope, Gord Hannigan and Hannigan's fellow Porcupiner Willie Marshall.

Over the summer, Tim had taken it upon himself to do a little recruiting of his own back in Sudbury. Red McCarthy had completed his second season as a Copper Cliff Redman, and was considering overtures from Hap Emms to go to the Barrie Flyers— he had signed a B-form with Barrie's sponsoring club, the St. Louis Flyers of the American league. Tim worked on him, convincing him to go to St. Mike's. The tug of war actually produced a confrontation on a Nickel Belt ball diamond. McCarthy was umpiring a juvenile league game when Tim and Emms squared off over McCarthy's future. "There was sort of a confrontation," says McCarthy, "with Tim telling Hap, 'Red's going to go to St. Mike's.' But Emms always liked Horton, and he might have said to Tim, 'Well, why don't you come too?' "

Tim didn't, and Red came to St. Mike's, moving into House 90, a dormitory next door to the main St. Mike's building.

On October 13, the Majors travelled to Barrie to match wits with Hap Emms' Flyers. The exhibition game generated three major and thirteen minor penalties. Tim collected four of the six St. Mike's infractions and scored once as the Majors lost, 3-2. Three days later the Majors were in Windsor, playing the season-opener for both teams. In a penalty-filled game, the Spitfires scored five power-play goals and buried the Majors, 9-5. Tim left the ice with no points and one minor penalty, but he was clearly the star of the Majors. His monicker of the moment was "The Nugget": good as gold.

Conn Smythe was having a rough autumn. There was the bewildering Dan Lewicki fiasco, the tug of war over George Armstrong and then the matter of the crafty operator named Punch Imlach who crashed the Leaf training camp.

Imlach would be hired in 1958 by Conn Smythe's son Stafford to be the coach and general manager of the Maple Leafs, and would guide the Leafs to four Stanley Cups. But in 1948 Punch Imlach was a punk to the Leaf brass. The former Torontonian, as player-coach of the Quebec Aces of the Quebec Senior league,[3] showed up at camp while the Leafs were shaking down their amateur prospects, mooching around the edges of the talent pool. On September 22, Dean McBride, a Senior Marlie, didn't show up for practice. The defenceman had been trying to land a starting spot with the Hornets, but it looked like the Leafs would send him to the Los Angeles Monarchs of the Pacific Coast league. Smythe heard that Imlach had offered McBride $3,500 and a job if he'd come back to Quebec with him. He'd made the same offer to Ray Hannigan,

Gord Hannigan's older brother.

Connie Smythe was beside himself. He had the signatures of these players on C-forms. How dare Imlach try to steal them away from him!

Max Ray, sports editor of the Fort Williams *Times Journal,* sarcastically put Punch Imlach's feet in Conn Smythe's shoes. "It's easy to understand the Leaf attitude in the matter…They were forced to go to a lot of trouble, looting the amateur ranks of these players, and it would be palpably unfair if the amateurs were permitted to steal them back again. After all, professional hockey has the inalienable privilege of hijacking anything they like in amateur ranks."

Criticism like this, when he heard it, must have rankled Smythe. No matter what else anybody said about him, his word was good: a deal was a deal. And the NHL teams had a deal with the Canadian Amateur Hockey Association wherein the CAHA was compensated for amateur players placed on reserve lists. Conn Smythe wasn't going to stand by mute while something he had paid for was swiped back by the group that sold it to him.

But that didn't assuage widespread local sentiments that the professional game was robbing the admittedly unamateur amateur system of its greatest talents. Like Frank Mathers, for example. When Smythe traded Wally Stanowski, along with Elwyn Morris, to the Rangers that summer, he received in return Cal Gardner, René Trudel and Bill Juzda, as well as the rights to Mathers. A handsome six-foot-tall rushing defenceman from Winnipeg, the twenty-four-year-old Mathers had been a key member of the Ottawa Senators Senior team for the past three years, and had reached the Allan Cup finals with them in 1947; he was also a halfback with the

Ottawa Roughriders. Mathers had just got married, and while he had agreed to come to the Leaf camp, he was an unusually pragmatic candidate for professional hockey. Frank was a student at the University of Ottawa (a classmate was Ron Caron, who would become general manager of the St. Louis Blues in 1983), and had completed two years of science studies. He was willing to consider a career in professional sport, but while some friends told him he was better at football than hockey, there was no money on the gridiron—a player then might pick up $500 for an entire season. Still, his enthusiasm for hockey was measured. If he couldn't crack the Leaf lineup, he'd pursue a career in dentistry. The Pittsburgh Hornets or Los Angeles Monarchs didn't fit into his plans. The biggest compromise he was willing to make was a position on the Senior Marlies, which would allow him to study dentistry in Toronto. If he played with the Leafs, he could continue his studies at the University of Manitoba for two more summers and at least finish his B.Sc. "Don't know whether it will do me any good," he admitted, "but a guy can never get enough education."

Conn Smythe had always been of the mind that a guy can very easily get too much education. He put on his career-planning cap, fired up the abacus and lobbed his conclusions into the daily press. Why would a young man even be considering dentistry when a career in professional hockey was there before him? It would take Mathers ten years to finish his education and get a practice going profitably. In those ten years, Smythe calculated (factoring in bonuses), Mathers could bring home $100,000 as a Maple Leaf.[4]

Smythe's persuasion hit the mark. Stanowski was

gone and Smythe needed a defenceman. Mathers signed on with the Maple Leafs. "This means a lot to me," Mathers said. "I hope I produce. I've made my choice and I think it's for the best."

Red McCarthy was enjoying one of the perks of being a St. Mike's Major that fall, a spot in the press box at Maple Leaf Gardens, when the Leafs found themselves down by one goal late in the game. Hap Day pulled the goaltender in favour of an extra attacker. Onto the ice came Mathers. Smythe, who was in the press box, blanched. "Oh, don't put that guy on," he moaned.

"And if it wasn't Mathers who made the play that got the tying goal," says McCarthy. "I was so happy for the guy."

Frank Mathers saw only intermittent ice time with the Leafs that fall, playing in fifteen games, mainly on the power play. He had one goal and two assists. On December 6, Conn Smythe shipped Mathers to the Hornets. The Leafs only called him up for eight more games during the course of his professional hockey career. He never attended a university class again.

Tim's transformation into an offensive threat halfway through his first season at St. Mike's had been no aberration. In an October game against St. Catharines—playing against Zellio Toppazzini's younger brother Jerry and two former Redmen teammates, Gord Byers and his old defence partner Specs Telford—Tim *was* the Majors, scoring both goals as they tied the Tee-Pees 2-2. Then in November, Tim thrilled the partisan Gardens crowd by scoring on a penalty shot, contributing an assist (and logging one minor) as the Majors crushed

Guelph 6-1.

This new role on the ice for Tim was inevitable. At the first practices of the 47/48 Majors, Tim had clearly been one of the most talented offensive players on the ice. It was a role, Don Rope reflects, that Tim would by necessity have to step into, and playing defence, he would be on the ice for more minutes per game than the average forward. As long as he was out there, he would have to get the Majors on the scoreboard.

"Primeau thinks Tim Horton is terrific," noted the *Globe and Mail*, "as who doesn't?" Gentleman Joe Primeau really did think Terrible Tim was terrific. The Majors coach and Lady Byng honouree got him involved in Mercantile League games at Ravina Gardens, and as Joe Jr. recalls, Tim made Gentleman Joe think not so much of Bill Barilko as Bill Ezinicki, the tough, penalty-prone right-winger of the Leafs. Wild Bill was about Tim's size—both had their official dimensions overstated at five feet, ten inches. While Tim was on the shy side of five-nine, in a team picture of the '48 Leafs Ezinicki is shoulder to shoulder with Les Costello, who appears to be exactly the same height and is officially listed at five-eight. (On his opposite side, Harry Watson, a gentle giant at six-one and 200-plus pounds, dwarfs Ezinicki.) Neither Tim nor Wild Bill did their damage through sheer bulk. They were about 170 pounds, were very muscular and had the same barrel-chested build, which they put to use running into opposing players straight-up—hence the "bouncing" quality of Tim's game. "When Bill hit," says Gus Mortson, a star of the Leafs defence corps from 46/47 through 51/52, "he hit very clean. He wore padding on his chest, at least one inch thick, and he threw his chest out when he hit." Ezinicki was six years older than Tim, a Winnipeg-born twenty-year-old when he played his first Leaf game in 44/45. In 48/49 and 49/50, Ezinicki took over from Barilko the distinction of being the league's most penalised player. (Barilko had taken over from Gus Mortson in that department in 47/48, and Mortson would take over from Ezinicki in 50/51, giving the Leafs a five-season lock on the league's tough-guy bragging rights.) Wild Bill was a defensive-minded forward, and Terrible Tim was turning into an offensive-minded defenceman, and somewhere in the rink's neutral zone their games overlapped.

Tim's performances in November 1948 show why the comparison between him and Ezinicki was so apt. In three consecutive games, he was kept off the score sheets, but escorted twice to the penalty box in each of them. And in a game against Galt at the Gardens that the Majors won 3-1, "Tim (Terrific) Horton was a show in himself as he sparked St. Mike's to victory," according to the *Globe and Mail*. "After Burcham pushed the Rockets ahead, Horton stick-handled through the entire Galt bunch to even matters... Horton belted every Rocket he could reach. He caught Pete Tkachuk with a thump in the first period and flattened Bronko Horvath so hard in the second, the Port Colborne lad was carried off on a stretcher. Horvath came back, but twice had to limp off with a knee damaged by the early impact." For this extra effort, Tim earned three minor penalties on the night.

Once Tim did move up to the NHL, differences between his play and that of Ezinicki emerged that were not so apparent when Tim was roaming the ice as a Major, demolishing opponents. Ted Kennedy is one of the great connoisseurs of hockey players. The centre played twelve and a half seasons with the Leafs, beginning in 43/44, and served as its captain from 48/49 to 54/55, with a stint as co-captain (with Jimmy Thomson) during his half-season comeback in 56/57. While Tim could hit, Kennedy considered Ezinicki a breed apart. "I've never seen a more devastating body-checker for a forward," says Kennedy of the old teammate he calls Ezzy. "It was just cruel. I could name three or four players that had to crawl off the ice, or couldn't crawl off. He would do it up on the forward line, catching guys with their heads down or sliding across the blueline. He would move in off his wing and just meet them head on."

"Tim was solid when he hit you," says Cal Gardner, who played with the Rangers, Toronto, Chicago and Boston over more than twelve seasons. "The difference between Tim and Ezzy was that Ezzy would drop the shoulder and lift his knee and all of his body would hit you at one time. And it wasn't dirty. It was a clean body check."

"When Tim took the man out," says Ray Timgren, who played with Toronto from 48/49 to 52/53, "it was right against the boards. Gus Mortson did a lot of that, too. Ezinicki would catch you on the wing. He'd go down the wing with you inside, then circle round and hit you. You'd think he wasn't there, but he sure could arrive."

"Mostly he used to check the opposite winger," says Mortson. "He used to come back on his own wing, and when the winger came down, if he happened to cut in and cross the defence zone, Ezinicki would cut in the other way, and the other guy never saw Ezinicki coming. The trouble was, if

Ezinicki missed the guy, you had to look out your-self, because he might end up hitting you."

On December 9, Lou Pieri was at it again. The owner of the Providence Reds of the AHL was on the receiving end of the biggest deal in NHL history for a minor-league player. The New York Rangers bought Allan Stanley from Pieri for $60,000 and the rights to centre Ed Kullman, who would play a dozen games with Boston in 49/50, and Elwyn Morris, who had been a Leaf defenceman in the war years. The deal was so shockingly expensive that it made Conn Smythe feel better about the Dan Lewicki fiasco.

The twenty-two-year-old acquisition was a six-foot-two, rock-solid defenceman who was the pride of the Stanley clan of Timmins. Allan's dad was the town's fire chief; his Uncle Barney had been in the manage-ment of the Chicago Blackhawks, and another uncle, Ab, had played Senior hockey with the Hamilton Tigers. The Bruins had signed him in 1943 after his Holman Pluggers won the northern Ontario Juvenile title two years running, and had been with the Boston Olympics' Quebec Senior team before coming to the Reds in 1946. For Stanley, being sold to the lowly Rangers was the cul-mination of a lifetime dream to play in the NHL. A decade and three trades would pass before he was paired with the defence partner with whom he became synonymous.

Red McCarthy enjoyed his year at St. Mike's, though he didn't play the best hockey of his career. It was something just to share the ice of Maple Leaf Gardens on a Saturday afternoon with Tim Horton, when the crowd could exceed 10,000 and included students from the local girls' schools. "When Tim touched the puck," says McCarthy, "everybody stood up. He was an explosive rusher. He wasn't a dipsy-doodler, because half the time he went through you, over the top of you. He was very, very exciting."

"Tim was the star of the team," says Dick Trainor, who had come down to Toronto to study law and found part-time work at Maple Leaf Gardens, first as an usher, later in the ticket sales office. "People used to go to the games just to watch him. They loved him. He couldn't get that out of his system, and I don't blame him, in a way."

Red and Tim shared a few double dates together, which were initiated by a young woman from Espanola who had a crush on Tim. She was attending nursing school in Hamilton and had a friend in Toronto. She would talk Red into dating her friend so she could go out with Tim. One night a week, the St. Mike's students were allowed out until midnight. On these double dates, they sometimes had trouble getting back before curfew. Tim had no trouble making his way back into the Jew's Flat—Father Crowley, his flat master, tended to look the other way. But House 90 locked its door after midnight. On one occasion, when his roommates decided not to open it for him, McCarthy was forced to climb a tree and enter through a window.

The problem with dating was that it consumed the one night a week the students were allowed out late, and that meant the Majors players couldn't go to a Leaf game on Saturday night if they'd been out on Friday night. They came up with all kinds of schemes to get out the door two nights in a row, along the lines of "My uncle's in town and he really wants to see me, father..."

After a late night out on Saturday, Red would try to catch up on sleep the next morning. But Tim, who had been out with him, either on a date or at the Gardens, would be up at the crack of dawn, putting on his best clothes and heading to Metropolitan United for the morning service. Red is still impressed by the commitment someone Tim's age made to attending church, with no one standing over him, making him do it.

Tim enjoyed special privileges at the Gardens as a property of the Leafs. One of them was frequenting Conn Smythe's personal box, which held no more than eight people. Sometimes he was able to bring Red along. "I remember Tim giving me all the rules: don't leave, don't make a lot of noise, Smythe needs to concentrate and he doesn't like talking. We have to be in there before he gets there. He doesn't want anybody crawling over him. And we don't get out till he gets out."

As strict as this might have seemed, Smythe was exceptional in allowing himself to be surrounded by teenage amateur prospects. Players—never mind prospects—on some other NHL teams were lucky if they even encountered their general manager more than once a season, at contract time.

The first half of the season ended on a positive note for the Majors, with an overtime defeat of the Oshawa Generals, but when play resumed in the new year, the odds of St. Mike's securing one of the five playoff spots in the eight-team league became increasingly long. In three successive January games, the Majors blew solid leads. Up 5-0 on Stratford, they lost 6-5; up 2-0 on St. Catharines, they lost 5-3; up two goals in the third period, they lost 8-6 to

Windsor. Tim continued to accumulate goals, assists
and, naturally, penalties. He notched four minors in
a 4-1 loss to Galt, and in the 8-6 loss to Windsor,
picked up two minors to go with his goal and assist.

The loss to Windsor had been a particularly brutal game—twenty penalties were handed out in all,
including four majors and two misconducts. Hockey
hadn't become any tamer in the year that had
passed since Rocket Richard left the penalty box in
Boston to discuss his infraction with the referee, and
had to be escorted by police from the Gardens. In a
January game against Galt, which St. Mike's lost 7-2,
Gord Hannigan was slapped with a misconduct for
firing the puck at the referee. In the three-team
Cape Breton Senior league, 635 penalties had been
meted out to date on the season in sixty games,
including twenty-four majors, twenty-nine misconducts and one match penalty—in all, 1,740 minutes
in penalties for 3,600 minutes of hockey. Even the
chief referee had been charged with assault after
attacking a player. Officials of the Ontario Minor
Hockey Association were deeply concerned about
rough play, which included spectators taking to the
ice to get involved in altercations. Play had become
so vicious in the western Canadian Senior league
that on February 7 the mayor of Edmonton ordered
city police to start arresting players to put an end to
brawling and stick-swinging. A few days later Judge
Joseph Archambault of the Montreal Superior Court
felt duty-bound to pronounce NHL hockey a sport
bound for disaster. "As long as Clarence Campbell is
president," he stated, "I feel the rules will not be
adhered to according to the true interpretation of
the rule book." Campbell was unperturbed. "Some
people like their hockey played differently from

others," he responded. "The public seems to like what is being presented."

On February 20, the Toronto Maple Leafs were playing Chicago when Blackhawks left-winger Red Hamill, a genial player who would only record sixteen penalty minutes all season, poleaxed Leaf defenceman Vic Lynn, knocking him unconscious and sending him to hospital for observation and eight stitches. (Lynn had already been carried, unconscious and bleeding, from the ice of the Montreal Forum in the spring of 1947 after Rocket Richard similarly laid on the lumber during the Stanley Cup finals.) The apologetic Hamill received a $250 fine and a one-game suspension. The Leafs came out of the weekend with four injured starters, three of them right-wingers. A slash by Blackhawks defenceman Bill Gadsby had fractured one of Howie Meeker's toes; Bill Ezinicki and Harry Taylor had twisted knees. The only healthy right-winger the Leafs had left was Don Metz; the team was down to fourteen regulars. To fill in for Lynn on defence, Conn Smythe called up former Majors star Gus Mortson, who had just been sent to Tulsa. And to plug the gap in right-wingers, the Major turned to two current Majors, Gord Hannigan and Tim Horton.

The Majors season had ended on the evening of Friday, February 19, the night before Lynn was struck down. Tim had set up two goals and earned one minor, but the Marlies, powered by George Armstrong's goal and two assists, prevailed 5-3. The win allowed the Marlies to squeak into the final OHA playoff spot, two points ahead of Guelph; St. Mike's had finished second-last for the second straight season, besting only Galt in league standings.

At first, Joe Primeau had tried to bring Hannigan
and Horton up to the Senior Marlies for the playoffs, once his Junior Majors were clearly out of the
playoff running. The Marlies applied for their
transfer on the grounds that they were members of
a lower-series club in the same municipality, but the
OHA turned them down. So instead, Hannigan and
Horton were working out with the Maple Leafs at
the Gardens on the Wednesday following the debilitating Blackhawks game. Tim continued to be something of an anomaly in this defence-obsessed era of
hockey. He was a defenceman who could put the
puck in the net and lead a rush. His offensive skills
had made Jim Dewey see him at first glance as a
right-winger, and Conn Smythe was now thinking
along the same lines. It was not altogether unusual
at this time for players well on their way to becoming professionals—even players who had become
professionals—to undergo a wholesale on-ice transformation as a coach or general manager converted
them from defence to offence, or even vice versa.
As a player, Hap Day had been moved from the
wing to defence. Similarly, Boston star Dit Clapper
had moved from the offensive to the defensive side
of the blueline in mid-career. One of the most
famous examples is Red Kelly, who played twelve
and a half seasons as a defenceman with Detroit
before starting fresh as a centre with Toronto. Conn
Smythe in particular liked to experiment with players, moving them from one side of the blueline to
the other in an effort to make them, and the rest of
the team, click. Later in the season, Smythe would
order Gord Hannigan tried out as a defenceman
after watching him practice with the Senior Marlies.
Appropriately, Tim was slated to stand in for the

injured Bill Ezinicki, the player whom Tim made Joe Primeau think of the most. He would play on a line with centre Cal Gardner and left-winger Harry Watson.[5] Alas, Tim's big break was not to be. After watching Tim and Hannigan work out with the Leafs, Smythe decided they weren't ready to wear Leaf uniforms. The *Globe and Mail,* which had built up their pending National league debuts, let the boys down gently. "The kids tried hard, skated well, but they lacked the condition and skating ability to keep up with their big brothers." Smythe instead rummaged around in the roster of the Senior Marlies and came up with two Porcupine prospects: Gord Hannigan's older brother Ray and John McLellan.[6]

With their call-up to the Leafs a washout, the Senior Marlies tried a second time to gain OHA permission to move up Horton and Hannigan for the playoffs. This time Marlboro president Harold Ballard wanted permission to use them on the grounds that two regulars, Ray Timgren and Eric Pogue, had been lost to the pros. (Timgren, a left-winger, had been called up by the battle-scarred Leafs.) The OHA could grant such a transfer, but the CAHA, which oversaw the Allan Cup playdowns, could not. Horton and Hannigan would be lost to the Marlies once the playdowns began, and that was the whole point of bringing them aboard.

Even though he couldn't put them on the ice in a game, Joe Primeau brought up Hannigan, Horton and Rope as a forward line for Senior Marlies practices as the team made its stab at an Allan Cup appearance. Having arrived at St. Mike's as a centre, Rope had been converted to left wing by the observant Primeau. Paired with Horton on the opposite

wing and Hannigan at centre, the trio terrorised the
Marlies scrimmages. "It was when I played my best
hockey," says Rope. "When we practised with those
guys we put a little extra into it, and they always
dreaded it, especially with Tim on the wing."

The Senior Marlies advanced to the eastern playdowns of the Allan Cup, losing to the Ottawa
Senators in six games. The Leafs went on to win an
unprecedented third straight Stanley Cup, sweeping
the first-place Red Wings in four games after finishing the season, albeit strongly, in fourth place with a
record of twenty-two wins, twenty-five losses and
thirteen ties.

But the Stanley Cup could not unfold without the
future of Dan Lewicki competing for media coverage. The Stratford Kroehlers' president, Harold
Wyatt, was promising to go to court over the issue of
signing minors to contracts.

"The owners of the club were pretty good people," says Lewicki, "and they explained to me what
the C-form was all about." With Lewicki's permission, they wanted to use him as a test case of sorts to
challenge the very legality of the C-form. Lewicki
readily agreed to open defiance of Conn Smythe.

As Toronto arrived in Detroit with a 2-0 series
lead, NHL president Clarence Campbell defended
the legality of the C-form and assailed all parties on
Lewicki's side of the dispute. Campbell was asked
what would happen to Lewicki if the case reached
the courts and the C-form was declared invalid. "It
won't do the player any good," Campbell said, pre-
emptively overruling the Canadian judicial system.
"He won't be able to play pro or amateur hockey
because he'll be under suspension." In essence, the
NHL would continue to see to it that Lewicki was

blackballed from the sport, even if the courts ruled invalid the very contract that led to his blackballing.

When the Leafs had wrapped up their cup win, Conn Smythe called a press conference at Maple Leaf Gardens, at which he spent ninety minutes defending the C-form and castigating Lewicki and those around him. He called the C-form "our protection against bootleg amateur clubs and operators," a remark clearly directed at Stratford. Smythe told the press that Lewicki was well aware of what documents he'd signed. "He will make at least $6,000 if he plays here [with the Leafs]," he announced—an interesting assurance, given that the C-form Lewicki had signed only called for a salary of $4,000.

In the midst of his press conference, Conn Smythe produced a C-form recently signed by "a St. Mike's standout" to show the gathering what one was all about. The player in question wasn't named, but there is an excellent chance that this was the C-form signed by Tim Horton. St. Mike's "standouts" in 48/49 were as rare as the Hope Diamond. Tim had been named top defenceman in the OHA Junior A, and only Gord Hannigan, Don Rope and Willie Marshall could be considered serious alternative candidates for the displayed form. Presumably Smythe would have wanted to put his best foot forward and show a C-form with the greatest value. On this basis he probably would have flaunted one signed by Tim.

The C-form detailed a $1,000 bonus upon signing a professional contract, and salaries of $2,000 for the Pacific Coast league or a Canadian Senior amateur club, $2,500 for the U.S. league, $3,500 for the American league and $5,000 for the NHL. That, in all likelihood, was the future Conn Smythe had planned for Tim Horton.

Smythe's diatribe did not win a full slate of converts. On April 28 the *Globe and Mail's* Jim Coleman touched base with a favourite former Leaf, Babe Pratt, and among other things asked him what he thought of the C-form. "Briefly, the Babe is against C-forms. He's against 'em for one reason. He can't see (and no one else can see it, for that matter) why a professional hockey team should have the right to tell a 16-year-old boy where he will play his AMATEUR hockey."

Dan Lewicki was in Stratford while the controversy raged, trying out at shortstop with the Stratford Nationals. Tim, having been voted the Majors' most valuable player by his teammates for the second straight season, was putting the finishing touches on his grade 12 education and preparing for another year at St. Mike's. The school newspaper, *The Double Blue*, in wrapping up the 48/49 Majors season, noted that "Next season [Joe Primeau] expects to have more to build his team around than he has had the past two seasons. On defence will be Tim Horton, who has been a standout on defence for two years." He was still young enough to play Junior hockey, and had one course still to go to complete grade 12. He got his geometry and his Latin composition (barely, with a fifty-one) on the second try, but French composition eluded him with a mark of forty-five. There was no reason Tim couldn't come back in the fall for another run at French composition.

Tim had yet to encounter Conn Smythe in full flight.

Chapter 7

School's Out

I t was an impressive display of Conn Smythe's reach into the amateur hockey system: on the St. Catharines Arena ice with Tim Horton were thirty-one other young up-and-comers culled from the lineups of twenty-one different teams, which included the Glace Bay Miners, Quebec Citadels, Fort Rouge Whirlaways, Porcupine Combines, Oshawa Generals, Edmonton Juniors, Stratford Kroehlers, Saskatoon Juvenile league, Thunder Bay Columbus Club, Brandon Wheat Kings, St. Mike's Majors, Sydney Millionaires, Inkerman Rockets and Toronto Junior Marlies. Smythe had gathered them in September 1949 for the annual Maple Leaf hockey school, held the week prior to the Maple Leaf training camp. Presiding over their drills, scrimmages, fitness routines, meals and 11 p.m. curfews were Hap Day and Bob Davidson, respective coaches of the Maple Leafs and the Pittsburgh Hornets. Assisting them was Turk Broda, the Leafs' stellar goaltender, who was always battling his waistline in the off-season and had found the school a good way to get into some semblance of shape before training camp.

Conn Smythe had been convening the school for the past four years, since returning home from the war. It allowed him to take stock of the talent his scouts, led by Squib Walker, had assembled through reserve and negotiating lists; to see his best prospects all at once, in competition with each other and, in the case of the very best of them who were invited to stay on, against his pros the following week; to see which players, in his own mind if not in theirs, should be playing somewhere other than where they were now.

Smythe had just endured his second foray into world war. He had assembled his own artillery company, and had been seriously wounded. He returned to Toronto to take charge of the Leafs (and in November 1948, all of Maple Leaf Gardens Ltd., as its president). On one level he maintained an officer's dispassionate, even ruthless, regard for his young charges. Joe Primeau, Jr. remembers his coal-black eyes with their piercing gleam—"like Rocket Richard's"—and how much they frightened him as a boy. Smythe was also intensely devoted and loyal to his favourite players and readily moved to public praise of them. But when he decided a player no longer measured up, he could move swiftly and boldly to rectify matters. The team ultimately came first; there was no money to be made from losers. Smythe was in the unusual position of running a publicly traded company, and in that context all players were essentially mining stocks——their talent and ability, which inevitably faded, qualified them as depleting assets, though some were depleting faster than others or weren't producing a satisfactory rate of return on the investment. As in mining, professional hockey had high up-front costs for prospecting and development, with no guarantee a particular find would ever actually prove profitable. When a player no longer panned out, or didn't fit the portfolio mix, the team tossed him onto the trading room floor.

The best trades involved unloading a player whose stock the market overvalued and receiving in return a player worth more than his book value. In all great trades there is a whiff of arbitrage.

Smythe provided a newsworthy preface to the 1949 school by trading away Tod Sloan, along with Harry Taylor and Ray Ceresino, to the Cleveland Barons of the AHL to get his hands on Bob Solinger. Sloan had only recently been Smythe's most celebrated Next Big Thing, by Smythe's own declaration "the greatest Junior prospect I have ever seen." But after the Falconbridge sensation played twenty-nine games for the Leafs in 48/49 and participated in the Stanley Cup victory that spring, Smythe had soured on him, sending him to the Hornets. He wanted Solinger, a Saskatchewan-born left-winger who would turn twenty-four in a few months. Solinger had been AHL rookie-of-the-year in 47/48, and while he had come up flat in his most recent season, Smythe saw stardom in him. Smythe's use of Sloan in a three-for-one trade package showed how low the St. Mike's alumnus had sunk in the Leaf magnate's esteem, and how any rising Junior star could easily turn into a shooting star in this business.

As it turned out, the Solinger swap was one of the Major's less inspired deals. Solinger played intermittently as a Leaf over four seasons, spending most of his career in the American league. The season that followed his trade, Sloan tied for scoring honours in the American league playoffs. Smythe was shortly working the phones to buy Sloan back for the very next season. Sloan, for his part, was discouraged to be returning to Toronto, having become disillusioned with what he viewed as the monolithic talent system of the Leafs. In the middle of the American league playoffs, he had been sure he was about to be picked up by the Blackhawks, where Charlie Conacher was coaching.

A young defence prospect like Tim Horton had to reconcile the "youth, youth, youth" message of the postwar league with the reality that, for the Maple Leafs at least, blueline talent was making for a buyer's market. In 1947 the Leafs had been able to win a Stanley Cup with a defence roster staffed by rookies: Jimmy Thomson, Gus Mortson, Bill Barilko and Garth Boesch. Just before training camp in 1949, Smythe settled contracts with Thomson and Mortson, the stars of the Leaf defensive corps. Bill Barilko also came to terms with the Major. The previous season, Alex Barilko, who was playing Senior hockey in Ottawa, had tried out with the Leafs in hope of forming a blueline pairing with his handsome younger brother, but he'd had to settle for a spot on the Senior Marlies. (He later became an NHL linesman.) They had gone into the appliance business together, opening a store carrying the Admiral line, Barilko Bros., on the Danforth, and were preparing to add a second outlet in the Beach as Bill Barilko signed on for his third full Leaf season. ("I signed my contract this week," he confirmed, "and I also sold Mr. Smythe a television set and a refrigerator.")

Smythe also still had Garth Boesch in his solid defensive corps. Boesch would turn twenty-nine in a month; he was married, with a six-year-old son, and had a 1,200-acre wheat farm to run with his dad in Riceton, Saskatchewan. Boesch held out hope for defence prospects—hockey was not a long-term proposition for the only NHL player with a moustache, and while he agreed to come back for this season, it proved to be his last. However, the retirement would not create a spot in the Leaf rearguard for a farm-system rookie. Bill Ezinicki and Vic Lynn went to Boston for defenceman Fern Flaman, who had played three and a half seasons with the Bruins. Smythe kept Flaman on the job for three seasons before dealing him back to Boston, where he played another seven seasons.

The Leaf rearguard was rounded out by one of Smythe's pleasant surprises. Bill Juzda, a.k.a. Fireman, a.k.a. Beast, was a defenceman "thrown in" (in Smythe's own words) by the Rangers on the deal that sent Wally Stanowski to New York in the summer of '48 and moved Frank Mathers' rights to Toronto. Juzda turned out to be a welcome stay-at-home addition, playing thirty-eight games in 48/49 before joining the lineup full-time in the fall of '49, and staying there until the end of 51/52. Smythe would remember him fondly as a "big body checker [who had], along with everything else, guts to burn." Juzda "gave every ounce, every game."

Smythe liked a five-defencemen lineup, but he planned to expand to six in 50/51, when the NHL would move from a sixty to a seventy game schedule, mainly at Smythe's urging. Smythe hoped to carry larger rosters all through his system, which meant some reassurance of genuine opportunity for the newcomers at his hockey school. Tim Horton was one of eleven defencemen invited to attend. Smythe liked players that could lay on the body, and while Tim was naturally so inclined, his wasn't one of the larger defensive bodies on the ice. Gord Hudson of the Inkerman Rockets weighed in at 202 pounds. Toronto's Frank Sullivan, an Oshawa

General, weighed 191 pounds, and Charlie Lumsden was a 192-pound Winnipeg Monarch. Tim had measured a comparatively spry 165 pounds, but weight was no substitute for ability or attitude, as Bill Ezinicki had overwhelmingly proved. Conn Smythe dropped in on the second day of the school and praised the St. Mike's star. Horton could be "a potentially great defenceman," he said. "I can see him knocking down those Montreal Canadiens now."

Don Rope and Gord Hannigan also came along from the Majors, and while they showed well enough to land positions with Joe Primeau's Senior Marlies, the offensive standouts were George Armstrong and Dan Lewicki. They were placed on a line with Jack McKenzie, who had played with Lewicki on the Port Arthur Bruins when they won the 1948 Memorial Cup, and was with the Brandon Wheat Kings when they were runners-up in the latest Memorial Cup. The unit looked good enough to pull on NHL jerseys. Smythe declared the Armstrong–Lewicki combo "the best pair I've seen together since Charlie Conacher and Harvey Jackson. And that's a twenty-year span."[1]

Smythe had made his peace with Armstrong the previous year, trading two Junior players and handing over a lump of cash to the Stratford Kroehlers to get him aboard the Junior Marlies. Smythe wasn't hurrying Armstrong; he had him pencilled in as a Junior Marlie for another season. As for Danny Lewicki—the prospect that had cost him $20,000 to move off the reserve list of the Providence Reds, only to be outbid by the Kroehlers for his amateur services—Smythe wanted him to join the Hornets. Lewicki had just renewed his C-form in August, and in the ensuing manoeuvres to get Lewicki where he wanted him the Major would make much of this. In truth, it was all but impossible for a player not to renew a C-form, unless he abandoned professional hockey altogether. Smythe had every intention of activating its report-to-a-pro-franchise clause. And now that Lewicki was eighteen, Smythe didn't need an amateur team's permission to call him up.

To Smythe's eternal exasperation, Lewicki was balking. He wouldn't turn pro. He wouldn't even report to the Marlies as an alternative, which is where Smythe decided he really wanted him. He wanted to stay in Stratford and be a machinist. He professed not to like Toronto, saying the city was "too big."

That was the profile of Lewicki the Toronto media allowed Smythe to project: a confused and fickle young man who didn't understand the meaning of a signature on a contract. As far as Lewicki was concerned, he had been duped into signing the C-form in the first place and didn't want Conn Smythe running his life. The machine shop talk was a defence mechanism, a way of saying to Smythe that he had more things going for him than simply hockey, even though the game had been the focal point of his life since the age of eleven.

Conn Smythe was in no mood to be defied. "If we can't make a deal [with Stratford for him to play with the Marlies], I'll offer Lewicki a pro contract," Smythe announced. "If he doesn't accept that, he won't play hockey at all."

At the end of the week of hockey school, Lewicki left for Stratford, the Kroehlers and the machine shop.

Six amateurs and Bob Solinger were invited to practise with the Leafs when their camp opened the following week. George Armstrong was one of them, and so was defenceman Hugh Bolton—they were scheduled to stay only a few days before reporting to the Junior and Senior Marlies, respectively. One other defenceman, Frank Sullivan, was invited along. Seven amateurs were asked to the Hornets portion of the camp, two of them defencemen: John Arundel of the Sydney Millionaires (the former St. Mike's Buzzer from Alberta) and Gene Martin of the Toledo Seniors team.

Tim Horton packed his equipment and returned to Toronto to practise with the St. Mike's Majors. His exit from the camp was not a sign of failure, as a third year on the St. Mike's blueline was planned. The Leafs issued a statement saying that Tim was returning to play for St. Mike's, but interestingly added that his future was still to be decided.

St. Mike's had been able to attract two strong professional prospects to the school for 49/50. Bill Dineen was a seventeen-year-old right-winger who would spend four years at St. Mike's before playing five seasons in the NHL, the first four with Detroit. Leo Labine was an eighteen-year-old right-winger from Haileybury who had also come to St. Mike's for grade 12. He would play eleven seasons in the NHL, all but the last season-and-a-half with the Bruins. They would be joining Willie Marshall, who was coming back down from Kirkland Lake for his grade 12; "Wee Willie" had been the second-highest scorer on the Majors the previous season. Marshall would play thirty-three games, spread over four seasons between 52/53 and 58/59, with the Leafs at centre while playing a record twenty seasons in the American league.

Despite the fact that the week of practice with the Majors after the Leaf amateur school proved to be the only hockey they would play together, Labine and Horton did get to know each other better with time. Tim's family moved to North Bay in the summer of 1949, and in 1954 Labine, too, located in North Bay. The pair would see each other as opponents during the NHL season, then off the ice in North Bay, as Tim visited family and tended to his business ventures that took root there in the 1960s.

"We were under the impression that Tim was going to be with us at St. Mike's," says Labine of the first Majors practices in the fall of 1949. Horton, Marshall, Dineen and Labine would have made for a potent core to a resuscitated Majors team. (Also moving up to the Majors from the Buzzers was Bob Sabourin, a sixteen-year-old from Sudbury who would stay at St. Mike's playing Junior hockey until 1952 and go on to play for the Hornets.) But Conn Smythe had other plans.

Smythe was singlemindedly determined to build himself a Memorial Cup champion out of the Junior Marlies. He had Armstrong, and he was damned determined to have Lewicki; now he wanted Horton, even if that meant hurting another team in his own farm system.

Smythe always had the upper hand in these encounters, because, force of personality aside, he held the ultimate trump card: the promise of a career with the Maple Leafs. The NHL was the goal of all aspiring amateurs, and some clubs were aspired to more than others. The Leafs, the Canadiens and the Red Wings had the greatest heritage; the Blackhawks, the Bruins and the Rangers were perennial also-rans. The Bruins had been the last team outside the big three to win a Stanley Cup, in 1941, and while shrewd scouting would produce strong Bruins teams in the 1950s, twenty years would pass before one of the three have-not teams, the Blackhawks, again broke the stranglehold the top-three clubs held on the Stanley Cup. The Canadiens by tradition had their development roots in Quebec's francophone community—the old Maroons franchise was the Montreal anglophone team—and unless an English Canadian kid had come up through its development system, he probably wasn't going to play in Montreal. Detroit was an honourable place to play, but in the heart of a young Canadian anglophone, the Leafs were the pinnacle. "The Leafs weren't the greatest paying team in the league by any stretch of the imagination," Dan Lewicki reflects, "but they just had a pride you'd go through the wall for. The money was secondary. The fact that you made that team was the key, rather than the dollars and cents."

The pride in the Leafs was due entirely to Smythe's determination and particular hockey genius. He was widely admired for turning the Toronto NHL franchise into a sporting marvel, for going against the economic grain and marshalling the construction of Maple Leaf Gardens during the Depression, above all for bringing the city the Stanley Cup in 1932, 1942, 1945, 1947, 1948 and 1949. He had done so with teams of exceptional character, led by captains Hap Day, Charlie Conacher, Red Horner, Syl Apps, Bob Davidson and Ted Kennedy. Since the war's end, the team had been led by Apps and then Kennedy, who were exemplary in their dedication to the game, to the team and to the ethic of doing things with class, on and off the ice. Tim Horton fell into the camp of players who were attracted to the Maple Leafs by that ethic and spirit.

Smythe's reputation was not pristine. Some observers were wont to dismiss him as a charlatan; players who held a grudging admiration for him called him the Major or the Old Man, a nickname borrowed from the Philadelphia Athletics baseball manager Connie Mack; others who didn't called him the Old Bastard. He was without question fiery, and he made his share of enemies, among them Frank Selke, whom he suspected of engineering a coup against him while Smythe was overseas during the Second World War and ended up managing the Canadiens alongside coach Dick Irvin, who had also left Smythe's employ back in 1940. Yet Smythe never left wounds—his or those of others—untended if he could help it. "I was in Smythe's office when Dick Irvin was dying of cancer, and Smythe phoned him," says Ted Kennedy. "Smythe said, 'Teeder, I'd like you to talk to Dick.' And Dick didn't like me because Montreal had had my rights, and I had left to join Toronto."

"Living with him from day to day," says his son Hugh, "he could be terribly angry with us for something or other, and then three days later there would be nothing left of it. If he had something on his mind, it came out. Once it came out, it was not something that smouldered away, motivating him years later.... In the revisionist times, they'd say he was a paternalistic bastard, but he took a very great personal interest in anything that involved the players."

In the fall of 1949, Conn Smythe was taking a very personal interest in Tim Horton. Tim was nineteen now, which put him in exactly the same situation Armstrong and Lewicki had found themselves with Smythe—once over eighteen, a player who had

signed a C-form could no longer be saved by his
amateur club from being called up to play professionally. The Old Man wanted Tim to come over to
the Junior Marlies. If that didn't appeal to him,
Smythe could exercise the C-form and send him to
Pittsburgh.

Tim was not going to give up St. Mike's willingly,
despite the fact that he wanted nothing more in life
than to wear a Leafs uniform. This made it extremely difficult for the young man to defy Conn Smythe,
but he balked at the Marlies proposition, categori-
cally refusing to play against St. Mike's.

"I hadn't had that great a year," says Red McCarthy of
his 48/49 season at St. Mike's. He saw little or nothing of Tim over the following summer—the Hortons
had moved to North Bay. That fall, McCarthy went to
training camp at Midland for the St. Louis Flyers,
with whom he had signed a B-form. While McCarthy
wasn't going to make the American league team,[2]
Hap Emms of the Barrie Flyers was there, and he
told Ebbie Goodfellow, the St. Louis coach, to let
him know if Red changed his mind about going back
to St. Mike's.

Red did go down to St. Mike's, though his mind
was far from made up about attending the school
for another year. He found Tim equally torn by the
choice between staying in school and turning professional with the Hornets—switching to the Junior
Marlies was out of the question.

Classes at St. Mike's had already started when
Tim told Red he was going to walk down to the
Gardens to talk with Smythe and Day. Red kept him
company, and waited downstairs while Tim had his
meeting. While waiting, he made up his own mind

about his future. He phoned Hap Emms and said
he was interested in playing for the Barrie Flyers.
Emms told him to hop on a bus and come on up.
He would get forty-five dollars a week.

Tim came back downstairs.

"What did you do?" Red asked.

"I signed," said Tim.

Although the coercion is not alluded to, an article
by *Toronto Star* reporter Gordon Campbell in a
53/54 Maple Leafs program covers the essence of
Tim's reluctant decision to turn pro. Campbell
reported that over the weekend following the amateur portion of the Leafs' 49/50 training camp—it
actually would have been a weekend later, after Tim
had been practising with the Majors for a full
week—Smythe offered Tim a three-year contract
with the Hornets. Tim called his parents in North
Bay, "and Pop Horton, although he felt his son
should complete his schooling, left the decision up
to the boy. He decided to accept." Campbell came
close to the nub of the tale when he wrote that Tim
"probably wouldn't have been there [at his first
Hornets practice] if it hadn't been planned to play
him with Marlboro juniors. Tim balked, saying he
didn't want to play against his old St. Mike's teammates, and that had a bearing on his decision to
turn pro." In other profiles of Tim in Leaf programs during the fifties, it was noted that Conn
Smythe personally drove Tim to his first practice as
a Hornet in St. Catharines after getting him to sign.

At a time when the top Junior players routinely
switched teams, seeking out the best team and the
best deal for themselves, Tim's refusal to play for
the Marlies against the Majors, a stand on simple

principle, was noteworthy, and was typical of his life:
he did the right thing, because it was the right thing
to do. His obstinacy undoubtedly surprised Smythe,
who must have thought that churchgoing Tim, a fellow Irish Protestant to boot, would welcome the
opportunity to escape an Irish Catholic institution.

In his negotiations with Dan Lewicki over the
young man's future, Smythe would bark, "Are you
going to be a hockey player, or a scholar?" It's easy
today to hear the Major giving Tim the same hockey-
or-scholar treatment as Tim made whatever case he
could for a third season at St. Mike's. In his Maple
Leafs program profile, Campbell quotes Tim four
years after the fact, undoubtedly accurately: "I decided if it was to be hockey instead of school, I might as
well get right at it." Conn Smythe couldn't have said
it better himself.

Regardless of educational concerns, in 1949 the
momentum of the Leafs' Junior hockey system was
with the Marlies. While Smythe would continue to
support the St. Mike's Majors program for the next
decade, his enthusiasms had plainly shifted to the
Marlies empire. As it happened, 49/50 would be
Joe Primeau's last season as the Majors' coach. The
next season, when the St. Mike's high school moved
into its present home at Bathurst and St. Clair,
Primeau began coaching the Leafs.

A week after training camp had opened that
month, the Maple Leafs organization was celebrating signing Tim to a three-year contract that would
make him a Hornet. Smythe called him "the number one defence prospect in Canada." Reported the
Globe and Mail: "The hard-hitting defenceman
showed little respect, or regard for the opposition.
He continued to impress scouts and top-level hockey

officials at the Leafs' annual hockey school two weeks ago."

Russ Gioffrey, a close friend of Tim's in his Leaf days, remembers Tim telling him that his first Leaf contract was worth $4,000 a year, $4,400 tops. Coincidentally, $4,000 a year for two years was what Dan Lewicki was rejecting to play professionally. If the C-form displayed by Conn Smythe the previous spring during his Lewicki diatribe belonged to Tim, then Tim was paid $1,000 to sign with Pittsburgh and a $3,500 salary. Tim would tell Gioffrey's kids that he would have paid the Leafs to let him play, if he'd had the money. (Tim's customary description of his profession was that he was paid to practice—he played for free.)

The decision to become a Hornet was not a difficult one for Tim, according to Dick Trainor. "Tim really wanted to turn pro. He wanted some money, and he wanted to buy a car." In 48/49, according to Trainor, Tim had been chafing under the knowledge that Smythe was paying George Armstrong $175 a week, plus room and board, to play for the Junior Marlies while he was toiling for the Majors in exchange for a free education, room and board, and ten dollars a week.

As it turned out, Tim received less money to play for the professional Hornets than Lewicki did to play for the amateur Junior Marlies. Suspended by the CAHA for defying his C-form call-up, after about two months off the ice Lewicki came to an agreement with Smythe to play as a Junior Marlie. Lewicki figures Smythe finally got to Stratford by threatening that, unless they stopped protecting Lewicki and agreed to cough up his amateur rights, Smythe would send them no more players from his

reserve list, the most noteworthy recent example
having been George Armstrong.

But Lewicki still played hardball. Despite his
avowal today that the money was secondary, he was a
remarkably self-assured teenager in his negotiations
with Smythe. He signed what amounted to a one-
way minor-pro contract to play for the Marlies.
Lewicki had wanted $10,000 a year and a $2,500
signing bonus; as to where he played, pro or amateur, that was up to the Leafs. In the end, he got a
$3,500 signing bonus and a $4,500 salary and was
assigned to the Marlies. Technically, under CAHA
regulations on amateur status, Danny Lewicki
should never have been a Marlie. Practically, nobody
in the amateur hockey system cared.

The Leaf organization, in its orgy of self-congrat-
ulation over the signing of Horton, put a very
strange spin on how they had come across this
bright prospect. As the *Globe and Mail* recounted,
Tim "enrolled in St. Michael's College in 1947, and
was almost immediately put on the Leafs' negotiating list. Squib Walker, chief of the Leafs' scouting
organization, discovered him with an assist from Joe
Primeau. 'Joe called me one day and suggested I
take a run out to Royals Rink and look over a
youngster trying out with St. Michael's. It was Tim,
and he looked like the type of defenceman for
which we were looking. I didn't wait for the practice
to end, but went to the nearest telephone and contacted the NHL office in Montreal.'"

It was a nice little anecdote that played well in
newspaper type, but bore no resemblance to truth.
There was no mention of the Leafs' northern scout,
Bob Wilson, making sure Tim was on the Leafs'
negotiating list back in the spring of '47 and signing

him to a C-form. Nor did it explain just how
Protestant Tim in Sudbury wound up "enrolling" in
St. Mike's and "trying out" with the hockey team
without the introduction of the C-form and Charlie
Cerre's connections. None of it made any sense,
except in the context of Squib Walker's being loath
to credit Tim's discovery to Wilson, who had since
switched to scouting for the Chicago Blackhawks.[3]

Tim joined the Hornets in practice in St.
Catharines the day after his signing, then travelled
to Fort Erie with them for an exhibition game
against the Buffalo Bisons of the AHL. Paired with
Frank Mathers, the recruit whom Conn Smythe had
talked out of dentistry, Tim immediately demonstrated professional-league poise and talent.

Mathers and Horton would play together on the
Hornets for three seasons, as a defensive pair for
one of them, and win the Calder Cup together in
Tim's final Pittsburgh season before he was called
up for good by the Leafs. They were instant
friends—Mathers would even serve as Horton's best
man. "He was such a good hockey player in the
minors," says Mathers. "I really admired his ability.
He'd get that puck and come out of a bunch of players and he'd be gone. A great stickhandler, a strong
skater. Very strong, physically. And he could shoot
the puck very well. He was destined to be in the
NHL." Danny Lewicki sums Tim up as well as anybody: "He could skate like hell. He was a goal-scorer
too, and he had a hell of a shot. And he was as
strong as an ox."

On October 5 the Leafs and the Hornets travelled
to Oshawa for a Kiwanis benefit game. "He's got a
lot to learn defensively," Conn Smythe said of Tim
after the game, "but he certainly has the natural

ability. I don't think I was far wrong when I said he was the best defence prospect in Canada."

Jim Vipond of the *Globe and Mail* was there for the game, and the columnist immediately recognised a great talent. "A fast-travelling, hard-hitting youngster who hardly has had time to dry the ink on his professional hockey contract served notice here tonight that he rates serious consideration for a major-league post in the near future. His name is Tim Horton and although his team, the AHL Hornets, were defeated by the NHL Toronto Maple Leafs, 4-2, he was one of the most impressive two-way players on the ice. It was Horton who set up both Pittsburgh scoring plays in the third period, the second being particularly spectacular as he skated through the entire Leaf team to put the puck on the stick of waiting Andy Barbe. A few minutes later he had rushed into the Toronto zone to flip Ray Hannigan a perfect pass to put Pittsburgh on the score sheet. Defensively, Horton...stepped into the Leafs with absolutely no regard for reputations." Bill Ezinicki nailed Tim early in the game, but Tim did not shy away. He took on every ounce of Leaf muscle—Ezinicki, Mortson, Barilko, anyone else who was interested. "He thrilled a sellout crowd with a bumping duel with Bill Ezinicki in the second period," Vipond summed up, "and was to be found in the thick of the action at all times."

Bumping with Wild Bill. Tim Horton truly had announced his arrival.

Chapter 8

Missing in Action

As an aspiring player, your worst nightmare was to be assigned to a minor-league club by the NHL team holding your professional contract and be forgotten there like some dog tied up behind the barn. At first you dutifully reported to Cleveland or Pittsburgh or Buffalo or Hershey or Tulsa or wherever because that, with few exceptions, is what you did as a teenager embarking on a professional hockey career. The minor league was your finishing school—you went there to prove yourself and polish your skills and wait for the call-up. When the call-up came, it often came because a starter was injured. You put in a game or two, or even a few—even the better part of a season. But then you got sent back down again when the star mended, or when the team said that you needed more seasoning. And you strove to remain positive, even though the next wave of teenagers was arriving and the parent team was signing more hot prospects just like you, or making trades to fill the position on the fourth line you thought would be yours. The lineup for a starting assignment with the parent NHL club was getting longer, and you were not necessarily at the head of it.

With the advent of the seventy-game season in 49/50, Conn Smythe for one had hoped that teams would be able to increase their roster sizes to twenty

players. At the end of the 48/49 season, Smythe was
envisioning a skating lineup of three forward lines,
six defencemen, and a penalty-killing unit. But team
rosters were pegged at seventeen skaters plus goaltenders (generally just one) that season. In 52/53
the league owners sought to cut costs by cutting roster sizes, reducing the "skater" limit to fifteen on the
road and sixteen at home. The "skater" limit went to
a straight sixteen the next season, and in 54/55
teams were permitted to carry eighteen skaters up to
December 1, but in 60/61 teams were back to sixteen skaters again.[1] At the same time, the NHL was
not expanding as was being constantly forecast, the
Pacific Coast league folded after the 50/51 season,
and the American League shrank from a high of
eleven teams in 47/48 to six in 53/54. The job market for professional hockey was shrinking, competition was intense—fights at training camp were par
for the course—and fate and circumstance could
conspire to deny a very good player an NHL career.

Some great players got lost in the minors in the
early 1950s. With only about seventeen active players
on each NHL club, there were just 102 employment
opportunities. With teams generally opting for four
forward lines, there were a total of seventy-two openings for forwards. This meant that, even though
defencemen accounted for 40 per cent of the
skaters on the ice at any given time, they accounted
for less than 30 per cent of the spaces in the dressing room.

Teams emphasized forward lines over defencemen because more forwards meant more fresh legs.
Defencemen throughout the Original Six era were
not expected to be as strong skaters as the forwards.
Eddie Shore had been a prototypic rushing

defenceman in the 1930s, and Red Kelly in Detroit and Doug Harvey in Montreal played the position with offensive skill in the Original Six era, but the defenceman was still largely what his name suggested: a defensive player who wasn't expected to tear up and down the ice, much less cross centre ice. They weren't yet fully integrated into the offensive game, and when they did join in for an all-out assault inside the opposition's blueline, it was known as a "ganging attack." A five-defenceman lineup translated into two regular pairs and an alternate, and those regular pairs by force of mathematics could expect to be on the ice about thirty minutes a game, with some relief from the alternate.

On average, there were only about thirty jobs available to defencemen in the NHL during the Original Six era, and if you were a left-hand shot, which dictated that you play left defence, then the number of jobs dropped to fifteen. The only opening harder to come by than defenceman was goaltender. Teams were only required to carry one full-time goaltender until league rules made two dressed-to-play goaltenders mandatory in the 65/66 season.

But job opportunities were even narrower than these figures suggest. There weren't thirty defensive positions to apply for. In reality, there were only the five on the team that held your contract. If that club had a surfeit of talent in your particular position, you might never emerge from your initial minor-league assignment. It might be that you had plenty of talent, that you deserved to have a career in the NHL, but that your playing style didn't mesh with that of the parent club. Your only hope was a trade, but trades did not always come to a player's rescue.

Sometimes you were just too valuable to the minor-league team to let you get away. It was even believed among the players that sometimes you were too good to let another National league club have you—your team didn't want to play you, but neither did it want to play against you—and so you were kept in perpetual cold storage in the minors, all overtures from other teams wanting to trade for you being turned aside. Sometimes you had, in the eyes of the parent club, misbehaved, and so were shipped to the minors as punishment, and the other National league clubs were told that you were there for a good reason, and that you were not available under any circumstances. Sometimes your brilliant career melted before your disbelieving eyes.

And sometimes you didn't want to leave the minors, once you were there. Sometimes it was easier to be the big fish in the small pond, to be the star in a smaller market, making more money than you could as a fringe player in the National league, above all sleeping at night because you weren't worried that if you had two off games in a row management was going to ship you down for the umpteenth time. Sometimes this reluctance grew out of the fact that the parent club had left you down in the minors so long that you'd put down roots. You'd bought a house, your kids were in school, you and your wife had a social life. It was hard to give up, and some players actually dreaded the call-up.

It took more than pure hockey talent to make it from the minors to the NHL. It took a consistently high effort, game in, game out. You could not float for a game or two in the National league and get away with it. You had to perform under a degree of

pressure from management, the fans and the press
that didn't exist in the American league and elsewhere. "You've got to have a little bit of killer
instinct and character," says Larry Hillman, who
made his first acquaintance with the NHL as an
eighteen-year-old on a call-up with Detroit in 1955,
and was one of the Leafs' best defencemen when
they won the 1967 Stanley Cup. "Meanness was
sometimes the difference between one player and
another."

A good example of a player whose stardom was
strictly an American league phenomenon was Pete
Backor, captain of the Pittsburgh Hornets. Backor
was a Fort William product, a six-foot-tall, 185-
pound left defenceman who had come up from the
St. Catharines Saints, an OHA Senior team, at age
twenty-five to play thirty-six games with the Toronto
Maple Leafs in 44/45 but didn't see any playoff
action as the Leafs won the cup. The next season,
while Toronto was missing the playoffs altogether,
Backor was down in Pittsburgh. Conn Smythe
would haul up a raft of Hornets when he rebuilt the
club for the 46/47 season, but Backor wasn't among
them, even though he'd notched thirty-one points
in sixty-one games in Pittsburgh and been named a
first-team All Star. Smythe chose Thomson, Mortson
and Boesch instead for his new defence, none of
whom had been All Stars.

"I remember Pete when he played Senior for St.
Cath-arines because I was raised just down the street
in Port Colborne," says Ted Kennedy. "He was a
great offensive defenceman, an excellent passer,
pretty good in his own end at covering a man, but
he wasn't a body-checker. Absolutely not. I don't
know if he had an inferiority complex or not, but he

was anything but an outgoing person. Pete could do it all, he was a natural talent, but when you move up, there are pressure situations, or situations where pressure is put on you from coaches and managers. Not that it affected his play too much, but it affected him. He couldn't play under those conditions. It would bother Pete. He wasn't made for that."

Backor stayed in Pittsburgh for the rest of his professional career, which lasted through 53/54. He was a first-team All Star five times in six seasons, and might have made it six straight had he not missed twelve games of the 46/47 season.

Some teams could care less about a player's moral fibre, but Conn Smythe cast a discerning eye over a player as much when he was in street clothes as when he was wearing his skates. Billy Harris, who joined the Leafs in 1955 and played on three Stanley Cup winners, notes that Smythe's admiration for Syl Apps and Ted Kennedy "wasn't just because of what they did on the ice. He looked at how they handled themselves off the ice in his total assessment."

The 1950s produced numerous quality players who, for one reason or another, never cracked the starting lineup of an NHL team. Frank Mathers was one of the most obvious. His absence from the NHL during that decade is still a cause for wonder. "He was one of the best defencemen in the American Hockey League and they never brought him up," says his Hornets teammate Andy Barbe. "He wasn't rough or dirty. He was very capable with the puck, and he would take his man out. Nobody ever got around him."

Conn Smythe had been pleased with Mathers's progress with the Hornets after sending him down in late '48—so pleased that he intended to call him up to the Leafs for the playoffs in the spring of '49 when the Hornets missed the American league playoffs. But in the first period of the last game of the Hornets season, Mathers separated his shoulder. In contrast, Gus Mortson, who was bound for Tulsa in February when called back to replace the injured Vic Lynn, clicked with Jimmy Thomson and became a Stanley Cup standout. Mathers's chance to showcase himself passed as the Leafs won their third straight cup; after the victory Mortson headed north with Bill Barilko to prospect for uranium, his position in the Leaf defensive corps rock solid.[2]

But even after the Leafs swept Detroit, Mathers was still on Conn Smythe's mind. Looking to the next season, Smythe announced, "We will have six defencemen with the addition of Frank Mathers." It didn't happen, despite the Major's best intentions, because he didn't get his way on an expanded roster as he did with a seventy game season for 49/50. The window of opportunity for Frank Mathers opened and closed.

"I thought he was terrific," says Bob Davidson, who coached Mathers in Pittsburgh in 48/49 and 49/50 before becoming the Leafs' chief scout in 1951. "He should have played in the National league."

Dan Lewicki, that sensational Junior prospect whose professional rights had cost Conn Smythe $20,000 and who had made headlines by defying his C-form call-up, never did have the NHL career he deserved.

In his memoirs, Conn Smythe confesses to punishing an unnamed young player in 1950 who married when he promised Smythe he wouldn't.

Smythe shipped him to Pittsburgh for two seasons
and then traded him. Some suggest that the offend-
ing player was Johnny McCormack, who aroused
Smythe's ire by marrying in mid-season. Smythe did
banish him to Pittsburgh within a week of the wedding and he did trade him away, to Montreal, but
McCormack never spent two seasons in
Pittsburgh—he was traded to Montreal the very
next season. The scenario fits exactly the strange
saga of Dan Lewicki, who could have been part of a
Leaf resurgence had he not been buried in
Pittsburgh for two seasons and then dealt away to
the Rangers.

Lewicki's defiance as a Junior ultimately resulted
in a Pyrrhic victory. "The C-form was probably the
biggest stumbling block in the relationship between
the Leafs and myself, and I don't think it ever got
healed," he now says. At the end of the 49/50 Junior
season, when the Junior Marlies were eliminated in
the playoffs by Windsor, the line of Lewicki, George
Armstrong and Jack McKenzie was moved up to the
Senior Marlies and won the Allan Cup. The next
season, Lewicki turned pro with the Leafs and won a
Stanley Cup, while Armstrong was sent to the
Hornets, to play with Tim Horton. (McKenzie chose
teaching over professional hockey.) "The odd time
they'd bring George up from Pittsburgh, but they
never put us together," Lewicki recalls, still mystified. "I could never figure that out."

What Lewicki did figure out was that Conn
Smythe had never got over the C-form debacle, and
Lewicki's marriage in 1950 only seemed to aggra-
vate the Major more—Smythe was never big on
young players having family commitments in a team
he ran along regimental lines. (In a letter home to

Squib Walker during the war, he mentioned his plans for what he called "my soldier defence.") Having been at first enthralled by the sight of Lewicki and Armstrong playing together, Smythe appeared to do everything he could to keep them apart. The greatest pairing since Conacher and Jackson would never play together as professionals, despite being in the same organization. Armstrong came up to the Leafs for the last twenty games in 51/52 but was kept away from Lewicki on the ice. Rather than attempt to play them together as a unit, the Leafs instead set out to make Armstrong a right-winger too. When Armstrong joined the Leaf lineup full-time in 52/53, the Leafs shipped Lewicki to the Hornets—he had only produced thirteen points in fifty-one games with the Leafs in 51/52— and left him there for two seasons, calling him up for only eleven games.

Down in Pittsburgh, his skills impressed Frank Mathers. "Danny was a good, smart hockey player who could skate well. He *thought* his way around the rink."

Ultimately, Lewicki's curse seems to have been that he was born in the wrong era of hockey. "Danny was a very talented hockey player," says Ted Kennedy. "He wasn't very big, you know, and in the rough going he wasn't at his best. But in this era, he'd be as effective around the net as Gretzky. He was *that* talented. Offensively tremendous, but in playing for the Leafs then you had to be a two-way player."

"Gretzky," notes Billy Harris, "would have driven Conn Smythe nuts."

In 53/54, when Mathers was named to his third straight first American league All Star team, his

teammate Lewicki was a second-team All Star.
Lewicki was seventh on the scorers' list, fifth in
goals. Instead of making him a Leaf, Smythe sold
him to the Rangers on July 20, 1954. He became an
immediate star in New York, making the league's
top-ten scoring list with fifty-three points and only
eight minutes in penalties, and was named to the
second All Star team. He tied for fifth in goals with
Gordie Howe, with twenty-nine. But the following
season Lewicki was caught in the crossfire of a front-
office shakeup: coach Murray "Muzz" Patrick
moved up to general manager, and former veteran
Ranger Phil Watson took over as coach. Watson had
played the opposite wing to Lewicki for twelve and a
half seasons, and the two had very different ideas
about how a winger should conduct himself. Over
the next three seasons, Lewicki's performance
steadily suffered. Left unprotected in the 1958
intraleague draft, he was picked up by Montreal,
and after a solid training camp was looking forward
to a fresh start. Before the season could begin he
was dealt to Chicago, where he aroused the ire of
Chicago management by advising rookie Stan
Mikita to ask for a scoring bonus in his contract.
The Blackhawks didn't even invite Lewicki to training camp the next season. Deeply disillusioned, in
1959 the twenty-eight-year-old Lewicki took his
game to the American league for four seasons, the
first with the Buffalo Bisons, the last three with the
new Quebec Aces franchise. The same season that
Zellio Toppazzini left the American league to coach
Providence College, Lewicki stepped behind the
bench of the Hamilton Red Wings in the OHA
Junior A. It didn't suit him; the game ate him up
and he took it home with him. His general manager

suggested he try something new, like sales. Which is what he did, very successfully, for fourteen years with the Toronto media company CHUM Ltd. and later with the auto parts company Acklands.

Years after Lewicki left the Leafs organization, he ran into Conn Smythe at a sports banquet. "The Old Man came to me and said: 'I think I've made two mistakes in my life in players that I've traded. One was Flash Hollett, and the other was you.'" The implications of that statement still give Lewicki visible grief.

"Danny Lewicki was as good a player as any that came out of the north," says Sam Bettio, who played against him in the American league when Lewicki was in Pittsburgh and Bettio was in Hershey. "But they didn't like him in Toronto. He was fantastic. Willie Marshall, too. What a hockey player."[3]

Destiny did deliver for Tim Horton, but not overnight. Some players, like Lindsay, Howe and Kelly, made the leap into the NHL straight from the Junior ranks, and became immediate stars. Tim's talent was not so overwhelming, and Smythe's heralding of his new signing as "the number one defence prospect in Canada" had a kiss-of-death ring about it, considering how great a prospect Smythe had once pronounced that other Nickel Belt and St. Mike's product, Tod Sloan, before coldly dealing him away. The cream tends to rise, but for Tim, it was a case of there being too much other cream to rise through. It was also a case of coming to play the game the way the Leafs wanted him to. He served three full seasons of apprenticing with the Hornets before the Major granted him a starting position with the Leafs.

Tim's stint with the Hornets was an unusually long minor-league hiatus for someone who was supposed to be a hot NHL prospect. In 46/47 the Hornets saw five players—Jimmy Thomson, Gus Mortson, Garth Boesch, Joe Klukay and Bill Ezinicki—graduate into the Leaf lineup after spending about a season each in Pittsburgh as Smythe rebuilt the team.

"I think the first year Tim was in Pittsburgh was a disappointment for him," says Ray Hannigan. "I think he had greater expectations. It was a really big adjustment year for him, that first year, because everybody expected him to be with Toronto, and he did himself. There was confusion about what their expectation was for him. I think the Leafs expected more of him, and they kind of gave up on him, but you could see his skills just developing and developing. And Backor and Mathers, all those guys, really helped him."

When his first Pittsburgh season was over, the Leafs called Tim up for one game in the Stanley Cup semifinals against Detroit, which the Red Wings won in seven games. Tim's contribution was less than minimal. "I got a piece of Ted Lindsay when he was coming down ice and got a penalty for it," he would remember. "That's the only action I saw." In 50/51 it was back to Pittsburgh and the minor-league charms of Duquesne Gardens.

The arena, a converted streetcar barn, was the property of franchise owner John Harris, who also owned the Ice Capades. Duquesne Gardens was in the Oakland section of Pittsburgh, close to Forbes Field, where baseball's Pittsburgh Pirates played, and to the University of Pittsburgh. Players lived in apartments and boarding houses close to the Gardens, a dingy shrine to hockey and figure skating. The walls were covered with photos of hallowed players and teams, and Ice Capaders. The Gardens could hold about 5,000 spectators, small even by American league standards, and its second tier of seats, four rows deep, was a balcony that practically overhung the small ice surface, which in the recollection of players was no more than 180 feet long. (Its official dimensions were considerably elastic. In the league's statistical "Red Book" of 49/50, the rink is listed at 85 feet by 200 feet—full regulation size. In the 51/52 Red Book, however, the width is down to 70 feet.) When slap shots boomed, it became a shooting gallery, and the Hornets tended to have an easy time of their home games. Players knew vividly when they were being heckled. A local acquaintance of many Hornets, a lawyer named Gil Morehead, would take roost in the first row of the balcony and let visiting players and officials have it with a bullhorn. The Gardens had character, and it was a structural nightmare. When it had to be demolished after the 55/56 season, Pittsburgh reluctantly lost its Hornets for six seasons.

Sam Bettio was impressed with the depth of the Pittsburgh Hornets. "When we used to play in the old Pittsburgh arena, you didn't have a good night if you scored two goals. You had a good night if you had two shots. They had such a good team, you were lucky if you touched the puck all night. I always thought that the Pittsburgh Hornets could have gone into the National league and done better than some of the teams that were already there."

During his three seasons in Pittsburgh, Tim shared an apartment with Andy Barbe, at twenty-six a veteran of the minor professional loops. A Nickel Belter,

Barbe was one of those names feeding the Sudbury
scuttlebutt about who was playing where when Tim
joined the Copper Cliff Redmen in the fall of '46.
Like many hockey players to come out of Sudbury,
he was also an accomplished baseball player. He
played a good half-dozen seasons with the Aces of
Coniston, his home town, and put in another season with Guelph in the old Inter-County league.

But hockey was his forte. By the fall of '46, the
twenty-three-year-old Barbe had already played one
season in Oakland and another in Los Angeles in
the Pacific Coast league. After a tryout with the St.
Louis Flyers of the U.S. league, which came to nothing when Barbe and the team couldn't agree on
money, he had returned to Los Angeles for another
three seasons. In 1948 the L.A. Monarchs had won
the U.S. hockey championship; the team also won
the PCHL title three seasons out of the four he was
with them. In 48/49 Barbe had been the league's
scoring champion, and that performance had got
him invited to the Leaf training camp in the fall of
'49. Barbe had been the only professional to work
out with the amateur portion of the camp, the camp
that resulted in Tim going to Pittsburgh. Barbe
joined him.

Barbe found Tim terribly shy and terribly frugal,
someone who was nearly impossible to separate
from a nickel. As the son of a railway mechanic,
Tim wasn't accustomed to spending money, and he
didn't exactly rush to part with his salary. Six years
older than his roommate, Barbe also found himself
serving as a surrogate father to the young defenceman. Riding with Barbe on road trips, Tim would
plug away at Andy with a host of issues: what to
wear, what to say, what to drink, what not to drink.

He was a professional now, an adult, and he was determined to act like one.

About the only thing that broke Tim out of his shyness was alcohol. "He never drank much," says Barbe. "A couple of beers and that would be it for him. But after a couple he'd loosen up a bit."

Sometimes he loosened up a lot. Frank Sullivan well remembers one incident. "Bob Solinger and his wife threw a lovely party. They had a turkey prepared. A lot of us had had a few. Tim had a few beers and started to manhandle the turkey. Without tools. Obviously, Solinger wasn't very happy, and they started to tussle." Sullivan says the animosity quickly dispersed. "It was all over the next day."

He still had a small-town naivety, which made him an easy mark for pranks. Ray Hannigan remembers Tim's teammates baiting him with the possibility that he was the subject of trade rumours emanating from Toronto. They were sharing a train with Eddie Shore's Springfield Indians, and no one was more feared as a boss than Shore, whose play during the 1930s in the NHL had verged on psychopathic. "We were kidding Tim that Eddie Shore was looking for him. What's it all about, Tim asked. We said we think it's something to do with the trade. He just pooh-poohed that, until Eddie Shore walked through the car, walked right up to Tim, stopped, and said, 'Nice game.' Tim turned white as a sheet. He was scared to death that he had been traded to Eddie Shore. We had him good."

Shore was, in fact, a consistent admirer of Tim, and offered to borrow Tim, train him properly, and then return him to the Leafs organization. They never took Shore up on the offer; in Tim's final season in Pittsburgh, the Leafs sent King Clancy down to work with Tim and the rest of their young recruits, like George Armstrong and Gord Hannigan.

Before coming to the Hornets, Clancy had spent two seasons coaching the short-lived Cincinnati Mohawks AHL franchise, where he was named the AHL coach of the year. His ambitions were directed back toward Maple Leaf Gardens, where his old teammate Hap Day was running the show with Smythe, and where Joe Primeau was coaching. When the coaching job in Pittsburgh became available in the summer of 1951, Clancy readily accepted the posting.

"Clancy used to sit in the ticker-tape room at Duquesne Gardens," says Frank Sullivan, "hoping to get called up to coach Toronto. He'd be watching the ticker tape saying, 'My God, Toronto is losing,' but I think he was cheering inside." At the same time, Clancy loved his Hornets. Like Primeau, he was a player's coach. As a referee, he'd had his heart broken when league president Clarence Campbell ordered officials to stop fraternizing with players. Clancy joined his Hornets at dinner after games, and when the ticker tape issued bad news from the Leafs, says Ray Hannigan, "he had mixed feelings, because he didn't want to lose any of us. They would always upset our team by bringing somebody up."

Tim developed a lifelong soft spot for Clancy, and it's clear Clancy thought well of him. Tim would recall how Clancy got involved past the point of no return in the action. He told of a game in which the Hornets drew a penalty and Clancy began shouting over and over again for a certain player to get on the ice and kill the penalty. When the players around him began laughing, Clancy realized that the player he was hollering for to get on the ice was the one in the penalty box.

"I really loved King's pep talks best," Tim would reflect. "We'd be sitting in the dressing room with our heads down and he would be giving us a good talking to. Then suddenly he'd throw in the funniest line and it would break us up. Usually that was the end of the pep talk."[4]

In Pittsburgh Tim seemed to recognise himself as raw material to be moulded and refined. He devoted considerable energies to becoming something other than what he was, or what others thought he should be. The self-confidence he had exuded while at St. Mike's was challenged by his first season in Pittsburgh. It would not be so simple to become a Maple Leaf after all. Rather than sulk, or rebel, he bent himself to the task of transformation.

It became one of his most essential qualities: the determination to hone himself, not only physically, but mentally and spiritually as well, to create from himself a better person. It was not a matter of turning bad into good. Never considered anything less than a decent person, Tim in his quiet personal crusade of improvement nonetheless represented the idea that any innate "goodness" in a person rested on the willingness and the determination to achieve that very quality. This left room for outward shortcomings: he was not perfect, but he was very determined to get there someday.

Faith, ambition and pride were all qualities that could be attached to him. While any one of those three could provoke arrogance, it never showed in Tim. He had exquisite self-perception, which choked off any possibility of gloating or grandstanding. He knew exactly who he was, but, more important, who he wanted to be.

Tim kept up his wrestling, finding new victims in his roommates. Barbe and Horton shared their apartment with other players—Ray Hannigan, John McLellan and Rudy Migay. Tim would take on Barbe and Hannigan at the same time and win.

His mania for fitness expressed itself in new ways. "The one thing I really remember is he kept gum balls that he would squeeze with his hands," says Barbe. "And then he had those wire things with handles you squeeze with your hands. He always carried them. He'd have them in his pocket. He'd use them all the time—on the train, on the bus."

Tim was making a concerted effort to improve the strength in his hands. They were small and wide, and his fingers were stubby. Weak hands were one thing that stood in the way of his being a decent baseball player (the other was his terrible eyesight), and they hampered his ability to shoot with any effectiveness. At the time, the wrist shot was the basis of the game, and Tim's shot practically floated toward the goal. "Tim had such a poor shot for such a strong guy," says Ray Hannigan. "I could squeeze Tim's hands and hurt him. He hated to shake hands because that was one way you could get even with him."

His game's salvation lay in improving his grip and mastering a relatively newfangled device called the slapshot. Hockey tradition has it that Bernie "Boom Boom" Geoffrion, who entered the NHL with an eighteen-game tryout with Montreal in 50/51, invented the slapshot. There's no doubt that he was the first to use it in the Original Six era of the NHL. "Geoffrion was the first guy we saw slap a puck, and he could wire it," Cal Gardner recalls, remembering a game in which Leaf defenceman Hugh Bolton was struck in the mouth while trying to block a Geoffrion blast from the point. But the shot in some form had been around for at least several seasons, perhaps even more than a decade. If Geoffrion was the first to use it in the NHL, Tim Horton was a close second.

Geoffrion and Horton developed the shot independently. Geoffrion was using it as an amateur in Quebec in the late 1940s, as was Jean Beliveau. "I've always thought there were at least two kinds of slapshot," says Beliveau. "The one with the short backswing, and the one with the very long windup. I think mine was the very short kind." National Film Board footage showing Beliveau as the star of the Quebec Aces Senior team underlines his recollections precisely. "I used the slapshot one against two, you have no speed, you're at the end of your shift, so you're just at the blueline or inside the blueline and you let it go. Closer to the net I preferred the wrist shot because I felt it was more accurate.

"I thought with the long windup, eight out of ten shots are deflected, because it gives the opponent time to deflect it. Jacques Laperrière had a decent slapshot, but his backswing was so high it was a good thing in a way that he was a defenceman because most of the time it was deflected. I think Tim had a short backswing."

Beliveau began playing Junior hockey in 1948. That season, Frank Mathers moved down to Pittsburgh from the Leafs and encountered the slapshot in the hands of Pete Backor. "Pete was the first player I saw use the slapshot consistently and well," Mathers says. "I know I learned the slapshot from Pete, and I think Tim did, too." Frank Sullivan (who had been at the 1949 Leaf amateur school with Tim and joined him in Pittsburgh after playing with the Senior Marlies) agrees that Backor had the novel shot down pat, and that he passed it along to teammates. "Definitely. He was the first guy I ever saw with one. And that was a big deal going down to Pittsburgh and having a Northlands stick, which we didn't have in Toronto."

Phil Samis, who played in Pittsburgh in 48/49 and 49/50, notes that Stan "Buddy" Kemp, Backor's defence partner, was also using the shot. Kemp confirms this, and says that he developed it on his own when he arrived in Pittsburgh in 46/47. Backor had already been a Hornet for one season; Max Kaminsky was in his third of three seasons coaching the Hornets.

"Max Kaminsky said to me, 'Buddy, if you don't have it, you can never get it,'" recalls Kemp. "I spent hours and hours on it, and I finally perfected it. Some players had a big windup, some had a half slap, half wrist shot. I had more of the windup."

Kemp does not take credit for inventing it. He passes that distinction back to the great Fred "Bun" Cook, a left-winger with the Rangers from 26/27 to 35/36 (with a final NHL season in Boston in 36/37). Kemp's recollection is buttressed by Jack Riley, who became the coach and general manager of the Rochester Americans and the Pittsburgh Penguins. Riley adds to the list of slapshot pioneers the names of Frank Bathgate (older brother of Andy), who made it up to the NHL with the Rangers in 52/53, and Bathgate's fellow Winnipeger Alex Shibicky, who played with the Rangers from 35/36 to 45/46.

Tommy Gaston, a volunteer in the archives of the Hockey Hall of Fame and a one-man memory bank of hockey lore—he can claim to have been at Maple Leaf Gardens on opening night in 1931—traces the slapshot back to a prototypic "shovel shot." The idea was that as the puck was moving in the same direction you were, you swept your stick along the ice from behind and swatted the puck forward. Carson Cooper, who played with the Bruins and the old Detroit Cougars/Falcons franchise from 24/25 to 31/32, had this shot, says Tommy. He also suggests, highly logically, that the slapshot began its serious postwar development through the popularity of golf among players. Winding up with a club and whacking a stationary projectile must have seemed equally applicable to stick and puck.

It's clear that Tim could have learned the slapshot's rudiments from at least three different Hornets, who were all using it before Geoffrion brought it to the NHL: Pete Backor, Frank Mathers and Buddy Kemp. And by the time Tim Horton was exposed to the slapshot in Pittsburgh, the shot had also taken root within the Senior Marlies.

But as far as Ray Hannigan, who played on the Senior Marlies and the Pittsburgh Hornets, is concerned, Tim's slapshot was the first proper one he ever saw. "He developed it to a fine art. He learned to slap a puck, and I'll tell you, that was like another light went on. Some of them might have been experimenting with it, but he could do it. He picked it up almost overnight. It made an incredible difference from the point. I don't know whether it was his wrists or what. He couldn't snap a shot, but boy could he slap it." Tim suddenly had

an offensive weapon of which almost no one in the
NHL, save Geoffrion, could boast.

One of the most remarkable aspects of Tim
Horton's career was that he managed to have any
kind of career with such poor eyesight. There's no
question that it was a disability Tim struggled with.
At several points, he tried wearing contact lenses, to
no avail—his astigmatism prevented them from fitting properly. Frank Mathers remembers Tim trying
to play with hard contacts in Pittsburgh, developing
bubbles of air behind the lenses, and having to reap-
ply them in mid-game. But while his Leaf defensive
mate of the 1960s, Al Arbour, wore his glasses on
the ice, Tim never tried to follow suit.

Ray Timgren, who played with Tim during his
first seasons in Toronto, recalls him once trying to
circle behind the net and skating right into the
goalpost. Most friends tend to downplay the disability, but it does underline the tremendous natural
skill with which Tim played. It was critical for a
defenceman like him to be attuned to the ebb and
flow of attack and retreat. When players speak of
"seeing" the game, they mean more than the puck
and the uniforms. Seeing means understanding and
reacting to the nuances of the play, the shifting pat-
terns, the opportunities opening, the dangers sur-
facing. Tim Horton could hardly see a thing, yet he
saw everything.

One of the greatest friends a Pittsburgh Hornet
could have was a local character named Adolph
Donadeo. He was in the food business, and was
mainly known as the chef at Churchill Valley
Country Club, where team members would retire to

play a round after practice. He was also known to work at Fox Chapel Golf Club—he might have been the club dining room's *maître d'*. He also worked as a caterer and would supply the food for team parties. He knew all the best places to eat and spoiled the players with freebies like plates of shrimp. Several times a season he would join the team on road trips at his own expense, and he made it his business to tend to every need of a player. When Donadeo decided Andy Barbe belonged in the West Pennsylvania Sports Hall of Fame, he nominated him, and Barbe was duly elected. He once made up his mind to do something about the virginity of one Hornet, and supplied him with a gross of condoms he purchased from a golf-ball salesman. When the player went on a road trip, his nosy landlady found the stupendous prophylactic supply. Upon returning to Pittsburgh, the player found his bags packed, his presence no longer desired in the boarding-house.

Donadeo has been credited with serving as a matchmaker of sorts for Tim Horton in his romance with Delores Rose Michalek, who by all indications was his first true girlfriend. Born on New Year's Day in 1932, Delores—henceforth known as Lori—was the second-youngest of seven children in a family of five girls and two boys. Her father worked in a meat-packing plant, and had provided for the family through the Depression as a house painter. She was a bright student, but the family's finances meant there would be no post-secondary education for her. She has sometimes been described as a former Ice Capades skater; in truth, she had been taking skating lessons since age fourteen with the Ice Capades classes at Duquesne Gardens but never actually skated professionally. Did Lori have dreams of joining the skating show? "I don't think I had my heart set on it," she says. In any event, in the spring of 1951, when the Hornets were just starting the playoffs, Lori was introduced to Tim at Duquesne Gardens by Donadeo. Lori downplays the idea that Donadeo was playing matchmaker. "Actually, I had just met Adolph and I was speaking to him, waiting to go on the ice, when Tim came along. Adolph said, 'Lori, have you ever met Tim Horton?' And he introduced us."

Nonetheless, there is an undeniable element of a fix to the encounter—Donadeo making his acquaintance with Lori Michalek, then making sure that she formally met the painfully shy Tim Horton, who just happened to be in the neighbourhood.

Lori and Tim dated "maybe three or four times" that spring, in Lori's recollection. The Hornets had enjoyed a late-season surge, and finished third in the Western division by winning thirty-one, losing thirty-three and tying seven. They swept aside Springfield, the third-place team in the Eastern division, with wins of 6-0, 9-0 and 7-2. Then they got past Hershey, the second-place team in the east, in the semifinals, which vaulted them, in defiance of all expectations, into the finals against Cleveland. Johnny Bower was Cleveland's goaltender, and proved to be one of the series stars when the Barons defeated Pittsburgh, but only after being taken to the full seven games.

Though disheartening, the season's outcome was an exceptional one for the Hornets. Bob Solinger, Rudy Migay, Ray Hannigan, John McCormack and Andy Barbe topped the playoff scoring race, while George Armstrong was eighth and Frank Mathers ninth. Tim was fourteenth, with nine assists. His sixteen minutes in penalties, collected in thirteen games, was fourth-highest—Ray Hannigan outdid him with twenty minutes, which included two fighting majors, while Tim collected minors exclusively.

When the playoffs were over, Tim headed back to North Bay. He hadn't played a single game in Toronto that season, and the Leafs won the Stanley Cup through Bill Barilko's heroic overtime goal. A month before training camp for the 51/52 season, Barilko was dead in a plane crash. There was an opening that urgently needed to be filled in the Leaf defence roster. If Tim had made it, he almost certainly never would have seen Lori Michalek again. He didn't make it. When Tim returned to Pittsburgh that fall, he resumed his relationship with Lori. In little more than a year, he would be a Maple Leaf, a husband and a father.

Chapter 9

Life After Bill

With a talent like Tim Horton's, it is less a case of whether or not a career will unfold than how it will unfold. There is no single accepted way for a career to unfold. Destiny often depends on those mutually supportive phenomena known as fate and circumstance. Fate and circumstance helped launch Tim's career as a Maple Leaf when Bill Barilko's floatplane disappeared from the skies north of Cochrane in August 1951, after his overtime goal in game five of the Stanley Cup the preceding April gave the Leafs their last cup victory for the next eleven seasons.

Less than three minutes into overtime, with the score tied 2-2, Barilko had dashed in from the point when Harry Watson's point-blank shot from the slot hit the skate of Montreal defenceman Butch Bouchard. In attempting to feed Rocket Richard with the loose puck, Bouchard sent the puck skittering across Hollywood Bill's field of vision. Lured out of position by the talisman of open ice, Barilko nearly collided with his own centre, Cal Gardner, as he gathered up the puck on his backhand and shovelled it over the fallen Canadiens goaltender Gerry McNeil. The effort of the shot lifted Barilko off his feet; he crashed to earth on his elbows as the goal forever sealed his fame.

Barilko had scored his famous overtime goal by

leaving his position on the point and dashing in like an uninvited stranger. He was out of position, out of turn, out of character, out of the blue. He could not have been more of a surprise had he jumped from the spectators onto the ice. His appearance and breathtaking success was a delightful discovery to the Leafs. To the Canadiens, the Cup had been lost to the least expected adversary: a Maple Leaf defenceman abandoning his post at a critical moment in a pivotal game. "That was a playoff series where every game ended in overtime," says Harry Watson. "It was important for you to stay where you were and do your job." After Barilko scored, the Canadiens on the ice removed themselves from the scene of Leaf revelry in disgust. The Leafs had won the wrong way. They had lost the wrong way. Only Butch Bouchard, after at first turning away from the Leaf celebrations at the Canadiens' goal crease, took the time to study the wonder of their mutual failure.

Barilko's death as much opened a character role as a specific position in the Leaf defence corps. In his final season he garnered eight times as many penalty minutes as points, although his performances over his final three seasons, each ringing up less than 100 minutes in penalties, were far tamer than the 147-minute spree he offered in his first full season, although his devastating body-checks put players like Milt Schmidt, Ed Sandford and Bill Gadsby on the disabled list. Barilko's heroic final game and his tragic death, focused his contribution to the team, perhaps even exaggerated it. If another player came along who reminded Conn Smythe of Bill Barilko, or at least captured some of his essence, there was assuredly a place for him in the

Leaf starting lineup.

For Tim, the role was there both to embrace and to resist. He was capable of playing as fiercely as the game called for—by his own admission in 1968, it was only by controlling his temper that he avoided collecting more penalty minutes than he did when he finally reached the NHL. "I was young and reckless in my early days in the league," he would recall. "I had a very bad temper. I guess I still have one, but I've managed to contain it as much as possible. Otherwise, I would have spent much more time in the penalty box." It was a surprising confession from a player who has always been regarded as one of the more unflappable, even-tempered players to take to the ice. His outer temperament was the result of a conscious decision to control and submerge his inner one.

He could easily have become one of the succession of Maple Leafs to lead the league in penalties, but he was determined not to. Nothing speaks louder of his self-discipline than his refusal to play the kind of game the game itself welcomed, the kind of game to which he was emotionally disposed. As for the kind of game he had shown he could play—the game of electrifying end-to-end solo rushes in which he had revelled at St. Mike's—well, there wasn't much call for that kind of skill in the defensive corps of an NHL team coached or managed by Hap Day. The slapshot he developed in Pittsburgh did give him a valuable offensive weapon: unlike Barilko, Tim would not have to leave his post at the point to shovel after loose pucks. He could wait for the puck to be fed back to him, and tee off with devastating results. But the Leafs were still looking for a strongman, and the slapshot would not be enough to guarantee him a starting position. He was going to have to get tough.

"He knew he was going to get there eventually," Frank Mathers says of Tim, "and he could have gotten there sooner if he'd been more aggressive—by that I mean a Bill Barilko type."

The summer that Barilko died, King Clancy was hired as the new coach of the Hornets. In his autobiography, Clancy would recall his trepidation at the possibility of losing a star player like Tim just as he was taking over the Hornets. "The Leafs made periodic sorties into my camp to take away boys they wanted to look over. They were in dire need of a replacement for Bill Barilko... Naturally, they kept taking some of my best talent, and I had conniptions when Sullivan, Horton and Mathers went to Toronto camp for tryouts. I wished them well, but as a 'greener' I needed all the strength I could get. When Hughie Bolton snaffled [the Barilko position], I heaved a sigh of relief that could be heard all the way to Pittsburgh."

Ironically, Bolton only recorded seventy-three minutes in penalties in his first Leaf season, and was shipped right back to the Hornets for two seasons.

"Tim never had a mean bone in his body," says Ray Hannigan. "A lot of the coaches tried to get him to play mean, but he never could. He could hit you, but it was always clean. They wanted him to play like Barilko. He was a gentle giant, and his finesse improved every year he played."

Tim's career path may have been muddied for him by his own Junior hockey record. His penalty minutes at St. Mike's may have suggested to the Leaf organization a born brawler, but his Majors teammate and roommate Don Rope felt that Tim attracted an unfair number of infractions. In addition to retaliatory penalties Tim was suckered into committing, there were infractions handed out on clean hits that looked illegal when Tim delivered them, simply because of the damage they did. A routine body check from Tim could send a player on an eye-catching trajectory, or leave him crumpled on the ice, encouraging referees to dispense a boarding or charging penalty.

Certainly his reputation had been that of a player accustomed to doing damage. An enthusiastic profile of Tim in a 1949 edition of *The Double Blue* of St. Mike's offered this scenario:

> "Who is this guy Horton?" scoffed the gay young blade as he tightened his laces before his first game against St. Michael's College Majors. All he got from his team-mates was a few pitying glances.
>
> Fifteen minutes later, the not-so-gay young blade awoke to the odour of smelling salts. He stared blankly about the white-washed walls trying to collect his scattered senses. Suddenly, he gasped through the wide open spaces once occupied by his front teeth.
>
> "So! That was Tim Horton!"
>
> Exaggeration? Possibly. But there is still many a young puck-pusher who would rather pass that biscuit than attempt to pass Tim Horton.

It was as if Tim was haunted by Barilko. In the six games he played as a Maple Leaf during his Pittsburgh years, Tim conducted himself more the way the Leafs expected, collecting no points and ten minutes in penalties. But in Pittsburgh he was slow to warm to the pugnacious role the Leafs expected of him. Acquiring the slapshot, his scoring was very respectable—twenty-three points in his first season, thirty-four in his second, thirty-one in his third. On the physical front he started tentatively that first season in Pittsburgh, with a relatively tame eighty-three penalty minutes in sixty games. But that changed. He had 129 minutes in his second season, and in his third season, the one that followed Barilko's death, he ran his misdemeanours up to 146 minutes. As each season passed without a posting in Toronto, Tim got the message.

Frank Mathers watched his teammate bounce his way through one game after another. Mathers and Horton were both offensive-minded defencemen, similar to Gus Mortson, says Mathers, in their ability to move the puck. But Mathers was never a scrapper like Mortson or the young Tim, and never would be. The Leafs had a superlative defensive system: strong in goal and behind the blueline, with forwards who could back-check relentlessly and a few, like Ezinicki, who could hit without mercy.[1] One reason Tim was down in Pittsburgh was to improve his work in his own end, but the Leafs also thrived on an aggressive, intimidating style: clean, but fearsome.

"Tim was more of a fighter than I was," says Mathers. "Tim was young and eager and he'd get involved. He was a very strong individual. Just in the manner he played, he'd throw people around and get them excited. And he was never one to back down." Tim commanded immense respect from the league's pugilists. "Not many people would fight with him," Mathers remembers. "They weren't going to win. He was involved in quite a few, but they were over quickly. He would move in just like a bear and pick them up and flatten them."

Ted Kennedy agrees wholeheartedly with the comparison of Gus Mortson and Tim Horton. "Absolutely. The only player you could compare Tim to was Gus Mortson." (Mortson himself agrees with the comparison.) "Gus was not a great body-checker," Kennedy explains, "nor was Tim. Tim was a very, very powerful man. If he got you along the boards in his end, you didn't come out. That's where you stayed. He put you down." In style of play, Kennedy saw Bill Barilko and Tim Horton as entirely different entities. "Barilko was a much bigger man, had a much bigger back, and was an actual body-checker. He could hit and hurt."

Barilko also stood out for the mischievous way he telegraphed his body-checks when he caught his victim unawares. Just before he made contact, says Cal Gardner, he'd announce his impending arrival with a Roadrunner-like "boop-boop"—sometimes it was the last sound a player heard before the lights went out. Gardner recalls Barilko catching Zellio Toppazzini, traded by the Bruins to the New York Rangers, crossing centre ice with his head down during the 50/51 season, Barilko's last. One *boop-boop* later, Toppazzini was on the ice. "He really nailed him," says Gardner. "Barilko went over to him and said, 'Now, you've got to keep your head up, Mister Toppazzini.'"

"I can remember Bill making those sounds," says Gus Mortson, "but I don't know if he made them every time he went to hit somebody. When he hit them, he would line them up and then take about three steps on his toes." On comparisons between Barilko and Tim, he observes: "Bill wasn't as strong as Tim. Tim was a more muscular person."

Tim wasn't a scrapper in the Barilko style. "Tim was never a brawler," says Andy Barbe, "but he was rough."

"Tim was strong with his arms," says Kennedy. "He could wrestle you. He wasn't a fist-fighter as much, but he was a very courageous man, and if he ever got his arms around you, you were going to go down."

"One of the remarkable things about Tim was that he could never hit anyone in the face that I knew of," says Dick Trainor. "Tony Leswick used to know how to trip Tim without getting a penalty when he was winding up. He used to hit Tim right between the top of the skate and the bottom of the shinpad, and dump him. It would infuriate him, and one day Tim couldn't take it any longer. They got in a battle and Tim had both his knees on Tony's arms, pinning him to the ice. He drew his hand back to strike him, but couldn't do it. I never saw him punch anyone, but he could really wrestle."

"He would never use his fists," says Johnny Bower, who joined Tim as a Maple Leaf six seasons after Tim finally cracked the Leaf lineup. "He would grab a hold of you and squeeze you until you turned purple, and that was efficient enough. You would very seldom see Timmy swing at a guy in a fight. Maybe he was afraid to use his dukes, that he would hurt somebody because of his strength. Everybody on the hockey team, when there was a fight, had to grab somebody. You couldn't leave one guy floating around, because that floater would probably grab a hold of you from the back. When Timmy would grab a hold of somebody, he would grab big, tough guys. He wouldn't grab the easygoing guys. If there was a guy like John Ferguson on the ice, he would grab a hold of him instead of a guy like Beliveau, because he knew he could hold him down if he had to."

"He could untangle a pileup quicker than anyone I've seen," Leaf trainer Bobby Haggert would reflect. "If there was one of our guys on the bottom of a pile, he'd just wade in and throw everybody off. The players would pair off during brawls. Horton would usually grab a couple."

"Tim was not an aggressor," remembers Frank Sullivan. "He would never deliberately hurt anybody." But if an opponent committed an offside against Tim's blueline of proper conduct, he could be formidable. "I remember we were playing in Pittsburgh against Buffalo. Tim was very close to Frank Mathers. They were good buddies. Somebody, I think it was Harry Dick, really rapped Mathers. Horton got mad because he'd hit his buddy, and he chased him around the rink and caught him. He picked him up by the shoulder and the crotch and threw him over the boards. Dick had to weigh 220 stripped. Tim was a small man, but incredibly strong. I always said he had a waistline like a girl's and just shot out from there."

In his third season, Tim and Andy Barbe shared the apartment without additional roommates, and they regularly double-dated—Barbe's girlfriend, Frances Swearingen, was a student at Carnegie Tech who sang in churches and with the Pittsburgh Opera. Gord Hannigan arrived in Pittsburgh that year from the Senior Marlies to form Pittsburgh's top line, with George Armstrong and Bobby Hassard, and began dating Anne Conboy, who had been in Lori Michalek's skating class and performed in a hand-

ful of Ice Capades shows. Harris forbade frater-
nising between his figure skaters and his hockey
skaters, so Lori had quit her classes and concentrat-
ed on Tim.

"He *was* shy," Lori says. "He wasn't a dancer,
ever." She agrees with Andy Barbe that Tim was
"concerned about not being correct. When he met
me I started doing the same thing as Andy"—giving
Tim pointers on rights and wrongs of style and etiquette. "I would put out his clothes, although he
really wasn't very big on wardrobe for a long, long
time."

Romance blossomed on all fronts. Andy married
Frances, Gord married Anne, and Tim married
Lori. Lori left the Catholic faith to be married in a
Protestant church, a decision that made Gord
Hannigan, a devout Irish Catholic, furious with
Tim, and for a while he wouldn't even speak to him.
A wedding date of April 17 was selected by Tim and
Lori, and invitations mailed. Then the playoffs
began, and it turned out the Hornets were slated to
play the Providence Reds in the Calder Cup finals
on that date. The wedding date was quickly moved
to the twenty-third, and it then transpired that,
because the Pittsburgh Pirates were holding their
season-opener at Forbes Field on the seventeenth,
to avoid a conflict the seventh game of the Calder
Cup series, if necessary, would be played in
Pittsburgh on the twenty-third. Tim may or may not
have had in mind saving his wedding plans when he
scored a goal in game six as the Hornets won the
Calder and left him free to marry Lori on the date
planned. Ray Hannigan scored the overtime winner
in Providence, and the Hornets, led by captain Pete
Backor, made a triumphant return to Pittsburgh on

the twenty-second. The city hadn't won anything of
sporting consequence since baseball's Pirates captured the National league title in 1927, and the
population was thrilled with the Hornets' success.
The next day, the Horton wedding went ahead. The
future Frances Barbe sang, and Frank Mathers
served as best man. "Frances," says Lori, "had a lovely voice."

Even before Barilko's death, fate and circumstance
had already aligned for Tim Horton. It happened
in St. Catharines Arena in September 1949, while
Tim was back in Toronto, practising with the Majors
at Maple Leaf Gardens and contending with Conn
Smythe's request for him to switch from the Majors
to the Marlies or heed the call-up to Pittsburgh.
The Leaf organization was through with the amateur school portion of camp, and on September 19
the professionals' camp formally opened. At the
heart of the action was Aldege "Baz" Bastien, a goaltender who had turned pro with the Leafs in 1945
after returning from the army. Born in Cornwall,
he'd been a member of the Cornwall Army team
coached by Punch Imlach. He played five games
with Toronto in 45/46, put in a season with the
Hollywood Wolves and had been minding the net in
Pittsburgh ever since. At playoff time the Leafs
would call him up from the Hornets to back Turk
Broda (who had also been in the service, though
overseas), but in the three seasons that followed his
league debut Bastien didn't play in a single game.
In the meantime he was winning accolades in
Pittsburgh: for three seasons straight he had been
the American league's top goaltender. Bastien was
newly married, and about three weeks before camp

opened he turned twenty-nine. Both he and the
Leaf organization were playing a waiting game.
Turk Broda had enjoyed an extraordinary career,
eleven seasons in all, with two years of wartime army
service dividing them. He'd won the Vezina twice,
been second three times, and had his name on four
Stanley Cups, with a fifth to come. He was now thirty-five, driving a truck at Smythe's sand pit during
the summer, heading for retirement. Bastien was
being groomed to replace him.

Four seasons of grooming came to an end at the
first day of camp when Don Clark, a former St.
Louis Flyer and Springfield Indian hoping to crack
the lineup of the Senior Marlies, let a shot go from
the blueline that threaded through a screen of bodies and struck Baz Bastien in the face, cracking his
cheekbone and smashing his eye. Rushed to hospital, Bastien's eye was removed; his playing days were
over.[2]

Another goaltender was also struck in the face
that day. This left Howie Harvey, the former St.
Mike's Major and current Senior Marlie goalie, next
in line. He took a sobering look at the day's carnage,
revealed he had a skin rash aggravated by nerves,
and announced his intention to attend university.
Suddenly, the Leafs were without an heir to Broda,
or even a starting goaltender for the Hornets.
Within two weeks they had bought Gilles (Gil)
Mayer, a diminutive star of the OHA with the Barrie
Flyers the previous season who had just started with
the Buffalo Bisons of the American league. Mayer
was sent to Pittsburgh and the grooming began all
over again. Broda played another full season in the
Leaf net, relieved for two games by Al Rollins, who
had been with Kansas City of the U.S. league.

Gil Mayer never made it out of the American league. He was named an AHL All Star five times and the league's outstanding goaltender four times over the next six years, yet he was only called upon by the Leafs for nine games over seven seasons. Meanwhile, Rollins played forty of seventy games in 50/51 (Broda took the other thirty), recorded a paltry 1.77 goals-against average, and won the Vezina as the Leafs won the Stanley Cup. The next season he played every single game for the Leafs, posted a very respectable 2.22 goals-against average, and finished second to Terry Sawchuk in the Vezina race. But it wasn't enough. The Leafs thought they could do better.

Harry Lumley was almost exactly the same age as Rollins—they were born a month apart in 1926—but Lumley had been around the league since 43/44. Of late he had been striving, valiantly, to keep the woeful Blackhawks competitive. From 46/47 to 51/52 the Blackhawks finished last five seasons out of six, and were second-last in the only other outing. Lumley had been with them since 50/51, when the Blackhawks allowed twice as many goals as the regular-season champions, the Red Wings. No one was blaming poor Lumley—for three seasons running, he'd been the Vezina trophy's runner-up. Where Rollins had the support of a superlative defensive corps on a defence-obsessed team, Lumley was earning his living in Bill Tobin's shooting gallery. He had long ago proven what an outstanding goaltender he was. Eighteen years old in his rookie season with Detroit, Lumley had held the Leafs to nine goals and shut them out twice in the seven-game defensive gridlock that was the 1945 Stanley Cup. The Leafs may have won that series, but

Lumley had won Conn Smythe's admiration. (He'd also endured a considerable dose of Smythe invective. Late in the sixth game of the '45 cup, Smythe took to heckling Lumley mercilessly from a rinkside position near the Detroit goal.) In 47/48, Lumley was on the receiving end of a four-game Stanley Cup sweep of Detroit by the Leafs.

Harry Lumley would not come cheaply. Within days of Bastien's injury, Bill Tobin of the Blackhawks had been willing to come through with a goaltender, provided the Leafs were willing to give up a proven defenceman, either Jimmy Thomson or Gus Mortson. Lumley, however, was playing for Detroit at the time. To get him three years later, Conn Smythe gave up a Vezina winner in Rollins and a star centre in Cal Gardner. He also gave up Ray Hannigan from the Hornets, but most of all he gave up his prized defensive star Gus Mortson, the player Tobin had long hankered after.

With Mortson gone, Smythe needed a defenceman who could move the puck. Down in Pittsburgh, he had two such All Star players to choose from. Both Tim Horton and Frank Mathers were named to the first team in 51/52. But Smythe also needed somebody with Mortson's tenacity. Mortson had clocked 142 minutes in the penalty box with the Maple Leafs in 50/51. Tim Horton clocked 146 minutes with the Hornets in 51/52. Frank Mathers had fifty-nine minutes. While Tim was given the starting position with the Leafs in 52/53, Frank was called up for two games, the last he ever played in the NHL. Horton's presence made the Mortson trade possible; the Mortson trade made the start of Tim Horton's Leaf career possible. And Baz Bastien's terrible injury, three seasons earlier, had made it all possible.

When the decrepit state of Duquesne Gardens forced its demolition in 1956, John Harris was forced to close down the Hornets with it; the team disappeared for six seasons, and the Leafs moved their American league affiliation to the new Rochester Americans team. The rink demolition finally compelled Andy Barbe to quit hockey and join his wife in the regional Coca-Cola bottling business she had inherited. He was the only Hornet to settle in the Pittsburgh area, and he's still there with Frances.

The demolition also put Frank Mathers in the position of reassessing his life and future. By the time Tim was chosen over him to fill the gap in the Leaf defence formed by the Mortson trade, it had become clear to Mathers that a career in the National league was not to be, and his contract was picked up by the Hornets. He had played on through four more seasons, earning a first-team All Star selection in every one of them. At the end of the 55/56 season, with five consecutive first-team selections to his credit and rubble for a rink, Frank Mathers was thirty-two years old and without a hockey club. He was still going back to Winnipeg every summer, and began to think seriously about getting "a real job." Then he got a call from John Sollenberger, president of the Hershey Bears.

"I really wasn't that interested," Mathers remembers, "but he was a pretty insistent guy." Hershey, a.k.a. Chocolate Town, was a small Pennsylvania community, the idea of which didn't appeal to him, but the people treated him very well on his visit, so well that he decided to make a second visit with his wife. He could see a future there. "If John Sollenberger hadn't called me and if Pittsburgh hadn't folded I would never have come down. But it was the best move I ever made." He has been in the Hershey area nearly forty years now.

Six other Hornets followed him to Hershey, all top quality: Willie Marshall, Les Duff (brother of Dick), Bobby Hassard, Bob Solinger, Jack Price and Gil Mayer. Mathers became their player-coach from 56/57 to 61/62, winning the Calder Cup in 57/58 and 58/59. "There wasn't any more of a gentleman around for doing that job," says Pete Conacher, who played for Mathers in Hershey when his NHL career was over. Mathers coached the Bears to another Calder Cup in 68/69 after taking on the general manager's duties as well in 1968. He was named the league's coach of the year in 1969. Three more Calders followed—in all, the Bears made it to the league finals fifteen times with the help of Frank Mathers.

During these years, Frank and Tim by force of their careers drifted apart. "We kind of lost each other. I'd see him the odd time. Whenever I got to Toronto, which wasn't often in those days, I'd call him up. He was a fellow that you had to like. A great personality. A regular person."

In 1973, Mathers became the Bears' president, and held the post until his retirement at the end of the 90/91 season. He was twice named the league's executive of the year. In 1987 the National Hockey League—the league that could never quite find a place for his playing talent—honoured him with its Lester Patrick Trophy, given to the person who best exemplifies "outstanding service to hockey in the United States." In 1992, Frank Mathers was elected into the Hockey Hall of Fame in the "Builders" category. Two of his old jerseys, one from the Bears, one from an All Star team, are on display in the Hockey Hall of Fame. On a square footage basis, Frank Mathers occupies more display area of the Hockey Hall of Fame than all but a handful of star NHL players. With the exception of Fern Flaman, who played the bulk of his career in Boston, not one member of the Leafs' great defensive corps of the immediate postwar era—not Bill Barilko, not Jimmy Thomson, not Bill Juzda, not Gus Mortson, not Garth Boesch, not Bob Goldham—has made it into the Hall of Fame. Maybe Conn Smythe was right after all to have talked Frank Mathers out of dental school.

Chapter 10

Setback

The fifties all but passed the Leafs by. The scramble for fresh talent late in the Second World War and in the handful of years rounding out the forties had been critical: the stars would play for better than a decade, and whichever teams scouted and signed the right players and combined them in the right formula would rule the league. The Toronto Maple Leafs, with one of the most ambitious scouting and farm-team systems in professional hockey, came up short on a few players and the formula.

The Leafs were never short of defensive skill, and the team was a model of two-way strength, a lineup dominated by polished generalists, as exemplified by captain Ted Kennedy, who excelled as much through courageous determination as through innate skill. And while these Leaf teams played with exceptional heart and character, they were unable to muster the kind of offence a powerhouse club required in the fifties. The Leafs under general manager Hap Day (only an arm's length from Conn Smythe)[1] lived and died by a disciplined system of play that seemed to have no place for flashy individualists. Conn Smythe's attitude to the relative merits of scoring stars was underlined by his extraordinary observation in his memoirs that Bobby Hull was "overrated," that Chicago lacked balance because of him.

It is one of the myths of Leaf lore that the team excelled so much as a team that stars were superfluous. This tends to obscure the fact that the last time the Leafs won the Cup, in 50/51, they did so with tremendous firepower. They produced a stellar season: forty-one wins, sixteen losses and thirteen ties, finishing second overall to Detroit and scoring the second-highest number of goals (212) while allowing the fewest against (138). Five Leafs—Max Bentley, Ted Kennedy, Tod Sloan, Sid Smith and Cal Gardner—were in the top-ten scoring list, a feat that has never been repeated. An extraordinary final series against the Canadiens, capped by Bill Barilko's overtime goal, gave the Leafs one of their most impressive Stanley Cup victories. Joe Primeau's masterful coaching proved that a defensive forward could hold the reins of an explosive two-way team.

But Primeau stayed on for only two more seasons. In 51/52 the Leafs finished third overall and were eliminated four-straight in the semifinals by the emerging Red Wings. In 52/53 the Leafs missed the playoffs altogether, and Primeau gave up coaching to concentrate on his block business. As the Wings and the Canadiens took charge of the decade, the Leafs began to crumble. Some of their star scorers of 50/51 disappeared. Cal Gardner (along with rushing defenceman Gus Mortson) was traded away before the start of the 52/53 season to Chicago in the Lumley deal. Max Bentley went to the Rangers after the 52/53 season. Some of them stayed. Sid Smith played on with the Leafs for a little more than six seasons after the '51 victory, and captain Ted Kennedy led the team for another four seasons, winning the Hart Trophy as the league's most valuable player in 54/55. But the Leafs, perhaps hampered by Smythe's insistence on well-rounded two-way players, were unable to come up with a new generation of scorers to replace those traded away—above all, a dangerous offensive star, someone of the calibre of a Howe, Lindsay, Beliveau or Richard, who could produce sixty to ninety-point seasons. Tod Sloan, who had been aboard the 50/51 cup team, and Sid Smith were the only Leafs to crack the top-ten scorers list over the next decade. Bob Solinger, for whom Conn Smythe had initially dealt Sloan away while Sloan was still with the Hornets, never made it full-time into the Leaf starting lineup. It's a matter of conjecture how much worse off the Leafs would have been had Smythe not immediately bought Sloan back.

George Armstrong, despite his prolific years in Junior hockey, had been slow to find a starring role with the Leafs. Playing as a right-winger instead of as a centre, the position that had brought him the OHA Junior goal-scoring record, and hampered by injuries, the Chief struggled through his first three seasons. In 54/55 he had only twenty-eight points in sixty-six games, and went for two months at the end of the season without scoring once. Although more productive seasons lay ahead for him, he was not proving to be the Leafs' offensive solution, and there was simply no one making it up through the Leaf development program to ease his burden in the early fifties. Ultimately, Armstrong emerged as a team leader, not as an individual star: in nineteen and a half seasons in the NHL, all of them with the Leafs, he was never named to an All Star team.

When it came to Tim Horton, either the Leafs were unable to shoehorn an obvious talent into their system, or that talent had not been sufficiently refined to reach its potential. The Leaf program's profile on Tim in his rookie 52/53 season was titled: "Is This the Year for Horton?" The Leaf program's profile on Tim Horton four seasons later was titled: "Is This Tim's Year?" The unchanging headline captured the befuddled anticipation perfectly.

What were the Leafs planning to do with Horton? He became the talk of league managers, who wondered whether the Leafs were going to fit him in, figure him out or deal him away. After spending the summer of 1952 moving beer cases in a Brewer's Retail in North Bay, he and Lori moved into a Toronto basement apartment as he began his rookie season; Tim was on the road when their first child, Jeri-Lynn, was born on November 26. It was a tentative first tour of duty for Tim: he collected sixteen points and eighty-five minutes in penalties. In his final season, Bill Barilko had twelve points and ninety-six penalty minutes; the Leafs were expecting more from Horton.

As the heir apparent to Gus Mortson and/or Bill Barilko, Tim inherited the frustrations Mortson himself had felt. "I used to like to carry the puck," says Mortson, "and all the time I played with Toronto, with Hap Day there, he'd limit me. 'Once a period, that's all you get to go the red line,' he'd say. 'As soon as you get to the blueline, you pass it.'"

"When I first came up," Tim would reflect in 1968, "Hap Day was the coach[2] and he stressed defence about 95 per cent and offence about 5 per cent. You could carry the puck, but not all the way. I wouldn't go in deep. If you did, you might hear about it."

"Tim sat beside me in the dressing room when he

first came up," says Harry Watson, a great bear of a left-winger who defied the expectations created by his intimidating size (and his nickname, Whipper Billy) by routinely recording fewer than ten penalty minutes per season. "The thing I really remember about Timmy was that he was a good skater and a good rusher and could always get back into the play, but the Leafs were always on him about rushing too much, and if he quit rushing they would say, 'Well, you should carry the puck more.' And I used to say to him, 'Tim, bite your tongue, don't say anything and just go out and play the best way you can.'"

"Tim used to tell me that that was one of the things he was unhappy with," recalls Red McCarthy. "With the Leafs at negotiating time, they'd say, 'Gee, Tim, you've only got so many goals and so many points. We don't know if we can give you a raise with those numbers.' And he'd say, 'Yeah, but don't forget, you told me I couldn't carry the puck over the blueline.'"

In his sophomore season, Tim exceeded his rookie season's output in the first twenty-nine games. His first goal that season gave the Leafs a 2-1 win in Chicago on November 8. When the season was over, he had nearly doubled his scoring effort of 52/53, with thirty-one points, only one point behind George Armstrong (who admittedly had played seven fewer games). He was named to the second-team All Star lineup; Tim's selection was as much a tribute to his season as it was to the determined defensive style of the Leafs. That season Toronto set a league record (which still stands) for fewest goals against—131—which earned goaltender Harry Lumley the Vezina and his first of two consecutive first-team All Star berths. At the same time, the

Leafs only scored 152 goals. Tim's points production meant that he had been involved in one of
every five of those goals, a career high. The next
season, 54/55, goals against were held to 135, while
scoring sank to 147, an offensive misfire still on the
record books. That the Leafs were able to finish
third in the standings with such an anaemic offence
in 54/55 illustrated the gap between the best teams
in the league and Smythe's squad. Detroit and
Montreal finished 1-2 in the standings with forty-two
and forty-one wins respectively; Toronto, in third,
had only twenty-four.

Unlike Montreal and Detroit, Toronto hadn't
been able to come up with a potent power play. The
Leafs had once conducted their man-advantage ses-
sions with reasonable success using a lineup of
Jimmy Thomson, Max Bentley, Ted Kennedy, Tod
Sloan and Sid Smith. When Bentley was traded to
New York after the 52/53 season (the following sea-
son with the Rangers proving to be Bentley's last in
the NHL), the Leaf power-play formula seemed to
go with him. In 53/54 the new Leaf coach, King
Clancy, put together a power play of Jimmy
Thomson, Harry Watson, Tod Sloan, George
Armstrong and Tim Horton, with Tim in Clancy's
mind filling Bentley's skates.

"Horton can shift, he can shoot, trap the puck
and get back fast if anything goes wrong," Clancy
praised. Just to be sure Tim filled not only Bentley's
skates but his uniform as well, Clancy gave Bentley's
old number, 7, to Tim, who had been wearing 16
until then. There was an added measure of honour
in this gesture, as it had also been worn by Clancy
himself. It was an unusual number for a defenceman (Ray Hannigan had worn it in Pittsburgh,

while Tim wore 3, his St. Mike's number), but
appropriately it had also been worn by another St.
Mike's star, Fleming MacKell, while he was with the
Leafs. Tim would wear 7 for the rest of his Leaf
career.

Tim delivered with scoring punch and earned his
All Star berth, but the season that followed, 54/55,
was a setback for Tim in every way. While Tim was a
favourite of his coach, having helped Clancy win
the Calder in Pittsburgh in 51/52, he was struggling
to deliver the kind of game the Leafs expected of
him. In 54/55, Tim's points production fell by more
than half, to fourteen, and his penalty minutes were
down from ninety-four to eighty-four minutes.

The Leafs overall were struggling, winning only
two of their last fifteen games. As the playoffs
approached, Montreal was in first, just ahead of
Detroit; Toronto, some twenty points behind, was
third, just ahead of Boston. The four games left in
the Toronto season were all on weekends. The first
of them, on Saturday, March 12, was on home ice,
against the Rangers. There was trepidation about
the game within the Leaf camp. On the one hand,
the Rangers were out of the playoff picture and
weren't expected to put up too much of a fight. On
the other hand, New York had Bill Ezinicki. Ezzy
had not been seen in the NHL for more than two
seasons when the Rangers called him up from the
Vancouver Canucks of the Western Hockey League
on February 23 for a game against the Leafs.
Rumours that Ezinicki, who would turn thirty-one
on March 11, had lost interest in body-checking in
his advanced years proved greatly exaggerated
when he showed up to play his former team.
Wearing red, white and blue on the Madison

Square Garden ice, Ezzy had sent Eric Nesterenko limping onto the Leaf disabled list with a badly wrenched knee.

The Leafs checked the Rangers so tightly in their rematch at Maple Leaf Gardens that New York wasn't able to get a shot on Harry Lumley until twelve minutes into the first period, when defenceman Bill Gadsby let one go from the blueline. But the Leafs were in the meantime unable to get anything past the Ranger netminder Gump Worsley. At last, at 7:31 of the second period, the Leafs went up 1-0 on a goal by Tod Sloan, assisted by Parker MacDonald and George Armstrong.

With less than three minutes to play in the period, Tim Horton decided to embark on one of his race-against-the-clock rushes. Tim gathered up the puck in his own end, saw open ice, and moved into the neutral zone.

In hindsight, Bill Ezinicki was not the player to be feared that night. He was only on the ice for about nine minutes. It was Bill Gadsby, playing nearly thirty minutes, who was lying in wait.

There was some inevitability about the confrontation between these two defencemen. Gadsby's slash, which had broken the toe of Howie Meeker in February 1949, had resulted in Tim's call-up from the Majors for a tryout with the Leafs. In 53/54, when Tim made the second All Star team, he had been paired with Gadsby. And the trade that had sent Gadsby to New York had sent Tim's future defence partner, Allan Stanley, to Chicago. On this night, the careers of Gadsby and Horton truly converged.

In the stands that night was a young St. Mike's player named Frank Mahovlich. "It was almost as if it was meant to be," Mahovlich says, reflecting on the peculiar way the two bodies gravitated to one another. He saw Tim looking down and doing an odd, awkward dance, as if the puck had become caught up in his feet and he was trying to kick it forward to regain control of it.

"Gadsby started from his blueline and skated into Tim as Tim was coming out with the puck, with his head down," says Ted Kennedy, who was watching from the bench. "The puck could have been bobbling because with his experience—he'd been in the league for a while—he wouldn't have been caught with his head down like that. He might have been trying to get control of the puck, or to make a pass."

It is possible that Tim simply wasn't looking where he was going. Ron Hurst, who played right wing for the Leafs in 55/56 and 56/57, recalls that "a lot of times when Tim started out, to get up speed, if he had a little bit of room, he'd put his head down. It depended on the situation."

An account of the game suggests that Tim was bearing down on Ranger defenceman Ivan Irwin when he cut in sharply, as if to split the defence. Instead, he veered into the path of Gadsby, who was three inches taller than Tim and about the same weight.

Tim's head was down: that's mainly what Gadsby remembers: "Being a body-checker, every time you see a guy with his head down, you try to get his attention." Unlike Bill Barilko, Bill Gadsby didn't go *boop-boop* to let Tim know—albeit too late to do anything about it—what was coming. And Gadsby was well aware of how devastating a well-delivered body check could be. In 50/51, Barilko had tattooed

Gadsby with sufficient force to dislocate his shoulder. ("I remember that," says Gus Mortson. "The game was in Chicago. The hit was just outside the Leaf blueline. They carried Gadsby off the ice on a stretcher. Barilko crawled to the boards on his hands and knees.")

"When Gadsby saw that Tim was looking down, he just moved out to hit him," says Brian Cullen, who was playing his first season with the Leafs after starring in the St. Catharines Tee-Pees' Memorial Cup win of the previous spring. "And when he hit him you could hear everything crack."

"That was like the roof falling in on Tim," says Kennedy. The tibia and fibula of Tim's right leg fractured and his jaw was broken.

That night, Gadsby was quoted saying the hit on Horton was the "hardest body check of my career." Today his opinion is very different. "I hardly felt the check," he says. "I know my shoulder hit him in the high chest area and chin area. His leg must have twisted as I hit him. I knew he was hurt—it knocked him right out. It scared the living hell out of me, I'll tell you, because there was blood coming out of his ear and the side of his mouth as he was lying on the ice.

"I felt like horse shit. I went right up to Chadwick ten seconds after it happened, and I said, 'Clean check, right?'" Bill Chadwick, who refereed in the NHL for sixteen seasons, gave him no argument. But Chadwick did not escape unscathed from the incident. The *Globe and Mail* would allege that Chadwick had refereed "like a man with his mind on the golf course."

Gadsby then headed for the bench. "The guys on the bench said, 'Christ, you really nailed him.'" And

Conn Smythe was waiting for him in the hallway by the Rangers bench. "You son of a bitch!" Gadsby remembers Smythe railing. "I'm going to look at the films! Chadwick is blind! He missed the call! That was a dirty check! You're going to be suspended!" (When Hap Day reviewed the game film, he pronounced Gadsby's hit "as clean a check as you'll hope to see.")

"I'm sorry it happened," Gadsby told the press after the game in which he demolished Tim, "but what can you do? You can't ease up, or you're beat." He then revealed a large bony lump on his left shoulder, his souvenir of the Barilko hammering. "It doesn't bother me; it just wasn't set right. These things happen."

"I really, truthfully, felt bad," Gadsby emphasises, "especially when Conn Smythe got on to me. I thought, 'He's hurt pretty bad. I'm in trouble. I don't want to hurt anybody.'" (Kennedy laughs today when told of Smythe's outburst. "He'd lost his star!" he says. "Horton was a star player. He didn't think too kindly of that.") "I guess it set Tim back a few years," says Gadsby, "but you know, I hardly felt a damned thing. It really was a light check. I've hit guys harder and not hurt them at all. I've hurt myself doing it a couple of times. That was a very strange feeling."

Pete Conacher, who had been traded from Chicago to New York that season with Gadsby, was watching from the Rangers bench when the collision happened. "I wouldn't have thought it was that thundering a check that caused all that damage," Conacher says. "I don't think Gadsby, as good as he was as a player, was noted as a really heavy hitter. I think it was a case of two big men colliding and one of them being not quite ready for it. Horton could skate, he could have a head of steam when he was wheeling like that, and Gadsby was a solid guy. I don't think Gadsby went looking for that." Certainly Gadsby was never known as a goon, despite the Meeker incident and the Horton collision. His sixty-one minutes in penalties in 54/55 was one of the lowest totals in his twenty-season career. As a defenceman he was one of the most respected in the league. A second-team All Star in 52/53 and 53/54, he would make the first team three times and the second team again before the decade was out.

Still, Gadsby was known for the odd wild outburst, and nobody knows better than Frank Mahovlich. "Bill and I are now good friends. Our wives hit it off and they became very close. But when I played with the Leafs he almost took my head off. I ducked and his stick hit me on the shoulder." Gadsby was still with the Rangers, and, says Mahovlich, "the New York papers had a picture of me going down swinging right at his jaw, and it looked like a sucker punch but it wasn't. Some fan of his sent me the picture and cursed me to death. There was a big brawl and I got thrown out of the game."

"It was so obvious that Tim was badly hurt," Lori Horton would reflect ten years later. "You could hear his leg crack all over the Gardens. Yet two men behind me yelled, 'Get up and skate, you phony!'...I went into shock. I would have sat in the Gardens all night if an usher hadn't led me away."

"I'll never forget that as long as I live," Lori says today. "I was a new bride at the time. I wasn't a hockey fan and I'd never seen Tim hurt. All of a sudden he's down and he's not getting up."

Thirteen years after the incident, Tim would pass his own judgment on the collision. "I made a foolish move," he said. "I came across the blueline and watched my own pass. Gadsby's shoulder pad caught my face and the impact of his hip check sent me spinning. Only my leg, with the skate caught in a cut in the ice, didn't spin. It just snapped. But I learned my lesson. I learned not to watch my passes so much and keep my eyes on the other guy."

On the day of the fateful game, says Lori, "before dinner, he lined up all his shoes and polished them. After that, he only polished the pair he was wearing."

"I was there with Mr. Smythe, watching the game with him," says Dick Duff, who had been called up from the St. Mike's Majors for a three-game tryout, but was sitting out this game. "Tim was taking the puck up the ice, and had his head down momentarily. The defenceman stepped up, like they're supposed to do. A young guy looking at that would say, 'This is a serious game to be involved with.' And that's exactly what it was. There was no penalty on the play. Fifty guys didn't jump off the bench. It was just something that happened."

Hugh Smythe loved hockey, and like his older brother Stafford he became immersed in his father's business as a youth. At fifteen he had his name engraved in the Stanley Cup when he served as the stick boy for the 1941/42 Maple Leafs. In years that followed he acted as an in-game messenger service between his father and coach Hap Day. But when it came time to choose a career he decided on something he thought was totally different from the game that consumed his father and his brother. In 1949 he graduated in medicine from the University of Toronto. Ironically, while Dr. Hugh Smythe would make a name for himself as one of the city's leading specialists in arthritis, medicine promptly steered him right back through the doors of Maple Leaf Gardens. He became one of the two team physicians Conn Smythe kept on call for his beloved Maple Leafs.

"I had learned nothing about sports medicine at medical school," says Hugh Smythe. "It wasn't taught in those days." One of the leading authorities, of all people, was Conn Smythe, and Hugh learned much of his rinkside methodology from his father. "His experience had been that team doctors tended to be fans and wanted to be coaches and managers." Conn Smythe also expected the doctors to be more than boxing's cut men, who did quick-fix repairs to battered and bleeding pugilists. Smythe didn't want his players simply patched up in any old fashion and tossed back on the ice. He might get another game or two out of them that way, but if the injury was aggravated to the point of compromising or ending a career, his investment in the player was ruined. "He was very firm that we were not to allow a player to practise, let alone play, until we were willing to declare them 100 per cent. Our assessment overruled the coach and the manager. That was a given, and put us in a very strong and responsible position, and one which we enjoyed very much. It also meant that the players learned to trust us." Not only the Leafs, but players from other NHL teams, who would parade their ailments before the Leaf doctors whenever they were in town.

During the regular season, Conn Smythe had no qualms about having an injured player, even a star, out of the lineup for whatever time it took for him to heal. If a doctor's opinion meant having a star convalesce for two weeks, then so be it—the main thing was for the team to be as healthy as possible for the playoffs. A side benefit of this policy was that sitting out a starter during the regular season meant being able to call up a prospect from Pittsburgh to see if he was indeed capable of playing at the NHL level. Players well understood this and were sometimes reluctant to owe up to injuries. A few days' rest while a hungry minor-leaguer took your place might spell the end of your NHL career.

In the playoffs, Conn Smythe's attitude toward injuries shifted gears. Players regularly performed with pulled muscles and other injuries, the pain deadened by freezing. They did so mainly out of their own desire to win, and they did so with Conn Smythe's enthusiasm and blessing, with one caveat: an injured player only took part if the risk of a career-threatening re-injury was low. The team doctors were the ones who had to rule on that risk, and Hugh Smythe found it a tremendous responsibility.

There would be famous examples of Leaf players rising above their injuries in the Stanley Cup, particularly in 1964, when Bob Baun played with a leg frozen to dull the pain of a fractured fibula and Red Kelly played with a damaged knee ligament frozen. But in the 1960s, when Conn Smythe was no longer in charge of the team, players found themselves being stuck with needles during the regular season and sent out to play hurt. Dr. Jim Murray in particular was belittled by Punch Imlach, who ran his team by the motto: If he can walk, he can skate. Still, Hugh Smythe is proud of the team doctors' track record during his twenty-year association with the team. He can't recall a single player being forced to retire through knee or back injuries—and George Armstrong injured his knee nine times.

When Tim Horton crashed into Bill Gadsby on March 12, 1955, the Leafs and their physicians were clearly dealing with one of those rare injuries that threatened a player's career. Hugh Smythe examined Horton before he was rushed to the hospital. "He must have been suffering terrible pain," he said at the time, "but there was no complaint out of him."

"That was typical of Tim," he says. "In fact, one of the problems we faced as team doctors was people like Tim, Bobby Baun, Ted Kennedy and many others, who never complained of pain. We had to spot the fact that they were walking or skating a little awkwardly and go after them and find out what was wrong. Others, of course, would be complaining when you couldn't find very much wrong, but for the majority of the team at that stage, their ethic was not to complain, and Tim in particular had a very high pain threshold."

Despite the fact that Gadsby was sure the check had knocked Tim cold, the story was told in the press that Tim talked Hugh Smythe out of taking him to Wellesley Hospital, which was only a few blocks away. Tim wanted to be sent to East General, which is on Coxwell just above Danforth, so that it would be easier for Lori to visit him from their home in the Scarborough neighbourhood of Wexford.

Today, Hugh Smythe has no particular memory of that night, but as it happened, East General was probably the most sensible place for Tim to be sent, whether he requested it or not. The team's other doctor, Jim Murray, was associated with East General. Murray was also a plastic surgeon, and the task of repairing Tim's face fell to him. It turned out his cheekbone was cracked as well, and a tooth had to be removed because of the jaw's fracture line. The leg fractures required pins to secure. Lori stayed with Tim until 2 a.m., when she was sent home.

He was consigned to the hospital for a full month, sustained by a liquid diet. Four days into his hospital stay, Tim was visited by Dick Trainor, who had been at the game.

"I was in shock," Trainor recalls. "I didn't believe anything could hurt Tim. It was the same when he died."

Tim was drinking chocolate milk through a straw. "I'll never play again," he managed through his wired jaw.

Toronto finished the season with seventy points: three more than Boston, and twenty-five less than first-place Detroit. Conn Smythe stunned King Clancy by publicly predicting that the Leafs would win the Stanley Cup—at the beginning of the season the Major had been his customary understated self and vowed that the Leafs would do no better than fourth overall on the regular season.

A TV was arranged so that Tim could watch the playoffs. It only took the Red Wings four games to eliminate the Leafs, as they were swept 7-4, 2-1, 2-1 and 3-0. It was an ignoble end to the fine career of captain Ted Kennedy, who retired after the last game.[3] Detroit advanced to meet and defeat the Canadiens in the cup finals. Montreal had been enervated by the suspension of Rocket Richard. The

night after Tim had been hospitalised, Richard took
his stick to the head of Bruins defenceman Hal
Laycoe, a former teammate, after Laycoe had
clipped him with a high stick, and gave linesman
Cliff Thompson a shiner when he tried to intervene.
The resulting suspension moved Montreal's fans to
riot during the first game of the home-and-away
series between Montreal and Detroit that wrapped
up the season and saw Detroit move past Montreal
into first overall. The fans attacked Clarence
Campbell in his seat at the Forum, lobbing tear gas
and going on a tear through downtown Montreal.

The future of the Leafs appeared fragile.
Kennedy's retirement left a yawning gap in team
leadership and offence, and overall the Leafs admit-
ted to lacking depth in their forward lines.
Observers bemoaned the players that had got away.
Most of all, there was all that talent on the Red
Wings that had once been the Leafs', or in the
Leafs' farm system: Bob Goldham, traded away in
'47 and now playing the best hockey of his life; Red
Kelly, snubbed by the Leaf scouts while at St. Mike's;
Ted Lindsay, also passed on while at St. Mike's; and
Gordie Howe, overlooked as a fifteen-year-old amateur prospect. The 54/55 All Star team did have
Harry Lumley and Sid Smith on the first team, but
there was the nagging fact that a surprising number
of former or could-have-been Leafs were sharing
the honours with them. Red Kelly was on the first
team. Both second-team defencemen, Bob
Goldham and Fern Flaman, were players the Leafs
had traded away. And Dan Lewicki had been named
to the second team. Tod Sloan, named to the second team in 55/56, would be the last Leaf to be
selected for an All Star team until 59/60. People

were beginning to discuss the need for the Leafs to benefit from the sort of mercy trades Conn Smythe had once magnanimously conducted to help out also-ran franchises like Chicago and New York.

Less than two weeks before the end of the season, Leaf general manager Hap Day recounted a conversation with his Canadiens counterpart on their respective depths of talent. "Frank Selke told me he thought the Canadiens were well stocked for years to come with the talent they have now on their minor teams. It looks that way, too. But you never can tell. We've felt at times we were in the same position, with championship contenders from Pittsburgh right down the line. But when the time comes that you need a fellow to plug a hole, you suddenly discover the fellow you had in mind can't do the job in the NHL. That could happen in Montreal."

It proved to be wishful thinking. Montreal won the next five Stanley Cups, while the Leafs went downhill. The next season, nine of the record number of ties the club had managed in 54/55 moved over into the losses column; none became victories, and total wins remained at twenty-four. In 56/57 the Leafs missed the playoffs, slipping to fifth with twenty-one wins. In 57/58 the team again managed only twenty-one wins and finished last. The slide cost both Hap Day and King Clancy, two of Conn Smythe's oldest associates, their jobs. With a terminally ill Squib Walker already having been replaced as head scout by Bob Davidson in 1951, Smythe was embarking on a wholesale changing of the guard at Maple Leaf Gardens. That changing of the guard included himself. He moved into the background as he shifted control of the Leafs to a seven-man

committee chaired by his son Stafford. Slowly,
painfully, the rebuilding of the Leafs was launched.
Equally slowly and painfully, Tim Horton struggled
to make his comeback from the collision that very
nearly cost him his career.

Chapter 11

Recovery

T im spent about six weeks in hospital as his leg and jaw mended. "He had a private room and he hated it when he was confined to bed," says Lori. "When he was up in a wheelchair, you could never find him. He was visiting all his neighbours. We made a lot of friends in the hospital. One of them was a policeman, and I remain friends with him to this day."

Seven months' pregnant when Tim was injured in the Gadsby collision, Lori gave birth to their second child, Kim, on May 21. In early July 1955 the cast came off Tim's shattered leg. The injury had not only kept Tim out of the playoffs, it had also denied him the player's traditional opportunity to throw himself into an off-season job once the skates were hung up for the summer. Conn Smythe bailed Tim out by giving him a desk job at the sand pit once he was mobile. As kind a gesture as it was, the sand-pit job all but completed the *Pinocchio* analogy of the young hockey recruit: lured into the game by the ruffians who called themselves scouts, intoxicated by the Pleasure Island that was Maple Leaf Gardens, and then consigned to the salt mine.

But Conn Smythe had no intention of leaving Tim behind a desk at Smythe Ltd. Despite the disappointing statistics Tim had accumulated in his third NHL season, the Maple Leaf program, Smythe's house

organ, at the beginning of the 55/56 season flow-
ered with hope and praise for the defenceman. Milt
Dunnell wrote in it that the Leafs, at the end of the
54/55 season, "were convinced they had a
superduper defence star." He quoted Smythe in full
rhetorical flight: "I don't care if I have to keep
Horton out of hockey for a whole season. He's not
going to play one minute of a single game until I am
assured by all the doctors that he's completely recovered. We're taking no chances with this guy. I never
realized he was as good as he is."

Smythe's declaration of his surprise at the quality
of Horton was classic Conn. In his public pro-
nouncements, it was never possible to be entirely
sure that he meant what he said. He routinely predicted middling performances from the Leafs in
the regular season at the start of every season. He
had flattered George Armstrong and Dan Lewicki
by comparing them to Busher Jackson and Charlie
Conacher, two players he later claimed to have
loathed. If Smythe had "never realized he was as
good as he is," why had he declared Tim to be "the
number one defence prospect in Canada" when he
had signed him to a Hornet contract in 1949? Was
his original praise all hype, or was his newfound
admiration a bit of disingenuous posturing?

There's no doubt that he did take Tim's rehabilitation seriously. It was very possible that Tim would
never play hockey again. A handful of games into
the 56/57 season, a multiple leg fracture would
bring to an untimely end the playing career of Leaf
defenceman Hugh Bolton, who had been at the
1949 Leaf amateur camp with Tim. Smythe was
determined to get Tim back on the ice.

Daily over the summer, Tim was put through an

exercise regimen of running, swimming and basketball at the YMCA and underwent therapy to
strengthen his leg at East General. Smythe also
reached into the Marlie system and came up with a
nineteen-year-old defenceman named Robert Neil
Baun to serve as Tim's gofer and help get him back
in shape.

Bob Baun was still a season away from playing his
first Leaf game. The previous spring, he had been a
member of the Junior Marlies team that at last
rewarded Conn Smythe for all the attention he had
lavished on the club by winning the Memorial Cup.
Also on that team were Billy Harris, Bob Pulford, Al
MacNeil and Mike Nykoluk, all four of whom would
shortly turn pro with the Toronto organization, all
four of whom would go on to coach in the NHL.

The graduating class of Marlies would be the key
to the resurrection of the Maple Leafs franchise,
but there were still several seasons of dreadful hockey ahead of the team. It was a period in which Tim's
career came close to derailing. He was struggling to
come back from a serious injury while the club and
professional hockey in general was in turmoil. The
team was going downhill, and its management was
going through a bewildering series of changes, all
of which was played out against the backdrop of the
attempt to form a players' association led by Ted
Lindsay of Detroit, Doug Harvey of Montreal and
Jimmy Thomson of Toronto.

Howie Meeker had taken over as coach from
King Clancy in 56/57. In his first season behind the
bench in Pittsburgh, in 54/55, the Hornets had
won the Calder Cup, and the following season, the
last for the Hornets franchise, Meeker had produced an even better won–lost record, though the

league title eluded him. His time as the Leaf coach was short and not at all sweet; the Leafs missed the playoffs, finishing fifth. The storm clouds gathered over Meeker in the weeks before the 57/58 season. Only days before the first game, Meeker was fired. "It has been decided at a meeting of the hockey committee that, in the best interests of the club, Howie Meeker be immediately discharged from his duties, for obvious reasons of inexperience and incapability with the new setup," Stafford notified his father. Billy Reay took over as coach.

The "new setup" was precipitated by the extraordinary departure of Hap Day the previous spring, which in turn was brought about by the rise of the players' association movement. The March 1957 press conference Conn Smythe had held following the Leafs' poor season had been a humiliating one for Day. "Whoever signs my men next year," Smythe declared, "will have to know whether they are going to understand that they have to give 100 per cent hockey loyalty to the Maple Leaf association and also that they know that they are going to play; when, how and where, our organization tells them."

Smythe apparently felt that Day was "soft" on the players, a remarkable assessment, given Day's disciplinarian lead-by-example reputation. Day got the message and left both the Leafs and Smythe's sand pit, never looking back. Following Day out of the Leaf camp was captain Jimmy Thomson. Smythe had been compelled to bring Ted Kennedy out of retirement to serve as Thomson's co-captain during the 56/57 season, when the players' association began to take shape. Thomson's role as vice-president of the association was unforgivable to Smythe, who saw Karl Marx centring a line with Lenin and

Gorky when he saw the players joining together. "I hated the very idea" of an association, he wrote in his memoirs, and traded Thomson to Chicago to be rid of him. The Red Wings did the same with Lindsay and Glenn Hall; only the Canadiens could not stomach losing their association organiser, Doug Harvey, and refused to trade him away. Tod Sloan, who along with Dick Duff and Sid Smith became one of three co-representatives of the Leafs on the players' association after Thomson's dismissal, was sold to Chicago on June 4, 1958.

As politics soured the Leaf camp, Tim's progress in recovering from the Gadsby collision was doubtful. The season that followed his injury, 55/56, he had played tentatively, favouring his leg and shying from the hard hitting. After playing only thirty-five games, the leg had to be reset and he missed the rest of the season.

Tim would remember Hap Day being ruthlessly impatient with his recovery. "I was out for some time with those injuries and it took me a little while to get back in shape," he said in a 1969 article. "But it didn't take Hap Day very long to fine me. In fact, after only three games he slapped a $100 fine on me for indifferent play. And what made it worse was the fact you never got your money back. With Imlach you had a chance to make up for it, but not with Day. When Day fined you, you'd get a receipt from a charitable organization thanking you for your contribution. I really got mad at him after that season when he called me into the office and wanted me to take a pay cut. I don't think I've been as angry since. But there was nothing for me to do but agree. In those days they didn't have to waive anybody out of the NHL. They handed you an airline or train ticket and you were gone."

When Tim came back for the 56/57 season, he almost didn't come back as a Maple Leaf. "There was a team meeting early that season," Billy Harris recalls. "It was the day of a game, a home game. I remember Bobby Haggert [the team's trainer] telling Tim, 'Hap Day wants to see you after the meeting.' I talked to Tim that night or that weekend. He said he went up and Day told him, 'You going to be home all afternoon?' 'Yep.' 'I think we're going to complete a deal.' Boston turned it down at the last second because they didn't think he'd ever be healthy enough to play."

The experience is still vivid to Lori Horton, and it essentially dovetails with Harris's account, although Lori remembers Montreal being the team he was supposed to be traded to. "We were still living on Warden Avenue. I had three little ones. [Their third child, Kelly, was born Sept. 1, 1956, just before training camp.] He came home from the meeting on game day. He was going to get a phone call that afternoon and we went through a long, agonised afternoon. The call never came. I never knew what happened. I don't know why the deal fell through."

With Tim remaining in a Leaf uniform, there seemed to be hope, but also frustration with him. "This boy can do everything," said King Clancy, who had moved up from coaching the Leafs into the Maple Leaf Gardens Ltd. management. "He can skate; he can handle a puck; he can check well; and that slapshot of his isn't bad either, although I don't like too many slapshots. But I'd like to see him get mad at somebody. He never took a backward step in his life, and he has all kinds of moxie. But you just get the feeling that if he ever became angry, they would never top him in the league."

But far from getting meaner, Tim was settling into a role as a player so physically intimidating that he didn't have to intimidate. In 56/57 his penalty minutes dropped to seventy-two.

Harris captured precisely the disorienting state of the Leafs at the beginning of the 57/58 season in his book *The Glory Years*. "As a team we were certainly struggling at ice level, and there was total confusion at the management level. Clancy had been replaced as coach by Howie Meeker; Hap Day resigned as general manager; Conn Smythe replaced Meeker with Billy Reay; Stafford fired Howie Meeker, who had been G.M. for a couple of hours. When the dust settled, the Leafs did not have a general manager, and King Clancy was his assistant."

Harris recalled in *The Glory Years* that the Leafs were trying to trade Tim at the beginning of that season. "That could happen within a month," Stafford Smythe told Harris. "We are trying to complete a deal and move Horton." As in 1956, the Leafs failed to move Tim. He stayed with the turbulent team, if only because no other team would risk trading away the level of quality player the Leafs would demand in hope that Tim truly had a future in the game. The career-ending leg fracture of fellow Leaf defenceman Hugh Bolton (the player originally chosen to replace Bill Barilko) in 1956 only helped emphasise the fact that Tim's chances of recovery might be no better than Bolton's. He was an early-season holdout over his pay, and because of his late signing he wasn't eligible to accept an invitation to play in the All Star game. (Because only

twelve players were officially named to the team
that played the defending Stanley Cup champion,
additional players would be invited to round out
the squad.) With Reay as his coach, Tim spent
much of the season riding the bench, steamed that
the Leafs would neither play him nor trade him.
His ice time further cut back by a knee injury, he
officially played in fifty-three games, but the fact
that he still produced twenty-six points and garnered the All Star invitation indicates that his skills
were as sharp as they had ever been and that he was
still held in reasonably high regard in the league.

The beginning of the 57/58 season saw as much
action off the ice as on. The new players association
filed an anti-trust suit in New York and Toronto,
naming the six NHL team owners and league president Clarence Campbell as codefendants. The association charged that the owners had "monopolised
and obtained complete domination and control
and dictatorship" of the sport since 1926. Years of
chafing against C-forms and negotiating lists and
voluntary reserve lists for retirees and the domination of the amateur system by the professional game
exploded in one primal scream of writ-serving.

 Conn and Stafford Smythe, accompanied by
MLG lawyer Ian Johnston and Clarence Campbell,
paid an extraordinary visit to the Maple Leaf dressing room on November 4 as the team prepared for
practice. The MLG annual general meeting was
four days away, and November 18 would bring the
provincial certification hearing for the association
as the bargaining unit for Leaf players. The foursome did their level best to frighten the players out
of pursuing their certification. They were assured,

among other things, that they would no longer be able to negotiate their own packages if they formed a collective bargaining unit—everyone would get the same pay scale. Smythe wanted a vote then and there from the players to decertify. Instead, they voted 10-7 to meet on their own the next night.

A full contingent of eighteen players met at the Gardens with Ian Johnston, Milton Mound, who had organised the association at Ted Lindsay's behest, and lawyers representing individual players. George Armstrong took along two old high-school hockey teammates who'd gone on to get their law degrees: Ossie Hinds, who was also his brother-in-law, and Dick Trainor.

Armstrong was in an extraordinary position. As a player he was sympathetic to the movement to organise, though he was never a tough bargainer with Smythe. As he would tell it, his contract negotiations would consist of Smythe presenting him with a contract and showing him where to sign. He was also the team's new captain. With Thomson gone, Conn Smythe "insisted that George Armstrong be named captain," as Smythe related in his memoirs. "I would have made him captain before, but had left it to the hockey committee and Hap, who had chosen Thomson instead."

As team captain, he had duties to be a leader along the lines laid down by the team ownership, and participating in a certification drive wasn't what Conn Smythe would have had in mind. To complicate matters further, Armstrong was also a shareholder in MLG—he'd been one since the Major had paid him in Gardens stock for his services as a Marlie. Smythe's own notes in preparation for the AGM reveal that Armstrong held 250 shares.[1] (Joe

Primeau had 262 shares and Foster Hewitt held 2,120, with a further 100 held by Foster Hewitt Broadcasting Ltd. The voice of hockey was not going to be counted on by the players for public support of their cause.) By carefully tallying Armstrong's shares along with those of Hewitt and Primeau, perhaps Smythe had been hoping to count on Armstrong's proxy to oppose the union at the AGM. But Armstrong chose to stand with his teammates—all eighteen present resolved to proceed with the certification. Tim Horton was one of them, and his enthusiasm was firm but understated. "I think he was supportive," says Tod Sloan, "but he wasn't too vocal."

Another player who voted to proceed with certification was Frank Mahovlich, who was in his rookie season as a Leaf. The St. Mike's star had just signed to play for $10,000, but he had come to the Leafs already annoyed with Conn Smythe. At St. Mike's he had looked forward to moving up from the Junior B Buzzers to the Junior A Majors. He was getting $75 a week as a Buzzer, and had figured that being a Major would be worth at least $350. To his chagrin, at the insistence of Smythe (and others like the Barrie Flyers' Hap Emms) the OHA teams instigated a salary cap of $60 a week just when he was arriving in Junior A. He actually took a pay cut moving up to the Majors. Smythe had been paying George Armstrong nearly three times that much when he was a Junior Marlie back in the late forties.

Conn Smythe went into the Gardens' AGM with a definition of communism attached to his agenda. This might seem somewhat hysterical today, but in November 1957 the Red Menace was everywhere. In particular it was up in the sky—Sputnik II was launched on November 4, the very day Smythe made his dressing room visit.

George Armstrong hung in as captain. But there was no future in Toronto for Tod Sloan. The players' association fell apart, not because of waffling in Toronto, according to the authors of *Net Worth*, but because of wavering and divisiveness in Detroit and Montreal and bland promises from the league to right its own alleged wrongs. The Leafs finished the season in last place and Sloan was sold to Chicago. For 58/59, Stafford Smythe hired Punch Imlach as coach and general manager.

He could be tyrannical, overbearing, vindictive and egomaniacal, but as a character cast wholly against the coming change in player-management relationships, Punch Imlach succeeded in creating one of the most successful dynasties in the history of professional hockey. He created the Toronto Maple Leafs that got to the finals in 1959 and 1960 and won four Stanley Cups between 1962 and 1967, and he did it by employing the talents he had at hand and making some of the game's most inspired trades and acquisitions to build in remarkably short order a league powerhouse.

All doubts about Tim Horton's future as a Leaf following his collision with Gadsby were quickly erased with the arrival of Imlach in the fall of 1958. A memorandum Conn Smythe had written following a 5-5 tie with New York in January 1958 shed a gleam of light on a restlessness within the Major on Tim's role. He had complained that "Horton is used on defence and that breaks up the Baun–Reaume pair." Where else did Conn Smythe think Tim Horton should be used? As a forward? Was the Major preparing to execute one of his occasional alchemic transformations of a player? Was he back in 1949, calling up Tim from St. Mike's for a tryout on right wing?

It didn't happen. Imlach would on occasion employ Tim on the wing when he was short a few healthy bodies, but he made one of his shrewdest personnel decisions when he let Tim play the game as he knew how to play it: with sound defensive fundamentals and an offensive spark. Imlach came to refer to Tim as the General, the player who could direct and mount an attack from the blueline forward.

His friend Dick Trainor came to sense that success Tim found under Imlach had been forged through the adversity of the Gadsby collision. Trainor had become a litigation lawyer in Sudbury, and would one day be appointed to the provincial bench. Once his schooling was over and he was back working in Sudbury, he would drive down to Toronto to see Tim play on Wednesday nights, and he was frequently Tim and Lori's guest at their Scarborough home. "Tim had carried the puck in the NHL about like he did in high school," says Trainor of Tim's pre-injury days. "He carried it end to end. He was not a very good playmaker in those days, except that he made great plays for himself by beating the whole opposing team. It was exciting, and the papers wrote it up. They called him the Pony Express. He was a very good skater, fast, and he wasn't afraid to go through you or around you. But I didn't think he was as good a defensive player then, and when he fractured his leg, as tragic as that was, from then on, he turned into a much better playmaker, and a much better defenceman, because I think to some extent it slowed him down."

"I discount the hockey skill in anybody," says Dick Duff, who became a teammate and close friend of Tim in these years. "Everybody had some skill to some degree. That's why we were all there, whether we were excellent skaters or a great goaltender or a team player... It was the other qualities that made the guy stick and stay for a long period of time and overcome all obstacles. That's to the credit of all those people, Tim included. He came back from that injury, and that was the hard part. There would be a lot of guys looking to fill in that spot fast. Coming off an injury like that, some guys would never surface again. They couldn't go back and face the music, knowing it might happen again the first day they were back. Tim came back and became an even better player."

From the perspective of Tim Horton's career, Imlach made two immediate and critical changes in on-ice personnel. On his first preseason scouting swing, he stopped in Saskatoon and acquired Johnny Bower from the Cleveland Barons. At thirty-four, Bower was at last going to get a real shot at the NHL. He had begun his professional career in Cleveland in 45/46, and with the exception of a stint with the New York Rangers in 53/54, and seven games with the Rangers over the next three seasons, he had been a career American league netminder. He'd had a good season in New York in 53/54, playing all seventy games and recording a very respectable 2.60 goals-against average and five shutouts, an effort that compares favourably with his best seasons as a Leaf. But the Rangers also had Gump Worsley, and they went with Worsley as their starter until 63/64, when Worsley became a Canadien.

Bower had attracted the attention of Imlach by playing "a heck of a good series" in his own recollection against Imlach's Springfield Indians in the American league semifinals in the spring of 1958. The Indians had needed the full seven games to defeat Bower and the Barons. (In the finals, Imlach came up against Frank Mathers's Hershey Bears and lost in six games, despite his team's outscoring the Bears 20-18. It was Mathers's first Calder Cup as a coach.)

Bower was hardly a shot-in-the-dark discovery by Imlach. In 57/58 he won the American League's most valuable player award for the third straight season. It was also the third straight season he had been the league's first-team All Star goaltender, an honour he held five times. The season also brought him his second straight—and third career—top-goaltender award.

Imlach would not be disappointed by Bower; the veteran of twelve American league seasons would have his name engraved on the Vezina and help the Leafs win every one of the four Stanley Cups that lay ahead.

Then, while he was in Quebec for an exhibition game between the Aces and the Leafs that same fall, Imlach cut a deal with Boston for defenceman Allan Stanley. Imlach was assuredly aware of Stanley because Springfield was tied into the Bruins system. He sent Leaf defender Jim Morrison and $7,500 to the Bruins, and received in return a ten-season, thirty-two-year-old NHL veteran who proved the perfect match for Tim Horton. Imlach immediately made Stanley an assistant captain, and he wore the A on his sweater for the rest of his Leaf career.

It had taken Stanley nine seasons to come into his

own. As a New York Ranger, he had been heckled
mercilessly by the notorious balcony boo-birds. The
Rangers dealt Stanley to Chicago in 54/55 with Nick
Mickoski and Richard Lamoureux in exchange for
Bill Gadsby and Pete Conacher, and after a season
as a Blackhawk he was sold to Boston in October
1956. With the Bruins, Stanley had blossomed as an
offensive threat, producing thirty-one points in
both seasons.

Stanley was much bigger than Tim Horton,
standing six feet, two inches and weighing 190
pounds, but he didn't have Tim's powerful skating
style and he recorded only modest penalty minutes,
in most seasons well under fifty. Still, he was a capable playmaker and he'd been around the game
long enough to make an art of defensive minimal-
ism. As a less than sparkling skater, Stanley was not
going to tear all over the rink in pursuit of opponents. He knew how to get the job done with quiet
efficiency, and he was able to pass along those tricks
of the trade to Tim.

At the beginning of the 58/59 season, Imlach
had five defencemen: the newly arrived Stanley;
Tim; Marc Reaume, who first had been called up
when Tim broke his leg in 1955; Bob Baun, who was
starting his second full season; and rookie Carl
Brewer, who like Baun was a product of the Marlies
system.

For two weeks of practice, Imlach tried Stanley
with Brewer, a rushing defenceman in the Tim
Horton mould who eagerly collected penalty minutes. "Actually, I thought we played pretty well
together," says Stanley. Then Imlach tried Stanley
with Tim, and Brewer with Baun, with Reaume the
utility. Suddenly, the Leafs had a defence. "We hit it

off from day one," says Stanley. "You put it together and man, it felt comfortable."

They worked their differing playing styles to their advantage. Stanley wasn't as mobile as Tim, but he knew how to play the man and the angles. When a rush developed against them, their modus operandi was to have Stanley confront the puck carrier just before he got to the blueline. "I stayed out, tried to shake him off the puck, get them to go the long way around, and hell, maybe they'd get around me, but Tim, he'd cut over and take them over there into the corner or to the boards." Generally, if Tim Horton got you anywhere near the boards, you weren't coming out again, at least not with the puck.

The only danger with this system was that, in herding the puck carrier, Tim would end up on the wrong side of the rink. "If I know Tim's in my corner," Stanley explains, "I go straight to the front of the net. There's no problem." There was no problem because in practice, for example, when confronting line rushes, Tim and Allan would switch positions. They got to know both sides of their end of the rink, and covered for each other relentlessly. "How we explained it is like this: you're never out of position so long as you know where the other guy is."

"Allan was a heck of a guy," Tim would reflect in 1970 after Stanley retired. "Everyone said I did the rushing and he played defence, but he had an uncanny sense of when the play changed from defence to attack and often would be up there leading the charge himself."

At first, Stanley was known just as much as a points producer as Tim. From 59/60 to 61/62, Stanley produced 33, 34 and 35 points, while Tim produced 32, 21 and 38 points. By the time Stanley

and Horton won their first Stanley Cup in 1962,
Stanley was thirty-six and Tim was thirty-two.
Stanley, who had been a second-team All Star in
59/60 and 60/61, began to fall back into a more
exclusively defensive role, and let Tim continue to
roll up the points.

"I think Allan Stanley was probably one of the
best defencemen for angles," says Johnny Bower,
"but Timmy was great on angles, too, easing the
other guy into the corner for a bad-angle shot.
Timmy was always good in front of me, because he
would come back and you could talk to him, give
him a pat on the back and he'd give you a pat on
the pads. He'd give you encouragement. He was a
good, solid competitor, probably one of our best
defencemen. He didn't care how big a guy was, he
could still move him away from in front of the net.
And Timmy worked very hard in practice. He didn't
go through the motions like a lot of other guys did
at the time.

"He wasn't afraid to go down on shots, and he
would come up with a lot of bruises—ankle bruises,
shoulder bruises—and never complain at all. I used
to see him block shots for me and get some real
good hard shots, and there were times I'd look at
him and he'd just tighten up a little and feel the
shot go through him, but he'd never say anything.

"Tim was a good, steady defenceman. Not colourful. He was a goaltender's defenceman. He'd do
anything to protect you. When Horton was on the
ice, not too many guys would take a run at me. The
defenceman's job was to protect the goaltender too
and there were times when the goalie had to go out.
Timmy, if he knew the guy was going to come at me,
he would take the guy out, or yell, 'Look out!' at

me. He always gave me a good loud warning that something was coming in at me.

"His shot from the point was a good, heavy shot, but it wasn't what you'd call accurate. He liked to get the puck and carry it to the blueline and fire it, and most of the time he missed the net by about two feet. Punch always wondered I guess how his eyes were. But Timmy wasn't looking for points. If they'd come his way, great. But he'd give the puck up to the guys and say, Hey, I've gotten it this far, now you take it the rest of the way. And if he got an assist, great.

"I had to get along well with my defencemen. If I didn't I'd be in a lot of trouble. I just couldn't speak well enough of the guy. He was a tremendous player while he was with the Maple Leafs. Very seldom do I mention him when I'm asked to pick an All Star team. Usually you're not supposed to pick a team-mate. It's always Doug Harvey or Bobby Orr.[2] But if I picked anybody, I'd pick Tim Horton. And there were so many great defencemen in those days, too, I'll tell you. I could never forget a guy like him."

Tim at the age of 16 with his father, Aaron Oakley ("Oak").

The Copper Cliff Redmen of 1946/47. Tim missed the photo session. George Armstrong is back row, center. Jim Dewey is second row, left. The front-row players are Tatter McClellan, Yacker Flynn and Sam Bettio.

Copper Cliff (shown here in 1936) was a scorched-earth mining town, and the site of Inco's main mines, smelter and headquarters. It was also the site of the Inco-funded Stanley Stadium, home ice to the Copper Cliff Redmen.

After starring as a Copper Cliff Redman, Sam Bettio's professional career included four seasons with the Hershey Bears of the American Hockey League.

Zellio Toppazzini enjoyed a stint with the Boston Bruins before becoming a star in the American Hockey League.

'Tim' Horton Best in Junior "A"

TIM HAS BEEN A STAR ON THE MAJORS DEFENSE FOR TWO SEASONS

TIM PLAYED MINOR HOCKEY IN COPPER CLIFF BEFORE COMING TO ST. MICHAEL'S

TIM HORTON

COPPER CLIFF

CHOSEN THE BEST DEFENSEMAN IN THE JUNIOR "A" OHA DURING 1948-49

"TERRIBLE TIM" HORTON

Tim was the subject of this caricature in a 1949 issue of the St. Michael's College newspaper, The Double Blue.

The 1948/49 St. Mike's Majors featured (left to right) Tim Horton, Connie Bonhomme, Gord Hannigan, Willie Marshall and Red McCarthy.

The 1950/51 Pittsburgh Hornets. Tim is middle row, center. Other players: Ray Hannigan (7), George Armstrong (8), Pete Backor (5), Frank Mathers (2), Andy Barbe (16).

Toronto's St. Michael's College has been one of hockey's most unusual, and productive, finishing schools. When its new arena was opened in 1961, four alumni who were starring with the Toronto Maple Leafs came out: Red Kelly (class of '46), Frank Mahovlich (class of '57), Tim Horton (class of '49) and Dick Duff (class of '55).

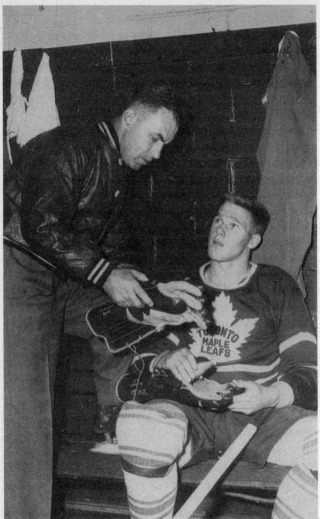

Leaf coach "Gentleman Joe" Primeau confers with his rookie defence-man Tim Horton in 52/53. Primeau had also coached Tim for two seasons at St. Mike's.

Imperial Oil—Turofsky—Hockey Hall of Fame

Tim skates in on Glenn Hall.

Billy Harris

Tim celebrates a Stanley Cup victory with his defence partner
Allan Stanley.

Imperial Oil—Turofsky—Hockey Hall of Fame

This staged Maple Leafs publicity photo shows Tim in the summer of 1955 recuperating from the terrible Gadsby collision—at the wheel of a dump truck at Conn Smythe's sand pit. He is chatting with Hap Day, who ran both the Leafs and the sand pit for Smythe. Tim actually was given a desk job as his leg and jaw mended.

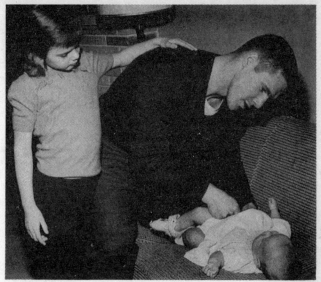

Jeri-Lynn looks on while Tim tends to Traci.

Jeri-Lynn, Kim, Lori, Tim, Kelly and Traci take in a Maple Leaf family skating party.

Tim and the family pose with the Stanley Cup in this Christmas card from the 1960s.

Tim pitched in and oversaw the construction of his custom home on Bannatyne Drive in the summer of 1965. The distinctive brown brick, supplied by his old St. Mike's teammate, Joe Primeau, Jr., was later used for the donut shops.

The first Tim Horton franchise, on Ottawa Street in Hamilton, opened in 1964. Three franchisees later, it was bought by Ron Joyce, who became Tim's partner in December, 1966.

Ron Joyce in 1994.

A dapper, longer-haired Tim is presented with the Buffalo Sabres' most valuable player award after the 72/73 season by franchise chairman Seymour Knox III.

Tim Horton was killed at 4:30 a.m. on February 21, 1974. That night, his teammates wore black armbands and observed a minute of silence at their home game against the Atlanta Flames. Left to right: Rocky Farr, Larry Carriere, Jim Schoenfeld and Craig Ramsay. Schoenfeld wept openly: "I was overwhelmed." Goaltender Dave Dryden could not bring himself to play and was given the night off.

Chapter 12

Hustling

Dick Duff takes a drag on his cigarette, levels his gaze at his interviewer, and launches into a soliloquy. "People who came from small communities, from solid backgrounds, they were quite aware of what the impact of being an NHL player was on anybody who made it, whether they were from Flin Flon or from Kapuskasing or wherever they were from." Duff, who was from Kirkland Lake, played left wing in the National league for more than sixteen seasons, the best of them with Toronto, New York and Montreal. "They knew that they were going to be nationally known, and respected, and we were special in the people's eyes. I don't think Tim was unlike a lot of players in those days who were quite aware of the factory worker and the miner and the farmer out west, that we were really playing for these guys. We were locked into something: we can do it, we're never going to be overpaid at this job, not the way it's set up, and we're going to make more sacrifices than we're going to get back. That's the way it was, whether it was Grey Cup weekend or Christmas or New Year's, you're going to be playing. There's one league, they make the rules, and that's it. You do your job well, you respect the city and the team that you play for. And I think you're right. I think Tim loved to play for the Leafs. Who wouldn't? That was our team. It was out of respect for the guys that played before us that we were going to make our mark on the league ourselves. But that comes with the support of the system. We didn't build Maple Leaf Gardens. Hap Day was a great coach and manager, just like any of the people that followed him. The players, they're all part of it. Our part was good, and it didn't come without a price, and our price was that we were willing to do it in the prime of our life, and make all kinds of sacrifices, and that at nineteen and twenty years old you had to think and act and be as emotionally strong as a guy twenty-five years old or you wouldn't be there. It was not a place for kids to be. Growing-up time was somewhere else. Pick another street. Go somewhere else. Give yourself five more years to grow up, but we need guys who are grown up when they come here. Guys like Tim would have learned it early. They had to go spend some time in the American league, in a place like Pittsburgh, and get paid accordingly. People will never understand how badly these guys wanted to play hockey, or what they would play for in order to get there. And having arrived there, somebody's going to give you $7,000 for being a national hero."

Dick Duff tilts back his head and exhales smoke with tight laughter.

The 60/61 salary and bonus records for the Maple Leafs are the only such team record to survive in the Conn Smythe Papers. They provide a fiscal snapshot of the Maple Leaf lot when the team was on the cusp of greatness, when Tim Horton's attentions were expanding beyond hockey as he marked his thirty-first birthday and his twelfth season of professional hockey.

There were great disparities in the salaries of players. Some had handsome performance bonuses; others received no bonuses at all. The records uphold the reputation the Leafs had for paying less handsomely than other clubs. The top-paid player was Red Kelly, who had been acquired from Detroit on February 10, 1960, in a brilliant one-for-one deal for Marc Reaume engineered by Punch Imlach. On a team where the average earnings were about $12,700 and the team captain, George Armstrong, earned $14,500, Kelly was paid a whopping $21,000—$20,000 in salary and a $1,000 performance bonus for the Leafs' second-place finish. (Kelly also won the Lady Byng that season while a Red Wing, but the honour for gentlemanly play brought no bonus from the Leafs.) Next in line was Bert Olmstead, who had won four Stanley Cups with Montreal and had come to the Leafs in 1958. Olmstead commanded a salary of $19,000, plus a $500 bonus for the team's finish.

Third was the team's young scoring star, Frank Mahovlich. By converting Red Kelly from an offensive defenceman to a playmaking centre and putting him on the same line as Mahovlich, Imlach had finally allowed Mahovlich to blossom into the offensive threat his performances at St. Mike's in the mid-fifties had promised. In 59/60, Mahovlich had produced thirty-nine points; in 60/61 he ran them up to eighty-four. Fortunately, he had a contract that rewarded him appropriately. Mahovlich earned a base salary of $15,000, then was paid $500 for scoring thirty goals, another $750 for reaching thirty-five goals, and another $1,000 for reaching forty goals (he scored forty-eight in all). Adding on his $1,000 first-team All Star bonus, Mahovlich took home $18,250. (Mahovlich had long been a focal point of performance incentive clauses. When he moved up from St. Mike's to the Leafs in 57/58, the Leafs agreed to pay the college $2,000 if Mahovlich was named rookie-of-the-year or if the Leafs made the playoffs. Both scenarios panned out.[1])

Tied for fourth in salary were Bob Pulford and Allan Stanley. Pulford collected a flat $15,500 in salary–he played only forty games that season, collecting no bonuses. Stanley, beginning with a base of $14,000, earned $500 for the team's second-place finish, another $500 for having a greater goals-for than goals-against record while on the ice (usually referred to as a plus–minus record, it's a rule-of-thumb test of a defenceman's skills) and another $500 for being named to the second All Star team.

Tied for sixth at $15,000 were Johnny Bower and Dick Duff. Duff took home a salary of $14,500 and a $500 bonus for the team's finish. Bower was a classic "money" player. He began with a salary of $11,500, and watched it grow through a series of bonuses: $1,000 for the team making the playoffs (the only Leaf with such a performance incentive), $500 for allowing fewer than 200 goals, $1,000 for winning the Vezina, and another $1,000 for being a first-team All Star.

Eighth was George Armstrong. The captain earned $14,000, augmented by the $500 team-finish bonus.

In ninth place, in the middle of the team, was Tim Horton. It was not a career season for him, with a back injury limiting him to fifty-seven games. (Tim had a slight curvature of the spine and hurt it rough-housing with his kids. He passed his time on the disabled list making mosaics.) He began with a base salary of $12,000—$2,000 less than his defence partner, Allan Stanley, who had the greater reputation, having been named to the second All Star team for the past two seasons, whereas Tim had only one All Star appearance, with the second team in 53/54, to his name. Tim picked up the same basic bonus package as Stanley—$500 for the team's finish and another $500 for his plus-minus record. He received another $100 on the recommendation of Imlach to finish the season at $13,100.

Tenth was Ron Stewart, the journeyman right-winger who was paid a straight $12,500 with no bonuses. Eleventh was Carl Brewer. The young rushing defenceman, in his third full season with Toronto, had been held to fifty-one games by injuries. He began the season with a $12,000 salary, the same as Tim, and finished it with not a penny more.

Tied for twelfth were Brewer's defence partner, Bob Baun, and forward Billy Harris. Baun started with a salary of $10,750 and added $500 for the team's finish and $500 for his plus–minus record. Not surprisingly, this was the same basic bonus package earned by Tim (and Allan Stanley), as Baun and Horton always compared notes at contract time. Harris's $11,250 salary was increased by the $500 team-finish bonus.

Fourteenth was Larry Regan. The right-winger was in his fifth and final NHL season, and had played only thirty-seven games. He earned a $10,000 salary and the $500 team-finish bonus. Fifteenth was the team's star rookie, Dave Keon. The centre from St. Mike's had produced forty-five points and been named the league's rookie-of-the-year, but he was paid a pittance by the Leafs. His base salary was $8,000, which was $400 less than Tim's old Redmen teammate, Sam Bettio, received as a Boston Bruins rookie in 1949.

When Keon came to the Leaf training camp in the fall of 1960, little was expected of him. He'd had a tryout as a pro the previous spring with the Sudbury Wolves of the Eastern Canadian Professional League, which hadn't gone well. Murph Chamberlain, a teammate of Jim Dewey on the Frood Tigers, was the coach, and didn't think much of Keon; Sam Bettio was the captain, and he at least had been impressed with Keon. Keon's own expectations with the Leafs were modest. "I had hoped that I would play for the Leafs," he says, "but I guess I thought that I was going to play in Rochester." His reward for making the Leafs was a low-ball contract with no bonuses specified whatsoever, not even the near-standard $500 top-up for the team's finish. (Eleven of the nineteen players received some kind of bonus based on the team's performance.) However, the club plainly recognised his contribution by awarding him a $500 sundry bonus for his play in the final month of the season, and he took home another $1,000 for his rookie honours. Total income for one of the game's new stars: $9,500.

Sixteenth was Larry Hillman, the Leaf's spare defenceman who was in his seventh season and on his third team. He had already played in Boston and Detroit, and would play another eight seasons for Toronto before moving between Minnesota, Montreal, Philadelphia, Los Angeles and Buffalo (with some of those teams for a matter of hours or days) in five seasons in the expansion era before jumping to the WHA in 73/74 with his brother

Wayne. In 60/61, Hillman was paid $8,750 plus the $500 team-finish bonus for a total of $9,250.

Seventeenth was another outstanding rookie, Bob Nevin, who had moved up from Rochester. Like Keon, Nevin earned a base salary of $8,000. Unlike Keon, Nevin earned a $500 bonus for scoring at least twenty goals. Nevin scored twenty-one goals and produced fifty-eight points. Keon also scored twenty goals—exactly twenty goals, and forty-five points—but his contract didn't have such a scoring bonus. Nevin collected another $500 for finishing second in the rookie-of-the-year voting to Keon, for a total of $9,000.

Eighteenth was Eddie Shack, who was acquired that season from the Rangers for Johnny Wilson and Pat Hannigan (younger brother of Gord and Ray), with a straight salary of $7,500. And nineteenth, at $7,000, was rookie John McMillan.

Then there was Punch Imlach. Although his salary does not appear in the 60/61 records, hockey committee records indicate that in May 1959 he agreed to coach and manage the Leafs in 59/60 for $15,000 and a company car.

In addition to their salaries, players were provided with an expense allowance for road trips. It was not grand. A breakdown of permitted spending dated December 17, 1958, reveals the following allowances, tied to the number of days a particular trip would last: Chicago, $10 (1.5 days); Boston, $13 (two days); Montreal and Detroit, $5 (one day); and New York, $9 (1.5 days). A free training meal and taxi fare were also provided on the day of a game.

Hockey salaries are traditionally thought to have begun escalating at the end of the Original Six era, when the league doubled in size in 1967, and with

the arrival of the World Hockey Association in 1972.
But for the Maple Leafs at least, salaries had begun
to increase in the late 1950s, when Punch Imlach
took over as coach and general manager and began
to build a winning team. Good players cost more
money; players who performed better because they
played on a better coached and managed team, and
were paired with better players, deserved higher
salaries (although they had to fight tooth and nail
for them). Including pro-rata payments to minor-
leaguers brought in to fill in for injured starters, the
Leaf payroll had been climbing steadily since 58/59,
Imlach's first season. The Leafs finished fourth that
year, winning twenty-seven games, an improvement
over their twenty-one wins and last-place finish of
the previous season, and they made it to the Cup
finals against Montreal, which they lost in five
games. Total player payroll that season was
$203,600. In 59/60 the team won thirty-five games,
finished second and again met Montreal, only to be
swept in four. The payroll was now at $228,099. In
60/61 the Leafs won thirty-nine games and finished
second to Montreal, but the Cup was contested by
Montreal and third-place Chicago, who snapped the
Canadiens' cup streak at five. The Leafs that season
were paid $251,181. Over the space of two seasons,
the payroll had increased nearly 25 per cent.

Not that every Leaf had experienced a 25 per
cent pay raise over those seasons. The journeymen
were still toiling for very modest returns. The
arrival of celebrity out-of-towners like Olmstead and
Kelly had helped inflate the overall payroll. But a
winning team creates winners as much as it is created by them, and players whose careers moved up a
notch as the Leafs caught fire in the 1960s were in a

position to exploit that renown, if not with their own employer, Maple Leaf Gardens, then out in the marketplace, where hustling could change from being a means of picking up some extra cash and marking time between seasons to being a genuine avenue to independence above and beyond the game they were paid to play.

Eddie Shack epitomised the raw hustle of some of the Leafs that came to win Stanley Cups for Toronto in the 1960s. Born and raised in Sudbury on the same street as Tim (Shack was seven years younger), he had no choice but to hustle, being one of the lowest-paid Leafs. Shack used his own innate savvy to get ahead off the ice. The Hat Expedition is a typical tale of Eddie Shack resourcefulness. In this entre-preneurial scenario, Shack buys an old car in Toronto and drives it to Guelph, where he fills it up with factory seconds from the Biltmore hat factory. Then it's on to his hometown of Sudbury, where Shack sells all the hats on the street corner, sells the car too, and hitches a ride back to Toronto.

In the 1960s, some Leafs would try to take short-cuts to personal fortunes by playing the penny stock market, a strategy that made winners of some, like Shack, and losers of others, like Duff. Tim Horton steered a less hair-raising course toward financial gain, although his off-ice pursuits were more of a diversion for him than a concerted effort to strike it rich. That diversion was the auto trade, and he came upon it by way of Bob Baun.

In choosing Baun to help Tim Horton recover from the injuries suffered in his collision with Bill Gadsby, Conn Smythe could not have come up with a better pairing of therapist and patient. On the surface, Bob Baun and Tim Horton appeared to be

far apart. Tim was six years older than Bob, and
they had come to the Maple Leafs along very different routes. Tim had moved steadily southward,
from Cochrane to Sudbury to St. Mike's to
Pittsburgh, before doing a U-turn for a Leaf starting
position in Toronto at the age of twenty-two. Baun
had grown up in Scarborough and come up
through the Marlboro system; Maple Leaf Gardens
was home ice, and he made the jump to the Leafs at
the age of twenty without having to put in the years
of apprenticing that Tim was called upon to serve
with the Hornets. Baun had attended his first Leaf
camp just after his sixteenth birthday in September
1952; it had also been Tim's first camp as a full-
fledged Maple Leaf.

Yet there was much common ground. On a
superficial level, both were defencemen, about five-
feet-nine and 180 pounds. More important perhaps
was the fundamental similarity in their backgrounds. Both sets of parents were in the auto service business. After moving from Sudbury to North
Bay, the Hortons had opened a Shell station in
1953. Oakley Horton had made a signal change of
allegiance from rail to road as the automobile, the
highway and suburbia conspired to change the
landscape. Horton Shell occupied a pie-shaped lot
bordered on three sides by roads. It was a superb
location, near the shore of Lake Nipissing on
Lakeshore Road; Highway 11, the southern
approach to northern Ontario's gateway city, fed
into it. If you were coming into North Bay from
Toronto, you couldn't help but encounter Horton
Shell, and the station was located near the neighbourhood of waterfront motels strung between
North Bay and Callandar.

The Bauns were at least ten years ahead of the Hortons in embracing the automotive revolution, but their experiences were remarkably similar. During the war, the Bauns had operated a Texaco station on Kingston Road (Highway 2), which until the MacDonald-Cartier Freeway was completed in 1956 was the only major road into Toronto from the east. Like the Hortons, the Bauns lived on the property, on the top floor of their station. In 1941, Baun's dad was the largest Texaco dealer in the country, thanks in no small part to Baun's mom, who would attract customers by putting on the shortest skirt she could find, standing at the side of Kingston Road, and creating a traffic jam a half-mile long in either direction from the station. They were operating a service garage at Cornell and Kingston Road, across the street from the Toronto Hunt Club, when Bob was assigned to the task of rehabilitating Tim.

Baun also felt that his parents and Tim's were much the same in that neither family was ruled by stereotypic hockey parents who wanted their kids to have an NHL career. "They probably didn't even know their son played hockey, just like my mom and dad. They probably just got tired of paying a buck and a half or two and half for a hockey stick. When St. Michael's said, 'We'll pay for his schooling and his hockey equipment,' they probably said, 'Good.'" That essentially had been Baun's parents' reaction to his opportunity to play for the Marlies. How about that: somebody who'll buy this kid his sticks.

During Baun's eleven seasons in Toronto, he was as close to Tim as anyone on a team that in those years was already exceptionally close-knit. Coming

from families who ran service centres and being
young men who liked fast cars, Bob and Tim gravitated naturally toward automobiles. Bob was the
first into high-performance, becoming known as a
Corvette man. He took Tim for a drive in Tim's first
sports car, a Sunbeam Alpine with a big Chrysler
engine that you practically sat on.

In Baun's first season, 56/57, Tim took him along
on the inevitable speaking engagements that were
part and parcel of being a Maple Leaf. Bob quickly
discovered that Tim wasn't one for public speaking.
Bob the rookie ended up doing all the talking while
Tim the veteran signed autographs. That set the pattern for the next eleven years, Bob and Tim out on
the speaking circuit, Bob doing the speaking.

"He was an amazing type of individual," says
Baun. "A very private guy. He never told anybody
what he did." If you ask Baun or other players from
his Leaf days—even those from his Hornet days—
what they could remember Tim saying about his
decision to turn pro rather than play for the Marlies,
for example, you'll draw a blank. They don't know,
because Tim wasn't one for such reminiscing.

When George's Spaghetti House opened at the
corner of Sherbourne and Dundas in 1956, Bob
Baun was among its first patrons. It was one of
North America's foremost jazz venues, and while
with the Leafs Baun came to manage the second-
floor room, the Castle George, for the owner, an ex-
cop named Doug Cole. George's was only a few
blocks from Maple Leaf Gardens, and through
Baun it became an inner sanctum for the team. "It
was our main meeting place after practice," he says.
"A lot of things were decided there. Most of us
worked at the time, so we didn't have that much

time to be together. That team was very much a 'together' team. So we'd meet there for lunch and have a couple sandwiches. Some of the guys were hangers-on and stayed much longer, but Tim and I were always hustling."

In a six-team league with a seventy-game season and only two tiers of playoffs, players had plenty of spare time on their hands if they were inclined to hustle. Training camp began in September, the first official game was played in October and the Stanley Cup winner was decided by the end of April. That left four months of empty calendar between the end of one season and the start of the next, more for players on teams that missed the playoffs altogether. And during the season, players had enough free time between games and practices in which at least to monitor a side venture.

A few players, like Billy Harris, Dick Duff and Bob Pulford, used some of their off-hours to earn university degrees part-time, despite the persistent scholastic scepticism of Conn Smythe (and Punch Imlach). Almost every player had some kind of off-season or part-time job, and some strove to establish businesses of their own. And while players earned a good middle-class wage, the pragmatic ones well understood that their careers could not last forever and were conscious of the need to develop alternative avenues of employment. Not everyone wanted, or could expect, to stay in hockey through the front office, coaching or scouting. Too many of them, of course, did not find any suitable alternative. They had been doing the same thing since they were six years old, and when a few years of professional hockey were behind them they faced a lifetime for which they were completely unprepared financially,

intellectually or emotionally. Sustained by measly
pensions and unable to adjust to life beyond the
game's limelight, they self-destructed, often in a
haze of alcohol.

Those who did establish themselves in business
had to do so by wile and force of personality, more
than by financial weight. They weren't the players
of today, who can take a lump of their earnings and
make an instant and sizable investment in some
venture. Hockey players often had little more to sell
than their own name, but that was enough to land
them an off-season stint in a sales position, where
their persona could be put to lucrative use attracting customers. When Tim became a Leaf many players had summer jobs as "beer travellers." They were
paid by a brewery to drive around handing out free
samples of its product or buying a round at a hotel.
George Armstrong and Tod Sloan once kept themselves busy this way. Overwhelmingly during the
Leafs' Imlach years, off-ice sales positions were in
the auto trade, and it was common for players to
land a promotional role with a car dealer in
exchange for a car. (This still goes on today with the
Leafs.) Others took the car business more seriously,
and Baun was one of them. He became a General
Motors man, starting out in sales with Hearn
Pontiac Buick on Lakeshore Boulevard West, then
moving to Addison's on Bay, a Cadillac and Buick
dealer, for several years. When Alex Irvine opened
his dealership in Scarborough in 1961, Baun
hooked up with him, and along the way Baun
attended GM's management school.

Others followed him into the auto trade, in particular the Cullen brothers, Brian and Barry, who
joined the Leafs about the same time as Baun and

started in leasing at Hearn after Baun left there. The dealership's owner, Herb Kearney, was a sports enthusiast who was well known to both Bob Baun and Bob Pulford. (The dealership sponsored Milt Dunnell's "Hearn Sportscast" on CHFI.) Brian Cullen thought the world of the two Bobs, and named his eldest son after them. "I got involved because I went to a father-and-son sports banquet one night with Bob Pulford," says Brian Cullen. "When we went, Herb happened to say to me, 'My son broke his leg and he couldn't attend the banquet tonight. We live only a few blocks from here. I was wondering if you and Bobby could drop by on the way out.' We did, and a friendship started." The leasing business at Hearn became Brian's livelihood when his wife's poor health compelled him to quit hockey in 1962 and concentrate on cars. He opened Brian Cullen Motors, a Pontiac–Buick dealership, in Grimsby, between Hamilton and St. Catharines, in September 1966. (His brother Barry became general manager of the Hearn leasing operation.) "I brought in Tim, Bobby Pulford, Bobby Baun, Frank Mahovlich, Eddie Shack, seven or eight more of the Leafs for the opening. You couldn't get within four miles of the dealership." The players were like a flying squad of promotional gold. "They couldn't do enough for you when you went into business and needed a boost to get off the ground and be well known," says Cullen.

After returning to the Leaf lineup for half of the 55/56 season, Tim had moved his off-season interests from pushing paper at the Smythe sand pit to pushing classified advertising for the Toronto *Telegram*.[2] This brought him into contact with the city's used-car dealers. Between talking car dealers

into taking out ads in the *Telegram* and talking to
Baun about the business of selling cars, Tim was
drawn into the car business himself.

"Tim was a very astute guy," says Baun, who could
tell this "by the things we talked about when we
were on the road, when I was in the car business.
That's what got Tim interested in cars." He says Tim
got started by "buying old junkers and selling them
to the rookies who came into camp." (Baun was
strictly a new-car man.) From 1958 on, the Leaf
training camp was in Peterborough, and some people recall Tim arranging with a used-car dealer in
town to use his lot for his sales efforts. (Others, like
his defence partner Allan Stanley, never knew him
to do this.) Sometimes he just sold them right out
of his house. Tim became notorious for selling
lemons. He sold the Buick convertible he was driving to one hapless rookie prospect. On his way
home to the west, the car self-destructed. Tim's reputation for generosity toward rookies at camp during social outings, when they were normally
shunned by the veterans whose jobs were on the
line, takes on a slightly different colouring through
these tales.

Tim had very little time for the more traditional
leisure pursuits of hockey players in the off-season.
He played one golf game every summer, the tournament supporting the NHL old-timers, in a foursome
with Billy Harris, team doctor Jim Murray and trainer Bobby Haggert. "Tee-off time was at eleven-thirty," says Harris. "The three of us would be on the
tee. Thirty seconds before eleven-thirty, Tim would
show up in a pair of running shoes with a golf bag
he'd take out once a year. He was a respectable
golfer, considering he only played once a year. Tim

always had other projects. He was going to car auctions. To give up five or six hours to play a round of golf was ridiculous to him."

About this time, Tim bought a BP service station with a partner named Fred Care. Gerry Horton believes Care had been working at Anderson Pontiac when Tim met him, and Lori agrees, adding that Tim had met him through his classified ad sales job; there was a Fred Care living on Wildwood in Willowdale at the time, and the BP station was on the east side of Yonge Street in Willowdale, across the street from the Towne and Country Plaza just south of Steeles Avenue. In addition to pumping gas, Tim Horton Motors offered repairs, as well as a collection of used cars and the Triumph sports car line from Britain.

Lori and others say the dealership lasted a few years, but, strangely, Tim Horton Motors never appeared in a telephone book or city directory. Dating this business is a challenge; a profile of Tim by Lawrence Martin in *Canadian* magazine in 1973 dates the enterprise to 1961, but this may have been the year it closed. Dave Keon feels it could have been open as early as 1959, the year before Keon joined the Leafs. Lori is sure it was 1958. "We were still living out on Warden Avenue when he started that," she says. She recalls taking a vacation to Florida with Tim at the end of the 58/59 season. "I remember feeling very guilty because Fred was working his butt off all winter and made very little money, and we took off to Florida." If Fred had been working at the dealership all winter, then it most likely had opened the previous year, which was 1958.

In 1960, Tim's brother Gerry opened Tim Horton Motors on the family's Shell station property

in North Bay, which advertised Hillman and
Sunbeam sales and service. Triumph was soon
added; by 1963 the operation was promoting
Studebaker in place of Triumph. Gerry ran the day-
to-day business, though Tim was involved, scouting
around for used cars for Gerry, sometimes running
them up to North Bay, indulging his passion for
speed on the open road. Jeri-Lynn Horton remembers her father paying drivers twenty dollars to run
cars up to Gerry for him when he couldn't make
the trip himself.

It is difficult to picture Tim Horton as the stereotypic used-car salesman—an unctuous extrovert
with little concern for his client's welfare. By all
indications, at this time he was the same old Tim:
shy and reserved in public, the last person one
would imagine going into sales of any kind.
Ultimately for Tim, a far more compelling example
of what a hockey player could accomplish off the
ice was taking shape in Alberta through the indus-
triousness and ingenuity of two old cohorts, Gord
and Ray Hannigan.

Tim was extremely tight with the Hannigan clan.
For several summers, when he was going to St.
Mike's with Gord and then playing in Pittsburgh
with Ray, Tim practically lived in Schumacher with
the Hannigans. He often visited on weekends as
well. Tim's family had moved to North Bay by then,
and it was a reasonable run up to the Porcupine
from there. The Hannigans' mom adored Tim and
treated him like another son.

Tim was especially close to Gord, for whom suc-
ceeding in professional hockey was the focal point
of his life. He had to work harder at it than Tim did,
as he was only five-seven and about 160 pounds.

"Gordie was a husky guy and he didn't have the height," says Frank Mahovlich, who grew up with the Hannigans in Schumacher and roomed at St. Mike's with Pat, the third hockey-playing Hannigan, who was six years younger than Gord. "He was built like a bulldog," says Andy Barbe, who played with Gord in Pittsburgh. Mahovlich notes that while Tim, too, lacked height, "he was a stand-up skater so it made him taller. He bent at the knees but his back stayed straight." Mahovlich thought that Tim's sense of balance was exceptional, that he must have had a remarkably low centre of gravity to land on the ice as seldom as he did. Gord, on the other hand, was not only even shorter than Tim, but as a forward skated with a bent-over style, which further diminished his size.

"Gord was an intense competitor, with a tremendous desire to pursue hockey," says Don Rope, who played on the Majors and then the Senior Marlies with him. "But his skating was weak for the NHL, and he didn't play all that much in 49/50 when we won the Allan Cup. That summer, he worked hard on his skating." (As Gord's son Mark recalls, his father's nickname was "Chop-along.") The McIntyre Arena in Schumacher had ice all summer long, and Gord made the most of it. "He came back," says Rope, "and had a great year." Promoted to the Hornets in the fall of 1951, Gord was a star on its most productive line, with George Armstrong and Bobby Hassard. The line was broken up when Armstrong was made a Leaf late that season, but Gord was on hand with his older brother Ray and Tim Horton when Pittsburgh won the Calder Cup that spring.

Tim, Gord and Ray all headed for the Leafs'

training camp the following autumn, hopeful that their performances in the Calder Cup would earn them a starting position alongside George on the Leafs. Gord and Ray drove down from Schumacher together, and on the way they heard on the car radio that the Blackhawks had just traded Harry Lumley to Toronto in exchange for Cal Gardner, Gus Mortson, Al Rollins and some minor-leaguer named Ray Hannigan. While Gord and Tim made the Leafs, Ray was sent packing to the Blackhawks' affiliate team in the Western Hockey League, the Edmonton Flyers.

Ray would play with Edmonton from 52/53 to 54/55, but during his first season there he decided he needed more financial stability in his life than hockey could offer. On a road trip to Seattle, Ray got to chatting with a businessman who was a director of the Edmonton exhibition board, which ran the team. "I asked him what business you could get into without a lot of capital," says Ray. As the team bus whizzed through the northwestern U.S., the director spotted a Dairy Queen. He told the driver to pull over. Ray and the director got out and stared at the thing. "That's the kind of business that would go well in Edmonton," Ray was told.

It was 1953, and there were no Dairy Queens in Canada. Ray contacted Gord, who was in his rookie season with the Leafs, and the brothers decided to write to the Dairy Queen people asking for a franchise in Edmonton. "They wrote back and said they felt we lived too close to the Eskimos," says Ray.

Undaunted, they went into business for themselves. Chipping in $2,000 each, they opened Hannigan's Dairy Freeze on 109th Street in Edmonton in 1954. Pat came out to lend a hand for the summer. Frank Mahovlich remembers Pat returning to St. Mike's that fall, twenty pounds overweight from being in close proximity to Hannigan milk shakes all summer. "He *liked* the product," Ray confirms.

Maybe the Dairy Queen people had been right. Maybe Edmonton was too close to the Eskimos. The next year they switched the store over to burgers, and Ray left the Flyers and professional hockey for good at the end of the season. Having been spurned by Dairy Queen in the first place, the brothers renamed their operation Hannigan's Burger King.[3]

In the meantime, Gord had been struggling to make his way in the game. In 52/53 he outshone his fellow Leaf rookies and most of his teammates, collecting thirty-five points in sixty-one games. He was named runner-up to Gump Worsley of the Rangers in rookie-of-the-year voting, but unlike Tim Horton and George Armstrong, Gord was unable to stick with the big league. After recording only eight points in thirty-five games in his second season in Toronto, when Tim was making the second All Star team, Gord was sent back to Pittsburgh.

"They thought he was lazy," says Pat. "He had mononucleosis. He was playing when he had it, and he didn't know it." Adds Ray, "He thought he was out of shape and he would stay after practice doing stops and starts. He was a really determined guy, and he never recovered his strength after that."

Gord made it up to the Leafs for sixty-one games over the next two seasons, but the points wouldn't come. When the Hornets folded at the end of the 55/56 season, Gord moved to the Leafs' new American league farm club, the Rochester

Americans, and served as their captain. He had a fine season, producing sixty-one points in sixty-four games (with only eleven penalty minutes). But by then, Gord and Anne had five kids, with four more to come. Hockey was not coming through for Gord as a means of supporting his burgeoning family any more than it was for Ray, who was raising seven children of his own. He quit the game and headed west to Edmonton, to join Ray in the newfangled business of drive-in restaurants. Except for his 57/58 season with the Flyers, Gord devoted himself fulltime to the business.

Within a year of changing their operation from ice cream to burgers, the Hannigans were on an expansion spree. The original site was sold and replaced with an outlet on 118th Avenue in the northwest section of town, and they opened a second Edmonton outlet on Calgary Trail. Through a combination of Hannigan-owned operations and franchises, they expanded into Wetaskwin, Red Deer and Whitecourt. Fame and fortune came their way through the Hannigan Steer Burger, for which they ground their own meat. The restaurant concepts were innovative: the modular designs set on cinder blocks were tailor-made for small-town locations. With the exception of one outlet in Edmonton that offered interior seating, they were all in the drive-in mode. The Hannigans also picked up a franchise for Heavenly Chicken. When anyone asked them about the name, they said it was because they burned the hell out of it.

The Hannigan boys never lost touch with Tim. "Tim was like a brother to Gord," says Lori. Whenever the Leafs made a preseason exhibition tour through the west, Tim always made a point of dropping in on the Hannigans. They in turn kept Tim apprised of their business's progress, showing him plans as they expanded their restaurant empire. "Gord encouraged him to think about getting into business because of the uncertainty in hockey," says Ray. Gord's full-time foray into fast food came just as Tim was struggling to rebuild his career after his leg and jaw fracture. His career was by no means assured of a rebound, and he must have taken his old St. Mike's quarterback's call to heart. "Tim," says Ray, "was really, really interested in what we were doing."

Chapter 13

Hughie

In October 1955, Tim Horton attended a Halloween party at Bloorview Hospital and Home for Crippled Children, a few blocks from Maple Leaf Gardens. Twelve-year-old Hughie Phillips was dressed as a clown; Tim Horton was dressed like a gentleman in suit and tie. The Leafs were playing in New York, and on All Hallows Eve Tim's career was still in doubt. Kept out of the line-up by the leg fractures of the previous March, and with his own children—Jeri-Lynn was not yet three, Kim was five months—too young to trick or treat, Tim had headed for Bloorview on one of the good-will appearances for which Conn Smythe's Leafs were famous. Disabled children were a favourite charity of the Major's—he was very involved with the Ontario Society for Crippled Children and its Variety Village.

Hughie has no idea why Tim picked him for special attention out of the crowd of kids. It may have been Hughie who did the picking. He was nuts about hockey, and while Tim Horton wasn't a familiar player to him—not like a Teeder Kennedy or a Rocket Richard—he was the real thing, in the flesh, and that's what mattered. Tim was introduced to him, and Hughie thought: I've *got* to get to know this guy. He got to know Tim better than either of them could ever have imagined. "We talked and talked," Hughie remembers of that night. Nearly twenty years later, only days before Tim's death, they were still talking.

Lori Horton recalls that Hughie made his biggest impression on Tim not at the Halloween party, but on a subsequent encounter that winter. "Tim walked round the back of Bloorview and there was Hughie, who has cerebral palsy, trying to skate. He would stand up and fall down, stand up and fall down, for a good half-hour. He was determined to learn to skate. Then Tim found out that Hughie had built the rink. Tim just admired his guts. He had to be the gutsiest little guy he had ever met in his life."

Hughie was an illegitimate child, born to a Toronto woman, fathered by a married American. He was made a ward of the Children's Aid Society, and when he was about eleven, living in a Toronto foster home, he was informed that his father had died. The news meant nothing to him; he had only met the man once, and he might as well have been told that a neighbour down the street had passed on. When his cerebral palsy necessitated surgery, Hughie was moved to Bloorview, and within a year or two he met Tim.

At fifty-one, Hughie Phillips needs crutches to get around, although he drives and has been receiving physiotherapy and acupuncture to regain lost mobility. He runs his own landscaping business out of his house, a modest attached brick structure in Toronto's Danforth—Woodbine neighbourhood. As a kid, he was quite agile, playing football, baseball, hockey, golf, soccer—virtually anything that came along. His mobility then was limited not by his illness but by his circumstances. Bloorview wards were

not allowed out of the building unsupervised.
Without a chaperon, Hughie was a prisoner of the
facility whose name he loathed. (It would later be
renamed simply Bloorview Children's Hospital.)

Tim changed that for him, becoming for all
intents and purposes his surrogate father. It's
tempting to view Tim's initial attraction to Hughie
in light of his own circumstances. His hockey career
hanging in the balance as he fought back from his
terrible injuries from the Gadsby collision, in
Hughie he may have found someone with whom he
could identify. Indeed, war veterans like Smythe
were attracted initially to the plight of disabled children through their own experiences with injury
and their efforts to improve rehabilitation facilities
through organizations such as the War Amps.
Although there is no comparing a sports injury, no
matter how career threatening, to Hughie's circumstances, Hughie could provide Tim with a remarkably analogous relationship. Tim could help
Hughie through influence and attention, but in
turn Hughie could affect Tim positively too. By
nature a charitable man, Tim could also learn from
Hughie a certain humility about his own circumstances and the relative weight of his own burdens.
Hughie was no passive victim. He had spunk and
determination, an effervescent personality and an
extraordinary singlemindedness.

"I remember him saying to me, 'Hughie, if
you've ever got a problem, you just give me a call.'"
By that, Tim meant financial help. "I don't forget
things like that. I once said to a girlfriend of mine,
'You know, I could have taken advantage of him.'
And she said, 'No, Hughie, you wouldn't have.
Because if you would have, Tim would have known

that, and he never would have offered it.' And you know, she was right. Because if I asked him, I would have needed it. But I never did ask him. Sure, sometimes it wasn't easy, doing what I was doing. I couldn't afford this house when I bought it. No way. But I'm determined when I do something. There's no way I should be where I am today. No way. I wouldn't be where I am without Tim." He reconsiders this. "I would be there, but I wouldn't have gotten there as fast."

The first leg-up Tim gave him, Hughie is sure, was a spot in the educational programs of Variety Village when he was sixteen. He can't prove Tim was responsible, but he doesn't see how it could have happened any other way. Variety Village was Conn Smythe's charitable territory, and Hughie didn't have the education required of its enrolees. "In those days," he says, "I couldn't make change for a dollar. Pretty sad. But that's the way it was at Bloorview then."

The biggest leg-up Tim gave him was, in Hughie's words, "being there." When he was still living at Bloorview (he left at sixteen to enter a group home on Riverdale Avenue when he began the Variety Village programs), Tim would shuttle back and forth between the Gardens and the hospital, taking him to games and practices. After practices, Tim brought him along to George's Spaghetti House and the players' lunches and bull sessions. Tim was regularly on a diet under Punch Imlach's orders and Lori's supervision, and Hughie would watch him dutifully adhere to it. "Lori would say, 'Now Tim, you're going to have this today.' And Tim would have that today."

Hughie's greatest thrill in his Bloorview days

came from the Union Station send-offs. The players would head for the station right after a home game to board the train for a road trip. The families would gather to wish them well, and Hughie, who had been brought to the game by Tim and was to be driven home by Lori, would be part of the intimate crowd. "They were all kissing their wives goodbye, and you really felt so good. As if you were almost part of the team."

He was a regular guest at the Horton home in Willowdale on Wedgewood Drive and in the custom-built home on Bannatyne Drive that followed it. He hung around in the generous yard on Wedgewood while Tim made one of his rare acquaintances with his golf clubs. "'Keep your head down!' he'd shout. He didn't have a clue what he was doing."

When Tim tended to business at his ill-fated service station and car lot in Willowdale, he often took Hughie along. Hughie was not impressed with Tim's partner, Fred Care. Hughie adored Tim, and would not tolerate any opinions that ran contrary to his view of his benefactor. "I remember he said, 'Tim Horton Motors. That name has done nothing for us.' I'm only a kid, and that really hurt me. I felt like punching him. Tim used to work like hell."

Sometimes Tim's charity was all too transparent. While living on Riverdale, Hughie decided to take in a Leafs game. The Rangers were in town; it was near the end of the season. Hughie and a friend named Barry from his Bloorview days went down to the Gardens to get tickets, and came away with the best they could manage, standing room. Tim would customarily swing by Hughie's place and pick him up on the way to the game. When they told Tim they had standing-room tickets and would be going to the game, "I know Tim and Lori must have talked and decided 'We can't let those guys stand.' When Tim picked us up, he said, 'Lori isn't feeling too good tonight. She's staying home. You guys go in there and get rid of your standing room, and here are these tickets.' They were middle blues, which are now the golds."

On another night, Hughie and Barry paid the Hortons a visit. Barry, says Hughie, was an amazing musician who could play virtually any instrument by ear. On this occasion he had an organ in the back of his truck. "Beautiful," says Hughie. "It does everything but talk. I'm trying to talk Tim into bringing in the organ. 'Bring in the organ, bring in the organ, bring in the organ…' I must have bugged him for an hour, and he wasn't going to bring it in. Finally Lori said, 'Tim, why don't you give us all some peace and bring the thing in.' She knew I wasn't going to shut up till he did.

"Tim says, 'Okay, but where are we going to put the pipes?' "

The pipes? Tim had this idea that there was some great church organ out in his driveway.

"Oh, Tim!" Lori shouted at him.

"Well, I don't know anything about these things," he complained, and went outside to bring it in.

"Barry helped him," says Hughie, "but you know who did most of the lugging. Barry played, Tim and Lori enjoyed it, and then we put it back on the truck and went home."

Where are we going to put the pipes? "Tim was *smart*," says Hughie, delighted, "but he was *dumb*."

Chapter 14

Turnaround

Only three Maple Leaf games of the 1960s have emerged from the vaults of the CBC to be copied from film to videotape. One is the third game of the 1962 Stanley Cup final between Chicago and Toronto; the game is in Chicago and the Blackhawks win, 3-0. Another is the decisive game six (or, at least, eight minutes of the second period and fourteen minutes of the third) of the 1967 final between Montreal and Toronto, which Toronto wins 3-1 on an empty-net goal by George Armstrong. The final relic is the fifth and deciding game of the 1963 semifinal between Montreal and Toronto, which the Leafs win five-nil.

This relic might be the most precious of all, because of an oddity of broadcasting policy. At the time, NHL team owners could not shake their suspicion that television cameras would compel fans to stay home and watch the game in the comfort of their living room, and so "Hockey Night in Canada" broadcasts were not permitted to begin until the second period, the logic being that anyone who wanted to see the game in its entirety would have to buy a ticket. The deciding game of the 1963 semifinal survives in its entirety because the cameras were rolling and recording throughout the first period, waiting for the broadcast crew to get the signal that they were on the air and to begin the play-by-play.

And so for almost the entire first period of this game, the surviving footage delivers the game as it never was on television, without comment or intervention. The cameras watch, the play unfolds and the only sounds are the sounds of the game itself: the shouts of players, the slap and smack of stick and puck, the crescendo and decrescendo of the rapt crowd.

The game had not yet been exploited: neither by thuggery, which would find its tactics in the subjective nature of the rules, nor by television, which still only broadcast the play, rather than dictating its rhythm and framework. The game had yet to acquire its frantic showbiz patter of presentation, or its garish commercialism. Its back was still turned to the lens. Even when the play-by-play begins in the 1963 footage, the intrusion is minimal. There is no advertising painted garishly on the ice surface or the boards. There is no break in play to accommodate commercials. Advertisements for Esso Outboard Oil and Molson Export Ale are briefly superimposed in white-line animation over the picture during routine stoppages. There is no frantic rock music being pumped into the building at the slightest delay; if the Gardens organ is playing, it cannot be heard. The game is astonishingly pristine. It can still be imagined taking place out-of-doors.

It is a different *feeling* game, and the way the game feels today causes some of the players from the Original Six era to doubt the skills they had. A friend of George Armstrong's says when he watches a game with the Chief today, the former Leaf captain dismisses his own playing days, noting how much bigger, faster and harder shooting today's players are. The players in the CBC footage certainly do not skate as fast as players today, but they do move with a remarkable fluidity. The game curls and unfolds and swirls, moved along by a minimum of interference. A visiting player grabs at a home player's arm as they sweep along the boards in pursuit of the puck and the crowd roars its outrage. The clutch-and-grab and stickwork of today's game would have compelled these fans to storm the ice and lynch the referee. No fierce jousting duels decorate the slot in front of the goaltender. Hits are solid, sometimes jarring, but no one is running anyone else into the boards after every pass. The players with few exceptions wear no helmets; many goaltenders still wear no mask; none of the players have their names stitched across their shoulder blades.

The power plays lack a system—Punch Imlach, for one, never bothered drilling his Maple Leafs in the finer points of playing with a man advantage or disadvantage. The game proceeds more by force of personality than by rigid tactics. The style of the great players makes them unmistakably individual. Red Kelly picks up the puck behind his own net and methodically leads the rush all the way down into the Blackhawks' defensive zone in the 1962 game, and at once you know he is a forward who for a decade was a great rushing defenceman. The wrist shot has not yet approached the brink of extinction, so that when the puck comes back to the point and Tim Horton steps into it with a blistering slapshot that rings off the goalpost, you are at once aware of something unusual, something that is a trademark of the player.

Tim takes many faceoffs in his own end—this was the style of the game before the 64/65 season, when bodily contact at faceoffs was outlawed. Until then it was customary to send a force of nature like Tim to take the faceoff, and when the puck was dropped he simply charged into the opposing player, driving him away from the dropped puck and allowing a fellow Leaf to collect it.

In game footage he has moved far beyond the stay-at-home role in which defencemen were indoctrinated when Tim was first playing professionally. In the first period of the Chicago game, Red Kelly breaks out of the neutral zone and Tim jumps into the rush with him. Kelly's effort sweeps him right past Chicago goaltender Glenn Hall, but Tim is only a few strides behind and takes up position on Hall's doorstep to await a centring pass. In the first period of the 1963 semifinal game against Montreal, Tim is seen gathering speed behind his own blueline, carrying the puck right into the Canadiens' end in a rush that fizzles when two Canadiens flatten Tim a few strides across their blueline. You see Tim do this, and more like it, and you see Jim Dewey on the ice of Stanley Stadium in 1946, watching Tim play and wondering if he should be up on right wing.

He is at the height of his game in these films from the 1960s. He plays with finesse and daring, an offensive spark who has not forgotten his defensive duties.

Tim would acknowledge Punch Imlach's responsibility for letting him carry the puck the way he had never been allowed to under Hap Day. But Tim also believed that Imlach's success as a coach was due to the fact that he was also the general manager. He had authority over trades and demotions that others hadn't. Tim would reflect that had Joe Primeau,

Howie Meeker and Billy Reay been given the authority that Imlach had secured, they would have been just as successful.

Letting Tim play the way he knew how to play was partly a matter of Imlach resigning himself to what he viewed as Tim's obstinacy. In the first crack at his autobiography, *Hockey Is a Battle,* Punch Imlach is grudging in his praise of Horton. "He never said much…or listened much, for that matter. He's a stubborn so-and-so. The story with him is that he just keeps getting better all the time, so naturally he has faith in the way he does things. But this can be aggravating for a coach sometimes. He's going to play it the way he wants to play it. There is not much you can do about it. I've seen me say to him, lookit, you did this or that wrong. And he'd say, what the hell, I've been playing this way for 15 years, what's the use of changing? That would get me mad. Sometimes I'd say to him, 'I don't care the way you played 15 years ago, this is the way I want you to play now. After all, I'd say, if everybody else played it his own individual way, we're gonna lose.' But with Tim sometimes I'd just save my breath. I'd just look at him and walk away. But in his own way sometimes he'd listen to what I said and if *he* decided it made sense—if *he* decided—then maybe he'd do it my way."

After coaching them for more than a decade, Imlach seemed to have more respect for Allan Stanley and George Armstrong than Tim. "They had it all in their heads," he said in praise of Stanley and Armstrong. "On the ice, they knew where to go and also where not to go. In all the time they'd spent playing pro hockey you knew they knew—but in later years, of course, they weren't staying as strong physically as Horton was, I mean in skating and everything else. It was a case with them that they always knew where to go, but maybe in the last couple years they were having trouble getting there... Some people never learn, but the good ones do."

Johnny Bower is surprised at the way Imlach described Tim in *Hockey Is a Battle*—but then, many people have been surprised by what Imlach has said about one person or another in his memoirs. His opinions, which tended to be off-the-cuff and quickly modified, take on a finality in print they probably don't warrant. "Maybe before I came he was a little stubborn," Bower says of Tim, "but to me he was a good, solid competitor." And since Bower arrived when Imlach did, one does have to wonder why Imlach's praise of Tim was so measured, at least on paper.

There's no question that Tim was, if not stubborn, then at least a man with his own mind. He respected Punch but never kowtowed to him. Tim and Imlach, says Allan Stanley, "got along fine. We listened to whatever Punch had to say, took the best out of it and left the rest alone. Tim was very independent that way, because he came up the hard way. He spent time on the bench and worked his way up, and in those days you practically did it on your own. Nobody taught you much. Punch's strong suit was he put the talent together to make it work. We didn't have any secret plays. We'd been doing this stuff forever. Nobody would bother Tim. He went about his business in as straight and as forward a manner as anybody could. Being so honest, and given the honest effort, it was pretty difficult to single out anything to give him hell for. Some guys were scared for their jobs, wanted to be the coach, were scared of the owner, scared of the manager. Tim wasn't scared of anybody. He didn't try to hide anything from anybody. Some days Punch put on curfews or said do this, do that. Hell, if it was unreasonable, we'd go out and do it anyway. ["Yeah," says Bower, "and if we got caught we got fired."] Nobody was going to intimidate us that much. Everything was the game. The manager has a job, the coach has a job, you've got to let them do their jobs, you can't fight everything they're saying. But you do your own business."

"Tim and Punch had a great relationship," says Dave Keon, noting that Tim used to take the liberty of addressing Imlach by his Christian name, George. "When Punch first came, he didn't have to be a rocket scientist to realize that in Tim you had a very special person and a very special hockey player. Tim was, as far as I was concerned, the backbone of the hockey team. He was always there, he wasn't hurt very often, and even when he was hurt he never said a word. He just played right through it. He was a great player, teammate and friend. We had great times together during the season. Off-season, we didn't see each other a whole lot, only periodically, because he was working. But he was a man's man. He was fun to be around, he was a leader, he was just a great person."

"He was a prince of a guy," says Johnny Bower. "As a person you couldn't beat him. He was quiet in his own way, and he liked to go out, too, and have some fun with the guys. He mixed up real well."

"Tim," says Stanley, "was kind of a fearless guy. He had no fear within him. I don't think he was envious of anybody, for anything. Talk about fearless—I wasn't there at this time, but after a game on the road they were in some bar, and the Dallas Cowboys were in the same bar. These big mothers all had their cowboy hats on. Tim decided: I like those hats. He walked up to the biggest guy. He had to jump up, but he grabbed the hat. Everybody went, 'Uh oh,' but nothing happened. He did it in such a manner that it wasn't offensive. He was never offensive to anybody, no matter what he did. Not in a jovial manner, but in a mischievous, no-malice, let's-have-some-fun manner."

Dave Keon remembers the night with the Cowboys, how the hatless Cowboy asked for his ten-gallon back and Tim cheerfully replied, "But I'm not finished with it yet," and how the hatless cowboy simply said, "Okay."

"I guess 'fearless' is a good description of him," says Keon. "To a certain degree he thought he was indestructible, because we called him Clark Kent. I always said that if they wanted to move the Gardens he could grab one end and they could get a whole bunch of guys on the other end. He would just say, 'Make sure you guys don't drop your end because I won't drop mine.'

"I think it was '64, when we were in the playoffs in Detroit," Keon continues. "It was the night before the sixth game. We stayed at the Dearborn Inn. The Ford Motor Company was right there. Here we are in the parking lot and Horton's got the hood up on this guy's car. The guy comes out and says, 'What's going on?' 'Oh,' he says, 'I recognise this as the new Mustang, and I just wanted to look at it.'" As with the Cowboys, the confrontation went no further.

"He was always one of the easiest guys to get along with," says Dick Duff. "There would be very few reasons why you would dislike the guy. *Nothing* would come to mind. This guy had a lot of character. He was taking life head on, he had a lot of concerns about other people, about his teammates, about his family, the young kid [Hughie Phillips] he helped out and has his own business. I always felt Timmy had it from his family. His parents always seemed to be very nice people, and whatever his experience was at St. Mike's helped.

"He was always a guy who was wondering about what this world was all about and what his place was in it, and how he could best go put his talents to good use. And dealing with other people, it always shone through. Everybody has setbacks, but he always seemed to deal with them really good. Maybe he was well liked because he always indicated a greater concern for other people than for himself. I think that was the attractiveness of him. His home was open for anybody, for Christmas parties, for the team, but I think in some ways Tim liked that, too, for people to be around him. He was good to his daughters, they were high on his list, he was good to his parents... He was a great teammate. He was good to be around. It doesn't mystify me. These people come from small communities, from solid backgrounds."

"Tim made friends of the opposition," says Larry Hillman, who joined the Leafs in 1960. "There was a friendly respect. He wasn't a huge man, but a strong structural man, with big arms and shoulders on him. He was a clean, hard-playing individual, and I think that's what they respected. You might have someone like a John Ferguson, who's rough and careless, and is going to get you one way or another. Tim would get you, but in the legal part of the game, with a crushing body check or with his strength in the corners. Your head wasn't going to be taken off at the same time."

Jerry Toppazzini, who came out of the Nickel Belt one season behind his brother Zellio and Tim, saw plenty of him during his twelve NHL seasons on right wing, most of them with Boston. "Timmy was a very quiet person," says Jerry. "He wasn't a real extrovert. And in those days we didn't fraternise.[1] He was what you would call a soft-spoken animal out there. He wouldn't hurt you, wouldn't punch you, but if you stepped out of line he'd certainly let you know. He'd pick you up and crash you down on the ice. He was very strong. He was a tremendous offensive defenceman. He could skate, he could carry the puck out of his own end. He was a leader for the team. An All Star defenceman, no doubt about it. And he was the kind of guy you wanted on your hockey club."

"There were defencemen you had to fear more because they were vicious and would slam you into the boards from behind," said Bobby Hull after Tim's death. "But you respected Horton because he didn't need that type of intimidation. He used his tremendous strength and talent to keep you in check... Few players had more dedication or brought more honour to the game. He was my idea of a super pro."

"I've always thought that Toronto played a very close-checking game," says Jean Beliveau, "and I've always had a lot of respect for Tim. He was so strong. I remember meeting that great oak tree—solid. He was hitting hard, but nothing dirty. When you crossed the blueline and he was on the ice, you looked around. You knew that you were going to

get hit, or he was so strong you couldn't move him.
I know, because I used to be in front of the net, and
I don't think I was weak. He played the game
according to the rules, and I always respected that.
And on a regular basis he would take one of those
rushes. He had that good shot, too. Basically, I
think he was a defensive defenceman with this ability, when the opening arose, to step into it."

Most of the "Tim tales" have a similar theme, and
they take place either on a road trip or at training
camp. Tim goes out with some buddies on the
team, and hoists a few. When he returns to the
hotel, he wants to keep the night alive but finds the
door of a team member locked. Tim backs up and
puts his shoulder to the door, smashing it out of the
frame. Teammates learn not to lock their doors
until Tim is known to be safe and sound under his
own covers, so as to avoid being stuck with a $200 to
$300 bill from the hotel for the repairs to their
room.

    On the road, Horton and Stanley were room-
mates and partners in crime. Larry Hillman had
played with Stanley in Boston, and as a Leaf accompanied Tim on his visits to church; he was also
around when Tim got up to some of his more rambunctious hi-jinks. "Stanley was a statesman," he
says, "not as much of a prankster. It was probably
why Tim was roomed with Stanley. Tim made up for
Stanley. That was Tim's release from playing the
game."

    Horton and Stanley closed the bars together, and
back at the hotel raised a ruckus as they roused
teammates out of bed. They were particularly merci-
less with their two young stars, Frank Mahovlich and

Dave Keon, who were roommates. Mahovlich can remember a night when Tim came through the door and Mahovlich grabbed the television to defend himself. There was something very basic about Tim's predilection for walking through solid objects. He suffered from claustrophobia. If he wasn't trying to crash his way into something, he was trying to crash his way out of it, as happened when he was packed into an overcrowded team bus.

It was the self-appointed duty of Horton and Stanley to keep heads from becoming too swelled as the team found success and found itself with a new generation of stars. "I think we treated each other like family," says Stanley, "and what families do, you straighten guys out. Very seldom did they take offence."

"Tim and Allan would talk a lot together and they knew what bothered me," says Mahovlich. "They'd stick a needle in every once in a while to keep you relaxed and made sure that nothing went to your head. They'd keep you on level ground."

Dave Keon remembers Stanley being the more vocal of the pairing when it came to putting the young ones in their place. "Tim was more the steadying influence. He really didn't fluctuate a whole lot with the ups and downs, because his career had some ups and downs before he attained the success he had. He had that bad leg injury, and other injuries. He fought through all those things and then attained the success that was well deserved, but it never seemed to influence him in any way, shape or form."

While playing for the Rochester Americans, Larry Keenan would attend the joint training camp with the Leafs in Peterborough. He remembers Tim

Horton and Frank Mahovlich standing out for making sure rookies were involved in social outings,
when they were normally ostracised by older players
who feared they would take their spot on the team,
or that of a friend. He also remembers Tim being
quiet and unassuming for most of the camp. But as
the days passed, the veterans would begin shooting
each other knowing looks and saying, "Isn't it about
time Tim blew?" And he would, going on a rampage
in the hotel. The next morning, he could be seen
writing a cheque to cover the damages.

Billy Harris recalls a road trip when Horton and
Stanley arrived in Bob Baun's room one night to
find Baun eating a room-service dinner and watching television. Tim flipped the mattress and
dumped Baun, dinner and all, on the floor, and in
the process badly cut the top of his foot. They were
in Chicago at the time, and they located a sympathetic doctor who sewed up Baun so the team
wouldn't know.

With his heavy, horn-rimmed glasses, Tim's nickname on the team was Clark Kent, and it only took
a few beers to turn Clark Kent into Superman. The
combination of his usual social tomfoolery and a
dissolution of his inhibitions could prove daunting.
Anyone who played with or against Tim knew how
strong he was, but it was something else to see that
strength loose in the world, with Tim happily three
sheets to the wind. If you were Dick Duff, and Tim
and Allan Stanley decided that they were going to
hang you by your heels out the window of George's
Spaghetti House, two storeys above the intersection
of Dundas and Sherbourne, then that is what happened to you, and there was no one crazy enough
to try to save you. (When reminded of this incident,

that's precisely what Stanley says he was doing—saving Duff, or at least making sure somebody had a hold of the other leg.)[2]

Tim once decided that it was time to have fun and showed up in Bob and Sally Baun's bedroom to get the party started. He grabbed Sally by the feet and dragged her out of bed.

"Aren't you going to stop him?" Sally asked her husband as she headed for the floor.

"Are you kidding?" Bob replied, safe under the covers. "I'd get killed."

Tim sometimes, but not often, came out on the losing end. A beer party in the Baun family kitchen evolved to the logical consequence of Tim and Eddie Shack demonstrating the finer points of Greco-Roman wrestling to Bob Baun's sons. When it was over, Tim was being driven to the hospital to have ten stitches laced in his head.

Mahovlich and Stanley both remember well the "initiations" team members inflicted on one another. They often took place on a train trip, and they involved shaving all or selected parts of a player's body hair. When Dick Duff was initiated, teammates shaved a bare patch on his chest in the shape of a cross, since Duff was known to be contemplating the priesthood. Mahovlich was with Tim when they got the bright idea of initiating Foster Hewitt, who was in a sleeper, accompanying the team on its road trip. The team trooped off through the cars in the direction of Foster, with Tim leading the way and Frank right behind him. As they neared Hewitt's sleeper, Frank took a look back over his shoulder and noticed that the rest of the team had vanished. Hewitt was not only the Voice of Hockey—he was a significant shareholder in Maple Leaf Gardens. Tim waved off Frank's concern and headed on for the sleeper.

When Tim pulled back the curtain, Hewitt was white as a sheet, whimpering, "I knew you were coming, I knew you were coming..." Tim picked him up like a baby under his shoulders and knees, waved the board-stiff Hewitt back and forth a bit in the aisle, then gently returned Hewitt to his bunk as common sense closed in.

When the team decided it was Horton's turn to be initiated, a titanic struggle ensued to subdue him. "We used to say, 'We like a man who FIGHTS,'" says Stanley. Tim did, until he was pinned to the train car floor by a flying squad of players and Duff grabbed him by the scrotum. "If you don't hold still," Duff declared, "I'll rip this right out." Tim held still, and the razors went to work.

At the heart of Tim was a visceral enthusiasm for life. His values, his beliefs, his self-restraint, kept it in check, in much the way that the rules of the game keep hockey from descending into chaos. Occasionally, Tim allowed those restraints to fall away. It could come in a game, when he abandoned his own end of the rink for a thrilling end-to-end rush. It could come after a few drinks, when the hotel doors came crashing down. And it could come on the open road, when he depressed the gas pedal and turned the world into a tunnel-vision blur. It was when he became his alter ego, when Clark Kent turned into Superman. Far from being seen as a failure of character or self-control, these were moments when the hot spark of his essence found release: ferocious, daunting, even reckless. Meanness did not erupt: no Hyde crawled out of

Jekyll. Tim became the force of nature he spent his life striving to control and direct, and he seemed to understand that he could not keep himself pent up indefinitely. He would willingly release the valve, and those who knew him also knew enough to stand back a few extra paces. Repairs were made, spills mopped, heads shaken and forgiveness—for the most part—extended. Many found him terrifying as Superman, but few found him disturbing. Clark Kent always reappeared in time to make amends, and there was little doubt that it was Superman who was the occasionally seen alter ego, and not the other way around. Tim was determined to be Clark Kent, but he could not always resist the thrill of being faster than a speeding bullet.

The city hadn't seen anything like it since the end of the Second World War. When the Leafs won the 1962 Stanley Cup, ending the team's eleven-year championship drought, Toronto fêted the team with a ticker-tape parade that would have pleased an astronaut returning from a mission to Mars. After the 58/59 miracle season, the fans were primed for a cup victory, but the team couldn't quite convert their transformation under Imlach into a league championship. In 59/60 the Leafs won thirty-five games, finished second overall to Montreal, eliminated fourth-place Detroit in six games, then were swept in four by Montreal in the finals. In 60/61 the Leafs had their greatest season of the Imlach era, finishing second to Montreal with thirty-nine wins. But fourth-place Detroit, with only twenty-five wins, had eliminated the Leafs in five games in the semifinals, then met and lost to the third-place Blackhawks.

In 61/62 a fully satisfying season at last came their way. The Leafs won thirty-seven games, eliminated the Rangers in six games, and then met the defending-champion Blackhawks. When the Leafs won game six in Chicago and brought the cup back to Conn Smythe's Gardens, no fan was more caught up in the delirium of the victory than Hughie Phillips. His friend and idol Tim Horton had been instrumental in bringing the cup to Toronto, and the city—and large swaths of the country—adored him.

Hughie couldn't help himself. He headed down to Maple Leaf Gardens to soak up the atmosphere as the parade's beginning was being marshalled inside.

"I went around to the back where the players went in," says Hughie, "and Lori and all the wives and kids were there. Lori said, 'I can't let you in,' and I said, 'Yeah, I know that. I understand that.' I was just hanging around, having a good time." Suddenly his day took on an entirely new direction. Billy Harris came out of the Gardens, and brought Hughie in. He was soon riding in a convertible with Tim Horton and two of his daughters (there was no room for Lori), saturated with a public's affection.

"I've got to tell you, it was the biggest thrill of my life. Here I am in a convertible... What's this? I'm not ready for this!"

On the way up Bay Street to city hall (the old city hall, now a courthouse), the car stopped at an intersection. A lady on the street corner caught Hughie's eye and sweetly asked, "And who are you?"

It was a good question. Hughie was nineteen, plausibly old enough to be a player, but hardly of the dimensions of Tim. Then again, he didn't quite look like one of the Horton children, the oldest of whom, Jeri-Lynn, was ten.

"What am I going to say? Who's Hughie Phillips, anyway? Big deal. And I didn't know what to say, so I just looked at her and smiled."

The woman turned away in disgust. "Look at that," she declared. "They won't even speak to you."

"That hurt me and bothered me," says Hughie. "That was a lot of years ago, and I still remember that."

It was a lone note of pain in a day of unimagined excitement. "*What* a thrill. People throwing confetti at you. Oh my God. At city hall, all the kids and all the wives. Al Arbour's wife, she had a handful of kids, so she asked me to watch her purse. I'm all caught up in all the stuff that's going on, I'm not paying any attention. The players, the families, all went inside. And here's me, stuck outside of city hall. And there were so many people you couldn't see the sidewalk. Here I've got her purse. I panicked. I didn't know what to do. Finally a policeman took me inside. Thank God he did. He had to haul me up the stairs because I couldn't see the stairs.

"After the reception with the mayor we went back to the Gardens. They had two Stanley Cups, done in ice. Then Tim drove me back home. I was living on Riverdale Avenue in those days, because I had left Bloorview and was going to Variety Village." Hughie Phillips had had his moment in the limelight, and it had lasted far longer than the prescribed fifteen minutes. He has never lived a more memorable day.

One of Punch Imlach's more notorious declarations came in preseason 1964 when he boasted that with George Armstrong, Red Kelly, Dave Keon, Tim

Horton, Allan Stanley, Johnny Bower and a dozen nobodies he could win the Stanley Cup.

George Armstrong had undergone a wondrous transformation in the opinions of Imlach. Punch's initial instinct had been to get rid of him. A memo from Imlach to Stafford Smythe on January 5, 1959—halfway through Imlach's first season with the Leafs—laid out a wish-list of trades for which he needed Stafford's approval, as chair of the hockey committee, to pursue. Imlach was in the hunt for a high-scoring forward—in short, he was hunting for another Tod Sloan, who produced sixty-two points in only fifty-nine games for the Blackhawks. He had his eye on Alex Delvecchio of Detroit, Ed Litzenberger of Chicago, Camille Henry of the Rangers and Jerry Toppazzini of the Bruins. All of them, save Toppazzini, whose point production was consistently in the forties, were registering better than fifty points a season. Armstrong, who had produced forty-eight, forty-four and forty-two points in his past three seasons, was on his way to only thirty-six points in 58/59.

Imlach advised he was "still interested in Litzenberger for Armstrong or Stewart." Ed Litzenberger, captain of the Blackhawks, was having a sensational year, producing seventy-seven points. Ron Stewart was a right-winger who was in his seventh of thirteen seasons as a Leaf, and could be counted on to contribute point totals in the mid-thirties. "Understand Toppazzini available from Boston—would give up Armstrong for Toppazzini. Would try somebody less but can't see how could possibly be worked...."

Stafford Smythe's notations indicate that the hockey committee was not at all opposed to trading away their captain if the deal could be swung. But no deal ever was, at least not with Armstrong a part of it. (Litzenberger was finally acquired by Imlach, in 61/62, though his high-scoring days were behind him and he only played another season and a half.)

Armstrong came through for Imlach as the Leafs tore after the final playoff spot in the spring of '59. He went on a scoring binge, getting three goals in one game against New York, the team they edged out for the final playoff spot by one point. This Cinderella team, led by Armstrong, made it all the way to the Stanley Cup final before bowing to Montreal in five games.

Ten years later, after winning four Stanley Cups, Tim would insist that the "miracle finish" of the 58/59 season, Imlach's first behind the Leaf bench, remained his most memorable experience. With five games left, they were seven points behind the Rangers, who were in fourth. "It didn't look very promising," Tim recalled, "but we kept fighting for that last playoff spot. Then it came down to the last night of the regular schedule. We played in Detroit against the Red Wings, and the Rangers were host to the Montreal Canadiens. We were trailing the Red Wings 2-0 at one stage of the game, when we found out the Canadiens had beaten the Rangers and that it was now up to us to make it. It was the lift we needed. We came back, won the game 6-4 and finished in fourth place. It was a tremendous feeling."

The following season, George Armstrong broke the fifty-point barrier, and would do it twice again in the next six seasons. In all he played twelve more seasons in Conn Smythe's Gardens after Imlach couldn't deal him away: it was the only NHL rink that ever represented home ice to him. The Leafs'

four Stanley Cup victories in the 1960s would have
been impossible without him.

Time and again during the heyday of Tim's Leaf
career, players and pundits would shake their heads
at how he so often seemed to get overlooked when
it was time to hand out awards. He never won the
Norris Trophy for best defenceman, though he was
a runner-up twice, in 1964 (to Pierre Pilote) and
1969 (to Bobby Orr). His cheerleaders were scan-
dalised by the fact that in 1961/62 he neither won
the Norris nor made it onto the All Star team.

That season, the Leafs had finally won the
Stanley Cup in their tense, six-game series with
Chicago. They won it in a raucous Chicago Stadium
on a late goal that broke a 1-1 deadlock.

Punch Imlach would recall how Bob Nevin had
tied the game. "And then a few minutes later Tim
Horton started out from our own end with the
puck, the way only Timmy can burst out when he's
going his best. On the way up the ice he handled
the puck three different times, passing and getting
it back, before he made his final pass to Duff, who
put it in."

"We were on a power play," Tim would remember. "I carried the puck up ice, gave it to George
Armstrong and 'Army' went in deep and passed the
puck back to me. As I was being checked, I sent a
pass to Dickie Duff. Dickie did a great job of turning around and sending the puck into the net for
the winning goal." After logging thirteen seasons of
professional hockey, Tim Horton finally had his
name inscribed on the trophy that had last been
won for Toronto by Bill Barilko, two seasons before
Tim had joined the Leafs' starting lineup. That very

summer, Barilko's remains were recovered from the northern Ontario bush, still in the passenger seat of the crashed aircraft.

Tim's assist on Duff's series-winning goal gave him sixteen points for the playoffs. He outscored every other Maple Leaf and set a new league playoff points record for defencemen in the process. (Stan Mikita produced the most points, twenty-one, of those playoffs.) It capped a superlative season in which he'd produced thirty-eight points with ten goals and twenty-eight assists. And yet, the first-team defencemen that year were Doug Harvey and Jean-Guy Talbot; the second-team spots were claimed by Pierre Pilote and Tim's teammate Carl Brewer. Admittedly, All Star voting took place at mid-season, which meant playoff performances couldn't be factored in, but Tim's first half to the season had been strong enough to warrant more ballots.

At training camp in Peterborough the following season, former Red Wing major domo Jack Adams was hanging around. When Tim went by him in a restaurant, Adams declared, "There goes the best defenceman in the National Hockey League—last season. I wonder if the Leafs would have won it all if Horton hadn't had such a great year? Horton should have won the Norris Trophy in a breeze."

Tim shrugged off the lack of silverware with a grin. "I don't know if I got any votes at all," he said at camp. "All I know is that Doug Harvey took it." Asked if being overlooked for the honour bothered him, he said, "I don't think so. But I might have missed the money." The Norris carried a $1,000 bonus. So did a first-team appearance. A second-team appearance would have brought him $500. For now, fame would have to do.

Tim would never have another playoff series like it. When the Leafs won the cup in '63, he scored four points in ten playoff games; in '64, his scoreboard contribution was four points in fourteen games. He was never overly concerned about scoring, in the regular season or the playoffs; it was not the standard by which he judged his own game. In addition to providing near-impermeable defensive services to the Leafs, he had a growing reputation as an iron man. Tim was on the ice for every game during the Leaf franchise's finest seasons of the 1960s, which included all four Stanley Cup victories. Between February 11, 1961, and February 4, 1968, he played in 486 consecutive games.

But voting for All Star berths tended to favour above all point-scoring defencemen, and the voters must have begun the 62/63 season slightly cowed for having overlooked Tim in 61/62 when he was such a critical part of the Leaf offence. In scoring he had a modest year in 62/63, picking up twenty-five points in the regular season. The voters were sufficiently impressed to make him a second-team All Star. Carl Brewer, who also gathered twenty-five points on the season (and 168 penalty minutes), made the first team.

Tim opened the 63/64 season on a tear. By November 16 he already had twelve points on five goals and seven assists. On November 14 he won the game for Toronto in New York by firing a shot from centre ice that skipped past Jacques Plante. "This guy has probably the toughest slapshot in the league," said Plante after the game. "We brace ourselves against it, it still gets through. This thing bounced on me three or four times and had me fooled completely."

"When they go in," said Tim, "they go in."

Twenty games into the season, Tim played in his thousandth NHL game. By mid-December he had eighteen points, only one less than team-leaders Mahovlich and Keon. His points production was less frenetic in the final half of the season, as he wound up with twenty-nine. But when All Star votes were tabulated at the mid-season, enough votes had been cast his way to at last make him a first-team All Star. He missed the Norris Trophy by eight votes, as Pierre Pilote was named the top All Star defenceman with eighty-eight votes.[3] Frank Mahovlich made the second team, the first-team slot for left wing having been awarded to Bobby Hull. It had taken twelve seasons with the Leafs, but in 63/64 anyone still bothering to wonder "Is this Tim Horton's Year?" could answer with an unequivocal *oh yes.*

Chapter 15

Wexford

The transformation of Scarborough after the Second World War from a rural sprawl of farms and small market villages into the country's first bona fide exercise in urban sprawl was ferocious and abrupt. Before the war, about twenty-five thousand people had made the township immediately east of Toronto their home. Five years after the war, the population had nearly doubled, and it kept doubling every five years thereafter, so that by 1960 nearly 200,000 people lived there.

The landscape was consumed so quickly that individual market-village names were blast-frozen into the virtually seamless suburban quilt that had all but smothered them. One such village east of the Little Don River was Wexford, whose centre of commerce, such as it was, had been the intersection of Lawrence Avenue and Pharmacy Road. In the mid-nineteenth century there had been an inn and a post office and a general store and a blacksmith shop and a temperance hall, as well as several churches. With the exception of places of worship Wexford survived the urbanisation only as a name on some maps, though during the 1950s the name did endure in telephone exchanges. As occurred all over Scarborough, where there had once been focal points of social and economic activity there was now a gridlock of suburban homes and cars, with the interstices filled by the strip mall, the invention that turned commerce by necessity into a linear sprawl.

Tim Horton came to live in Wexford with his new bride Lori and their expanding family (which would grow to four daughters) in 1953. They bought a bungalow on the west side of Warden Avenue, just south of Ellesmere, one door down from the Canadian Pacific line, which made a diagonal slash through Wexford on its route to Peterborough and Havelock. The site was under development at the end of Tim's rookie season when they bought the house-to-be. "We bought it sight unseen from a plan," Lori remembers, "and the tracks were not on the plan. We went to North Bay, and came back and there's this house on the railroad tracks."

Postwar Scarborough was a community of the young, settling down in new single-family dwellings, commuting to work in the city of Toronto or, more likely, to jobs produced in the township's enormous industrial corridors, one of which lay right across the street from the Hortons. Tim and Lori stayed on Warden until 1959, raising their growing family as Scarborough continued to pour concrete, lay asphalt, bury sewer trunks, build schools and recreation centres, squirrel away a few precious pieces of parkland and above all strive to rise above the reputation it was developing, contrary to its ambitions, as a suburban wasteland, a windswept "Scarberia" with no civic cohesion, a middle-class retreat with no soul. That wasn't entirely fair. There were some nice parts to Scarborough, in particular the stretches around Kingston Road along the lake (where Bob Baun had grown up) and the areas around Highland Creek and the Rouge Valley. But where

Tim and Lori lived, a no-nonsense expanse of housing and industry scrubbed clean of any nuance of
geography, Scarborough was dominated by the automobile, offering easy consumer gratification on
every block as shopping centres sprang up along the
main thoroughfares, competing for the consumer
dollar with the smaller strip malls.

Lori was very much a war bride, a description she
readily accepts. She had married a Canadian who
made his living playing a game she didn't understand, and had moved back with him to a country
that was entirely beyond her experience. Their first
summer together, they lived in North Bay. "North
Bay was *much* different," she says. "I'd never lived in
a small town before." When they did move down to
a basement apartment in the big city that fall when
hockey season started, "Toronto was a little better,
but I didn't know a soul. I had Jeri-Lynn a few weeks
after coming to Toronto. Tim was out of town, of
course. A taxi cab took me to the hospital and I
almost had the baby in the taxi. I met the driver
years later and he said he was still recovering."

Then, for six years, Tim and Lori were out there
in Scarborough, in that very modest house on that
increasingly busy street, their phone number unlist-
ed, Tim's hockey career maddeningly slow to sta-
bilise. He and Lori didn't go out much in those first
few years. (In 1971, Tim would look back on their
first year together in Toronto, in the basement
apartment, and say, "The only entertainment we
could afford was listening to a radio.") They liked
to read, historical novels mainly. Tim was happily
devoted to his kids, and entertaining was home-
based. Ray Timgren lived in the neighbourhood,
and when he was traded to Chicago during the

54/55 season he rented the house to Ron Stewart and his wife. The Stewarts would drop in, and so would Tod Sloan and his wife Jean, fellow defence-man Jim Morrison and Rudy Migay, too. Of course, they would see George Armstrong regularly, although when he got married and settled into a home of his own in the 54/55 season, his visits became less frequent.

"I was kind of scared when we first moved here. I didn't know anyone and had never been away from home before," Lori would reflect. But Harry Watson's wife Lillian "came right over, introduced herself and took me to meet all the other wives." During the regular season, when their husbands took to the road, the spouses would get together on Saturdays, some of them on Sundays. For home games Lori would go to Maple Leaf Gardens with Jean Sloan. They had seats in a section reserved for relatives of players on the visiting team, which made for some competitive cheering. During training camp, Frances Barbe would come up from Pittsburgh to keep her company and lend her a hand with the kids. Frances and Andy Barbe were steadily assembling a family of four boys, while Lori and Tim were on their way to a family of four girls.

Tim never attempted to limit his social life off the ice to those he knew on it. Many of his closest friends had no ties to the game at all. He remained close to Dick Trainor, his old high-school friend, and once settled in Wexford he began to make other friends. Tim's life moved in very different circles, and it was a measure of his affability that he was able to make these circles not just coexist, but overlap as well. From the perspective of his business future, this quality was crucial, and so was the location in which

he brought it off. If Tim had not moved to
Wexford, if he had not stayed there so many years,
if he had been traded away at the beginning of the
56/57 or 57/58 seasons, Tim Horton as a coffee-
and-donut phenomenon would never have happened. It could never have happened anywhere
else, or with any other people.

Russ Gioffrey tried real estate, and when that didn't
pan out, he went into the appliance retail business
with a partner, Larry Bunkowsky. That clicked for
him; Scarborough was growing by leaps and
bounds. Every day there was another streetful of
homes crying out for toasters and televisions—
Scarborough even had factories turning out home
appliances. Beginning with a store at the bottom of
Warden Avenue on Kingston Road,[1] Gioffrey and
Bunkowsky expanded Bestway TV and Appliances
rapidly across the city. By 1956 they had four stores
of their own and a trade-in depot, as well as two
associate outlets. They shortly added another store,
on Lawrence near Pharmacy in the heart of
Wexford, around the corner from Gioffrey's home.

One day in the mid-1950s, Gioffrey remembers
Tim Horton walking into his store—this was the
original one on Kingston Road at the bottom of
Warden. Bob Baun probably made the introduction, since the Bauns and the Gioffreys knew each
other well, and the Baun service centre was only a
block to the west of the original Bestway store. Tim
by now had some fame as a Maple Leaf, though he
was never someone to make a big deal out of this.
The two men discovered they were both from
Sudbury, and a twenty-year friendship was born.

By 1958, Bestway had contracted as rapidly as it

had expanded. The chain was down to the original store on Kingston Road and a second store on Lawrence, which had moved from its initial site on the north side near Pharmacy to the south side near Warden, fairly close to Tim's house. It became a habit for Tim to drop by the store after Leaf practice on Saturday mornings to have a coffee with the appliance dealer he called Rooskie and shoot the breeze. Their wives became good friends. It seemed that whenever one was pregnant, so was the other.

Gioffrey was in awe of Tim—not as a hockey player, but as a person. "I used to try to model myself after him," he remembers. "I never could. I thought you had to be a saint. He never said a bad word against anyone." They made a point of getting together for lunch at Fran's on Eglinton, and the meal always made Gioffrey feel sorry for Tim. Gioffrey's plate would be clean and Tim's food would scarcely have been touched. Tim was a methodical eater, but his speed wasn't enhanced by the fact that, from the moment he sat down and picked up a menu, Tim was mobbed by diners. "It didn't matter who it was, whether it was a young person or an old person," says Gioffrey. "He always had time for them. *Always*." Tim's explanation for his tolerance: "These are the ones that like me."

Friendship eventually drew them into the realm of business, and with Tim, it was inevitable that business would draw him into yet more friendships. His circles of friends widened and overlapped; he became the common ground for very disparate groups of people.

Gioffrey brought Tim together with John Dywan; Dywan and Gioffrey had come together through two sisters, Mary and June; and Mary and Dywan

had come together through the twists of fate
unique to wartime. Mary's husband, an air-force
pilot, was killed during the war. After the hostilities,
his surviving co-pilot, Dywan, made a point of paying her a dutiful visit. They fell in love and married,
and raised five children. Four years after the war,
twenty-one-year-old Gioffrey married her sister,
June, and became Dywan's brother-in-law.

Dywan was one of the few fully licensed real-
estate appraisers around and had a special sense for
the value of small industrial buildings, a particularly
marketable and profitable skill as greater Toronto
expanded exponentially after the war. "John was a
great investor," says Gioffrey. "Anybody that had a
few dollars, he made them pretty well all rich."

It came to pass that Dywan set out to make Tim
some money. By the summer of 1963 Tim was
beginning to have enough money to invest seriously. The Leafs had just won their second straight
Stanley Cup, and Tim had finally been rewarded
with the recognition his supporters said he had
long deserved by making it back onto the All Star
team after an eight-season absence, albeit the nomi-
nation was, again, to the second-team squad. They
decided to put an investment vehicle together,
which Dywan would manage. Gioffrey continued to
act as a matchmaker, bringing in a third investor for
Tim and Dywan. Ed Siekierko was in the business of
developing and managing the very kind of small
industrial properties John Dywan was so adept at
appraising. Siekierko had been a customer of
Gioffrey's father, who was in the industrial heating
supply business. Hockey players were nothing new
to Siekierko. He knew Joe Primeau through his
block company (they were also members of the

same parish), and through Joe he had met Busher
Jackson and Charlie Conacher, the other members
of the Kid Line. In 1963, Horton, Siekierko and
Dywan became partners in Tim Horton Holdings
Ltd., a modest undertaking that never had more
than a few properties in its portfolio.

Tim and Lori had moved in October 1959 to a
larger house with a sprawling yard on Wedgewood
Drive in Willowdale, the new suburban neighbourhood across town and north of the 401; on
December 27 their fourth and final child, Traci, was
born. Tim's foray into the car business with Fred
Care, begun the year before, was nearby on Yonge
just around the corner from Wedgewood. The
office of lawyer Ken Gariepy was also in the neighbourhood, and Gariepy's home was close by.
Gariepy was part of the Siekierko–Dywan–Gioffrey
circle, and crossed over peripherally into Tim's
world as a director of Superior Sand and Gravel in
Thornhill, which was in the same business as Conn
Smythe. Gariepy became a central figure in Tim's
business affairs; the Gariepy residence doubled as
an entertaining and business centre. Whenever
there were papers to be signed with respect to Tim
Horton Holdings, Tim, John Dywan and Ed
Siekierko and their wives would head to Gariepy's
house and make a party of it.

Of course, Tim and Siekierko became close
friends. "We clicked," says Siekierko. "We were good
buddies."

It was drumming that lured Jim Charade from
Montreal as an eighteen-year-old in the early
1950s—the idea that he could make a go of it playing the rhythms of Buddy Rich to the anglophones

of Toronto. His younger brother Paul had come to Toronto before him, but had returned home (though he would return to Toronto again). His older brother Charles had come and stayed, and Jim stayed with him as there proved to be no money in music, at least not enough to live on. The young Québécois tried a series of jobs, the most solid with the stationery company Warwick at King and Spadina, before at last finding his calling with a group of fellow transplanted Québécois, the Vachon family. In 1932, Arcade and Rose-Anna Vachon had begun charming La Belle Province with their Joe Louis snack cake. In the 1950s, their expanding business brought them into the Toronto market.

The Vachons could bake, but they couldn't speak much English. Charade's bilingualism was an appreciated skill, and in 1955 he was hired by the Vachon Cake Co., moving easily between the Vachon people back in Ste-Marie Beauce, south of Quebec City, and the monolingual monolith that was the Toronto operation's customer base. The Vachon plant was located in the heart of the industrial corridor paralleling Warden Avenue, on Crockford Circle just south of Lawrence.

Vachon was a wholesale operation, producing cakes and pastries for stores, caterers and restaurants. Charade thought the product line too sweet for the market: Quebec has always had a sweeter tooth than Ontario, and the company used a lot of sugar as a preservative for products that had to have shelf lives of up to four weeks. Charade began trying to sell the Vachons on the idea of donuts and butter tarts, which could be sold to Dominion supermarkets and corner stores. The Vachons agreed, and by

1958 Charade was on the other side of Crockford, overseeing a new donut plant. Married in 1956, in 1959 Charade and his wife Claudette bought a bungalow just around the corner from the plant, on the west side of Warden not far north of the Lawrence intersection.

When Charade had joined Vachon in 1955, the company had just one delivery truck. Now it had a fleet of twenty. Donuts were made early in the morning and delivered to customers around town by the fleet of Vachon drivers. Variety was minimal— Vachon made a basic assortment, with lemon and jelly fillings, honey dip and honey buns—and while it didn't make Vachon much money, says Charade, it did open doors for the company. The donuts also made Charade think about retail rather than wholesale. Why not open a store of their own, or his own, and sell directly to the public?

By now, the starter's pistol had been fired in the North American donut-store-franchising race, although the shot had scarcely been heard in Canada. A franchise company was already operating in California, but the Boston area was where most of the action was. Two brothers-in-law who'd had a falling out were running rival operations in the south Boston suburbs: Mr. Donut was based in Westwood, while the original chain, Dunkin' Donuts (founded in 1950), was in Randolph.[2] In 1960, Jim Charade flew to Boston to tour the Mr. Donut operation. He visited their shops and had a look around the training centre. "I was impressed with them and wanted a franchise, but on my way back to Toronto, I thought, Why do I want a franchise? I can do that myself."

Charade went to work on Paul Vachon, the son

of Rose-Anna and Arcade, who also had his own business, Diamond Products, which made condiments like ketchup and mustard. Charade says he convinced Vachon to help him start up a new enterprise, a chain to be called King Donuts. Jo-Lo Corp., which made the baking equipment and provided mix to Vachon, would do the same for King Donut.

But Charade says Paul Vachon couldn't get the approval of the rest of the Vachon board. The main concern was that by going retail, Vachon Cake would be competing with its own wholesale customers, its proverbial bread and butter. To stretch the metaphor, Vachon didn't think Charade could have his cake and eat it too. "I was sort of pissed off," says Charade. "I started looking for a place myself."

Still working for Vachon, he found something right around the corner from his house, a small retail space in the Colony Plaza strip mall on the north side of Lawrence, immediately west of the Lawrence–Warden intersection. There, Charade opened his first store, called Your Do-Nut Shop, on February 21, 1962.[3] It was a Saturday, and there was a snowstorm. The weather was so bad that on the walk from his house to the store, Charade lost his watch.

In spite of the inauspicious debut, the small shop proved quite successful, and he promptly opened a satellite outlet in midtown Toronto, on Avenue Road, siting it close to a Loblaw's and a Harvey's. However, the store quickly proved a mistake and had to be closed. He opted to stick to Scarborough, with a new satellite outlet due south of his main store on the Danforth near Warden.

By now all the pieces seemed to be in place for an encounter between Jim Charade and Tim Horton. But in fact, they weren't. Tim had moved away from Warden Avenue just as Charade was moving onto it. Charade had opened his Your Do-Nut in the mall right across the street from Russ Gioffrey's Bestway TV and Appliances store, where Tim kibitzed with Rooskie on Saturday mornings, but by the spring of 1962, when Your Do-Nut was up and running, Gioffrey had closed his Bestway outlet on Lawrence to concentrate on the original store on Kingston Road. The lives of Jim Charade and Tim Horton were close to intersecting, but not close enough.

Exactly how Tim and Jim came together depends on who you listen to. What's undisputed is that a young man named Dennis Griggs brought them together.

Griggs says he met Tim Horton in the summer of 1956, when he was sixteen years old and coaching kids' baseball at Manhattan Park in the neighbourhood on the east side of Warden. Baseball was never a major part of Tim's sports résumé, but he came out to Manhattan Park to be an assistant coach for a teenager ten years his junior because that's what you did when you were community-minded.

Dennis and Tim were friends for nearly twenty years, and as with almost every friendship Tim made, it was only broken by his death. "Tim was a beautiful human being," he says. "He never let on that he was anything more than a man." Dennis was solid and square-jawed, and could pass for a brother of Tim if people didn't know any better. Whenever they encountered a pack of kids clamouring for autographs, Tim would whisper to him, "Sign 'Kent

Douglas'," and Dennis would obligingly dash off the
signature of the young Leaf defenceman. They
jogged together, and Dennis became routinely
familiar with Tim's legendary strength. He watched
him curl 200-pound barbells. "He was *very* strong.
He could pick up the front end of a car."

As a kid, Griggs would accompany Tim on some
of his ad sales calls for the Telegram, and would
make runs to North Bay with him when he got into
the car business. He pitched in during Tim's brief
foray into selling cars with Fred Care, painting the
dealership fence. Sometimes he was a customer.
Tim sold Dennis a 1954 Olds, and Dennis in turn
sold his 1951 Dodge to Bob Baun's wife Sally. He
remembers Tim selling his wife a Triumph TR3.

Tim became even closer to Dennis's brother
Gordon. Two years older than Dennis, Gordon was
something of a hellion as a youth. He went to
Riverdale High (which Billy Harris also attended)
until grade 10 and played football there, but then
was "kicked out," according to Dennis. He finished
his high-school studies at Winston Churchill and set
his sights on the ministry, attending Waterloo
Lutheran (now Wilfrid Laurier University) and the
University of Toronto, with a significant amount of
financial help from Tim. Gordon was ordained in
the Presbyterian Church in 1967.

Dennis Griggs and Jim Charade met through
Griggs's company, VIP, which he had started after
trying life as a cop for a year on the streets of
Toronto in 1960. The two men became close
enough for Jim to serve as Dennis's best man.
Griggs was making signage and promotional
coupons for the original Your Do-Nuts. Griggs managed the Avenue Road satellite outlet, but when it

closed, he began minding the Lawrence Avenue shop.

By September 1962, Charade could no longer run Your Do-Nut and the Vachon donut plant, and had decided to leave the company to concentrate exclusively on the retail business. He soon cast in his lot with a group of Ottawa investors who were building a small motel and restaurant empire. In 1960 they had two motels in Ottawa, called the Bruce MacDonald Motor Hotel and the Bruce MacDonald Motor Lodge, as well as the Royal Burger Drive-In Restaurant.[4] Within two years, Royal Burger had grown to seven outlets in the Ottawa area and had entered the Kingston market. They had also opened a Royal Burger Drive-In in Toronto on Dundas West near Kipling, and in 1963 added a walk-in outlet in the heart of downtown, on Yonge near Shuter.

Charade struck a deal with the Bruce MacDonald people. He signed an employment contract and agreed to begin establishing a chain of "Royal" donut outlets for them in Ottawa. His employers, in turn, would buy the Your Do-Nut operation from him. In the winter of 1962/63, Charade went to Ottawa and opened the first Royal Donut Shop on Richmond, and the sign on the Toronto Your Do-Nut stores was changed to Royal Donut, but Charade decided to bail out. "I couldn't get along with the people," he says. "They were wacko and they worked with other people's money." He tore up the employment contract and walked away, still owning his Toronto donut stores but feeling the pinch of never having been able to collect the buy-out, which he says was pegged at $20,000.

Charade believes that he met Tim in the spring

of 1963—Dennis Griggs, he says, introduced them
when Griggs learned Charade was interested in buying a car, and he is sure he bought a Pontiac from
Tim. Griggs has a different version, with which Lori
agrees. Tim, Griggs says, came into the donut store
in the Colony Plaza one day after practice. Although
Tim hadn't lived in the neighborhood for more
than three years, he still got his trademark brushcut
at Benny's, which was next door to the donut store.
(Good old Benny's, at last inspection, was Cyndy
and Lynsey Unisex Hairstyling Salon.) "I told him
what we were doing and I set him up with Jim," says
Griggs. "Jimmy was the brains behind it, the one
who started the first donut shop, but it was me that
got Tim involved. I'm one of the founding fathers."

After Tim Horton did or did not sell Jim Charade
a car in May 1963, Charade in turn sold Tim on the
idea of going into the restaurant business. Tim
appealed to Charade as a partner on several levels.
For one thing, they got along. "Tim was a great
guy," he says. "He was my best friend." Claudette
and Lori also became quite close. And, naturally,
there was the matter of capital. Tim was not very
well off by any means, but he was comfortable in his
finances and what he couldn't kick in directly he
could arrange to borrow.

But most important, Tim brought that golden
intangible to the business: fame. Jim had read
about Gino Marchetti, who had starred with the
Baltimore Colts when they won the NFL season
championship in 1959 and had started a chain of
restaurants called Gino's. That was an intriguing
business model for Jim. You had someone the public recognised and admired. Put his name on the
restaurant, put him inside it as often as you could,

greeting the customers, pressing the flesh. That was precisely what Bob Baun was doing for Doug Cole at George's Spaghetti House—acting as a kind of publicist, host/*maître d'* and, when necessary, upscale bouncer all rolled into one. "People always feel you can't just go from sport, if you have a name, into another business," says Charade. "But I thought Tim could do it, if you took care of things and did it well and didn't mess people up and had the right attitude. I took him as a partner for his name, for his autographs. Even if you don't have the product, if you have the name at least you'll get them in the door."

That July, Ken Gariepy was a busy man. The lawyer handled the paperwork for two important items of business for Tim. In addition to overseeing the incorporation of Tim Horton Holdings Ltd., the property investment vehicle formed by Tim, Ed Siekierko and John Dywan, Gariepy also marshalled the documents creating the restaurant-business partnership between Tim and Jim, incorporated as Timanjim Ltd. Charade also arranged a licensing agreement to use Tim's name for his donut business, which he had plans for franchising.

In Tim, Jim Charade found a friendship that defied outward contradictions. Jim came across as a young rake, a jazz drummer with a French accent, silk suits and bright ties. Tim was a walking fashion no-no, someone for whom clothes were more of a disguise than a statement. No player was more generous with his autograph or more tolerant of fans in public places than Tim, but at the same time the adulation made him cringe. Jim felt that Tim liked to hide behind his thick-lensed horn-rimmed glasses. Tim was the Man of Steel, invisible to the public in his Clark Kent persona: quiet, self-effacing, eternally shy among strangers.

The persona was reinforced by his indifference to fashion. Tim was just plain folks, his plainness best illustrated by the Overcoat Story. The tailor of choice near Maple Leaf Gardens was Tony's, a few blocks south on Dundas. When Tim finally felt the need, or the pressure, to invest in quality outerwear, he was measured by Tony for a tweed overcoat. But Tony somehow muffed Tim's order, and when Tim arrived to pick up the coat, the tailor hastily brought out one he was preparing for Jean Beliveau, who was six inches taller and at least twenty-five pounds heavier than Tim. Tony draped the garment over Tim and moved the buttons over to the point where the coat was practically double-breasted. Tim agreeably left the tailor's shop wearing a coat whose hem reached his ankles and sleeve cuffs practically swallowed his hands. His friends and teammates were driven to hysterics by the sight of him, but Tim resolutely wore the coat for several seasons, only abandoning it when it began to fray. (Beliveau says he had no idea a coat meant for him ended up on the back of Tim Horton, but that he did get the coat he ordered from Tony.)

"It was a lucky coat," says Lori. "I bought him two new topcoats one winter because I couldn't stand seeing him in it. He wore one of them one night and they lost the game. It was months before he put it back on."

In a group of friends, above all at house parties, Tim was a different person from the public one who recoiled from his own fame. "He enjoyed company and people," Ed Siekierko remembers. "He loved entertaining, socialising. He used to come over to my place during the summer holidays. My wife would be up at the cottage with the kids, Lori would be up at his parents' place. Tim would stop in at my place with a couple of steaks. We'd put the barbecue on, pour some drinks and shoot the breeze."

Ed Siekierko's backyard in Etobicoke would turn into an open-air suburban facsimile of Fran's at lunchtime. The neighbours, the kids, would spot Tim Horton, Hockey Star, and the invasion would be underway. There would be children in his lap, twenty-five or thirty of them in succession, having their pictures taken. It isn't enough to say that Tim tolerated this—he revelled in it, not because the attention fed a star's ego, but because it reinforced his enthusiasm for families, children and suburbia. He loved the very idea of it: neighbours who knew each other, who watched each others' kids grow up, moms and dads and offspring off to church and Sunday school every week.

He had an indefatigable enthusiasm for children. Siekierko's daughter Cathy, who was fiercely devoted to the Leafs,[5] adored him. "He was like an uncle," she says. Indeed, over at the Gioffrey household, he was Uncle Timmy. "When he came over for a dinner party," continues Cathy, "after about half an hour he'd had enough of adults. He'd look out the window and see kids up the street playing ball hockey. He'd be out there, sitting on the curb with them, telling them how to play, getting them organised." Tim was like a Foghorn Leghorn who actually knew what he was talking about: No, son, you've got it all wrong. Hold the stick like this. Put your hands there, and there. Now let's see you shoot, and put some pepper on it.

"Tim couldn't tolerate bullshit," Russ Gioffrey says. "He got his sincerity from his kids and other kids."

"I do think the girls have more boyfriends because of their father's hockey," said Lori in 1966. "As soon as we move to a new neighbourhood the backyard fills up with little boys."

Boys in particular benefited from his attentions. As a boy himself, Tim had developed an enthusiasm for hockey that was not shared by his father, and while Oak and Tim were close, there was no handing down of on-ice secrets. (This was par for the course for players of his generation. Parents did not pack the stands to watch their kids play hockey.) As a new arrival to the professional ranks in Pittsburgh, he had benefited from the mentoring of older players like Frank Mathers, Andy Barbe and Pete Backor. He spent the rest of his professional career reciprocating with rookies—provided, in the expansion years, they weren't too full of themselves.

"Tim at an earlier time would have learned something from somebody else," says Dick Duff. "That's how our system worked. We wanted the guy next to come in line to keep it as good or make it better when we'd go. That's something we willingly did. It wouldn't come from the top. Guys just did it because they liked the young guy. They'd see him as someone who wanted to be a good player, was committed to what his job was going to be. But if the guy was some kind of flake, we could pass on him. Why waste the time with those ones? They won't be around in two years. They don't have the commitment to the job and they don't have the skill level. They're already making excuses to be out."

Tim had a mentoring streak a mile wide, with no

outlet for it within his own home, where he was the lone male and hockey was largely a foreign concept. Lori had been raised on baseball, and never entirely embraced the game Tim played. She came by her estrangement honestly. Late in Tim's career, Lori took her mother to a game in Pittsburgh. Her mother couldn't understand why, if the point of the game was scoring goals, the teams had goaltenders.

In an interview published in 1966, Lori said that Tim "tried to warn me what marrying a hockey player meant, but it didn't sink in. We were married in 1952 and later that year moved to Toronto. At first I was extremely bored at the games, and I found all sorts of excuses for not going. Sometimes I even sat in the stands and read," a behaviour the interviewer Sylvia Fraser accurately described as "an outrage in Toronto." Eventually Lori "started to find out what was going on out there on the ice. Hockey became a way of life for me, too." Still, even in 1966, her grasp of the game remained limited. "I watch Tim when he's on the ice, otherwise I watch the other defencemen. I don't actually know what a forward is supposed to do."

Tim was head-over-heels devoted to his daughters, but as with most girls hockey was not a priority in their lives, at least not when they were younger. "They never watch the games if they can help it," said Lori in 1966 of the children. "I take them to one a year, and it's terrible the way they fidget. The last time I took Traci, age six, a little boy got hit with a puck and now she thinks that's hockey."

He downplayed his own celebrity with them, insisting that he had a job like anybody else. "He tried to be a regular guy," says Jeri-Lynn. "It was a big problem with all of us growing up. We never

knew if people liked us for us, or because they wanted to meet Tim Horton."

As they grew up, his daughters did regularly
watch him play. "He used to take Traci to the
Gardens with him all the time," says Jeri-Lynn. Tim
tapped the ice with his stick to let his kids know that
he knew they were watching.

"Dad was very good, very patient with us," says
Jeri-Lynn. In their teenage years, she says, "We
drove him nuts. He was always there to talk to. No
matter where he was, he left phone numbers for us
to call. He was strict. He grounded us and disciplined us. Nothing we never needed. We were typical teenagers."

When they were younger, she says, "sometimes he
spanked us, but he controlled it. He had to, he was
so strong. He'd be wrestling with us and hurt us
because he didn't know his own strength. I remember him getting mad at one of my sisters when she
didn't clean up her room. He picked her up by the
back of the neck and the rear and tossed her up the
stairs. She hit the landing running."

"Tim was very close to his girls," says Russ
Gioffrey, but that did not insulate him from teasing
about his inability to sire a boy. When Lori delivered Kelly, thereby matching the Gioffreys with
three daughters, Gioffrey rang Tim up and by way
of congratulations needled him with: "Still don't
know how to do it?" That produced a "Smartass!"
from Tim, but when June Gioffrey soon had a boy
after three girls, Tim's response to the gloating
news from Russ Gioffrey was a loud "Screw you!"
and a receiver slammed in his ear. His old
Pittsburgh Hornets roommate, Andy Barbe, who
had four kids, all of them boys, similarly delighted

in needling Tim.

"Tim was very sentimental," says Ray Hannigan. "When my son Tim was born in 1955, Tim Horton came up to me with tears in his eyes. 'Thank you very much,' he said. 'For what?' I asked. 'For naming your son after me,' he said. Someone must have told him that I had, but I never had the heart to tell him that I hadn't. His chest would just go out every time I saw him. He was so moved."

Sons of friends were taken under Tim's wing. "I used to be on a construction site with Ron, our oldest boy," says Ed Siekierko. "Tim Horton would pull up, and that was it. I had the kid there to do some work, but Tim would say, 'Aw, get yourself a labourer.' Tim had a Sunbeam Tiger, a little bomb, and he'd drop the top and away they'd go. I wouldn't see my kid until five o'clock. Ron would come back stuffed with sodas. Tim loved his children, and it was always daddy this and daddy that. But he had four daughters, and Ron was just a treat for him."

Tim didn't isolate his daughters from his affection for high performance. Just as he enjoyed having his daughters at the games, he took Jeri-Lynn out in the Tiger to teach her how to drive when she was twelve. He had decided it was time his eldest appreciated first-hand the lure of the road.

"He was very down-to-earth," says Jeri-Lynn. "There were no airs to him at all. He took me to Bloorview a couple times, just to play with the kids. He'd go play floor hockey with them. These kids just worshipped him, and it brought me a lot down to earth, too. I was only ten, eleven years old, and there were kids with their faces and hands and arms burned off. That's a side of dad a lot of people never saw."

It wasn't a side of him that he particularly wanted people to see. Hughie Phillips remembers how a mention of Tim's visits to Bloorview once made it into the press, and how furious he was. He wasn't doing it for the PR, and he didn't want anybody thinking that he was. He had a very firm sense of what was the right thing to do, and he didn't look to other people for their approval before he did it. If people agreed with what he did, that was fine, but it really didn't make any difference to him what they thought. His religious convictions remained strong throughout his life, and he enhanced them with his enthusiasm for Norman Vincent Peale and his message of the power of positive thinking, which Tim readily translated into the power of positive doing.

Peale was one of the reasons Punch Imlach and Tim Horton had connected on an elemental level. Early in his tenure in Toronto, Imlach distributed copies of Peale's book while the team was on a road trip. Tim took to Peale's message instantly. Whenever he was in New York, he made a point of hearing Peale speak at Marble Collegiate Church; Lori can remember going to hear him speak during the play-offs with Tim, Billy Harris and Bob Pulford. Tim even had copies of Peale's weekly sermons mailed to the house. He cited Peale's work constantly, in the way that the Bible had been a particular source of inspiration for him during his second year at St. Mike's. Long before sports psychology had stormed the ranks of professional and amateur athletes, Tim had tapped into Peale's potent cross-pollination of Christianity and self-improvement. "He quoted him all the time," says Lori. "I don't think Norman Vincent Peale ever realized he had a fan like Tim." At times Lori found Tim's proselytizing wearying.

"Tim's favourite guy of all time was Norman Vincent Peale," says Gordon Griggs. "Tim was just fascinated by that man. I was a young minister and didn't have time for Norman Vincent Peale, the power of positive thinking. Later on someone gave me a copy of the sermons he gave each week. I really saw what Tim saw in it. It wasn't religion, it wasn't phony humility. It was: here's what I am. I'm related to God, and I'm not going to be embarrassed about what I am, and God and I are going to do certain things, and I'm going to do them as best I can.' That's what he got out of him. I would think that, if it were two thousand years ago, Tim would have chosen to be a disciple. There was nothing complex about him. He was straightforward in what he did, but it was always premeasured.

"Tim had this spirituality, and he was unashamed of it. Whether it came from his mom, it was there, a part and parcel of him that had to be developed just like your body and your mind. And he worked at that.

"I'm not trying to make Tim a saint, but when you look at the world we live in and our society, Tim was at least serious in his faith, and it wasn't a superficial thing that had only to do with the church. He was motivated by a very deep relationship with God, and he wanted to expand and understand that."

In Lori's mind, faith was something innate in Tim. While some do see his mother as an important influence, Lori notes that, from an early age, Tim was self-motivated in his convictions. "Tim was very religious. At the ripe old age of twelve, he would get himself up in the morning, get dressed and go to church. The family didn't go." His own children were sent to Sunday school, but like many kids, when they mustered sufficient control over their own lives they stopped going. Tim was the only dedicated churchgoer in the family. At the end of his life, when the family had a cottage near Huntsville, Ontario, Tim would get up alone on Sunday morning and travel by boat into town to hear his weekly sermon.

As Charade remembers, "Tim didn't know a donut from a hockey puck, but he liked them." He was intrigued by the donut business, but ultimately was far more interested in the potential of flame-broiled food. That interest was due to the enterprising example set by Gord and Ray Hannigan.

"Gord was instrumental in encouraging Tim because we were such a success from day one," says Ray. "When Tim was considering the donut franchising, he consulted with Gord quite a bit."

In Lawrence Martin's profile of Tim in a January 1973 issue of *Canadian* magazine, Tim streamlines and even mythologises his business history. His ultimate partner in the donut business, Ron Joyce, becomes an old friend who was on the Hamilton police force when they hooked up, when in fact Tim didn't know him from Adam. Jim Charade has dropped out of the narrative entirely, an inconvenient complication. He is loath to talk about his experience in the hamburger business: "Let's just leave it at that. They flopped." And he offers an unexpected epiphany from his days as a Pittsburgh Hornet. "There was this big, beautiful donut shop on the outskirts of town. I had never really thought of being anything else but a hockey player before, but the first day I walked into that shop, I thought that I would really like to own my own donut shop some day." In 1969 Tim would sum up his venturing into the donut business in a single quip: "I love eating donuts and that was one of the big reasons that I opened my first donut shop. Buying donuts was costing me too much money."

He may well have always harboured a desire to enter the donut business, but when out of the blue Jim Charade presented him with precisely that opportunity, he chose instead the business of drive-in burgers, a business in which neither he nor Charade had any experience. When opportunity knocked, the memory of that fabled donut shop in Pittsburgh obviously did not knock with it. Tim chose to ignore the opportunity of donuts and pursue the business in which the Hannigan brothers were successful. Only Charade seemed committed to the idea of donuts, licensing Tim's name for his donut enterprise.

The Timanjim partnership set out to establish a chain of burger-and-chicken restaurants featuring open grilles and stand-up counters around greater Toronto. In addition to the Hannigan model, their main inspirations were two Toronto-based restaurant chains, Harvey's and Swiss Chalet. Harvey's, with its open grilles and char-broiled burgers, was headquartered in Richmond Hill; founded in 1959, by 1965 it had eight outlets around Toronto and two in Hamilton. Swiss Chalet, founded in 1954, had three Toronto locations and a fleet of twelve delivery vehicles when Charade opened his donut shop in 1962.

Tim and Jim were soon off and running on an acquisition spree that mimicked the rapid expansion of the Hannigans' chain in Alberta. A local insurance executive with commercial real-estate investments had opened a pair of drive-in restaurants in Scarborough called Johnny Johnson's, one on Kingston Road east of McCowan Road, where an Arby's now stands, the other on Lawrence east of Warden. The executive was shutting both of them down, and leased the Kingston Road site to Timanjim. He had another property, formerly a Biff Burger, on Lawrence right across the street from the original Your Do-Nut, which had been renamed Tim Horton Do-Nut. Timanjim took this one, too, and the Tim Horton Drive-In Restaurant chain was launched.[6]

They opened another drive-in on the opposite side of the city, on Lakeshore Road in Port Credit (then New Toronto). Then they took over a spot occupied by a restaurant called Stop and Go on Yonge above Dundas, a good downtown location made even better by its proximity to Ryerson Polytechnical Institute. The owner was Benny Winbaum, whose Winco Ltd. owned the Steak and Burger franchise rights. The restaurant site has disappeared into the music retailing strip dominated by Sam the Record Man, which also benefits from its proximity to Ryerson. The open grille shared the front window with a display case for donuts driven down from the Colony Plaza store; in the back was a space that served as the head office for both the Horton restaurants and Tim Horton Holdings.

The restaurants weren't true drive-ins in the A&W model. There were no intercoms from which to order, or waitresses hustling between the restaurant and parking lot. They were drive-ins in the sense that, in the expanding Toronto typified by Scarborough, everybody was driving somewhere, and you were invited to drive right in and take advantage of the establishment's parking lot. The general floorplan the restaurants followed permitted only stand-up eating at counters for those customers who planned to hang around rather than return to their vehicles, but at the Kingston Road outlet there was a walk-in area with tables that increased the site's appeal in winter, just as the Hannigans had seating in one of their drive-ins. Out in Port Credit, the store delivered chicken as well, in the Swiss Chalet model, but the chicken also brought to mind the Hannigans' Heavenly Chicken outlet. For deliveries, they used an old VW van that Tim had scouted out and crowned with a Tim Horton Chicken sign. At the same time, Tim had found and sold to Jim's wife Claudette a used Karmann Ghia, which hardly ever ran. To ferry around their son André, Claudette would commandeer the chicken van. This produced the usual wisecracks along the lines of, "Funny, you don't look like Tim Horton," whenever she was at a stoplight.

The fifth and final Tim Horton burger outlet was opened in North Bay in the summer of 1964. Tim's brother Gerry built and staffed it; Tim provided the signage and design, and came up with Jim Charade to help Gerry open it. Naturally it was built on the Horton family's Shell lot, joining the car dealership that was already there. It was an A-frame structure inspired by the original Harvey's outlet on Yonge Street in Richmond Hill, which Tim and Jim patronised on trips to North Bay. (There was no Highway 400 then. A drive north meant following Yonge Street, which was Highway 11, the entire way.) What Jim Charade remembers most vividly about the grand opening (and Gerry agrees) were the shadflies. It had been a particularly bad summer for

them, and the lineup of people filing into the tiny
restaurant kept the door permanently propped
open. Flies swarming in clouds of charcoal and
grease typified the day.

The North Bay venture precipitated a small storm
between the brothers. "Tim had some equity in the
hamburger place," says Lori. "There was a bone of
contention about who owned it for about three
months. Tim went up, and he and Gerry were driving somewhere, and Gerry said, 'My hamburger
place,' and Tim didn't believe in 'my.' It was 'ours'
and 'we.' And Tim said, 'What do you mean?' And
Gerry said, '*My*.' They had a little falling-out. Tim
went up and had a conference with his parents, and
they certainly had their side of the issue, too. They
felt that there were things Tim had done which
would justify this [Gerry's position]. I had to agree,
and I think Tim did, too, and that was the end of it."

Others remember the car dealership becoming a
similar bone of contention between the brothers,
but Lori says the dealership "was never an item of
dispute. It was Gerry's place."

Right after the dispute over the ownership of the
hamburger stand, says Lori, "Gerry had his first
heart attack. Tim was really broken up about his little brother." Gerry was still in his early thirties, and
would have several more.

The hamburger stand, best known as "Number
7," was eventually closed, and after Tim's death was
turned into a German restaurant by Gerry. But by
the time Number 7 ceased to be, the rest of the
hamburger joints had also disappeared. Tim's second business venture had been headed toward failure virtually since the day it was launched.

Chapter 16

A New Trick

Spencer Brown was a twenty-year-old clerk at a Bank of Nova Scotia branch in Scarborough when he fell in with Tim Horton's would-be restaurant empire in early 1964. The Timanjim burger business was struggling to make its way, and Jim Charade was moving ahead on his plans to open donut franchises under his licensing agreement with Tim.

"This donut shop," Brown remembers, "had opened up at Lawrence and Warden." Dennis Griggs was busy at Tim Horton Do-Nut, and Jim Charade was around, as well as a little Scottish baker. Brown remembers that the satellite store had opened on Avenue Road, and that there were Tim Horton burger places across the road on Lawrence, in Port Credit, and downtown on Yonge Street. But he cannot remember precisely how or why he ended up in business with these people. "To this day I don't know how it all happened. One thing came to another, and before I know it I'm in the car with Dennis going to Peterborough." Spencer Brown, still living at home with his parents near Lawrence Avenue and Markham Road, was about to become the world's first Tim Horton Donuts franchisee.

Griggs and Brown were in Peterborough to investigate possible sites for such a franchise. Peterborough seemed to make sense as a franchise

locale, being the place the Maple Leafs held their
training camp every September. Griggs and Brown
had lunch at the Empress Hotel and scouted various sites. Old gas stations were popular because
they were roughly the right size for a restaurant and
came with lots of parking space built in. This made
for a logical business transition for Tim, from the
world of service stations to the world of drive-in
restaurants. Both businesses relied on location and
ease of access. It took someone whose family was in
the auto service business to be able to look at a gas
station and immediately see a restaurant.

While Tim was far from the scene as Griggs
worked with Charade in establishing a donut
empire bearing his name, Tim would prove to be
attracted fundamentally to the scouting side of the
business. He would become the Squib Walker of the
donut retail trade, driving into town, surveying the
best prospects, getting the feel of the location that
was going to deliver fame and fortune.

The Peterborough excursion was inconclusive,
with no property identified as a definite site.
According to Allan Stanley, season after season Tim
dithered over setting up a restaurant in
Peterborough. "We had our training camp in
Peterborough for ten years. Tim and I used to drive
down Lansdowne Street, and for years, every time
we went by one lot, he'd say, 'See that lot? Jeez, that
would be a good place for a donut shop.' The last
year, he said, 'I'm going to go in and see about
that.' And I think the week before, Country Style or
Dunkin' Donuts had bought the property."

While on the road back to Toronto, Griggs said to
Brown, "Well, we have this place we're just getting
ready to open in Hamilton. Would you be interested

in going over there?" Brown said he was happy to
take a look at it. Brown found a restaurant only a
few weeks away from opening, with nobody there to
run it. It was at the corner of Ottawa Street and
Dunsmure in the city's east end, across the street
from the world's first Canadian Tire franchise.

Twenty-five years later, as Tim Donut Ltd. prepared to celebrate its anniversary at this original
store with great fanfare, Lori Horton telephoned
Jim Charade. She was preparing herself for an interview with the local television station, Channel 11,
and a pertinent question had come to mind: "Why
did we go to Hamilton for the first franchise outlet?"

Jim Charade says he had picked Hamilton
because Hamilton wasn't Toronto. By then, Mr.
Donut had established its first franchises in
Toronto, and had none in Hamilton. Country Style
had also come to Toronto in 1963. In Hamilton
there would be no competition. Ironically, Jim
Charade was scrupulously avoiding establishing
franchises in the city in which the Tim Horton
name was best known.

Charade had found this old Esso station on
Ottawa Street. The property was owned by a
Ukrainian fellow in Kitchener, who agreed to build
to suit and would ride into town on his bicycle—a
round trip of seventy miles—to keep tabs on the
project. They wound up with a bleach-white building with a purple interior for about $200 a month.

The restaurant was stocked with used equipment,
and Brown tore up his arm on the lava rock in the
wall left over from the service station days, but he
liked what he saw. They agreed to a down payment
of $1,500 and a royalty rate that escapes Brown. (It
was probably the standard 2 per cent.) He went to

his uncle and borrowed every penny of the down payment, quit his job at the bank and headed for Hamilton. The Tim Horton Donut Drive-In Restaurant opened with little fanfare in April 1964, one month before Spencer Brown's twenty-first birthday.

Before it opened, Jim Charade passed an entire night counting cars on Parkdale Avenue to the east. It was the main commuter route for the steelworkers pouring out of the city's industrial northeast at the end of every shift, making their way up the escarpment to their homes in the new suburbia in the city's southeastern section. "I watched the traffic at three a.m., four a.m., because it was going to be open twenty-four hours. I thought, I've got to be crazy. But there was nothing to compare it to." He hoped that once people got to know the restaurant, they would make the detour to stop in at the end of their shift to meet, talk and eat donuts.

Brown stayed at the YMCA for a week, then found a room close by the store as he went to work. If Tim Horton didn't know a donut from a hockey puck, Brown didn't know a donut from a tire—as he puts it, they were both round and had a hole in the middle. Tim Horton, for that matter, was nowhere to be seen. Brown didn't even meet him until he'd been open for a week. Charade sent down his Scottish baker to help him get going. Brown was on the cutting edge of fast food, and he was about to help ignite a franchise revolution.

As it turns out, Charade could not have picked a better city in which to launch the first franchise. The city's blue-collar denizens literally ate up the concept. "It went super well," says Brown. "It was busy, busy, busy. For a kid that had been making about forty dollars a week in the bank, all of a sudden I'm making four hundred a week." At the end of a long day, he would keel over on a bag of flour in the kitchen, sleep for a few hours, then start all over again.

It was a long way from what Tim Hortons would become. Although coffee was on the menu, it was a very American drink at the time, in Canada something served in the home after dinner. Tea was the hot beverage of choice. Charade recalls that coffee contributed about 20 per cent of revenues then, when today it's responsible for about 60 per cent. But in donuts the men involved in the first franchise found a product that challenged the simile "Sold like hotcakes." The first Tim Hortons franchise was going great guns with a wide variety of donuts. "The big things were jelly and condiment-filled donuts," says Brown. The donut was pumped with goop and the outside sugared. "It was a really big deal: Venetian filled, jelly filled—apple and spice was a big seller—and honey dipped. Cake donuts were the only type people knew, and we didn't sell much of those. We had peanut crunch, macaroon, coconut crumble, you name it. We really tried hard to have at least forty different varieties there at any one time." Brown ordered tins of fillings from suppliers and went to work with Charade inventing a cultural phenomenon. "You ordered what you needed from a supplier for that week, and sometimes we had to order a second shipment because we were really selling a lot of product. It was terrific. It just went gangbusters." A dozen donuts were sixty-nine cents; two bits got you a cup of coffee and a donut. It was a snack break tailor-made for the bleary-eyed men off shiftwork: straight caffeine and sugar.

They didn't even sell off day-olds at a special price. "We'd put things in the proofer and keep them warm at 5:30, 6:00 a.m., before the shift changed at Dofasco. We'd walk by the counter with a tray of donuts that were probably about twelve hours old, saying, 'They're hot, excuse me, they're hot.' People would yell, 'I'll take six,' 'I'll take four.' We never had anything left over."

After a few months, Spencer Brown's rocket ride to donut fortune began to sputter. "Quite frankly, I got the impression that maybe [Charade] was a little underhanded or having a bit of a problem with Tim. Tim was off playing hockey and making a good name for himself that way, and Jim was screwing him in business. At least that was the impression I had."

Brown was not alone. Friends around Tim were beginning to take him aside and tell him his partner was ripping him off. The burger restaurants were doing badly, and they suspected that Charade was taking Tim to the cleaners. After all, this was Tim Horton, winner in 1964 of his third straight Stanley Cup, a second-team All Star in 1963, a first-team All Star in 1964. The Leafs had never been more popular, and Tim was easily one of the most popular members of this dynasty. Yet while the restaurants always seemed busy, Tim was perpetually losing money.

"Most of these people," Charade notes, "maybe they thought it was my fault that the business wasn't going, and maybe I didn't have the experience. I mean, I was just a young guy. When I opened my first donut shop, I was twenty-seven years old. I had the experience of Vachon, but that was wholesale."

By all indications, if Tim ever suspected Jim of ripping him off, he never directly accused him of it, or, if he believed it, ever held it against him. "Tim and Jim were friends," says Brown. Tim was straight as an arrow, and it is unthinkable that if he sincerely believed he was being scalped, he would have tolerated Jim's company. (Russ Gioffrey, who confronted Tim with the possibility that Charade was taking advantage of him, remembers Tim being stunned and managing only, 'I guess he needs it more than I do,' in reply.) The friendship endured the ride over a rocky road of financial calamities.

"I always found Jim easy to get along with," says Lori, who says that Tim didn't believe Jim was scamming him. "And I didn't believe it, either. I still don't believe it. I don't really think Jim was that kind of person. There was somebody working for them who was lifting money, but it wasn't Jim." That is not to say Jim wasn't playing fast and loose—and desperate—as business setbacks pushed him into a corner. "Jim was moving at fifty miles an hour and the car was moving at forty-five miles an hour," Brown sums up.

The root of Jim's credibility problems seems to have been his decision to move money from the hamburger business, in which Tim and Jim were partners, over to his donut venture to ward off a cash flow crisis. He did this, according to Lori, while Tim and Lori were away on a cruise to South America at the end of the 63/64 season. "When we got back," she says, "the money [at Timanjim] was all gone." Tim didn't hold it against him. It was an act of desperation, not deceit. Charade was so drained by their restaurant adventures that he had to sell his house to cover his debts. But the withdrawal from Timanjim did serve to create a rumour mill that Charade was systematically bleeding the burger business to the benefit of his donut venture.

"There was a lot of money coming in, but no profits," Charade says of the burger business. "We did a lot of specials—buy one, get one free. We used to have chicken at special prices, and the places would be just loaded with people, but we weren't making any money. We tried to get some business, let people know where we are, and if they liked it maybe we'll get some repeat business.

"We never had an argument," says Charade. "Tim was enthusiastic. He would call me in the middle of the night and say, 'I saw this in Chicago... I picked up this coffee cup...' It was always something like that. And people would bring him things because they knew he was enthusiastic."

They were constantly searching for new sources of capital, driving to lending institutions to make their case for yet another loan. "I remember going to Canada Permanent Trust, sitting in the car in the parking lot with Tim, waiting to meet a guy. Things were rough, saleswise and with the money. I was saying, 'Regardless of what happens, you'll be fine. Your name is there. We didn't do anything bad. We tried.' He said, 'Well, I always say, I can always dig ditches.' I said, 'Tim, Jesus Christ, you've got it made. It's me that's got trouble. I'm not a hockey player. Nobody's going to want my autograph anywhere.'"

Ironically, Charade was learning that Tim's autograph wasn't a guarantee of success in the restaurant business. For starters, it was tough to get him to come out and sign them. At the time, the Hortons were planning and building their custom home on Bannatyne Drive, and were in a constant state of decorating or shopping. Charade says Lori would call the restaurant when Tim came out and remind him they had an appointment. Tim would make a standard joke of this later whenever Lori wanted him somewhere—"I have to go pick out lamps." But he never refused to go, and while Charade and Lori had a perfectly amicable relationship, Charade came to feel that Lori's demands on Tim's time were hampering the fledgling restaurant business.

Tim himself didn't help. At an opening, the customary flying squad of teammates would come out to sign autographs, but Tim shrank from the spotlight shone on him during these appearances. He generally found an excuse to go back in the kitchen and watch over the chicken, while players like George Armstrong and Dave Keon manned the front lines, scribbling their names.

Jean Beliveau, the captain and star of the Montreal Canadiens, understood the trap built into the celebrity-based business several years later, when John Bitove acquired the Canadian franchise rights to the Big Boy chain. When he opened JB's Big Boy in Scarborough, Bitove had the promotional savvy to invite a fellow JB—Jean Beliveau—to the grand opening. "I became very close with the Bitoves," says Beliveau. "We've always been good friends. I almost had the Big Boy franchise for Quebec and the Maritimes. At the last minute, I stepped out. It's nice if after several years you end up with a few stores, but people would think that I should be there all the time, and that would be impossible if you have five or ten stores. You'd have to be everywhere." It wasn't enough for the enterprise to be owned by a famous name. People would expect to find him or her inside. If the celebrity was either unable or unwilling to support that expectation, the business was doomed.

Considering the Gino's model that had inspired Charade, Keon notes, "Gino Marchetti didn't only lend his name, he ran them. If you're going to be in that type of business, you're going to be a guy meeting the people, and it takes a certain type of person. A guy like Bobby Baun could do that, but Timmy felt uncomfortable.[1]

"He was happy to have somebody else take credit for things. Playing hockey, he enjoyed being an All Star, but he didn't particularly care for all the trappings that went with that. He would much prefer that when he stepped off the ice, it was over. He was a really humble guy. He enjoyed excelling at hockey, but I don't think he ever took it to be any more than it was."

"Tim *never* saw himself as a public persona," says Lori.

Charade was also frustrated by Tim's soft-heartedness. One of Tim's married teammates had a girl-friend on the side, says Charade, and he convinced Tim to give her a job in the modest Timanjim office at the Yonge and Dundas location. It was a payroll addition they could hardly afford. Tim turned crimson whenever he saw the young woman in the office, and headed in the opposite direction. After several months of needless salary, Charade finally convinced Tim to let her go.

Spencer Brown very soon realized that Tim Horton's name had nothing to do with the frenetic success of his small business. Charade had hit upon an explosive franchising concept, and had built the first one right where it had no competition and the perfect combination of location and demographics. He could have called it Jim Charade's Donut Drive-In and it still would have been bringing in $400 a week to the owner. Tim's affiliation was a quirk of fate.

Brown began to see his association with Tim Horton as a liability rather than an asset. "Franchising was such a new trick at the time," he says. "All of a sudden I'm seeing these bills coming in from the person supplying the boxes for the donuts, for example, or the paper, the yeast or the donut mix. Tim Donut[2] didn't have their own ware-housing. This was the first franchise. So with the guy selling the paper, the bill came to me with a price on it, but it was to be forwarded on to Tim Donut, and then they would send me back a bill. Hey, I might be young and green, but I look at this bill, and now it's marked up. I thought, I can buy this stuff directly from the paper goods place. I don't need this name out there that's costing me an extra how-many per cent."

"The burger places," says Brown, "were a mess. Winding them down was the best thing that could happen." Watching from the sidelines, Brown saw the new Red Barn concept pounding the Tim Horton drive-ins with fifteen-cent hamburgers. One opened in the heart of Wexford, at Pharmacy and Warden, just down the street from the first Tim Horton drive-in. There was another at Lawrence and Markham, across from Cedarbrae Mall.

Charade agrees that Red Barn was their principal nemesis. "We needed more promotion, more capital, more advertising."

Meanwhile, back in Hamilton in June, Brown says, "Business was good. Jim Charade tried to buy me out. I said no, no. I wanted to buy them out... take down your sign and I'll try this on my own. Well, that didn't fly. A lot of people were nosing around because the place was busy. George Sukornyk, who was president of Harvey's, was very interested in the whole deal. He'd just opened a place on Barton Street."[3] Brown says he finally agreed to sell back to Charade. Charade's impression of Brown's stint as a franchisee is 180 degrees from that of Brown himself. "I sold him the franchise but he was really nervous," Charade says. "He didn't think that he would make it. I had to take it back from him."

Brown says he got his $1,500 franchise fee back, plus $5,000 from the new franchisee, who turned out to be not George Sukornyk, but an Englishman with an older, wealthy wife. Brown paid back his uncle and had a nice bankroll. "I was gone... I've got this five thousand bucks in my pocket and it's, wow, here we go. George Sukornyk from Harvey's, I went to see him. He offered me the whole of Ottawa." So Brown headed to the nation's capital, and discovered that the site Sukornyk had fingered for the first Harvey's there was on Richmond Road, right next to an A&W and, of all things, a Royal Burger. "I looked at this. I just said, No, the competition's too strong. They went ahead and opened their location, and God knows how many other Harvey's they've opened in Ottawa. They offered me a location in Montreal. Fortunately, I didn't stay there."

Instead, he went to work for the Steak and Burger chain being run by Benny Winbaum's Winco Ltd.—the same Winbaum that had leased Jim Charade the Stop and Go location on Yonge above Dundas for one of the Tim Horton burger spots. Brown worked at Short Horn Steak House in London, Ontario, which was part of the Steak and

Burger chain, then moved on to manage a Winco restaurant, Peppio's Ristorante, at Davenport and Dupont in Toronto. Then there was a transfer to Winco's Gentleman Jim steaks-and-burgers franchise division, where he spent a few years selling franchises. This took him into the U.S. most of the time, and while he was stateside he came across a new franchise operation out of Ohio, a roast-beef-on-a-bun concept called Arby's. "I thought that was a great trick. I was going to bring that back to Canada. Winco caught wind of it, and for the first time in my life I was canned."

Out of the Winco employee roll, the Arby's scheme didn't come together for Brown, and he joined the Holiday Inn business, run by Scott's Hospitality, which also had the rights to the Kentucky Fried Chicken franchises in Canada. After five years at Holiday Inn, Brown had found a business niche he could call home, and struck out on his own. He's been very successful as a hotelier. Living just outside Kingston, he now owns hotels in Kingston, Cornwall, North Bay and Kirkland Lake, and operates them under the Best Western marquee. One of the Tim Hortons franchisees in Kingston is a friend of Brown's, and when the twenty-fifth anniversary of the Tim Hortons chain was celebrated in Hamilton in 1989, Spencer Brown was a guest of honour. He hasn't forgotten about the donuts and their allure.

"It was a novel concept, ideal for a cooler climate. It would be a big winner in northern Europe and Russia. A friend of mine from Oslo would come over with his kids, and they'd go nuts over filled donuts. There's nothing like that over there."

The franchisee that bought the Tim Horton Donut Drive-In in Hamilton from Spencer Brown was a disaster. Jim Charade was getting calls at all hours of the night complaining about the man's conduct— he was scooping money out of the till and heading down to Barton Street to drink it away at the Jockey Club tavern, and the operation was not spic-and-span. Charade reclaimed the franchise and started searching out yet another franchisee. At the same time, Tim and Jim came to an important change in their business relationship. No longer would Charade simply license the use of Tim's name for the donut operations. With the burger restaurants failing and Charade tapped out financially, they formed a new partnership on January 27, 1965, called Tim Donut Ltd. In exchange for injecting capital into Charade's donut venture, Tim got half the business.

Charade soon found the latest franchisee for the first, star-crossed outlet: a man who'd been running a Dairy Queen, an ex-cop named Ron Joyce.

Chapter 17

Tim and Ron

Ronald Joyce of Tatamagouche, Nova Scotia joined the police force of Hamilton, Ontario, on September 24, 1956, three weeks shy of his twenty-sixth birthday. He was a little older than the average recruit, who tended to be about twenty-three, as he'd spent the previous five years in the Canadian navy. He spent nine years on the force, and virtually every one of them was marked by protracted negotiations between the police association and the city for pay raises. It became routine for Hamilton officers to receive lump-sums of retroactive pay as negotiations consumed virtually all of the contract year.

By 1961, Hamilton police officers were closing in on the magical $100-a-week salary level (NHL players like Tim Horton were collecting about $200 a game). After accepting a three per cent increase that year, a first-class constable like Joyce was making $97.33. The officers opened their 1963 contract negotiations with an increase demand of 42 per cent, which would take their annual salary from $5,277 to $7,500. Officially, officers weren't allowed to moonlight to supplement their incomes. Unofficially, however, Ron Joyce, who had a family of four, was doing whatever he could to improve his financial picture. He drove a banana truck for Sam Netkin's wholesale fruit and vegetable business in his off-hours, and in 1963 bought a Dairy Queen franchise on Queenston Road in the city's east end, right across the street from Bishop Ryan high school.

In April 1963 the police association filed for salary arbitration. The following January, the arbitrators awarded all ranks an increase of just 5 per cent, retroactive to the preceding January. For Joyce, who would log his eighth year on the force in September, it meant a salary increase from $5,277 to $5,602. The chief would get a $1,200 raise, taking his salary to $15,400, which put him on par with many of the Maple Leafs winning their third Stanley Cup of the decade. The police association promptly filed its 1964 contract request: a 36 per cent increase. But by then Ron Joyce was moving away from police work. He would stay on the force until 1965, but his ambitions were already pointed in an altogether fresh direction.

The Dairy Queen had changed Ron Joyce's life. "I was a policeman, and frankly I wasn't very happy with it. I really fell in love with the Dairy Queen, because you were selling fun. It's pretty hard to sell a traffic ticket or sell locking up a drunk. Your product isn't fun at all, and I really didn't enjoy it. Then I got into selling food. People come to you, and it's a minor form of entertainment. People want a nice experience, and it was fun to sell Dairy Queen. I started looking for another one."

Dairy Queen was putting a new outlet in Bronte, an Oakville suburb about ten miles to the east of Hamilton. Joyce almost bought it, but the deal collapsed. He kept the one he had, and went looking for something else as he put policing behind him.

When he found out the Tim Horton Donut

Drive-In on Ottawa Street was available, he telephoned Jim Charade, who came to town and interviewed him. Charade remembers Joyce being tough to convince. Joyce remembers speaking with his lawyer, Buck Bennett. "He's one of the senior judges in the Hamilton courts now. He tried to talk me out of buying the store. 'There's nothing there,' he said. But I wouldn't listen to him. I was determined to buy the damned donut store."

As with Spencer Brown, Tim Horton was deep in the background, which probably didn't matter much to Joyce, who wasn't a hockey fan. Tim was in the middle of the 64/65 season when Joyce came aboard as the newest Ottawa Street franchisee on February 21, 1965, and he didn't meet Joyce until a grand opening was held for him.

It didn't take long for Joyce to wish he had taken Buck Bennett's advice. "When I got in the store," says Joyce, "the sheriffs were coming in trying to seize the cash register, the hot chocolate machine... They tried to seize the equipment a couple times, but I had a quit claim deed on the equipment. One sheriff came in, and me being an ex-policeman and young and healthy, we had a pretty good confrontation."

Then there was the Scottish baker from the Tim Hortons donut store in Wexford whom Jim Charade had sent to Hamilton to train Joyce in the world of donut retailing. "He was deliberately teaching me to fail," Joyce maintains. If Joyce crashed and burned, perhaps the baker could stay on and run it.

Charade says Joyce clashed with his trainer because the man had an exceedingly effeminate manner, and was probably not the best person to have behind the counter with an ex-cop in a steel town in the early hours of the morning while a counter full of mill workers clamoured for service. "I got a three a.m. call from Ron," says Charade. "He said, 'If you don't get this bastard out of here, I'm going to kill him. I'm telling you right now, I'm going to choke him.' "

"I threw him out the damned door," says Joyce. "It was true. He was deliberately teaching me to fail." Between his trainer and the sheriffs, Joyce had had enough. He was finally moved to call Tim Horton directly over the trainer kerfuffle.

"Tim said, 'I'll clean it up.' Once Horton got involved, that was the beginning of the end for him and Jim, because Jim didn't have any more money. Tim went out and borrowed the money to clear up all the debts against the equipment that I'd paid for.[1] The money I'd paid for the franchise went out to pay other bills. It was just coming down in all directions."

The Leafs failed to make it four Stanley Cups in a row that season. Their total wins dropped from thirty-three to thirty and they finished fourth overall, two points behind third-place Chicago. A bloody semifinal series saw Montreal eliminate the Leafs and go on to defeat Chicago in the finals. Tim didn't make a return to the All Star team, although Carl Brewer and Frank Mahovlich made the second team. Statistically, Tim had had a respectable season. He produced twenty-eight points, and scored three more goals than in 63/64, when he made the first team with twenty-nine points. He also collected his highest number of penalty minutes to date in the NHL—ninety-five, which was twenty-four more than the previous season.

There was one other, less cherished, milestone. Tim, and many, many other players, had to contend with the loss of Jim Dewey.

Dewey had been as active in sports as ever back in Sudbury. In the summer of 1946, before setting himself to the task of assembling the Copper Cliff Redmen team of which Tim was a member, Dewey had added golf to his exhaustive sporting résumé. He came to play it with a six handicap, and had been serving as president of Idylwylde Golf Club since 1961. He was diagnosed with leukemia in 1963. For two years, Dewey fought the disease into remission, but in early March 1965 it returned, and he had to enter Copper Cliff Hospital. His deterioration was rapid. After two weeks he was transferred to Toronto's Wellesley Hospital, a short walk from Maple Leaf Gardens.

His final week was also the final week of the 64/65 NHL regular season. The Leafs and the Red Wings were playing a home-and-away series to close it out. The first game was in Toronto on Saturday night, March 27. George Collins was in Toronto that weekend. He had been a friend of Jim Dewey's since Dewey's arrival in the Nickel Belt from Saskatchewan, and he was at the Royal York, catching a ride to the airport for a flight south, when he came across a knot of Red Wings in the hotel lobby. They were led by coach Sid Abel and included Gordie Howe. These sons of Saskatchewan had been to Wellesley to visit Dewey; his fame was far from forgotten back on the prairies. They told Collins not to visit Jim: he was too far gone.

In the Sunday night game in Detroit, two of Dewey's Copper Cliff protégés shone as the Leafs shut out the Red Wings. Tim Horton helped nullify

the Detroit offence and hit the goalpost in the first
period, while George Armstrong assisted on Don
McKenney's opening goal and on the final goal by
Dave Keon.

It's not known whether Tim Horton or George
Armstrong visited Dewey while he was at Wellesley.
"I certainly know that if George or Tim knew that
Jim was in the hospital," says Dick Trainor, "they
would have been there."

On the morning of Monday, March 29, Jim
Dewey, the greatest player ever not to play in the
National Hockey League, died at Wellesley Hospital
at the age of fifty-three.

Jim and Tim moved ahead on a second Hamilton
location, on Concession Street, a main road that
ran along the top of the mountain brow. It was both
a commuter route and a business district for the
new suburbia emerging atop the escarpment.
Quandamatteo Real Estate, run by a former
Hamilton Tiger-Cat football star, which was right
across the street from Joyce's Ottawa Street donut
shop, arranged the lease on the Concession Street
land for Tim Donut. Ed Siekierko came down to
give Tim a hand with the site work.

It was a busy construction season for Tim. That
same summer, he built his dream house on
Bannatyne Drive. Hughie Phillips was a regular visi-
tor at the Horton home on Wedgewood Drive in
Willowdale, and he remembers Tim and Lori "talking about staying there, because they didn't have
the money to move." They soon changed their
mind, inspired no doubt by Bob and Sally Baun,
who moved into a new custom-built home in 1964
on Ruden Crescent near Donalda Golf and

Country Club. (Bob, unlike Tim, was an avid golfer.) The Baun property backed onto the Don River Valley in the neighbourhood known as York Heights, just south of the 401. Maple Leaf Gardens was just a blast down the Don Valley Parkway.

The new Horton home was one major block west of the Bauns, between Bayview and Leslie. It was a peculiar but appealing site, a wedge-shaped corner lot that fell away in the back where a creek had once flowed, with a spreading willow anchoring one corner of the yard. The house was a family affair: Lori concerned herself with the interior design and decor (royal blue and burgundy), while Tim and Lori, in consultation with an architect, oversaw the basic design; Tim pitched in on the construction. It was built on four levels, with the top level devoted exclusively to four bedrooms and a bathroom for the girls. "He was very proud of building it," says Ed Siekierko. "I pushed him into it and kind of coached him on it. He wanted a builder to build it, but I said, 'Tim, what are you going to be doing all summer? You can use my sub-trades. I can give you a list of them. They'd be happy to do it for you.'"

Canada Brick was Tim's supplier for the house. Joe Primeau, Jr., who was working at Canada Brick at the time, dropped by the construction site to find a great hole in the ground. Tim clambered out of it and shouted "Joe, how the heck are you?" They hadn't seen each other since their last game as St. Mike's Majors in the spring of 1949. The distinctive brown brick Primeau supplied was later used for Tim Hortons donut stores.

Jeri-Lynn remembers the house with great fondness. When it was being completed, Tim and Lori let their daughters host a "paint party." They were

allowed to have their friends over and decorate
their rooms however they pleased. There was no
carpeting in yet, and a sheet was laid at the top of
the stairs. "There were forty of us," Jeri-Lynn recalls.
"We had a ball."

That June, Ron Joyce hosted a dinner party at his
home in Hamilton's east end, attended by Jim and
Claudette and Tim and Lori. It was the first real
opportunity for Tim and Ron to get to know one
another properly. "Ron cooked steaks and we had a
lot of fun," Charade remembers. "Tim could be
very funny. He liked to imitate French accents.
[Tim actually spoke passable French.] He drank a
little so he was in a good mood." Tim and Ron were
plainly hitting it off, and the evening promised a
friendly business future, if not outright friendship.

   "We had a hell of a party," Joyce agrees, but, he
adds "the evening deteriorated a little bit with Lori."
It seemed to Joyce that Tim was enjoying himself too
much for Lori, that she was feeling ignored by him.
"She demanded to go and got mad," says Joyce.
Suddenly the party was over, and Tim and Lori were
heading for Tim's Sunbeam Tiger, a powerful two-
seater sports car. Lori got in the driver's seat, and
Joyce could see her continuing to complain to Tim
about the evening. "Tim reached over and put his
foot on top of hers on the gas and put it to the
floor," says Joyce. "The car just fishtailed down the
street." Tim wasn't going to take his foot off the
pedal until Lori stopped talking. Charade remembers Tim laughing (and Joyce remembers watching
in alarm) as the car sped off into the night.
   Lori remembers this entirely differently. In Lori's
recollection, Tim simply had had too much to

drink. "We had all agreed that Tim shouldn't be driving, and that I should. Tim was of the opinion that if it was his car, he drove it." As a result, he was going to work the gas pedal, whether she liked it or not. "He had his foot on top of my foot on the gas. He did that all the way to Toronto. It was early in the morning, not too many cars on the road, no policemen. I was steering. I must have lost ten pounds on the drive home. It was frightening."

Regardless of which recollection of this night is the correct one, there is no question that Lori was beginning a turbulent period in her life, and by extension the lives of Tim and their children. Something had happened to Lori, and it was impossible not to notice. Not long after the new home on Bannatyne was completed, Gord Hannigan and his wife Anne paid an impromptu visit. Tim was away, but Lori was home. Anne remembers it as an unsettling encounter with a woman she had known since the early 1950s in Pittsburgh. "I said to Gord when we left, 'There's something drastically wrong.'" Jeri-Lynn was twelve at the time, and it was plain to her that her mother was in trouble.

According to her lawsuit against Joyce,[2] Lori was mentally incompetent during the period in which the Joyce house party occurred—she entered this state that year and would remain that way until 1987 through her battles with drugs and alcohol. That is not to say that she was necessarily incompetent at the party: her incompetence was apparently episodic and not constant. Nonetheless, alcohol and drugs would nearly destroy her life. While she would eventually recover from her problems, a recovery made possible by her return to Catholicism, in 1965 more than twenty years of living in various degrees of hell

still lay ahead of her. In 1964 she had been prescribed an amphetamine, Dexamyl, by a doctor at
Toronto's Western Hospital. On January 13, 1965,
Dr. John Fenn of Thornhill also wrote her a prescription for Dexamyl. It would be the bane of her
existence for the next two decades. Dr. Fenn's prescription was written the day after Tim's thirty-fifth
birthday, two weeks before Tim and Jim Charade
entered into partnership as Tim Donut Ltd.

Dexamyl, which is no longer on the market, was
most commonly prescribed as an appetite suppres-
sant. Lori had become involved in modelling part-
time with her daughters in the early sixties, and this
could have served as her introduction to the drug,
although Lori says it was prescribed as an antidepressant. (The girls did catalogue work and television commercials, and filled assignments at the
Sportsmen's Show and Canadian National
Exhibition. At one time Kelly Horton was one of
Toronto's busiest child models.) Dexamyl was pow-
erfully addictive, both physically and psychologica-
ly, and such diet pills became the enslavers of all too
many women. For Lori Horton, Dexamyl was either
a cause of the coincident crisis in her life, or a
debilitating symptom. It was about this time that she
began receiving regular psychiatric counselling
from Wellesley Hospital.

Lori may well have found the pressures Tim himself faced, through hockey and his struggling businesses, crushing, and her own dissatisfactions overwhelming. Married at nineteen, she had been introduced to a sporting and professional culture for
which she was completely unprepared. Unlike other
young Pittsburgh women who married dashing
Canadian hockey players, Lori faced more than

twenty years of being a hockey wife. Frances
Swearingen, who married Andy Barbe, saw her husband leave hockey in 1956 and join her in the Coca-
Cola bottling business. Anne Conboy saw her husband Gord Hannigan leave hockey for good in 1958
and enter the fast-food business with his brother
Ray in Alberta.

It is not difficult to find incidents in her life that
could have triggered corresponding crises in Lori.
The year 1965 was full of them.

Tim and Lori were building their new home, an
undertaking they had not been altogether sure they
could afford, and during the trial Lori would cite
the move as a factor in her condition. Tim had also
not had one of his better financial years. The Leafs
didn't make it to the Stanley Cup finals, and Tim
didn't make the All Star team—in 63/64, Tim had
collected bonuses on both accounts. (Lori would
say that modelling income paid for the house.) The
hamburger business was in a shambles and draining
his finances. Tim also experienced a double-bar-
relled calamity with his brother Gerry. First they
were estranged by the squabble over who actually
owned the burger outlet on the Horton family car
lot, and then Gerry suffered his first heart attack.

On the hockey rink, there were plenty of stress
triggers. In February 1964, Punch Imlach had traded away Tim's good friend Dick Duff, along with
Bob Nevin, to the New York Rangers. (Duff, like
Baun, would baby-sit for the Hortons.) In February
1965, Imlach's dealmaking again deprived Tim and
Lori of a good friend, when Billy Harris was demot-
ed to Rochester and then traded to Detroit.

Harris remembers warmly his halcyon days as a
Leaf and as an off-ice friend of the Hortons, and his

reminiscences suggest a happy, well-adjusted family in the early sixties, which only deepens the tragedy of the ensuing years. "Shortly after Traci was born [actually just before, by Lori's recollection]," he has written, "the family moved to Wedgewood Drive in North York. I was still a bachelor, and received frequent invitations to join the Hortons on special occasions. Lori was a good cook and we had some great meals. After supper Tim always gave me a choice. (We didn't watch much TV—we listened to records.) Tim would ask, 'Harry, who do you want to listen to first, Hank Williams or Woody Woodbury?' By the time I had had enough of both, the girls had had their baths and jumped into their 'doctor dentons' and up onto Daddy's lap for their goodnight kiss. I occasionally got a goodnight kiss too, not from Tim but the girls. Jeri-Lynn, Kim, Kelly and Traci today are adults, but they still call me 'Billy-bee'."

Bob Baun was a witness to the disintegration in Tim's home life (although he would testify at Lori's suit that he did not see any evidence of abuse of drugs or alcohol by Lori). "Lori was very demanding," says Baun. "The house was a shambles most of the time. Timmy would come home and do the washing, clean up. He was always in that turmoil. It was just like an electric bolt in there all the time. It was a very volatile relationship..."

Then, in the fall of 1965, Tim was one of five Maple Leafs involved in an unprecedented holdout for better contracts. Even though the Leafs had lost to Montreal in the semifinals (a series that has been described as "brutal and warlike") the previous spring, this was a team that nonetheless had won three straight Stanley Cups, and many of the players felt they deserved bigger paycheques. As the season began, Tim, Carl Brewer, Dave Keon, Bob Pulford and Bob Baun refused to play. In mid-October Carl Brewer, who had been a second-team All Star the previous season, stunned the fans (and management and many players) by quitting the game altogether that fall and enrolling in several courses at the University of Toronto. A few days later, on October 20, the logjam had begun to break for Imlach when Tim agreed to a one-year contract. "It wasn't what I want and it wasn't what they wanted," was all Tim would say publicly. "But I want to play hockey and the Leafs are keen on me doing so and we came to terms."

Even had 1965 been free of such incidents, Lori still would have been exercised by the fact that Tim's boss was Punch Imlach. As much as Tim respected Imlach, Lori loathed him. "Punch wasn't easy to get along with, but Tim liked him," Lori agrees. Imlach's arrival in 1958 ought to have been a cause for celebration for Lori. Tim had recovered his form after the disastrous Gadsby collision of 1955. Hap Day, who had fined Tim and cut his salary after the injury, who never enjoyed watching one of his defencemen cross the opposition's blueline (or even centre ice) was gone, and so was Billy Reay, who had made Tim ride the bench. Tim's career blossomed as the Leafs found success under Imlach.

But for Lori, Punch was the enemy. He was the inflexible autocrat who refused to acknowledge that players had wives and families. The idea that hockey wives and children suffered because dad was always on the road and not around like normal nine-to-five working stiffs is largely a myth, and one that Lori Horton readily rejects. "They weren't on the road all

the time. They had two road trips a year, week-long
road trips. Other times they'd leave Saturday night
by train and come back sometime Monday. Then
they'd have their Wednesday night game and then
could leave again. It seemed like Tim was home
quite a bit. They only practised an hour a day and
then they were home, too. There were no two practices a day, two-hour practices. They were pretty reliable. They'd go down for an eleven o'clock practice
and be home by twelve or one o'clock. Now, they
were gone that one week, and if my children chose
to be born the week he was gone, that's life, that's
the way it goes."

Lori's problem with Punch was that when something did come up that she felt deserved Tim's
attention or presence, Punch was unwilling to allow
him leeway. "He had no time for family. One time,
we had a huge snowstorm. They had one practice.
Our dog had to be destroyed that particular day
because she'd gotten caught in a snowbank and her
legs were bad. I had four kids at home with the flu
and I had to take the dog to be destroyed, and
Punch calls a second practice. Tim explained this
all to him, the kids are sick, but no way. Second
practice. He had no concern whatsoever. Traci was
born while they were out of town. Tim came back
on a Sunday and couldn't come and see me in hospital. They had a double practice for that day.
Punch had no consideration for families."

Lori Horton would receive no argument from
Frank Mahovlich in her assessment of Imlach's priorities. In November 1964, Mahovlich suffered a
nervous breakdown, and had to be hospitalised
early in the 67/68 season, so badly frayed were his
nerves by the pressure he felt trying to live up to

Imlach's expectations. "Imlach was never satisfied with anybody," he says. "He was a real queer kind of guy, a bit of a nut! He came out of the army, and he kind of ran the team like an army. You can't do that when guys have families. The thing was, the management let him do it, which made them stupid, too. It was a terrible, terrible situation. And I was so relieved to get out of the place. When I left, they finally fired him."

Johnny Bower effectively describes the man Lori Horton was up against. "I thought he was a very, very smart hockey man and manager. He was very, very strict. He was an army man. He always had the first word, and always the last word. If you listened to what he said, you were with the team. And if you worked hard, you were still with the team. But if you'd go your own way, you were in a lot of trouble."

Imlach cut Tim extra slack, not only because of his status as a team leader, but undoubtedly because of Lori's persistent objections. "I remember one time Tim was late for practice," says Dave Keon, "and we were all laughing because he was going to get fined. He came out on the ice and went over to Punch and gave him a note. It was a note from Lori: She was sorry Tim was late, but he had to do something around the home, and would Punch please excuse him. Punch said: That's okay, but don't let it happen again. That was the joke of the month— Lori had given Tim a note."

"Timmy used to take me on road trips occasionally," says Lori, "much to Punch's dismay." She once drove all the way to Detroit to see Tim, only to discover that the team was on its way back to Toronto. On one road trip, the Leafs were going to Los Angeles; Lori went ahead to visit friends who were also close to Punch and his wife Dodo. They all showed up at the airport to greet the team. "Punch comes by and says hello to our friends and ignored me completely. But he always ignored me. He never spoke to me at all. He would walk by me and avert his head. Of course, I was writing him these nasty letters as well."

Lori had launched a personal letter-writing campaign to vent her wrath at Imlach. She says Imlach never told Tim she was writing them until both Punch and Tim were no longer with Toronto. "I wouldn't have had the nerve when I first came up," she says. "In the days of Hap Day and Connie Smythe I didn't breathe out loud, never mind write a letter. It would have been cheeky. I got a little more self-confident after a while, with Tim's success. And I slowly became one of the older women on the team, and I took it upon myself to keep Punch in line."

Lori would never shed her feistiness when it came to standing up to management. Later in Tim's career, when he was playing for the New York Rangers, general manager Emile Francis tried to prevent a writer from interviewing players' wives about playoff pressure. Lori's response: the team has a contract with my husband, not with me. She defiantly gave the interview.

Her discontent during the Leaf days didn't stop with Punch. The kind of wild on-the-road behaviour that made for good "Tim tales" didn't go over nearly as well at home. Lori had no idea that Tim was smashing down hotel room doors with the Leafs. It was something Tim and his teammates kept quiet. When Tim—along with Bob Pulford— finally made headlines by being convicted of disturbing the peace in Quebec City during a preseason exhibition visit in 1962 (they had been kicking over large garbage cans in the middle of the night), Tim's penchant for occasional rowdiness on the road was finally made known to Lori. "I tried to call him but the hotel wouldn't put the calls through because reporters were trying to get to him. I was more than a little annoyed." But still the matter of hotel room doors remained hushed up.

Not that she hadn't seen Tim go through a few doors herself. "We went on a trip to Mexico, and the first night he broke down the hotel door. We had to replace the back door on our house at least three times, because every time he came in late I'd lock him out, so he came through the door." The kind of wild behaviour that is fodder for colourful anecdotes when they involve athletes on the road take on a different tone when placed in a domestic setting. Sally Baun, for one, was terrified of Tim.

Lori was also unhappy with George's Spaghetti House as a team hangout. "It was a cause for concern for a period of time. George's became a home away from home for Tim and the guys. You never knew when he was coming home. This was when success was new and they were either celebrating or drowning their sorrows. Tim came home with paintings—they're all gone—he brought from George's. It got to the point where there were beginning to be problems." The back door to the house was locked. New doors were purchased.

It would be wrong to assume that the Horton household was a model of suburban sobriety, with Lori manning the barricades. It hosted numerous raucous parties for team members and off-ice friends. "I got sent up to my room a lot," says Jeri-

Lynn. "The party's getting a little wild—girls, go to your rooms. I remember waking up in the morning and there were bodies everywhere. They played hard and they partied hard. It was a different life."

Although the house party at Ron Joyce's in the summer of 1965 had ended on a sour note, it was a turning point in Tim Horton's quixotic search for a successful off-ice business. Ron Joyce would turn out to be the steady partner that had always eluded him. Jim Charade was not going to be able to stick with it.

Tim's business dreams were failing outright or sputtering dangerously. The Horton burger chain was falling to pieces and the donut venture, while showing potential, wasn't without its problems. "Ron Joyce was unhappy that as a franchisee he wasn't getting as much help as he should," says Jim Charade, "but we weren't organised for it. We had problems like all small businesses. We needed capital, and when you don't have capital you take shortcuts, and that will kill you."

Having borrowed from his credit union to get the first store, Joyce went to his mother, his sister and others to fund his purchase of the second outlet. "The store was built," says Joyce, "but there were some financial problems, and the suppliers wouldn't release the furniture to them [Tim Donut Ltd.], so for some reason they released it to me. I think they'd become disillusioned with Jim a little.

"Jim was the idea guy," Joyce emphasises. "You've got to give him a lot of credit. The Tim Horton chain wouldn't be here today without him. Even though he couldn't execute, he was the guy who got it started. The one who made it run was me.

"It became very clear after the second store opened that there was no input from Jim, and he became a source of frustration for me, because I'd look for help, he'd come in, and with his limited knowledge of the business he would do what he could do, but when he got in a corner he would just have to leave. I was always struggling, trying to find my way through this business that I knew nothing about. Tim knew nothing whatsoever, and Jim a little bit."

"I could see by the end of the year that I wasn't making any money at this," says Charade. "I was married, and I had a son, and my wife had to work. I decided to take a job while I worked on the donut business."

Jim and his family made their customary appearance at the Horton household over Christmas. It was also the Christmas that Tim made a gift of a kitten to Charade's son André—the cat had started out as a Horton pet, but it was keeping Tim awake at night by scratching at the bedroom door. Fluffy was part of the Charade household for ten years, and Tim would sometimes make impromptu visits to the Charades, announcing "I've just come to see Fluffy" as he entered.

But the calamities of the fast-food businesses pressed down on Charade. Amid the Christmas cheer with Tim, "I said, 'Jesus, I'm not going to make it this way. I'm working night and day and nobody realises it and they think I'm screwing around anyway....' But when you have to run away from bill collectors and meet payrolls, and cheques are bouncing, what do you do? You have to rob Peter to pay Paul. It was not the easiest time."

It was becoming clear to everyone that there was

no longer a role for Jim Charade. "I signed over. I resigned as president [of Timanjim Ltd.] and surrendered my end of it. Tim would own it, as long as I wouldn't have the debt. Even at that the restaurants were closing, step by step. I had to go to these examinations with an arbitrator. They wanted to see the books. I was not going bankrupt. I was surrendering the charter and just saying that we couldn't make it, unless the creditors could make some other rearrangement. People from the coffee company, Mother Parker's, Jo-Lo Corp., would be there. And that was rough, to do that and to try to operate also."

"When things happened at the end, I think Jim just did what he thought he had to do," says Lori.

When the smoke cleared, Jim Charade was gone, and Tim Donut Ltd. had become the property of Tim and Lori Horton, with the equity split neatly between them. Charade had walked away from his equity in the donut side of the operation to extricate himself from the disaster of the burger enterprise, Timanjim Ltd.

Charade landed on his feet with Mr. Donut, living in Toronto while selling franchises in the United States. Tim tried to carry on without a partner, and managed to set up a third outlet in Kitchener–Waterloo on his own. Dore Carnahan was the senior Dairy Queen operator in Canada, probably the first one in Canada. Tim negotiated a deal with Carnahan to participate in the development of a property Carnahan had at the corner of University and Weaver. There was already a Dairy Queen on the site, and Carnahan leased out space for a variety store, and a Tim Hortons outlet. But Tim had no operator for the donut store, and Joyce ended up stepping in to run it for him. "I was living in Stoney Creek," says Joyce, "trying to run my two stores in Hamilton, plus my Dairy Queen, plus that store. It was one of the worst years of my life." Eventually, Tim and Ron found a franchisee, another ex-cop from Hamilton named Pat McGrinder, who still runs the franchise, although the outlet has since moved to a new location.

Joyce was not prepared to continue like this, as a franchisee scrambling to help Tim run his business while trying to take care of his own outlets. Joyce wanted to be a partner and nothing less. Tim demurred, and Lori was not happy with the idea of giving up her half of the business, but Joyce was persistent.

According to Allan Stanley, "Tim used to say, 'If we were to go into business and dedicate ourselves the same way we do to hockey, you've got to be a success, because you give 100 per cent. You live it, you eat it, you dream about it every night.'" But, as Stanley notes, as a hockey player Tim was only able to dedicate one day a week to the business during the regular season. "Monday was his day for business when he was playing hockey. He told Punch, he told anybody: Monday I don't skate. On that day you couldn't find him. He took off."

In hindsight, it would not have been possible for Tim to carry on without a partner. As Stanley says, Tim always had a partner in his business ventures, someone to take care of it while he played hockey.

The best partnership candidate to emerge was Ron Joyce. "He needed somebody who knew a little about the business," says Joyce, "and I was working there all the time. Once Tim accepted the fact that I wasn't going to stay there just as an operator, that it had to be more than that, because he wasn't contributing anything—he wasn't, because he didn't know anything about the business—once he accepted that, we became partners. That was done very amiably, and we became very good friends."

"Tim certainly did everything he could to develop the business," says Stanley, "and fortunately in his donut thing he had a guy who said he was happy to do the work, and he was a man of his word and did that. They worked well together, as far as I know."

Joyce says he and Tim shook hands on the partnership at the Leafs' training camp in Peterborough in the fall of 1966. They agreed to split the equity, with Tim president and Ron vice-president. It would be several months before the paperwork creating an official partnership was completed on December 1, 1966, with Joyce buying Lori's half of Tim Donut Ltd. for $12,000 and securing a right of first refusal on Tim's half for $12,500.

Between the handshake and the final paperwork, Tim was dealt a considerable personal blow. Gord Hannigan was felled by a heart attack on November 16, two months shy of his thirty-seventh birthday.

"I remember the death well," says Lori. "I think Gord had visited maybe six months previous, and they went to the restaurant [trade] show together. Tim was inconsolable. He cried for a few hours, and he wasn't a crying person." Gord's son Mark remembers Tim going to great lengths to hold a wake for Gord, attended by his widow Anne as she headed back to Pittsburgh to visit family.

All at once, at a critical stage in his business's development, Tim had lost both a close friend and a confidante. Gord had always been a phone call away, ready to provide advice and act as a sounding board. Tim's final decision to sign on a new partner could not have been more timely.

"The idea was there, it was good, it could work, but it needed a lot of work and a lot of assistance," says Jim Charade. "Ron was able to come in, and he had money available from people... When Ron came in, he was strong, and when he did something, he did it perfect. He took the ball and ran with it and he scored. Maybe I was able to snap the ball. That was my end of it. You needed somebody to conduct the play, and Ron Joyce was the guy."

Chapter 18

Chain Reaction

Ron Joyce was absolutely committed to the donut chain. He was bright, a detail man, and ambitious—more ambitious, it was generally felt, than Tim was about the chain. "They were different people," Jim Charade notes. "Tim was soft, and wanted to enjoy life." What has remained undisputed over the years, even in the course of Lori Horton's suit, was that Ron Joyce was a good partner for Tim. The business would never have grown and prospered the way it did had Tim simply found a caretaker manager or partner to run it for him.

"I don't think Tim thought the donut business would ever get to the size it is today," says Russ Gioffrey. "He wasn't looking for prestige, to be recognised like Conrad Black. With Tim it was something to do to keep himself occupied. He always let Ron Joyce run the business, even though he had control—he told me he had control. Ron I think had a lot of respect for Tim, not just as a hockey player but as a human being."

Charade didn't think Tim really appreciated the potential of the business, not like Joyce—or himself, for that matter. "That's why I was in it. I think people thought I was crazy. When I would order some of these things for fillings, people would say, 'What the hell are you doing? Donuts are donuts.'"

Which is not to say that Tim was disinterested. As

Charade remembers, Tim was enthusiastic about the business, and Allan Stanley recalls Tim taking the business's ledgers on the road with him. But Tim's enthusiasm during the first few years was focused on the burger side of the business, not the donut side. That was where the majority of his restaurants were, after all, where he had his partnership with Jim until Tim Donut was formed in January 1965, and both Jim Charade and Billy Harris remember Tim's active interest in moving more upmarket in the red meat realm. "He really had his mind set on a steak house," says Charade. He says Tim was impressed with the Tad's chain in New York City, where for $1.59 you got a steak, and then moved through a self-serve buffet, loading on salad and baked potato. "During the last couple of years that Tim and I were teammates," Billy Harris has written, "we started dropping into some of the fast-food outlets in Chicago and New York in particular, for a coffee after church. At that time you could see the proprietor barbecuing steaks through the window, and for 99 cents, you could buy a steak dinner. We wouldn't eat, but Tim would make a sketch of the floorplan showing the kitchen, tables, serving area and cash register, and he would estimate seating capacity."

"On the road," says Stanley, "there was always a restaurant he wanted to see. He had his interest in fast food for a long time. I used to go with him. We'd go in, and he'd talk to the owner and ask them about their business."

Charade says that the steak house plans even got as far as picking a potential site: the Rutherford's Drugs lunch counter on Yonge Street, across from Simpson's. (Lori Horton recalls that the steak

house would have been developed in association
with Benny Winbaum, who had the Steak and
Burger chain.) But the steak house never happened, the burger chain went down in charbroiled
flames, and Tim's retirement plans came to be
pinned exclusively on donuts—and, by extension,
on Ron Joyce.

Joyce's appreciation of Tim wasn't clouded by
being a star-struck hockey fan, since he didn't pay
much attention to the game. (He had played football as a young man.) "I thought that Tim was honest, fair, intelligent, astute," says Joyce. "He seemed
to be in so many ways easygoing. He very rarely
spoke ill of anybody." Yet Joyce also remembers Tim
as anything but a pushover. "He was really at his
best when someone was doing a number on him, if
he thought he was being taken advantage of." Tim's
little notebook of Esquire Room pool debts surfaces—he never forgot who owed him what. "When
I first got involved with him as a partner," says Joyce,
"he insisted we share the same office. Our desks
faced each other." The idea was that the two men
would have to look one another in the eye when
they were working together. The arrangement
brings to mind Tim's room at St. Mike's, where he
would study opposite Don Rope and Ted Carlton.

Like Jim Charade, Ron Joyce found Tim to be
someone who shunned the limelight. "It didn't
bother me, but I think it bothered him a little bit.
When we were doing a grand opening in Belleville
we announced he was going to be there. He had an
awful time. He was very uncomfortable, and he
showed it."

The reason it didn't bother Joyce was that he
brought a different business strategy to the partner-

ship from Charade's. Jim had been attracted to Tim as a celebrity around whom he could build a business venture. When Joyce came along, the business venture—the donut side—was so fundamentally sound as a retail concept that celebrity became entirely secondary. It was nice to have the fame of Tim the hockey player to draw business, and the appearance of Tim and his teammates at a store opening guaranteed a large crowd, but celebrity wasn't the be-all and end-all of donut retailing and franchising. The day after an opening, there were no hockey players, and something had to keep the crowd coming back. Tim, moreover, was seriously considering retirement. (Harris writes that it was on Tim's mind when he was scouting restaurants on road trips in 1964.) After a few years off the ice, Tim would be just another semi-celebrated sports figure; in a few more years, he would be little more than a name to the new breed of fans who had never seen him play. And if Tim wasn't working constantly at maintaining his public image once off the ice, there would be little reason to make his sporting fame the focal point of a long-range business plan.

Joyce would come to play down the hockey-star persona of the chain, even while Tim was still alive. He says Tim agreed, and it's easy to see why he would, given that Tim so dreaded the times when he was called upon to be a public figure for the sake of business. "The name was not important," says Joyce. "It was operations. How do you make it work? How do you make it happen? We developed the manual, the systems, because there was nobody there to teach us."

When Joyce and Horton formally joined as partners, Tim was in the middle of the 66/67 season,

when Imlach's Leafs were mounting their last great
reach for the Stanley Cup. In the on-ice celebrations after the Leafs did win, as captured by the
CBC, Tim is typically far from the limelight. The
players eagerly gather around captain George
Armstrong for a photo with the cup. When they dis-
perse, it can be seen that Tim is far in the back, off
to the right, and he skates away with a relieved,
now-that-that's-over-with look.

Tim put his Stanley Cup earnings toward the
chain's fourth store, the third one in Hamilton.
Joyce calls it "the turning point" in the pitching and
yawing saga of Tim Donut Ltd. The store also served
as the partnership's first venture into real estate. Sy
Freedman was a partner in the produce wholesaler
Netkin's, for whom Joyce had moonlighted as a
truck driver while on the Hamilton police force.
Freedman told him he had a "perfect location": a
wedge-shaped lot at King Street West and South
Oval in Hamilton's middle-class Westdale neighbourhood. The lot must have made Tim think of his
family's service station property back in North Bay.
Freedman presented the partners with a complicated lease–purchase agreement. Tim Donut would
have to build on the land, and they would lease the
land from Freedman for a five-year period, after
which they could buy the land at a predetermined
price. The rent was incremental, and would be
applied against the purchase price. They agreed to
sign the deal, but when the Westdale Community
Council caught wind of it, loud objections were
raised. The donut shop would occupy the land on
which the council had been planting flowers for the
past twelve years. But Freedman was tired of paying
$500 a year in property taxes on a slice of land that

wasn't generating any income, and the forces of donut progress won out. That May, Tim threw himself into building the store, just as he had built his house in the summer of 1965. It was something of a bonding exercise for the two men. "We had a lot of fun with that store," Joyce recalls. Tim decided he would rather get the store built—it was completed in late August—than report to training camp, and Imlach called constantly from Peterborough to make sure he was coming.

Early in the construction, Tim was digging in the footings when a group of schoolchildren heading to the library behind the store walked by. "He was all muddy and had rubber boots on," says Joyce. "One of the children recognised him and said, 'There's Tim Horton!' And the teacher said, 'Yes, and if you don't go to school you'll end up digging a ditch just like him.'"

Joyce remembers Tim being a serious holdout at training-camp time. There was a contract already prepared for him, but he refused to sign it. Tim bundled up a selection of donut scraps in a box and forwarded the package to Punch at training camp with a note attached which read: "With donuts like these, who needs hockey?" Tim did finally report, and Joyce feels that his holdout brought him his first serious pay raise. The three-year contract he ultimately signed paid him $42,500 per season, virtually doubling his salary.

Tim was famous for his dislike of training camp. For players like him, holding out was sometimes little more than a means of avoiding the bad-tasting medicine of getting into shape for the new season. "Our camps were always so long," says Larry Hillman. "With the Leaf organization, they started the first day after the Labour Day weekend and went for five or six weeks and then maybe we made a tour across western Canada to Vancouver. The older players would rather have had a two- or three-week training camp, and then start the season. The five- or six-week camp was something you tried to skip around."

Stores five and six were also located in the greater Hamilton area. Store five was built on the site of a mothballed Shell station on Plains Road in Burlington. The partners paid about $35,000 for the property; two former Hamilton policemen did the renovations. Store six represented their biggest investment to date. They paid $50,000 for land at the corner of Mohawk Road and Upper James on Hamilton mountain. This was a major intersection in the city's southern suburbs, and the partners had high hopes for the site. "It was going to be our number one store," says Joyce, "and it turned out to be an absolute dog for the first year or two. It ended up being number one, but we really hurt."

People who knew both men consistently say that their contrasting personalities worked to their advantage. Tim was more laid-back than Joyce, who was driven and somewhat excitable. Joyce's personality had the edge that was needed to push the company forward, while Tim had a way of (as Joyce puts it) "simplifying": of cutting through the panic or the frustration and keeping the crisis at hand in perspective.

This quality came to the fore when they were building their seventh location, out on Queenston Road on Hamilton's eastern border with the town of Stoney Creek. A piece of property was available next door to Gulliver's Travels, a motor hotel owned by two partners: Tom Gulliver, who used to be the sheriff for Stoney Creek's police chief, and Ian Fraser, a former minor-pro hockey player. The property belonged to Gulliver, and Fraser had designs on it, but Joyce beat him to it.

It was a great buy, but it stretched the cash flow of Tim Donut to breaking point. "The money crunch was coming down on us," says Joyce. "Everything had to work. We had to get the building permit in a hurry, we had to get the building up. It was bleeding us." When Joyce examined the building plans, he noticed that the main window would look out on an apartment building. He decided to have the plan flipped so that the view was out across the lush expanse of the Gulliver's Travels front lawn. It was the kind of attention to detail that was typical of Joyce. He told Tim about the change—it was Tim's customary role to deal with the contracting for the store fixtures.

"I went all through it with Tim. Somewhere along he forgot to do it. He screwed up." When the fixtures came, they wouldn't fit the building. In a few years, such a mistake would be an annoyance, delaying a store opening while the fixtures were reordered, but with store seven it meant a delay in cash flow the company couldn't afford. "The problem was no money. The moving truck is there with all the equipment, and we have to find a place to store the stuff. I'm livid." Joyce phoned up Tim and tore strips off him.

"Tim said, 'Ron, hold it. As I see it, we've got two choices. Either I'll drive down to the Skyway Bridge and jump off if that solves the problem, or I'll order new equipment. Now it's your choice. You tell me what to do.' He got it back in perspective. He didn't really lose his cool, and he got a little humour in there."

They may have had a manual, and they may have had a system, and they may have had a vision, but in one important respect, not much had changed from Jim Charade's days. "All the time we were doing this stuff," Joyce explains, "we had no money. We were borrowing it, signing notes. I was the one doing it, and Horton would get mad at me. It was a snowball effect.

"A whole lot of things we were doing were, not dishonest, but probably unorthodox. There were things we did to get money. We'd sell something and then mortgage it. It was never to defraud anybody, but we probably shouldn't have done that. We were just trying to get money to get the chain going.

"We were borrowing money off Barney Rosenblatt in Hamilton, and then he'd take a mortgage out. Mortgage rates then were 8 or 9 or 10 per cent. We were paying 18, 19 per cent because we were such high risk." (In September 1969, Tim complained in the *Toronto Star*, "The price of money these days is ridiculous. Why, on good, solid mortgages, people are demanding as much as 20 per cent.")

"Harold Ballard claimed that there wouldn't be a Tim Hortons chain without him," says Joyce. "I don't think that's quite true. But at one time during that period, because of some of the things I was doing, Tim had to borrow money. I really believed we could make it happen. Money was an intrusion or a problem for us, but I figured there was some way we could do it. Tim was probably more realistic, and he went to Ballard and said he needed some money for a lot of these things." Ballard and Horton discussed the matter while the Leafs were riding the train from Toronto to Montreal for a game against the Canadiens. "Ballard said, 'Go down to my bank, and just ask for it. They'll give you some money.' So he went down and signed a note for it. I think it was $25,000. Ballard said, 'Your word is good. I don't want a mortgage. Just take it. Just pay it back.' It wasn't a lot of money, but it got us out of a cash flow crunch."

Tim Horton and Ron Joyce weren't the only people in the business of pushing franchises. After decades of turning aside entreaties, the National Hockey League doubled in size in 67/68 by adding six new teams. Once a closed circle of arena owners who didn't want more teams—particularly out west—that would dilute earnings through travel expenses, the NHL suddenly joined the same world in which Tim and Ron were operating. Hockey was going into the franchise business, pushing itself as a product, conquering new markets. The NHL set out to be a dominant brand, coast to coast. The competitors weren't tier-two hockey leagues; they were the professional sports with an overlapping schedule, such as basketball and football, which were chasing the same discretionary consumer dollars and television audiences.

When the six new franchises were added, sponsored amateur teams and territorial rights were done away with to break up the monopolies on talent enjoyed by the most powerful of the Original Six franchises. Recruitment via reserve lists was replaced by recruitment via the universal draft. On June 12, 1969, nineteen-year-old Rejean Houle was

the first player selected in the league's new amateur
draft (a draft of non-reserve amateurs had been in
place since 1963). Eighty-four players were divvied
up that day at Montreal's Queen Elizabeth Hotel,
and Houle, a star with the Montreal Junior
Canadiens, was chosen by the Montreal Canadiens,
a parent club now only in name.

The arrival of the universal draft marked a para-
digm shift in the game the professionals of the
Original Six era had come to know. Almost
overnight, the essential fabric of the hockey system
unravelled and was reknitted into a new cloth. Total
NHL teams doubled, and kept growing; the
American league changed rapidly from a tier-two
professional loop with teams that had ties to NHL
clubs to an unabashed development league whose
essential purpose was to serve as a finishing school
for the NHL's new stars.

But perhaps the greatest change came in the way
the players related to the owners. The fresh recruit
was no longer signed as the property of a particular
club at age sixteen. He would no longer become de
facto property of a professional club while still in
Pee-Wee through that club's sponsorship of a small
town's hockey program. No longer would a player
who signed a C-form at age sixteen play with an
affiliated Junior club and have his amateur career
controlled and directed by a team like the Maple
Leafs. While there was a whiff of freedom in the
change, it also meant that young players were not
nurtured by a particular club, instilled with its
pride. No seventeen-year-old would ever again
know, as Tim Horton had, what it was like to be part
of Conn Smythe's development system: to be
coached by a former star like Joe Primeau in a

sponsored Junior team; to enjoy the perks of Conn Smythe's Gardens as a young man in high school, entering the sacred arena through the back door, accepting invitations from the Old Man to sit in his personal box or hang out in the press box as the Leafs entertained the hometown crowd. No teenager would ever again see his future mapped out before him as vividly as Tim had, or would ever exude that confident sense of destiny with which he had so impressed Don Rope while they were at St. Mike's together.

The draft would now decide, at the eleventh hour of their amateur careers, where they would play for a living. No scout would come calling with a sheaf of forms and rolls of bills. No one would ask him to come to North Bay or St. Catharines or Sudbury or Peterborough for a tryout. No team owner would load a player in his car the way Conn Smythe did with Tim Horton and personally drive him to training camp after the ink had dried on his first professional contract. The draft would help prevent the richer clubs from dominating the talent pool with their larger, better financed scouting staffs, and deny clubs like the Maple Leafs the right of first refusal for any amateur playing within their territory. A talented young player raised in the greater Toronto area was no longer destined to wear the Maple Leaf uniform. As onerous as the old system had been, there was no denying the sense of belonging, of team pride, that it could instil in a young player. From June 12, 1969, the best young amateurs in the country strove to attract the attention of scouts in hope that they would draft them, not in the hope that they would peel off ten ten-dollar bills, show them a C-form, and say, "Sign this, kid, and you'll be a Maple Leaf some day."

And in 1967 the NHL Players Association was born, in the process creating a new hub of power in the game in the form of Toronto lawyer Alan Eagleson.

Although Tim had been one of the eighteen Maple Leafs to vote to certify the stillborn players association of 1957 as their collective bargaining unit, he did not support the successful association drive a decade later. He was one of the "old guard," which included Johnny Bower and Allan Stanley, who remained loyal to Imlach, who was reduced to apoplexy by the idea of a union. Ironically, Tim has become something of a hero of the union drive through an anecdote in the book *Net Worth*, which described how, at the start of the 67/68 season, after the association had been successfully formed, Imlach couldn't resist one more kick at the despised cat. He banished its chief Toronto organiser, Bob Pulford, to the Gardens ice to do laps while he lectured the rest of the team back in the dressing room on the evils of collective bargaining. Tim reputedly got up in disgust and joined Pulford on the ice; the rest of the team followed, and Imlach's opposition was effectively nullified.

Allan Stanley and Johnny Bower say this never happened. "I read that and I was trying to remember that, but I don't," adds Dave Keon, who was one of the last Leafs to sign an association membership card, and whose scepticism at the time challenges the notion that resistance to the association was simply a matter of old-guard players feeling they owed Imlach their careers and prosperity.

"They wanted Timmy to join the association," says Bower, "but he laid off, and laid off. There were about five of us who wouldn't. I was one of them, and Timmy, George Armstrong, Allan Stanley, and I can't remember who the other guys were. [Keon was one, and so was Marcel Pronovost.] I remember Punch was very, very against the association. All the owners were. One day Punch came in the dressing room and he was really upset about the agents and the association and he said: 'All right, I want everybody that's involved in the association to go on the ice. The rest of the guys that aren't involved in it, stay in the dressing room.' So naturally, the guys that were involved with the association, three-quarters of the team, went on the ice, and there was just a handful of us guys left. Eventually we joined up. When things started up, we had to, I guess."

"I don't recall anything like that," Allan Stanley says of the incident where Tim supposedly went to Pulford's rescue. "Punch would have sent about six guys out there to skate alone. All of Eagleson's school buddies, they were the ones that brought him in. Pulford was the main one. They were humping Eagleson. The rest of us didn't know him [Eagleson] from a hole in the ground. I doubt that scene. I've never seen Punch single out one man and discipline him in front of anybody, ever. When he gave anybody hell, he gave the whole team hell. He didn't point his finger at any one player."

Lori Horton is equally sceptical of the story. "I don't see that happening, either, because Tim was a holdout from the association. He and Davey Keon were probably the last two to sign. Actually, what Tim said back then came true. 'You put Alan Eagleson in there—who's going to get him out?' He didn't like Alan. Tim couldn't stand him." Although Keon, for one, cannot remember Tim voicing a dislike for the

players' association president, others, like Bob
Baun, agree that Alan Eagleson was not Tim
Horton's favourite person.[1] Lori says the only reason Tim finally did join the association was to take
advantage of its dental plan for his teenage daughters, who were entering the braces years.

"There were players on the team who had signed,
and there were players who hadn't, and it wasn't
that the players who hadn't were against it," says
Keon. "They wanted to know what it was about.
They weren't going to sign on because somebody
told them it was the thing to do. I remember people
saying, 'Well, let's have the guy [Eagleson] come
and talk to us, and we'll make our decision, not
because so-and-so said it was the thing to do.'" Keon
says Eagleson never did come and give that talk.

In 67/68, the season that followed the formation
of the players' association, Bob Pulford lost the "A"
on his sweater (although he would regain it the
next season). Allan Stanley still had his, George
Armstrong was still captain, and they were joined by
two new assistant captains: Tim Horton and Dave
Keon.

The changes Tim Horton and his teammates had to
absorb in the few brief seasons following their 1967
Stanley Cup victory were the greatest the game had
ever experienced, far greater than those that arrived
with the end of the Second World War. The old
regime was gone. While the Original Six franchises
would retain an undeniable cachet, they were now
part of a league hell-bent on becoming a continent-
wide phenomenon. If kids from Copper Cliff in the
late-1940s were scarcely conscious of the Boston
Bruins, in the late-1960s kids from all over had to

become conscious of teams in places like Oakland, California, with garish uniforms and strange monickers like the Seals. But if a kid could put up with playing with a seal, or a penguin or some other baffling variation on sporting heraldry, emblazoned on his chest, he had a far better chance at playing hockey professionally than his predecessors of the late-1940s ever had. And he would be paid far better, with perhaps an agent now representing him. Suddenly there were too many teams and not enough talent to go around. With six teams in both the National and American leagues and stricter limits on total players per team, there had been little more than two hundred jobs available. By 1972 the American league had eleven teams, the National league fourteen, and the new, upstart World Hockey Association, twelve. Job openings had nearly tripled, and players who never would have had a major-league career in the Original Six days, and veterans who would have long before been put out to pasture in a tier-two professional or a Canadian Senior league, enjoyed several high-paying seasons with the new order.

For the players who had toiled for mean wages in the Original Six era, the seasons that followed the Leafs' 1967 Stanley Cup victory were like manna from heaven. If their bodies could just hang in for a few more years, they could bank more money playing a handful of seasons in a city that scarcely understood the game than they had in their entire preceding career. Players who had always taken to the ice fundamentally because they loved the game and the roar of the crowd were suddenly lacing up their skates in no small part for the money. Who cared if they were wearing a uniform that had no

heritage, no meaning, no heart? Who cared if no
one in Houston seemed to know what a puck was?
This was their chance—the chance they had never
imagined—to cash in, to make the kind of money
they had always thought they deserved.

Everything about the game seemed to be different. The owners could still get their message out
through media toadies, but the players themselves
were now a collective force in the game, partly
through the players' union, partly through the dilu-
tion of talent that enhanced the market value of the
skilled veterans, and partly through the option of
the WHA that allowed the stars to dictate their
terms to their employers in a way that would have
been unimaginable ten years earlier. Hockey was no
Sunday picnic, but neither was it boot camp any
more. The game still had its share of tyrants and
egomaniacs at management level, but now there
was room and opportunity for egomaniacs on the
players' side of the fence. A "difficult" player could
no longer be dealt with by burying him in the
minors. With his agent by his side, he could
demand to be traded, and get his way.

Even before the Original Six era ended, the
Maple Leafs of Conn Smythe were on the edge of
extinction. Only the building remained. The transfer of power had begun with the Major's withdrawal
from day-to-day management in favour of his son
Stafford and the other members of the "Silver
Seven" board in 1957. Four years later, St. Michael's
College cancelled its Majors program, and the Leafs
lost a vital link to their past. The elimination of
sponsored amateur clubs with the introduction of
the universal amateur draft in 1969 also cut the
Leafs loose from the Marlies system. St. Mike's had

given the championship Leafs Tim Horton, Dick
Duff, Dave Keon, Frank Mahovlich and (by way of
Detroit) Red Kelly. The Marlies had produced Bob
Baun, Carl Brewer, Bob Pulford and Billy Harris.
Billy Harris fingers two more factors that sapped
the Leafs of their glory. When Maple Leaf Gardens
agreed in 1966 to host a boxing match featuring
Cassius Clay, who had dodged the Vietnam draft,
the Major angrily resigned his directorship. And
during the glory years of the 1960s, when the Leafs
won four Stanley Cups, the Major's Gardens had its
atmosphere irrevocably changed as 3,400 more
seats were added.

But the heaviest body blows were landed immediately after the Leafs won the 1967 cup. In a matter of months, the twelve-team league would debut
and every new franchise would draw its twenty players from the ranks of the established teams. The
Leafs, like the other Original Six teams, were only
allowed to protect eleven players. It was a gut-
wrenching scenario for Leaf fans, a litmus test of
loyalty on the part of Leaf management. Imlach
would claim that the only reason rookie Mike
Walton was protected was because he had married
Stafford Smythe's niece that spring.

Imlach stood by the core of his Stanley Cup
defence, protecting Tim Horton, Allan Stanley,
Marcel Pronovost and Larry Hillman. But he left
Bob Baun unprotected; Baun had been benched
during the 1967 Stanley Cup as the pairing of
Hillman and Pronovost shared the workload with
Horton and Stanley. The Oakland Seals, whose new
coach and general manager was former Leaf Bert
Olmstead (who had been left unprotected by
Imlach after the 1962 Stanley Cup at age thirty-five,

and retired with some bitterness), snapped up his
rights. Eddie Shack was sold to Boston for $100,000
and the rights to Murray Oliver. The unkindest cut
of all was Imlach's decision to leave his team captain, George Armstrong, off the protected list.
"Well, heck," Imlach would explain, "you know he
was nearly thirty-seven and all the forwards I was
going to protect were a lot younger." Nearly ten
years after trying to trade Armstrong, Imlach as
good as left him off the team. But the expansion
teams passed on the Chief, and he played on in
Toronto for four more seasons, outlasting Imlach in
the process. Red Kelly retired after the 1967 cup,
and went to Los Angeles to coach the Kings,
resplendent, if dubiously so, in maroon and gold.

Larry Hillman's survival of the 1967 houseclean-
ing was a special triumph for him. It had taken
Hillman several frustrating years to find a place with
the Leafs. He'd broken into the NHL just a month
after his eighteenth birthday in March 1955, called
up by Detroit from the Hamilton Junior Tiger Cubs
of the OHA Junior A for a six-game tryout. He
signed his first of many one-year contracts: $1,500
for signing and $6,000 to play, $900 of which went
straight to the pension fund. After three seasons
with the Detroit organization, he was traded to
Boston, where he spent three more seasons and got
to know Allan Stanley; he followed Stanley to
Toronto when picked up by Punch Imlach for
60/61.

He played nearly a full season as a Leaf, but then
badly separated his shoulder. A tendon was transplanted from his leg to strap his shoulder back
together (Sam Bettio underwent the same operation while in the American league), but it proved

tight, and even today Hillman has limited mobility in his left arm. For most of the next four seasons, while the Leafs were winning three straight Stanley Cups, Hillman was a Rochester American, and won a Calder Cup as the Americans' captain with coach Joe Crozier in 64/65. But first he had to serve as a "charitable donation" from the Leafs to Eddie Shore's Springfield Indians of the American league in 62/63. Playing for Eddie Shore "was an experience, and maybe a worthwhile one in a player's career, because it certainly made you appreciate any team that you were with after being there." Finally, in 65/66, he made it back full-time to the Leafs. When Carl Brewer had said to hell with the Leafs and Imlach and quit in the 64/65 season, he left Bob Baun without a steady defence partner. "When Brewer left, Baun didn't have somebody carrying the puck out for him," says Hillman. "He was a tough, rugged hitter from the old school, and that was his big asset." Baun's presence was reduced to forty-four games in 65/66 and fifty-four games in 66/67 as Hillman and Marcel Pronovost became the complementary defensive pairing to Horton and Stanley.

The 66/67 Leaf season, says Hillman, "was the first year I got to really appreciate being a full part of it. I played the most ice time of the '67 Stanley Cup of any Leaf. I had more than half an hour of ice time per game. I killed over half an hour of penalties," he proudly recalls of his playoff effort in the semifinals against Chicago and the finals against Montreal, "and never had one goal scored against us."

When Hillman reported to training camp in the fall of '67 to negotiate a new contract, he had done his homework. In addition to mapping out his playing record, he had touched base with a number of

fellow defencemen around the league to find out
how they had made out. His younger brother
Wayne (with fourteen points in sixty-seven games in
66/67) was signing for $21,000 as a defenceman in
New York, and he decided to ask the same of
Toronto. The Leafs offered him $19,000. Hillman
offered to split the difference and come down to
$20,000. The Leafs, too, offered to split the differ-
ence and come up to $19,500. With $500 between
them, Hillman held out.

The Leafs told him he would be fined $100 for
every day he failed to report, then let twenty-four
days pass before bringing in Clarence Campbell as
arbitrator. The league president showed up at the
Royal York Hotel in Toronto and told Hillman he
would make $19,500, less the $2,400 in fines he had
racked up. He left the hotel with a salary of
$17,100, which was still more than he'd ever made
as a Maple Leaf. That season, Tim began playing on
his new three-year contract of $42,500 per season.

The next season, Hillman was left unprotected by
the Leafs. At the intraleague draft on June 12, 1968,
he embarked on a poker-chip's-eye view of the
National Hockey League. The Rangers picked him
up from the Leafs and placed him on their reserve
list, but before the day was over the Minnesota
North Stars had drafted him from the Rangers. That
November, the Penguins claimed him on waivers
from Minnesota, and dealt him the same day to
Montreal in exchange for some cash and Jean-Guy
Lagace. The following June, Philadelphia drafted
him from Montreal and two days later traded him to
Los Angeles in exchange for Larry Mickey. Allan
Stanley, Tim's defence partner for ten seasons, was
also left off the protected list in 1968. After playing

one season with the expansion Philadelphia Flyers, he retired to Bobcaygeon in the Kawartha Lakes to run the Beehive Lodge and hockey school.

In 1968, Frank Mahovlich's career with the Leafs ended. His nerves were so badly shot playing for Punch Imlach that the Leafs dealt him to Detroit. Mahovlich was relieved to be away from Imlach, and as it happened his best seasons by far in the NHL lay ahead of him, as a Red Wing and then as a Canadien.

The social revolution of the sixties was catching up with hockey just as hockey was going through its own revolution—expansion, the arrival of the players' association and the replacement of the reserve list with the universal draft. The absurdities of generational clashes erupted as Punch Imlach had to contend with a players' association he despised, the agents that stepped between him and his charges and the changing standards in dress and grooming of the era. The crew cuts and Sunday-best suits were on their way out; bell-bottoms, loud shirts and long hair were showing up. Imlach was incensed when goaltender Bruce Gamble arrived from Tulsa with bushy sideburns nesting on his cheeks.

"Imlach didn't want to change with the times," says Hillman, who was thirty in his final season with the Leafs. "As soon as we got off the plane on a road trip, the younger guys were flipping off the white shirt and tie and putting on a turtleneck, because that was the rage then. They didn't want to be told what to do, on and off the ice. You had to be respectable and represent the Maple Leafs organization, but it was getting to where twenty-four hours a day they were telling you what to do, and

Imlach wouldn't change. That's why younger coaches probably had more success than he did at the end
[of his Leaf tenure]. But he was one of the best general managers and coaches for getting the mileage
out of hockey players at the end of their line."

Tim did not quite join the Age of Aquarius, but
he did finally give up his crew cut and grow his hair
respectably long. He explained that his teenaged
daughters had been hounding him about doing
something about his hair—with his lantern jaw,
heavy brow and twenty seasons' worth of scars, he
made them think of Frankenstein's monster. "We
made him grow his hair longer," Jeri-Lynn agrees.
"It was embarrassing—scars everywhere and his
brushcut. There were scars on his head you could
see through his hair. He finally grew it, and he
looked a heck of a lot better."

"I think because other players let their hair grow
longer, he just changed to be one of them," says
Hillman, "to show he wasn't totally from the old
school, that he could change with the times."

His outer appearance as a whole changed. "He
dressed like crap for the longest time," says Jeri-
Lynn. "I think he was colour-blind." He shed his
indifference to the contents of his closet. Now shoes
mattered to him, and suits. He had the money to
dress himself stylishly, and now he was going to. "He
went from being a shy northern boy to being a very
sophisticated businessman who knew what he wanted," says Jeri-Lynn. "He came out of his shell."

Dressing the part of a thriving entrepreneur was
entirely appropriate: by 1970 Tim Donut was a business of consequence, with twenty-two stores,
perched on the edge of becoming a serious force in

franchising. The future for the business was all the brighter because of the excellent relationship between its partners. Tim seemed as impressed with Ron as Ron was with Tim. "They were very close," says Dick Trainor, who was still practising law in Sudbury—his appointment to the provincial bench would come later—when he met Joyce. "Tim spoke to me often about it. He made a point of saying he wanted me to meet Ron. Tim really admired him. They got along very, very well."

"For years and years, they were very close friends," Lori Horton says of Tim and Ron. After Tim's death, and before the lawsuit started, she says, Ron told her "that Tim Horton Donuts had become work. With Tim there, it had always been fun. They had a good time together." In 1973, Tim would remark, "The business has been a combination of hard work, common sense, good luck and fun."

"He brought a lightheartedness to the office in the summer," says Joyce. "He was a very, very kind man. I used to get all the dirty looks, and he used to get all the smiles, and I had to live with that. But I loved Tim, and we had a lot of laughs. We'd have moments with mistakes being made, and we'd always cover each other's ass."

There proved to be common ground for friendship between Joyce and Trainor as well: both were recreational pilots. Trainor hit it off with Joyce as solidly as Tim did. Twenty years after Tim's death, Trainor and Joyce are still good friends.

Joyce had become a pilot through the business in 1968, when he and Tim had decided that their next operating sphere outside of Hamilton should be the eastern Ontario corridor from Belleville through Kingston, Cornwall and Brockville. "I

thought it would be great if I had an airplane to go
down there, where you couldn't get by commercial
flights," says Joyce. "I got my licence, and the company bought a Piper Cherokee 235." The four-
seater prop plane also became a surveying tool,
with Tim clambering aboard and taking to the skies
with Ron to scout real-estate opportunities.

In the process of expanding into eastern Ontario,
Tim and Ron had skipped over Toronto entirely.
Charade had deliberately stayed out of Toronto
when establishing the donut franchises, and Tim
and Ron were in no hurry to veer from that plan.

"Tim didn't like Toronto as a place to do business," says Joyce. "He was afraid of Toronto.
Competition was everywhere." Mr. Donut and
Country Style were well established. Joyce is sure
that Tim wholly agreed with Charade when
Charade chose Hamilton as the best spot for donut
expansion. Doubtless both men had been thoroughly traumatised by their burger drive-in experience and wanted to stay well clear of a city in which
every restaurant concept, no matter how seemingly
innovative, was guaranteed to have at least two
fierce competitors.

Tim Hortons would not come to Toronto until
1970, when it had already opened twenty stores elsewhere in the province. Even then, says Joyce, "we
opened two stores and didn't do too well."
Absorbing a bankrupt donut chain gave them stores
twenty-one and twenty-two, but twenty-one failed—
it was one of the first the chain ever had to close.
Store twenty-two, at Kennedy and Eglinton, made a
go of it, and a year later they successfully breached
Etobicoke.

By the time Tim Donut had enough moxie to

tackle the Toronto market, it was on the verge of becoming a significant player, at least regionally, in the restaurant franchise game. But first it had to weather a crisis spawned by a lawsuit that technically had nothing to do with them, but on a practical level had very much to do with them. The Jirna case, as it was known, was the result of a lawsuit filed by a group of Mr. Donut franchisees in Toronto against their parent operation in the United States, charging it with wrongful profits. The suit had arisen from a common practice of franchise chains. The parent company would negotiate what would be considered a favourable price for goods from suppliers for its franchisees. But then a volume discount would be applied by the suppliers to the shipments as a whole, and that rebate would be given to the parent company, which wouldn't share it with the franchisees. The Jirna plaintiffs argued that Mr. Donut was telling them exactly who they could buy their supplies from, negotiating on their behalf and then denying them discounts that were rightfully theirs. In 1969 the U.S. court in which the suit was filed agreed with the Jirna plaintiffs. The franchising business as a whole was knocked for a loop, and Tim Donut was one of the companies scrambling to deal with the new reality.

It very nearly caused Tim to quit hockey for good. "Tim and I never really liked the rebate system," says Joyce, but they had been using it just like Mr. Donut had, and now they had a crowd of franchisees, empowered by the Jirna ruling, who wanted a new relationship. As it happened, the Jirna ruling was overturned on appeal. "It would have been very difficult for us if that had held," says Joyce. But the crisis gave Tim an opportunity to demonstrate one

of his genuine strengths in the business. The franchisees loved him, and his steadying presence was
critical in avoiding a meltdown of the relationship
between Tim Donut and its franchisees.

Jim Charade had been busy selling franchises for
Mr. Donut in the States when the Jirna ruling
brought his efforts to a halt. Having been as far
afield as Colorado selling franchises, Charade
returned to his Toronto base to tend to operations
in western New York and Ontario. He would drop
in on Ron and Tim, since his travels took him by
their head office in a house on Trafalgar Road in
Oakville, which had a store and a franchisee training centre next door. The trio retired to a nearby
restaurant one day at lunch, and were still there at
closing, rehashing old times.

Charade went to work for Tim Donut for about
nine months, selling franchises and then working in
operations, running store twenty-two in Toronto.
He recalls standing in the parking lot of the company's Oakville headquarters with Ron and Tim,
locked in an impasse over the best strategy for the
company. "It was just on the edge," says Charade. "I
wanted to stay with it and expand, but money was
tight. There was a recession. Ron was kind of weary,
worried about the money. Maybe we shouldn't go so
fast, maybe we should slow down. We were opening
shops, but only one to four a year. I wanted to go
faster, I thought there was no job for me. Tim was
agreeing with me and Ron was disagreeing with me
about the way things were going to turn out."[2]

Charade stayed a while longer, then headed to
Philadelphia in 1971 to sell franchises for Amco's
retailing properties. Best known for its transmission
stores, Amco also had the franchising rights to a gift

shop called Plumtree, a women's clothing chain called Red Rooster, and a wicker-import retailer called Cargo 7.

If the Jirna ruling had made Tim seriously consider retiring to concentrate on the growing donut business, the firing of Punch Imlach by Stafford Smythe after the Leafs missed the playoffs in the spring of '69 pushed him over the edge. Both Tim and Johnny Bower announced their retirements within minutes of learning of the Imlach firing.

"This is it for me," Tim told the *Telegram*, adding that he had come "within a whisker" of retiring two months earlier because of "business pressures"—an unelaborated reference to the crisis set off by the Jirna ruling.

"He was a great guy to play for," Tim elaborated. "He put a lot of money into our pockets. I had my fights with him, mostly when I did something wrong, but five minutes later it was all forgotten. That's the type of people I like. I did something wrong, he fined me and gave me a talking to. After that it was all finished. I said it before, that when Punch goes, I'll go out the same door."

Would Tim change his mind? "I'm very busy and I just can't find time for hockey. But who knows, I might feel differently next fall. We all are human. Right now I feel I've had it."

"I have to tell the front office," Bower told the paper. "But you can say this was my last game. I'm very sorry for Punch. I owe him a lot. He brought me to Toronto and he put money in my pocket. In a lot of our pockets, I guess. He's been good to me, and I'm sorry to have this happen to him."

The *Telegram*, looking for more examples of solidarity, buttonholed George Armstrong. The team captain was less resolute than Horton and Bower. "I don't know what I'll do," he said. "At this moment I'm thinking more about Punch than about myself. I don't want to say anything right now. If I said I was retiring, nobody would believe me, anyway."

Armstrong didn't retire. Bower played one more game, the next season, before becoming a scout for the Leafs. Tim set the pattern for his next five seasons of hockey—routinely announcing that this was his last season, then hammering out a deal the following September during training camp. Friends joked that he became a consistent holdout just to avoid training camp.

"Tim had a really close relationship with Imlach," says Billy Harris. "When Stafford fired Imlach, Tim's attitude changed. It was fun playing for the Leafs, it was fun playing for Imlach." (Harris himself didn't have that much fun playing for Imlach.) "All of a sudden hockey was a business. He took a different approach. He became much more difficult to deal with at contract time, more demanding. Hockey at that stage stopped being a fun time."

Chapter 19

The Future Considered

In the two seasons that followed the 1967 cup victory, the Leafs struggled in the new expansion era. They had taken the Stanley Cup from a younger, faster, flashier Montreal Canadiens club. With a team of poised veterans, the Leafs had extended the glory years of Imlach farther than, on paper, they deserved to be. Tim was thirty-seven when he won his fourth cup; Allan Stanley had just turned forty-one; Red Kelly was a few months shy of forty. Sharing the goaltending duties were Johnny Bower, forty-three, and Terry Sawchuk, thirty-eight. George Armstrong was thirty-six when he scored the insurance goal into an empty net with forty-three seconds to go in game six, which sealed the Cup victory. On the ice with him were Stanley, Horton, Kelly and Sawchuk, along with a comparative youngster, thirty-one-year-old Bob Pulford.

Imlach had always been keenly loyal to his old guard, and they to him. He had resisted the imperatives from upstairs to go with youth and clean house of the veterans. On the contrary, he continued to accumulate aging stars, bringing aboard Terry Sawchuk, Pierre Pilote and Marcel Pronovost. His loyalties may have cost the Leafs one of the greatest young defensive prospects the game had to offer: Brad Park, who had risen up through the Marlie system, in the Leafs' own rink. The Leafs didn't bother securing his rights when they had the chance in 1966, before the universal amateur draft took effect. King Clancy was known to lament, "I don't know how we ever let that boy get away," whenever the subject of Park was raised.

Not that Tim was running out of steam. In the seasons following the 1967 Cup win, he played some of his best hockey. Tim's defensive skills, honed over nearly two decades of professional hockey, were overwhelmingly evident when turned loose on the diluted talent of the first expansion years. A second-team All Star in 66/67, Tim made the first team in 67/68 and 68/69.

He had a career season in 68/69, using the expanded seventy-four-game schedule to set personal NHL highs of forty points and 107 minutes in penalties. In a home game against the Bruins on January 16, Tim had scored his one hundredth NHL goal, capping a third-period Leaf comeback. The Leafs had started the period trailing 5-3, and Horton's goal at 17:04 tied the game. Bruins coach Harry Sinden and general manager Milt Schmidt were furious because referee John Ashley had bumped into Boston's Ted Green as Green tried to carry the puck out of his own end. Paul Henderson had pounced on the loose puck, which somehow made it to Tim. He remembered little more than that he had shot it from the left side when it came off the boards. Bruins goaltender Gerry Cheevers, who had once been a young Leaf backup to Bower, fished the puck out of the net and batted it into the crowd in disgust. The Gardens' announcer requested that the spectators return the puck, since it was Tim's centenary goal, and did not disguise his own contempt by naming Cheevers as the perpetrator to the crowd. "That's bush, using a guy's name," Cheevers complained afterward. "Sure I'm hot, right? But he didn't have to use my name."

When Hughie Phillips saw the goal, all he could think of was getting the puck for Tim and having it mounted. He didn't realise at first that the Leafs would see to that. When he learned that the puck was taken care of, he went to a Dominion store the day after the game and ordered a cake. He had them write "Congratulations on your 100th goal" on it, with a Maple Leaf player in icing, then had it delivered to the house. He felt good about that.

Even though Tim was playing some of the most impressive hockey of his career, the Leaf dynasty that had begun with Imlach's arrival in 1958 was crumbling with alarming speed. The close of the 68/69 season laid on the disasters with a dump truck. First came the humiliation at the hands of the emerging Bruins, led by Phil Esposito and Bobby Orr, who swept Toronto four-straight in the semifinals, outscoring them 17-0. Then came the Imlach firing, which begat the retirement announcements from Horton and Bower. As if that weren't enough, in June the Maple Leaf Gardens board of directors voted to remove Stafford Smythe as president and Harold Ballard as vice-president as an investigation by the attorney-general's office into the business's finances, which had been ongoing since 1968, began to close in on Smythe and Ballard. The vote against them had been weak— only fifteen of twenty-three board members had been at the critical meeting, and their erstwhile partner in the 1961 takeover of MLG, chairman John Bassett, had cast the deciding vote. In December 1970, Ballard and Smythe, who had maintained their seats on the board, were able to engineer a countercoup, vote out the board members who had massed against them, force Bassett to withdraw from MLG and sell his shares, and get themselves reinstated in their executive positions. None of this mattered to the RCMP. In July 1971, Smythe was arrested on charges of defrauding MLG of $249,000, Ballard for doing the same to the tune of $82,000, and together swindling another $146,000 in cash and securities. In a lamely transparent scheme, they had been diverting ticket revenues into their own pockets, skimming from the Junior Marlies and using MLG funds to renovate their personal properties.

When Imlach was fired at the end of the 68/69 season, Jim Gregory and John McLellan—neither of whom had major-league management experience—were brought in as general manager and coach respectively in place of Imlach. McLellan had been a roommate of Tim's when they played together for the Pittsburgh Hornets and was Ray Hannigan's brother-in-law. George Mara, an original member of the Silver Seven hockey committee (and a member of Canada's Olympic hockey team in 1948) took over from Stafford Smythe as interim president.

At the end of the 68/69 season, Tim had one year left on the three-year contract that paid him $42,500 per season, and by all indications, he was serious about retirement. "I was tired and the season had been long and hard," he said of 68/69. "For the first time hockey was no longer fun. Also, my business partner had been after me for a long time to go full-time in our Tim Horton Donut Shop business."

He devoted himself to the business as much as he

ever had in the summer of 1969, as he and Ron
Joyce pushed their franchises in the eastern
Ontario corridor from Belleville to Cornwall. Their
foray into Belleville had gone well, and now they
were exploring Kingston. Tim did not report to
training camp and gave no indication of doing so.
George Armstrong was also holding out.

In the meantime, the Maple Leaf Gardens board
of directors had voted Tim the winner of its J.P.
Bickell Memorial Trophy, awarded (when the board
felt the trophy was deserved) to the most valuable
Leaf. Tim was honoured and mystified. "I read
about it in the paper," he said. "Maybe they couldn't
get in touch with me, but no one from the Gardens
told me about it." He never did get the trophy itself.

At training camp in Peterborough, the Leaf
defence roster had rarely looked so porous. At the
1968 camp, the Leafs had had Marcel Pronovost,
Pierre Pilote and Tim Horton, as well as newcomers
Mike Pelyk, Jim Dorey, Pat Quinn and Rick Ley.[1] In
1969 the Leafs still had Pronovost, but he was reaching the end of his career, which had begun in 1950,
and he would only play thirty-four games with the
Leafs that season. Also joining the Leaf defence in
1969 was twenty-three-year-old Brian Glennie, who
would remain a team member for nine seasons.

Without Tim Horton in the lineup, the Leafs
looked like a team preparing themselves for another long stroll in the wilderness, in the spirit of the
one that had occupied them from 1951 until 1958,
when Imlach's arrival had launched their renais-
sance. But unlike the last frustrating period of Leaf
history, no one could blame the brain trust for
stressing defence over scoring power. "It becomes
increasingly evident as you watch the youthful

Maple Leaf defense corps' frantic efforts in the
daily scrimmages that the return of Tim Horton to
active duty is a must," the *Toronto Star* concluded on
September 17. "We should pay Horton, get him
here in a hurry," said ex-president Stafford Smythe.
"This team needs him."

The Leafs had dumped their farm clubs in
Rochester and Victoria, and in the process lost the
grooming system that had underpinned the game
in the years before the universal draft. The turnover
in players from the great cup-winning teams was so
rapid that the Leafs also had no veterans on hand
to bring along the young and inexperienced
defencemen. All of the Leaf blueline greats—Baun,
Brewer, Hillman, Stanley and Horton—were gone,
and Pronovost was close behind.

At a September 3 press conference at the start of
training camp, Gregory noted that Tim wanted his
salary doubled. "If he sticks to that," said Gregory,
"he'll stay retired." Tim was exasperated by the
implication that he was the one pushing the negotiating. "I'm not really holding out," he insisted. "Mr.
Gregory is doing the talking. It's a difficult situation. A matter of personal feeling. Enough's
enough."

On September 26, Tim told the *Star*: "A lot of figures have been kicked around. Actually, no specific
sum was mentioned. Gregory asked me whether
there was anything that would change my mind. I
said, 'Sure, double my salary and I'll be back.' Jim
replied: 'That's a lot of money.' Was I serious? Well,
I suppose I was. We've talked money a few times but
there is no real pressure from the Gardens or the
fans to have me come back. I guess I've had the itch
to play again, since camp opened, but I'm so busy

in my doughnut business that I haven't time to think about it. The situation at the moment is that we're not bargaining. I had conversations with Mr. Mara a month ago, but we didn't even discuss a definite salary range."

Despite the fact that Tim was on the record saying it was Jim Gregory whom he had asked for the doubled salary, Harold Ballard was quick to assert after Tim's death—within hours of it, in fact—that the crucial conversation was with him. According to *Star* columnist Milt Dunnell, Ballard claimed he had met Tim on the street and asked, "Would you be interested in returning to the Leafs if somebody offered you a lot of money?" Ballard said that Horton replied, laughing, "If somebody doubled my salary, I might consider it." Dunnell contended that Tim later confessed he meant the figure as a joke. But Tim's double-or-nothing proposal may not have been so cavalier. Bob Baun, who was playing with Detroit, says Tim consulted him on his salary negotiations. "He talked to me about his contract," says Baun, "because he had heard how well I was doing, and I told him how much he should be making." (In Detroit, Baun's salary was closing in on $70,000.)

Globe and Mail reporter Dan Proudfoot caught up with Tim at the beginning of October at the donut chain's Oakville headquarters. Tim had forgotten he was coming, apologised, and then invited Proudfoot along as he and Joyce flew to Kingston to pursue a new franchise site. The three men boarded the company Piper Cherokee, made a pass over Oakville so Tim could inspect a new waterfront site from the air, then headed down the lake.

In Kingston they made the rounds of city officials

and hockey fans. Tim moved easily between them. In Proudfoot's story, he comes across as someone clearly immersed in the business, not simply a figurehead. He spoke of how the quality of their product suffered in refrigeration, about the percentage of cream that really goes into coffee whitener.

Once back in Oakville, Tim told Proudfoot, "Sure, you get involved and interested in the business. There are a lot of decisions to make and Ron likes to be able to share them with me, and he thinks I'd be just as far ahead to stay out of hockey. But at the same time he wants the decision to be mine. The decision will be mine, and it won't be too complicated. If they come up with enough money, I'll play. The business won't suffer without me. It certainly doesn't hurt for me to be known in hockey, and the worst part of the hockey season is over now. That's training camp. The best part of training camp is the end of it. I could be in shape in a couple of days—that's all it would take to get the legs and feet going. And if I were to play another couple of years, the business would be really established. If I don't play, we could open a few more franchises than if I do play. There's that to consider, too. We have a lineup of people wanting to buy franchises." At the time, a Tim Hortons franchise cost $38,000, including equipment; the franchisee paid Tim Donut a 3 per cent royalty on gross sales.

During the visit to Kingston, the sports editor of the *Whig-Standard* had pigeonholed Tim about his hockey future. "As of now," said Tim, "I am retired. However, for the proper amount of money, as you put it, I'd be a fool not to play. As a matter of fact, Jim Gregory is talking about a two-year contract. Figures have been bounced around, but this is going to be something that either side might have to give or take a little on... The firing of Punch Imlach had something to do with my retiring all right, but I had mentioned retiring as early as February."

"You can look for v.p. King Clancy to start negotiating with Horton," the *Star* predicted. "He has a way with reluctant Leafs, usually winning them over by taking the elastic off the bankroll."

King Clancy would have to remove a lot of elastics to get his way. Tim had been reasonably well paid under Imlach as the Stanley Cups and All Star team appearances for Tim had mounted. Doubling his income would make him one of the game's highest-paid players. "We need Horton badly, but not that badly," Mara reportedly responded. The *Windsor Star* concluded that Tim "is up against the SRO sign on Maple Leaf Gardens"—Toronto fans liked hockey so much they were willing to pack the building regardless of how well the Leafs played. But the Leaf manager proved not to be that cynical. The Bruins may have helped them change their minds about Tim's value. Having shellacked the Leafs in the semi-finals the previous spring, a makeshift Bruins squad called on the Leafs at their Peterborough training camp and thrashed them 5-1.

The 1969 camp was the first to follow the introduction of the universal draft, and as such was an early warning sign of what hockey was going to become. "I think that the players who came out of the sixties and those good farm systems always found work, because they were trained," says Dave Keon. "They were trained to be professional hockey players. Even the kids today who are drafted, they're trying to play professional hockey and they're not in any way, shape or form trained. As far as being trained in Junior hockey, it may happen in the very odd case, but in the majority of cases, if you're a great goal scorer you'll get drafted higher, and if you get a lot of penalty minutes, that means you're tough, so you'll get drafted higher. The average kid coming out, unless he's fortunate and has a coach who has his interest at heart, they're just thrown into it when they turn pro, and it becomes the responsibility of the team they're playing for to train them."

Within a week of Dan Proudfoot's trip with Tim to Kingston, the Leaf veteran holed up with Jim Gregory at the Gardens while an intrasquad game was underway. They went into a room together just before 8 p.m. An hour later they emerged with a deal. With Tim aboard, Armstrong, too, came to a deal, although the captaincy moved to Dave Keon and Armstrong played only forty-nine games that season—he hadn't played a full season since the Stanley Cup win of 1967.

Gregory held a press conference during the second period of the intrasquad game. Tim, he said, had asked for $85,000, but had received unspecified "certain considerations" that Gregory said would take his pay close to $70,000. *Hockey News* reported that the Leafs had come up with a $28,000 package of such "considerations" that would take his salary to $70,000.

"When I gave the Leafs a figure of $85,000," Tim said, "I believe I really wanted to quit hockey, because I didn't think they would meet that figure. Now times have changed."

For the first time in his career, Tim appeared to have agreed to play the game solely for the money.

It was a monumentally regrettable decision. Despite the bravura expressed in his interview with Dan Proudfoot that he could be in shape to play in a matter of days, Tim hadn't been on skates since the playoffs of the previous spring. He was thirty-nine years old and hadn't, as usual, done much of anything in the off-season to stay in shape. When asked what he had done to prepare for the season, he quipped, "I only stayed in shape enough to run faster than my wife—that's the main thing."

"I was quite sure back in May that I wouldn't be back in hockey," he told writer George Gross when the season was underway. "To change my decision required a lot of adjustment in many ways. It takes considerable mental and physical preparation to get ready for a hockey season. I didn't do either, of course. Now that I'm taking a crash course in both, I'm finding how much out of shape I really am. When I decided to come out of retirement it was with the understanding that I'll always give hockey my full attention. I can't play any other way. At my age you have to work at it much harder than, say, fifteen years ago. It's as simple as that." When Gross asked if his donut business suffered without him, he replied, "Not really. I have a very good partner in Ron Joyce. He looks after things when I'm not there and I do my share of the work when I'm finished with my hockey assignments."

Reflecting on Tim's seasons after Imlach's firing, Dave Keon says, "I don't believe he was playing strictly for the money. He might have been capable of doing it for a year, but not over a period of three or four years. You're at that age, and his business was starting to get successful. Who would want the double aggravation? If you don't like the game, and you're just doing it for the financial remuneration, then your performance overall is going to reflect that."

Money might not have been the only reason Tim agreed to be a Maple Leaf in the fall of 1969, but it was the sole issue that convinced him to give up devoting all of his time to the business, which Ron Joyce very much wanted him to do. It is unfortunate that he missed all of training camp before coming to an agreement with Jim Gregory. One season after being a first-team All Star and a runner-up for the Norris Trophy, Tim Horton was out of shape and playing poorly. He was suddenly the money player who wasn't giving the team its money's worth.

Jim Gregory was criticised for bending to the pressure of Gardens titans like King Clancy and to the catcalls of the pundits appalled by the Leafs' decline. On January 10, two days before Tim's forti- eth birthday, the Maple Leaf Gardens program car- ried a frank, if hopeful, story on Tim's thus-far lack- lustre season.

"I knew it would take him a while to get into the proper mental and physical condition to help us," lamented his coach, John McLellan, "but I didn't realize what a struggle he would have."

When it was noted that Gordie Howe, who was two years older than Tim, was still going strong in Detroit, McLellan responded: "Howe was preparing himself mentally and physically for the hockey sea- son away back last July. At that point, Horton had decided to stick to his donut business. When we finally coaxed him out of retirement, the training camp was completed and he had a long way to catch up to the rest of the players in the league." Now, said McLellan, Tim was beginning to find his old form.

The story noted that for a while Gregory, like Tim, "was the object of snide remarks. The critics pointed out that the only place Horton led the Leafs was at the pay wicket. They inferred that rookie G.M. Gregory had made a bad deal in luring Horton back to action."

Said Gregory: "Horton appears to be finding himself. We brought him back to steady our young defencemen, help them gain the experience needed in this league. It took him a long time to make up for that missed training camp. He still gives the puck away too much but his physical play has improved. We are entering a very rough period in the schedule and we need Horton at his best to anchor our defence. It would appear that he is ready to take charge of our defensive chores. If he continues to play well it will be a big plus for us."

All in all, it was an unusual story for a club program, as much a vote of confidence in their most celebrated and most expensive player as it was a warning to him to start earning his salary. The *Telegram* would contend that Tim's play had become a matter of dispute between two of his oldest cohorts: coach John McLellan and MLG vice-president King Clancy. Clancy, it was said, wanted McLellan to bench Tim; McLellan refused.

The Leafs struggled toward the spring and the final judgment of the playoffs, now only a pale shadow of what had, two seasons earlier, still been one of the greatest franchises in league history. Tim was sixteen years older than anyone else in the Leaf defensive corps. He was the most expensive player the team had, and he wasn't playing at an All Star calibre. On March 5, with the Maple Leafs mired in last place in the East division, Jim Gregory walked into the team's dressing room in Oakland, California, while the Leafs were suiting up to play the Seals, and told the players that Tim Horton had been traded to the New York Rangers for future considerations. Tim had been notified at 4:30 that afternoon.

"I knew it would have an emotional effect on the team," Gregory told Dan Proudfoot. "It had an emotional effect on me, too. I couldn't eat before the game, and I wasn't feeling very hungry when I tried eating afterward. The decision had to be Horton's. When a man has spent twenty-three years with an organization [counting back to when Tim signed his C-form] and performed the way Horton has, you don't just trade him… Horton had intended speaking to the team before the game, but he found he wasn't able to—emotionally. He just shook hands with some of the players. I felt something should be said, so I just told the players that we had made the deal for the good of the team, and that it had been up to Tim.

"We left it strictly up to him," Gregory avowed. "It was in his hands. If he didn't want to go, then the deal was off. He talked to [New York coach and general manager Emile] Francis and agreed to terms. I don't know what those terms are. Our end of it involves players to be transferred to our reserve list before the May 20 deadline for protected lists."

"It was a really traumatic thing," says Dave Keon. "He had played his whole career in Toronto. He was, oh, I guess…" Keon searches for the right word, then simply offers up: "disappointed."

Before the game, the *Star* reported that King Clancy was "silent and emotional"; Tim "was equally broken up."

"I knew King Clancy from Pittsburgh," says Lori.

"Tim was a favourite of his, and he was one of our favourites, too. When Tim was traded, King Clancy said to me that it wasn't because they couldn't afford his salary. It was because they couldn't afford any more hotel doors." Clancy's effort to inject some levity into the situation served as the first word Lori had ever received that Tim's penchant for going through locked doors wasn't simply something he was doing at home. The powerhouse Leafs of the sixties had proved to be a remarkably close-lipped organization. No one was telling Tim that his wife was writing scathing letters to his coach and general manager, and no one was telling Lori that Tim was bashing his way into hotel rooms.

Tim and Lori also had gotten along well with Stafford Smythe. It may have been easy for Lori to take a shine to Stafford—he had come to loathe Punch Imlach as much as Lori did. Two summers after Tim was traded, Lori was up north while Tim worked in the donut business. "I was up at Cleveland's House. I was invited down to a cottage across the street from Stafford's place. And because I was there the people called Stafford and got him out of bed. He came over and we sat and talked hockey all night, and he said he would never have traded Tim. The year Tim was holding out, Stafford wasn't in charge, he was having his tax problems. He said he would have told Tim to take the contract he had then, and he would make up for it the following year."

Stafford, however, hadn't opposed the raise. "Some of our directors told us we must be out of our minds," he said a year after the raise was awarded. "Of course, they were right, although I voted for it at the time."

Tim later said that the hardest part of being traded was walking into the Leaf dressing room in Oakland to collect his sticks and skates. While one newspaper agreed that Tim had known negotiations were underway, it reported that Tim wasn't aware he was going to New York until just before the game. "I don't know that he was that forewarned about it," Keon agrees.

"Tim didn't take change well," says Lori. "We were fully aware it was coming. We just didn't know when."

The enormity of what had transpired weighed on those involved. One of the last tangible links with the great Leaf teams—not only the Leafs of George Armstrong and Dave Keon and Johnny Bower and Punch Imlach, but the Leafs of Teeder Kennedy and Tod Sloan and Sid Smith and Joe Primeau and Hap Day—had just been discarded. Only Armstrong and Keon were now left from the 60/61 lineup. Tim was a marvel in that he was still capable of playing a first-class game in the NHL while being able to recall training camps with the likes of Hollywood Bill Barilko and Wild Bill Ezinicki. But such things no longer mattered in the NHL of the universal draft and expansion clubs. Loyalty was no longer a consideration, because there was no such thing as loyalty anymore, at least not with the Toronto Maple Leafs. There were no more sponsored amateur clubs; no more C-forms, however despised, with which a kid gave his promise to play for an organization. In the new game, the paternalism of Conn Smythe, whether benign or exploitive, was a distant memory. For future considerations, the past had just been mortgaged.

"I found I was bothered by the trade," said rookie

defenceman Brian Glennie. "It's because I really came to have a lot of respect for him. He always helped me. Whenever I had something come up, some problem in my game, and I asked him what would be the best thing to do, he would go out of his way to help. And off the ice he was just such a fine guy—very thoughtful."

George Armstrong was confronted by the reality that the man with whom he had been playing hockey almost uninterruptedly since 1946, the man who had signed a C-form with the Toronto Maple Leafs, as he had, in 1947, was not about to step out onto the ice with him that night, and never would again. He expressed a mixture of shock, resignation and anger. "Hell," Armstrong exclaimed, "we played together with the Copper Cliff Redmen when we were sixteen. When you go back that far, playing together, both of us always on the right side of the ice, you get to know each other's habits. You pick up a few things over the years—nothing you can think of, just instinctive things. There was a confidence I had in him. When we were in our own end, I knew the thing would be coming out, or it damn well wouldn't be his fault. And now those instincts aren't any use any more. All of a sudden he's gone. He had a large influence on this team. He was never a rah-rah guy, that's for sure, but if ever an important matter came up, he'd always speak up. If there was an argument, he'd drop in something that would make sense. The first damn thing about him is that he's a great hockey player. There's probably a little of Tim Horton in everybody in this team. Trades are part of the business we play in, eh? We know it, but we never accept it, I guess. We all know hockey is a big business now. But sometimes you get to thinking some things are immune to big business. A guy twenty-three years in the organization, maybe wrongly or rightly you get to thinking..."

George Armstrong didn't say what it was you get to thinking. He played one more season with no Tim on his side of the ice, and retired. He set the record for the most games as a Leaf—1,187, only two more than Tim had when he was traded.

The Leafs beat the California Seals that night 4-1. The team's management seemed to think the defence performed just fine without Tim Horton.

"In our building program," declared Harold Ballard, "we can't use guys over forty. Sure, we'd like to use Horton the way we are using Johnny Bower, sending him out to scout. He would be a great asset to our organization. But his $80,000 salary is a little steep." With that statement, Ballard, who had always been on good terms with Tim, who had loaned him $25,000 without collateral for his donut business, made it clear that hockey was a business and that this was business. He also made it clear that, despite Jim Gregory's assurances the previous October that Tim's package was worth no more than $70,000, the Leafs had indeed virtually doubled his salary to get him back. Of course, it's possible that Ballard was exaggerating to reinforce his case that the team could no longer afford Tim. That was to be expected: downplay the salary package when it was signed so as not to raise the hopes of other players, then blow it out of proportion after the player was dumped to show what happened to players who were paid more than they were worth. And when Tim died, the number grew larger in Ballard's recollection. On the day of Tim's death, the *Star*'s Milt Dunnell reported that Tim's salary had been in "the $45,000 bracket. The Leafs felt they needed Tim, but his money proposal staggered them. 'We finally got our offer up to $90,000,' Ballard revealed. 'He was worth it, too.'"

He didn't seem to think Tim was worth it when he was traded, and he exaggerated the return the Leafs would enjoy. "We will be getting about four or five players," Ballard explained. "A couple would likely be junior draft choices or young professionals from New York's farm teams in Buffalo and Omaha."

What the Leafs got was Guy Trottier, a compact, thirty-year-old right-winger in the Rangers' farm system who had played two games for the parent club in 68/69, and Denis Dupere, a solid nineteen-year-old left-winger who played his first NHL games when he reported to the Leafs for the last twenty games of the season. He lasted three more full seasons with only middling points production—his best season was 72/73, when he garnered thirty-six points. From 74/75 to 77/78 he played in Washington, St. Louis, Kansas City and Colorado. Trottier stayed only two seasons with the Leafs, contributing twenty-four and then twenty-one points, before jumping to the World Hockey Association.

"Not to say Guy didn't play well for us, and so did Denis," Keon reflects, "but when you look back at it, they didn't get very much for Tim." The Leafs didn't get anything at all for Dave Keon after fifteen seasons. In 75/76, after another quality, fifty-nine-point season and while still the captain of the Leafs, he became one more NHL star to jump to the WHA. He never came back.

Chapter 20

"I'm a Tired Old Man"

Once Tim left the Toronto Maple Leaf organization, which had been the focal point of his life since age seventeen, his life resisted falling into a predictable groove, in no small part because he could not decide what that groove should be. He was forty years old, one of the game's most senior players. He had no one else to look to as a role model in this situation. Hockey was entering uncharted waters; so was the restaurant business, and so, not surprisingly, was Tim.

During the two seasons that followed Jim Gregory's decision to trade him away, Tim moved through a flurry of upheavals, unable to please himself and everyone around him. His life had been changed irrevocably by the trade, which exacerbated problems in his personal life and ultimately forced a confrontation over his commitment to the donut business with his partner, Ron Joyce.

It was a time in his life that called for decisiveness. Instead, Tim seemed overwhelmed by options, and rather than choosing one of them, he kept them all open, waiting for life to give him some unequivocal sign that this was what was best for him. No sign came to him, and the path of least resistance kept leading him back to the rink. And although, for a player of his stature and calibre, it might have seemed the most logical path to follow, there could be no following it without consequences.

The Rangers of 69/70 were a team of both the present and the future. They had a legitimate shot at the Stanley Cup, and if that shot did not find the mark, there was always next season. The Leafs were at the bottom of the East division as the season drew to a close; the Rangers were in second. Two weeks before the Horton trade, New York had been in first place, but they were now limping badly as injuries sidelined key starters. Coach and general manager Emile "The Cat" Francis had lost two All Star defencemen to the infirmary: Jim Neilson was out with a knee injury and Brad Park had a cracked ankle. Also out of the lineup was forward Don Marshall, with a shoulder injury. Chicago and Detroit were breathing down their necks. The Rangers had last won a Stanley Cup thirty springs earlier, and the season that promised at last to return the elusive trophy was in danger of complete collapse. Word was that the league itself was pulling for the Rangers. New York was home to the head offices of NBC, ABC and CBS, and the league was pining for a national television contract. Maybe, if the Rangers won it all, the network executives would finally take notice of the game.

Emile Francis was an established fan of Tim who had been trying to cut a deal for him for some time. During the 67/68 season, he declared, "I'll tell you how strong Tim Horton is. He can hold three guys with one arm and clear the puck with the other. He does it to us all the time."

Ranger defenceman Arnie Brown was thrilled to learn that Tim was on the way. "Horton could be the difference between us being knocked out or going all the way to the Stanley Cup."

Tim, for his part, was quite happy to be going to New York. As painful as it was to leave the Leafs, it was no longer the team or the organization he had known, and the future for them looked grim. The Rangers were a league powerhouse, and their line-up brought plenty of fond memories. Four members of the starting lineup had been with Tim in Toronto in the early 1960s. Bob Nevin, Arnie Brown and Rod Seiling were three of the five players Imlach had traded away to New York in 1964 to get Andy Bathgate and Don McKenney for the Stanley Cup playoffs. Ron Stewart had been traded to Boston in 1965, and had found his way to the Rangers (via St. Louis) in 1967. (Terry Sawchuk also played his last eight NHL games with New York in 69/70, and died that year.)

In his first full season in New York, the twenty-six-year-old Nevin was made captain in Bathgate's stead as he regained the scoring touch that had steadily eluded him while playing for Imlach. Edged out by Dave Keon in 1961 in voting for the rookie-of-the-year award, Nevin had impressed Tim as the most dependable right-winger he had played behind. While with the Leafs, Nevin made regular pilgrimages to Horton's Willowdale home on Wedgewood to enjoy a beer with Tim and impromptu circles of other players. Lori became quite close with Nevin's wife (the Nevins subsequently divorced).

"Everybody looked up to him," Nevin says of Tim in the early 1960s, "especially on the ice. He was unbelievable on the ice. He was great with the younger guys. He had been with Toronto as long as anybody, and had seen the bad times, and was now revelling in the good times."

Francis understood perfectly what Tim could do for his club. "When Tim came to New York," says Nevin, "he was a complete veteran player, and just his presence added a lot to the team. The Cat would say, 'It's not what you make, it's what you leave,' meaning that it's not how many goals you score, it's how many goals you have scored against you. Tim fit right into that mould. He wasn't rushing as much as when I knew him in Toronto. He was basically doing a lot of defensive stuff."

Tim by then had resolved to put his barnstorming days behind him. "My style hasn't changed much," he said when he was thirty-eight, following the 67/68 season. "I don't rush up ice as much as I used to. I've learned that the most important thing is to check well in our own end. I'll only carry the puck more if we're behind." That season, he edged out J.C. Tremblay for a spot on the first All Star team by one vote. Twenty-four votes ahead of Tim was Bobby Orr.

Late in the 68/69 season, after again being named to the first All Star team with Orr, Tim's frame of mind was very much that of a stay-at-home defenceman. He lamented the fact that All Star selections and other honours like the Norris Trophy tended to go to defencemen who paid more attention to offence than defence. "They pay off in points," he complained. "So all the defencemen want their scoring points. Teddy Green has been a terrific factor for Boston for some seasons, but it wasn't until he began scoring points that he began getting All Star votes. Bobby Orr is a great player, maybe the greatest prospect to come into the league in several seasons, but he's much better offensively than defensively at this point and he's inspiring kids all over Canada to copy his rushing style. In this respect, he could be a bad influence, though I don't mean that in an unkind way."

This was the same Tim Horton who had delighted in end-to-end rushes as a St. Mike's Major, who led the Leafs in offensive production in the '62 Stanley Cup. As it happened, in 1972 Orr would break the playoff scoring record for defencemen set by Tim in 1962. "As a kid," Tim was willing to concede, "I wasn't as keen on defence as I was later. It's just as important to stop goals as it is to score them, but it's not as spectacular. The real good defensive defenceman, the good body-checkers, are all older men, like Leo Boivin and Marcel Pronovost. Tim Horton's an old man, too. It's an era of change in defencemen."

Tim may not have been able to admit that it was an era of change in Tim Horton, too. He was going through the same career adjustment that Allan Stanley had at this age, emphasizing his work in his own end over his rushing skills. The idea of being an "old man," once it had surfaced, would not go away. He referred to himself this way consistently for the rest of his career and his life. Nearing the end of the 68/69 season, he touched on the same themes. "I don't rush as much as I used to. Oh, if we get behind a goal or two I'll carry the puck whenever I get the chance. But over the years I've learned that the most important thing is to check well in your own end. This comes from once playing for Hap Day, I guess."

He was assuredly conscious of the change in team rosters. The players with whom he had come of age were steadily disappearing. Season by season, Tim was becoming the old guard. The accompanying change in the league, with expansion franchises, the elimination of the reserve and negotiating lists and the advent of the universal draft, further emphasized his seniority. Hockey suddenly had a generation gap, and Tim became nostalgic for what had once been.

In the 1973 profile by Lawrence Martin, Tim groused, "I miss the old days, when a rookie came into the league and kept his mouth shut for the first two or three seasons because he knew his place." Martin wrote that Tim missed the days "when bosses like Connie Smythe would boot a kid back to the minors just for putting in a bad practice session; the days, he says, when you knew every player in the six-team league and every move he had. Now, says Horton, 'the rookies think they can step in here and run the whole show. And now you don't know half the players or half the teams in the league, never mind what moves they have.'"

In coming to play for Emile Francis, he was returning in many ways to the hockey of his youth— if not the hockey he had wanted to play, then at least the hockey that disciplinarians like Hap Day had wanted him to. Or, for that matter, Jim Dewey, under whose tutelage Tim never recorded a single regular-season point as a Copper Cliff Redman. While Francis welcomed a rushing defenceman like Park, he strove to clamp down on the number of goals the team gave up every game. Francis had been a workaday goaltender in the NHL from 1946 to 1952,[1] and as a coach and general manager he proved to be a strategist whose priorities were never far from those of a netminder.

"At least I jumped twenty points in the standings," Tim said after his first outing as a Ranger, a home game against Detroit. "And I'm here with a lot of old friends like Stewie and Nevvie." Just playing the Red Wings was something of a trip down memory lane. Bob Baun, Frank Mahovlich and Carl Brewer (who had just returned to the NHL) were all with Detroit, and sent Tim their best wishes from the Red Wings' dressing room. Asked to comment on Tim's transformation from a Leaf into a Ranger, Gordie Howe replied laconically, "Nothing's changed. He's still wearing blue."

"When the opportunity came for me to come to New York," Tim said the year after the trade, "I jumped at it because the Rangers are an up-and-coming team very close to the Cup." He did his best to be diplomatic and not cast aspersions on the team he had left behind. "Johnny McLellan and Jim Gregory are real good guys," he emphasized after his first game as a Ranger. But there's no question he was taken with New York as a team and as an organization. A month after his arrival, he was ebullient. "We're treated so well," he sang. "I'm not used to it, coming from Toronto where everything is different. It's just that anytime you have to ask Francis for something, you don't hear him saying ask me tomorrow—he tries to help you right away. Little things like travel and accommodation are so much better." He hastily backpedalled in the implications of his comments. "Toronto wasn't bad, either—let's get that straight. Jim Gregory and John McLellan are fine. But, without being too specific, things are different here from the top."

"I spoke to Tim a number of times," says Keon, "and he said how much he enjoyed playing for Emile Francis. He thought it had turned into a really good opportunity for him. He really enjoyed how

Emile handled the players."

In the beginning, Francis handled Tim like a new toy he couldn't put down. In his first Rangers game, he spent nearly forty draining minutes on the ice, playing a regular shift with Arnie Brown as well as serving on the power-play and penalty-killing units. He appeared wearing number 3—Rod Seiling had number 7, so Tim reverted to the number he had worn as a St. Mike's Major and Pittsburgh Hornet. He was on the ice when Gordie Howe scored Detroit's opening goal, but Howe had been on Brown's side of the rink. While the Rangers lost 2-0, Tim's debut had gone over well with the fans, in part because of his crowd-pleasing body checks. On his very first shift, he hammered Nick Libett, to the crowd's lusty approval.

The reception was a relief to Lori, who had been in Pittsburgh when she received news of the trade from Tim, and had flown to New York to join him. She knew how brutal the New York "gallery gods" had been to Allan Stanley in the 1950s, and was worried that they would turn on Tim the same way. Her confidence hadn't been boosted by the fact that the number Tim had chosen to wear had been that of Harry Howell, another victim of the Madison Square Garden mobs, who had been traded to Oakland at the beginning of the season. His number had been conspicuously unclaimed since then.

Francis was pleased with his acquisition, despite the loss to Detroit. "He's been the class down through the years," he proclaimed, "probably one of the best defensive defencemen in the league. Who wouldn't have loved to have him? So we had to give up some players. We know what we got—a power All Star, a guy who doesn't panic when things get tight. And we had a commitment to the team. You have to give them some protection after they've got you this far. So Horton is our insurance."

The Rangers' slide continued unabated, despite Tim's arrival. They lost six, tied two and won one for the remainder of March, and wound up in a tie with Montreal for the fourth and final playoff spot in the East. The teams had identical records, and the Rangers only advanced to the playoffs instead of Montreal because they had scored more goals over the season—246 to 244. Had the Rangers not potted nine goals in their final game of the season, they would not have made the playoffs, after leading the East division for three and a half months until injuries had started their slide. For the second season in a row, Tim came up against the young, fast and aggressive Bruins in the semifinals. Arnie Brown's fear came to pass. The Rangers went down in six in the opening round, and Boston, another venerable Original Six franchise that had wandered the post-season wilderness for too long, went on to win its first Stanley Cup since 1941.

It was Tim's third unsatisfying playoff season in a row. "Last year was disappointing," he had said after the 67/68 season, which followed the Leafs' last Stanley Cup win under Imlach. "It really felt strange not to be in action while everyone else was playing for the Stanley Cup." The next season, the Leafs did make the playoffs, finishing fourth with thirty-five wins. But their reward had been humiliation at the hands of the Bruins. In the spring of 1971, Tim would remark, "Remember two years ago with the Leafs, for instance? I just couldn't cut it in the playoffs. Same last year. I was taking too big a load. I ran out of gas."

"I felt a lot of pressure the last while I was with the Leafs," he noted in 70/71, "because it seemed the club was relying heavily on me to do a whole lot of things. It wasn't much different when I came to the Rangers late last season. We were struggling to squeeze into the playoffs and it was a very uptight situation. This year, there's been none of that very exhausting strain."

In the playoffs with the Rangers in the spring of 1970, Tim produced only two points (a goal and an assist) in six games, but he also played his most belligerent NHL playoff hockey ever. He was assessed twenty-eight minutes in penalties—the closest he'd ever come to this total was in the 1967 Stanley Cup drive, when it took him twelve games to pick up twenty-five minutes. The last two regular seasons had been his most penalty-laced to date—he produced 107 minutes in both 68/69 and 69/70.

If Lori had found the news of Tim's trade to the land of the gallery gods stressful, the prospect of having to uproot the family and move to New York for the 70/71 season pushed her to the brink. It was the last thing someone in Lori's condition needed. A consultant's report prepared in May 14, 1970, at Wellesley Hospital—this was right after Tim's first playoff series with New York ended—had Lori noting she had been depressed and had been under continuous psychiatric treatment for five and a half years, initially taking Stelazine (an antipsychotic tranquillizer or sedative), then Etrafon (a combination of the antipsychotic perphenazine and the antidepressant amitriptyline) and Dexamyl. The family was deeply divided over moving to New York for the new season. The youngest, Traci, was excited. The oldest, Jeri-Lynn, was upset but resigned. The middle children, Kim and Kelly, were flat-out opposed. That summer, with the move to New York looming and her children far from uniformly enthusiastic about leaving Toronto, Lori was admitted to Wellesley on August 7 for a two-week stay to deal with her Dexamyl addiction. At the time, her consumption of Dexamyl had reached one hundred tablets a week. The trade to New York threatened to undermine a marriage that already had been to the brink of dissolution. "When I was sixteen [in 1968 or 1969]," says Jeri-Lynn, "they asked us to make a choice between which one we wanted to live with. They were coming down to a divorce, but they'd worked it out then. I was going with my dad."

During the summer of 1970, the league held an expansion draft to help stock its two new franchises: the Buffalo Sabres and the Vancouver Canucks. Francis was pleased with Tim's effort, but he couldn't help take into account that he was forty and so gambled by leaving him off the team's protected list for the draft in order to hang onto his younger talents, hoping nobody would claim him. Nobody did claim him, and it is interesting to note that Punch Imlach, the Sabres' new coach and general manager, was one of the league managers not to bite. Tim was capable, but he was coming to the end of his career while others who would be the futures of franchises were just starting theirs. He was also expensive, and there may have been concerns that any team taking him in risked setting off a salary escalation among its existing players. Indeed, that very fall Dave Keon was a holdout in Toronto, demanding an estimated $125,000 on the strength of what the Leafs had been willing to pay Tim the previous September. On September 22, 1970, Milt Dunnell alleged that Tim was being blamed for a general escalation in salaries. "It all started when they paid Horton that ridiculous salary," Dunnell quoted "a league big-wheel" as saying.

That fall, Tim reported to training camp in Kitchener with no guarantee he would actually make the team. In addition to his starting defence corps of Tim, Arnie Brown, Rod Seiling, Brad Park and Jim Neilson, Emile Francis also had newcomers Larry Brown, Ab DeMarco, André Dupont and Mike Robitaille. "I wouldn't want to have the job here of picking which ones to keep," said Arnie Brown, who was thankful Tim wasn't a left-hand shot and so wouldn't be in the running for his job.

"What the hell," said Tim. "If I don't make it I can always go back to selling donuts."

But he did make it, and so did Seiling, and Neilson, and Park.[2] When he had joined the Rangers at the end of the 69/70 season, Tim had moved into a suite in a hotel across the street from Madison Square Garden. Lori had joined him, and the children were looked after back in Toronto by Renate Pelletier, a neighbour and close family friend—the children of both families were involved in modelling together. Renate, recently widowed, came to serve as a second mother to the Horton children. In the new season, the entire Horton family came to New York and moved into the hotel while they waited for a house rented in the Long Island suburb of Manhasset to become available. During their stay at the hotel, Tim added another chapter to the Superman lore that permeates his life. The pop machine on their hotel's floor took Tim's money without surrendering a drink in return. By way of registering his complaint, he loaded the machine into an elevator and sent it down to the lobby. It took four men to get the machine out of the elevator.

In his first full season with the Rangers, Tim's penalty totals nosedived. He took only fifty-seven minutes, and never exceeded that total for the remainder of his career. It may have simply been a matter of ice time—the less Tim was in the game, the less chances he had to get into trouble—and when Francis brought Tim back for the new season, he was careful not to wear him out with forty minutes of game time. Tim said he had less ice time that season than in any of the last ten to fifteen seasons, and insisted he was being serious when he said he was taking "wheat germ oil and vitamin pills" to stay fit. He enjoyed himself thoroughly, both on the ice and in the city. He would call the season "the happiest of my career," an assessment that would not be made casually by someone who had won four Stanley Cups and been named to six All Star teams. He only produced twenty points, his lowest for a full season since 54/55, but he had found satisfaction playing the way Hap Day had meant the game to be played, and for that he was grateful to the Rangers. "Emile is a great person and a fine coach and he treated me well. They have good guys and great players on the team. We didn't go as far as we had hoped, but we had good success."

Boston was the runaway success of the season, winning fifty-seven games. New York finished second behind them in the East, with forty-nine wins. But the Canadiens, with forty-two wins and goaltender Ken Dryden, who had only played six regular-season games before the playoffs began, knocked off the Bruins in the opening round. New York met Chicago in the semifinals, and the series went all seven games, three of them decided in overtime, before the Blackhawks were able to advance—and lose to Montreal.

The season served to mark the passage of time for Tim in a novel way. His oldest daughter, Jeri-Lynn, had turned eighteen while in New York. Although she originally had been upset about his trade—her heart was set on nursing school, and she had a steady boyfriend in Toronto—she came to New York, completed high school and had a great time. "It was a good year, a lot of fun. I used to go out with the team a lot. I was drinking age down there."

A romance blossomed between her and rookie prospect Ab DeMarco. In the off-season he returned to North Bay, which was where grandpa Oak and grandma Ethel Horton were. Jeri-Lynn spent nearly the entire following summer with her grandparents so that she could see "Abbie," who was three years older than her. "I drove my grandfather nuts," she says. "I think he called dad to come and get me." The romance must have made Tim feel older than ever—his own daughter was dating a fellow player. Even worse, Tim had played against DeMarco's father (also Ab) while in the American League. While he did not entirely approve, neither did he make an issue of it with either his daughter or DeMarco. "I think it bothered him a little," she says. "He never said anything. I found out from friends afterwards that he'd say something to them, but it was only ten years ago that I found out about it."

When the season was over, Tim appeared at last to be through with hockey. "New York offered me a contract for next year, but I told them I wasn't interested in playing any more hockey. I have my plans, and they are all outside of hockey." The Rangers were still a powerful club, with a good shot at making the Stanley Cup finals. They would do just that the next season (and lose to Boston), but they would do it without Tim. The donut business had been expanding, but without Tim around full-time Ron Joyce had to go it alone in keeping the business growing without getting ahead of itself or behind in its debt obligations. "We were having to scramble for money," says Joyce. "We were trying to find franchising continually. And then he went to New York. When he was playing, he really didn't want to be bothered with business. He'd say, 'If it's really important, you call me, but I've got enough on my plate.'"

Francis took Tim at his word on his retirement plans, and left him off the Rangers' protected list. On June 3 the Toronto *Globe and Mail* had Tim begging off playing any more hockey, saying that "he needs more time to look after the chain of donut shops he operates." But Red Kelly, if he read this, paid it no mind. Since the fall of 1969, when Tim had held out in Toronto for twice his salary, Pittsburgh had been the coaching domain of Kelly, and in 70/71 he had also become the general manager. On June 8, Kelly claimed Horton in the intraleague draft, gambling the $40,000 fee due to the Rangers that Tim would change his mind about playing. When Tim found out, he protested, "I'm a tired old man. I've had enough hockey. Right now, I'm indifferent to it all. It would take a lot of inducing to make me play another year, but money is not the prime consideration."

Had it been virtually any other team, Tim might have been true to his retirement plans. Kelly tossed the Penguins' $40,000 into the pot, gambling that Tim could be persuaded to change his mind. This was, after all, Pittsburgh. Where he had played for the Hornets. Where he had met and married Lori.

On June 9, Kelly called Horton to tell him he'd been drafted, and encountered an unexpected complication. Lori had suffered an allergic reaction to an antibiotic, and in attempting to drive herself to her doctor had gotten into a car accident. On June 11, Kelly revealed to the press that he still hadn't been able to negotiate with Tim. "He was pretty shook up. He said Lori had been given a shot of a new drug and she had reacted to it in the wrong way. She passed out in the car and when the police found her, they had to rush her to hospital. Tim said it was a very near thing."

It is difficult to isolate this incident from the background of Lori's continuing drug problems when assessing Tim's motivations. During the summer of 1971 she was flying to New York once a month to obtain pills from several different sources. (When she had first arrived in New York, she had been able to have her Dexamyl prescription renewed by the Rangers' team doctor. She then secured a second one from a diet doctor.) Ron Joyce would also testify that Tim informed him in 1971 that Lori was in Wellesley Hospital for treatment of substance abuse. Tim had to make a trip to New York to collect her when she suffered an overdose there, and he threatened to divorce her if she didn't clean up. On another occasion, her family was called when she staggered off the plane. Two of her daughters found her wearing no shoes, with her

stockings shredded. She was carrying twelve different kinds of pills, mainly amphetamines and barbiturates (at one point she was taking Tuinol, a
potent sedative comprised of the barbiturates amo-
barbitol and secobarbitol). A doctor who was shown
the pills couldn't identify seven of them. In her testimony, during her lawsuit, Lori recalled flying to
New York every two weeks to pick up 150 pills at a
walk-in clinic, at $100 a visit.

At the beginning of September, Tim made one of
his increasingly familiar reversals and decided that
he was going to play hockey after all. The package
was believed to have been worth more than
$100,000. Horton publicly gave two reasons for
reversing his decision to retire: "My wife and Red
Kelly."

His unelaborated reference to Lori is not difficult
to interpret. Lori had family in Pittsburgh—Tim and
Lori still visited the city every spring and fall. It was
just possible that being in Pittsburgh would give Lori
the support network she required.

It was a festive occasion when they flew to
Pittsburgh to sign the contract with Red Kelly. Ron
Joyce did the flying, and in addition to Lori and
Tim, the partnership's new accountant, Mel
Rothwell, came along as well. Rothwell, who had
been with the firm Dunwoody since 1953, was a
good friend of Dave Keon, and Keon acknowledges
that in all likelihood he made the introduction.
"When Tim and I first met Mel, he was just a sweetheart," says Joyce. "We had had an accountant
doing our books with us when we first started out,
and the guy was always trying to figure out how to
get a piece of the company. Every time we went

there, he'd say, 'Well, if I do this, you sell me a third.' Mel just laid out his fees and what we should do. We both walked out of that meeting and took an instant like to the guy, and he to us. He and Tim became very close." In addition to servicing Tim Donut Ltd., Rothwell also served as the Hortons' personal accountant. According to Rothwell, Tim and Red handled the negotiations for the Pittsburgh contract on their own. Lori went house-hunting in the suburbs.

While Joyce had gone along on the trip to Pittsburgh for Tim's signing, he hadn't been happy with the fact that Tim was, once again, returning to hockey. "As soon as a season ended," Joyce says of their first years as partners, "Tim would be back into it, very aggressively pursuing real estate. The unfortunate part was that when the hockey season started he disappeared. I was hoping that he would retire and concentrate on the business."

Joyce had attempted to fully integrate Tim into the business by teaching him the hands-on side of it, which Joyce had long since mastered. Lori and the kids went up north while Tim showed up for donut-making duty at one of the outlets. Tim's stint as a trainee was a washout. "Ron took me aside for a week and tried to teach me, but I got burned all to hell," he would recall. "Baking donuts is worse than fighting a war. I intend to learn, though. I will when I get out of hockey." He never did get out of hockey, and he never did learn.

While they were equal partners in the company's equity, Joyce felt that he should also be compensated with a salary that reflected the hours he was putting into the business. "He had a real hang-up," says Joyce. "I was working in this business full-time.

The great thing about hockey is that you've developed your skills and it isn't very hard on you in terms of hours. You get up late in the morning, you have a practice, you have a snooze, and you play the game. Whereas this thing was twenty-four hours a day, seven days a week—very demanding. I would say that I think there should be a salary to compensate me for my time, and he didn't want any part of that."

When Tim agreed to play for Pittsburgh, they finally arrived at a revenue-sharing arrangement that Dick Trainor, who was aware of it, sums up as "remarkable." Tim arranged to have his salary paid directly to Tim Donut Ltd.; Tim and Ron then split that money between them and drew it as salary. Both also had a company car, leased from Brian Cullen. It was share and share alike, everything divided down the middle. Essentially, Tim was giving Ron half his hockey salary so that Tim could continue to play hockey, and in return Ron would run the business solo for at least eight months of the year.

Lori Horton remains bitter about this arrangement. "Ron demanded half the salary when Tim went back to hockey. The only way he would give Tim any peace and quiet was if he gave him half his salary. He was the one who begged Tim to take him in as a partner, and I don't know, but all of a sudden he was worth half Tim's salary just a few short years later."

Joyce maintains that the salary-sharing scheme was Tim's idea. "If you look at it in hindsight," says Joyce, "tying his salary to my salary here was probably a very smart thing. 'You let me play hockey, you run the business, and we'll share. We each have 50 per cent of the equity.'" Mel Rothwell will not discuss specifics of Tim's finances, but it is hard to imagine Tim entering into the salary-splitting arrangement with Joyce without Rothwell's input.

Before Tim began playing in Pittsburgh, he and Ron Joyce came to a formal understanding on inheritance with respect to Tim Donut Ltd. Their enterprise had grown far beyond the dimensions of the run-of-the-mill perilous small business. It had substance and potential, and they had come to grapple with the issue of what would happen to the company, and to the surviving partner, should one of them die while Tim Donut was a going concern.

The mechanism they chose was an unusual one: a share trust agreement. The partners each purchased ninety-six common shares at one dollar apiece from the company treasury. Each partner then sold, for one dollar, one of their shares to the other. This share was placed in trust under the proviso that it would be transferred to the other partner upon his death. In other words, if one of the partners died, through the share trust agreement the share held in trust would be transferred to the surviving partner, thus giving him ninety-six common shares, and the heirs of the deceased would have ninety-five shares. (One share would still be in trust, as only one of the parties had died.) The survivor would have control of the company with 50.5 per cent of the common stock. At least part of the logic behind the agreement was that the surviving partner would not find himself sharing control of the company not only with the deceased partner's widow, but with the widow's new husband, should she remarry.

This document would become the "cornerstone" of Lori Horton's 1987 lawsuit against Ron Joyce et al., according to Judge Patricia German, who presided over the case when it went to trial in October 1992. The suit homed in on clause 4, which stated: "The parties hereto acknowledge that this agreement is made in order that the Company may continue to flourish and prosper for the benefit of the survivor *and the heirs of the deceased party*." (italics added)

Lori Horton's case was that the share trust agreement denied her equal status to Joyce as the inheritor of Tim's estate; that by making her a minority partner the share trust agreement put Joyce in the driver's seat when he decided, a year after Tim's death, that he could not continue in partnership with her and proposed buying her out. (What Joyce said he actually proposed, which the judge accepted, is that either he buy out Lori, Lori buy out him, or they both sell to a third party.) Furthermore, her counsel would argue, in moving to buy her out rather than continuing as her partner, Joyce violated clause 4, which implied that the surviving partner was to continue running the company not only for his own benefit, but for the benefit of the heirs of the deceased party as well.

One can interpret the share trust agreement as a consequence of Ron Joyce's possible fear that Tim's death would leave him an equal partner with a widow in the grip of drugs and alcohol. In court, Joyce testified that he had no recollection of seeing Lori impaired by drugs or alcohol in the late 1960s or early 1970s, except on one occasion when she was unsteady on her feet and had to be assisted in to a Christmas party. Joyce's testimony was that Lori was "difficult"; that you never knew which way things would go between Tim and Lori. He recalled an occasion when he was drinking with several other men at Bannatyne Drive when Lori and her friend Renate Pelletier came in and Lori poured Tim's beer over his head.

"The drug I was taking at the time [Dexamyl] probably made my behaviour erratic and changed my personality," says Lori.

Joyce noted that Tim had made him aware in 1971 that Lori was undergoing treatment for substance abuse at Wellesley, and Judge German stated in her judgment: "I am satisfied he knew Mrs. Horton had problems." But it is not necessary to interpret the share trust agreement as something wholly of Ron Joyce's making. Tim would also have had good reasons to agree to it—even to propose it. The company, after all, had Tim's name on it, and he was the president. Were Joyce to die, Tim would probably want to be in a controlling position, and not have to start all over again with Joyce's heirs (and whomever Joyce's widow might choose to marry) as his equal partner.

Tim may also have been thinking of the winding down of the Hannigans' restaurant empire that followed Gord's death in 1966. It could have been particularly on his mind in 1971, since Ray Hannigan moved back to Toronto that year after his wife's death. Tim had long looked to the Hannigans and their experiences when making his way in the business world, and he would have wanted to ensure that his own chain continued to thrive for the benefit of all should he die suddenly, as Gord had.

The Hannigans had been unable to hold together the impressive restaurant chain they had so methodically built. A falling-out between Gord and Ray shortly before Gord's death led to the brothers'

splitting the chain between them as Ray moved to
Red Deer. As young hockey players, Gord and Ray
had been a feisty pair, boxing in Schumacher during the summer, taking on all comers on the rink in
the winter. Sometimes, recalls their Hornets teammate Andy Barbe, they even took on each other.
Frank Mahovlich remembers playing cards in the
Hannigan home in Schumacher one night when
the phone rang. Ray was home, and Gord was out
west trying to make a decision critical to the business. Pat answered the phone. "Gord wanted to talk
to Ray, so Pat said to Ray, 'When you're finished
talking to him, let him say hello to mom.' And
Gordie thought, well, business is business, and he
didn't want to talk to anybody but Ray, and would-
n't talk to his mom. Pat was mad as a son-of-a-gun,"
Mahovlich laughs. "They were all hotheads."

There was something about families and the
restaurant business that just seemed to be asking for
trouble. At about the same time that Gord and Ray
were splitting up their chain, Tim had experienced
his own falling-out with his brother Gerry over the
burger stand in North Bay. And the two biggest
donut chains going, Mr. Donut and Dunkin'
Donuts, existed as separate entities rather than as a
single collosus because of an in-law feud in the
Boston suburbs. After Gord's death, a younger
brother, Greg, had carried on managing Gord's
restaurants, but Ray sold his share of the original
chain. A successful restaurant operation that might
have stopped the fledgling McDonald's in its tracks
at the British Columbia–Alberta border (the first
McDonald's in Canada was opened in Richmond,
B.C., in 1967) faded from contention as a franchising phenomenon. In this context, the share trust

agreement Tim signed reads to some measure as a reaction to the fading of the Hannigans' empire.

Whether or not the share trust structure was, in Tim's mind, part of a safety net for Lori and the children is, ultimately, open to speculation. He never told Lori about the agreement.[3] Justice German's ruling was consistent with the school of thought on contract law that abhors debating inference and holds that what isn't there doesn't exist. "The paragraph [clause 4] does not state that the survivor agrees to operate the business for his benefit and the benefit of the heirs of the deceased party," Justice German concluded. In essence, the agreement did not require that the surviving party be chained to the heirs of his business partner for the rest of his natural life, even if that had been Tim's private wish. Joyce, in fact, maintains that the share trust agreement was Tim's idea entirely, conceived precisely to ensure that he would never have to share control of the company with Joyce's widow.

Although no longer a Ranger, Tim was still popular with his former teammates. Several visited him at the Pittsburgh training camp and presented him with a Superman T-shirt. Never mind the share trust agreement and its implications of mortality. Tim was now officially the Man of Steel. "He wore it," says Lori, "till it was in shreds."

He began the season at a furious pace, scoring twice and recording one assist in the first six games. The Penguins had won five of those games, the last four of them in a row (three of which were on the road), and were tied with Chicago for first in the West. Tim was racing after the puck to produce an icing call in the second period of a home game on

October 22 when he crashed into the boards, breaking his right ankle and damaging surrounding liga-
ments. It was the same ankle he had broken as a
Copper Cliff Redman in the spring of '47; the same
leg he had broken as a Toronto Maple Leaf in the
spring of '55. Ever superstitious, Tim joked about
three times being lucky, but there was nothing fortunate about the injury. He would be lost to the
Penguins until the new year. Pittsburgh had paid
the Rangers $40,000 for his rights and Tim about
$100,000 for his services, and after six games he was
lost for at least six weeks—which proved to be two
months.

At the age of forty-one, Tim had suffered the
most serious injury in his career since his leg and
jaw fracture of 1955. Perhaps his own mortality had
come to weigh heavily on his mind, for on
November 9 he finalised the will that would be in
effect when he died. Tim was approaching what he
had long jested as the likely end of his life. Lori
Horton describes Tim as being "fatalistic." "Tim
used to tell me that most hockey players died before
they were fifty from heart attacks because they work
so hard. When I first met him, he was going to die
before he was fifty because he was a hockey player."
While Lori says he never attached any deep serious-
ness to the comment, this conviction, as much as it
could be called one, could only have been reinforced by the deaths of Gord Hannigan and Jim
Dewey and by his younger brother's heart problems. Throughout his career, Tim had seen one
hockey player after another experience a brush not
just with a career-ending injury, but with death. Tim
had come to play for a Maple Leaf team that would
never forget how their captain Ace Bailey had

ended his playing days in 1933, as Eddie Shore tripped him from behind and fractured his skull on the ice. Until Bill Barilko died, Bailey's was the only number to be retired by the team. During the 1950 Stanley Cup playoffs, Gordie Howe, after colliding with Ted Kennedy, fractured his skull on the boards, and went under the knife to have life-threatening pressure on the brain relieved. In February 1958, Boom-Boom Geoffrion suffered a ruptured bowel in a collision in practice, and was administered last rites before pulling through in surgery. And Boston's defenceman Ted Green, for whom Tim expressed admiration, was skating around with a steel plate in his head after being viciously slashed during a pre-season game in 1969.

And then there were the lives that ended badly when their careers closed out. As Tim prepared his will the death of Terry Sawchuk was a recent memory. Sawchuk, only two weeks younger than Tim, had played with him in Toronto for three seasons, winning the Stanley Cup in '67; they were reunited in New York when Tim was traded by the Leafs. Sawchuk's career had begun darkly when he inherited the goaltending equipment of his older brother, who died of heart failure, and was beset by terrible injuries throughout it.[4] He had played only twenty-one games in his final two NHL seasons, and alcohol had boxed him in.

At the end of the season Sawchuk was divorced from his wife, separated from his seven children, and washed up as a player. On April 29 he fell into an argument with teammate Ron Stewart, with whom he was sharing a rented bungalow on Long Island. The subject was Sawchuk's share of the rent money and his indifference to cleaning the place up as they prepared to leave. Sawchuk attacked Stewart, and in the ensuing scuffle fell on either Stewart's knee or a barbecue. Rushed to hospital, he had his gall bladder removed, but a lacerated liver sent him back into surgery twice more over the next month. On May 31 he died in hospital. It was hard to find a more sobering example of how an exemplary life on the ice could end so badly off it. And only nine days before Tim was injured, another high-profile career in hockey had ended horribly. Stafford Smythe died at the age of fifty from complications following stomach surgery. Only days before his trial on humiliating fraud charges, Smythe had been consumed by the ulcer they had engendered.

Tim's will was a relatively simple document: it named Lori his sole executrix. In the event that Lori, too, died either fifteen days before or after him, Donald "Red" Alberts, the husband of Lori's sister Joanne, would serve as executor and trustee. Alberts was living in Pittsburgh, and his son, D.J. (Donald John), was an air force combat pilot in Vietnam. "The two got along so well," Lori says of Tim and D.J., who wrote Tim stirring accounts of dogfights with MiGs. "Tim used to carry his letters around with him for months." When Tim and Lori visited Europe at the end of the 67/68 season, D.J., who was stationed there, managed to clear away enough red tape to allow him to take Tim for a ride in a fighter jet. But Tim had turned down the opportunity, in part because of his claustrophobia.

The will's implications were thoroughly uncomplicated. If Tim died, Lori would inherit all of his assets, including his half of Tim Donut and his share of Tim Horton Holdings. (Tim also placed the family's real estate in Lori's name.) The will was witnessed by Ron Joyce and Tim Donut's lawyer, Ken Gariepy, who also provided legal services for Tim Horton Holdings, the property investment partnership. Joyce, Gariepy and Tim also bought about 150 acres of land together near Orangeville, Ontario.

It is a bald, compelling fact that, two days after Tim's will was finalised, making Lori his sole heir, Lori checked herself into Pittsburgh's St. Francis General Hospital. She left about two weeks later, on November 27, one day after the nineteenth birthday of their eldest daughter, Jeri-Lynn, with a final diagnosis of anxiety depression, Dexamyl dependence and migraine. On December 16 she again voluntarily admitted herself to St. Francis, and emerged in time for her youngest daughter Traci's twelfth birthday on December 27 (and her own on January 1).

The convergence of these events—Tim's will (which was preceded by the signing of the share trust agreement), Lori's voluntary hospitalizations, their daughter's birthdays—raises a host of questions not just about Lori's condition, but about Tim's attitude towards it and appreciation of it. Tim's decision simply to leave his estate to his wife without provisos is perplexing. He had not only Lori to think of but his four daughters as well, and two weeks after the will was signed his eldest daughter turned nineteen. Yet Tim made no immediate provision for his children in the will, even though they were reaching adulthood and Lori at this point was functioning poorly. He left behind no trust structure by which his children's interests could be addressed. They were only to benefit in the event that Lori died within fifteen days of him, in which case the trustee was to divide what remained of his estate after taxes and funeral expenses equally among his children "for their own use absolutely," provided they had reached the age of twenty-five. The will did not contemplate the possibility of Lori's surviving him and inheriting his estate as directed, and then being incapable of managing it, either in her own best interest or that of their children.

Tim was no doctor, and he may have been blind to the full extent of Lori's condition. But this is hard to imagine, given Lori's periods of crisis following Tim's trade to New York. One is forced to conclude either that Lori's condition was not as serious as it seemed, or that Tim, through love or ignorance or denial, produced a routine will that failed to recognise and accommodate Lori's condition.

Lori says Tim had difficulty understanding her condition. She was, after all, taking drugs prescribed by doctors, not freebasing cocaine. Although her need for Dexamyl and other drugs had compelled her to start doctor-hopping, she was still getting her drugs through legitimate prescriptions.

"Dexamyl was prescribed as an antidepressant, and over a long period of time, and it's highly addictive," says Lori. "After a couple of years, it's progressive. You have to take twice the number to get the same effect. But because it was being prescribed by a doctor I took them. It's something I don't understand. It never should have been. I have an AA book that says it takes a doctor thirty seconds to write a prescription where it would take an hour to solve the problem. I'm not blaming the doctors solely. I was the one that took them. And then Tim didn't understand it because they were being prescribed. How could he argue with a doctor?"

In fact, it seemed that whenever Lori tried to stop

taking Dexamyl, her condition worsened, which could create the perverse impression that the drug was helping her. A letter written by a Pittsburgh physician in connection with her second voluntary hospitalization there noted that Lori "has become both psychologically and pharmacologically dependent on this drug. In view of this, I think it is much easier to understand her feeling of depression and lassitude when she attempts to reduce the drug."

There is another, equally plausible reason for why Tim produced such a routine will despite Lori's problems. Tim may have thought himself as indestructible, as a person for whom a will would only become relevant when he reached old age. If anything, the lack of foresight in the will speaks of a distancing on his part from the very purpose of the will: to provide for an orderly inheritance should he drop dead the day after he signed it. A will so routine for someone whose professional and private life was so complex suggests that Tim considered it nothing more than a bit of legal work he had to have completed after the share trust agreement was signed, a few sheafs of paper with no real relevance to his life.

This view would seem to be buttressed by the fact that Tim was carrying no life insurance when he died. It wasn't that he could not conceive of the need for it, for Tim had in fact carried a policy, sold to him by his old Hornets teammate Frank Sullivan. In Sullivan's mind, Tim didn't cancel it because he thought he would live forever. "That went by the boards because it was not at the end a very happy marriage, so he wasn't too concerned about carrying on the insurance." All the same, if Tim cancelled it because at the time he didn't want to leave anything else to Lori, he didn't replace it with one that would make his children his beneficiary.[5]

Tim's true intentions with respect to his estate will never be known. One of the great difficulties in attempting to fathom Tim's intentions is that his point of view on any number of subjects—in particular his marriage, his plans to keep playing hockey, his enthuasiasm for an off-ice career—was far from static. In his final years, he was in an endless state of turmoil over the most essential aspects of his life. On the issue of where his life was headed—not over a period of years but simply over the next few months—he regularly changed his mind.

Tim was in rarefied territory for a hockey player. Few players had ever lasted as long in the game as he had, and certainly no one else had found themselves facing the choice of still playing when he was over forty or committing himself full-time to an off-ice business that was as promising as the donut chain. Tearing him in another direction entirely was his oscillating relationship with Lori and the turbulence of raising a crop of teenage girls. At the same time, money issues were causing tension between Tim and Ron Joyce.

With such a cloud of indecision and confusion surrounding him, all that can be said is that the inheritance mechanism he left behind either provided no more protection and security than he thought appropriate, or failed spectacularly to meet his intentions, based on the issues before him in turbulent 1971.

The move to Pittsburgh was an unqualified disaster for the family. "Dad was hurt, and we hated it," Jeri-Lynn sums up. "Mom thought it would be nice to go back and stay a year with her family, but..." There was a big difference between visiting relatives once or twice a year and living in and around them every day. The children rebelled. "Kim and Kelly kept running away back to Toronto," says Jeri-Lynn. In one ruse, Lori recalls, they borrowed the car to drive to the drugstore, and kept on going all the way to Toronto. Tim had to fly to Toronto to retrieve them. For her part, Jeri-Lynn was continuing her romance with Ab DeMarco by shuttling between Pittsburgh and New York. Lori's hospitalizations that fall in Pittsburgh were the nadir of an awful year for Tim, both personally and professionally.

As he prepared to return to play for Pittsburgh, he was interviewed by *Hockey News*. Out of action for two months, and having just turned forty-two, the desire to play again seemed to be ebbing. The donut business was drawing him back. "I feel about the business the way I used to feel about hockey," he said. "It's fresh and interesting and challenging. Hockey ceased being that for me some time back, though I still enjoy the game. I've had as much individual recognition as a man could want and played on more than my share of champions. And I can make good money in business, too. In fact, I've tried two or three businesses, but I found to make them go you really have to work at them. Your name isn't enough. We're expanding our donut operation and we build our own buildings. We franchise, but you have to get the right location, the right franchise holders and so forth. This is my future and I worry that if I don't concentrate on it, it may not work for me as well as it should." But the story noted another reason for Tim to finally give up hockey. "Tim and his wife, Lori, have four children, who are growing up and leaving home, and he felt it was time he spent more time with them." Tim may have come to the conclusion that continuing to play hockey was only exacerbating the blossoming crises at home.

But Jeri-Lynn doesn't think her father's quitting the game would have solved anything. "The problem [with Lori] was there since I was twelve years old. It was there all along, and would flare up, and calm down. Dad went through hell... Mom had her problems, and Dad did what he did [continuing to play] to kind of get away. I know New York was hell, and Pittsburgh, as far as that goes. New York was a good playing year for him, but not for him and Mom." (Lori says that it was the season in Pittsburgh, not New York, that was the disastrous one.) "And we [the children] weren't that great, either. I've got to admit we put him through hell. He was being pulled in twenty different directions."

Ron Joyce felt that Tim continued to play hockey, despite his repeatedly stated intentions to retire, "for a whole lot of issues," including his basic love of the game. "I think money had a lot to do with it, but it was also the difficulty he was having in his personal life. It got him out of an environment that he wasn't very happy in."

In early February, the prospect of committing himself full-time to the donut business continued to occupy him. Horton told George Gross of the *Toronto Sun* that the chain now had twenty-seven stores. "I think we've got as many as any other company in Canada. And we plan to open six more in the spring. So things are not looking too bad." But by month's end his hockey career was taking priority again, and the main reason seemed to be the impending debut of the World Hockey Association the following autumn. The WHA would usher in seven years of unprecedented bidding for the services of professional hockey players. Although the league iced a total of thirty-two teams as failures begat new franchises, and only four survived to be folded into the NHL, the WHA proved a fiscal bonanza for the players. As Tim returned to play with Pittsburgh, the Miami franchise had just lured its first NHL player—Toronto goaltender Bernie Parent—to the WHA with a five-year $750,000 package that would include a new boat, house and car every year. While the Miami franchise folded before the season began, Parent still jumped, to the Philadelphia Blazers, for one traumatic season.

Tim was astounded by the money being proffered by the new league. "First we had expansion—now this," he said to the *Toronto Star*'s Milt Dunnell. "You know it wasn't until expansion that I made over $25,000 as a Leaf? It included what I got for winning the Stanley Cup and being on the All Star team. Hell, they sign rookies for $25,000 now." At the same time, he noted: "My contract with the Penguins expires at the end of this season and I'm not sure whether they'll want me back. If they don't, there's still the World Hockey Association. Who knows, they might offer me a contract."

The Penguins didn't want him back. Before the season was out he had separated his shoulder in a collision with Detroit's Alex Delvecchio. He played a total of forty-four games, registered eleven points and forty penalty minutes, and the Penguins made a quick exit from the playoffs. In four games, Tim recorded one assist and a minor penalty. Red Kelly was convinced he had made the right decision in signing him. "He is one of the most powerful men ever to play hockey, and one of the smartest," he said in mid-season. "He makes plays you don't see much anymore. He is one of the oldest players still in the league, but also one of the ablest." At the beginning of the 72/73 season, he was still defending the signing. "I drafted Tim from the Rangers and it was one of the smartest moves I ever made in hockey. Just as I figured, some of Tim's polish rubbed off on our young players."

Tim had indeed been a positive influence, particularly on rookie defenceman Dave Burrows, and twenty-nine-year-old Bryan Watson, who was just beginning to find his place as a defenceman in the NHL. But at an estimated $100,000 in salary and $40,000 for his rights, the Penguins had spent about $1,100 for every period of hockey Tim had played. Kelly was prepared to sign Tim to another season, but Jack Riley, the former Penguins general manager who had moved upstairs to make room for Kelly as coach and G.M., was not. Their disagreement over the value of Horton has been cited as one of the reasons Riley took over as G.M. from Kelly the next season; Kelly was soon replaced as coach by Ken Schinkel.

By the start of the 72/73 season, whether Tim would or could play another season for Pittsburgh was moot. He had again retired from hockey at the end of the 71/72 season. And the following autumn, he was again unretired, and playing. This time it was in Buffalo—for the man who, as Tim said in 1969, had put so much money in his pocket.

Chapter 21

Carpe Diem

The Buffalo Sabres had the sort of rookie season one would expect of an expansion franchise in 70/71, winning only twenty-four of seventy-eight games, but the following season represented anything but progress. Punch Imlach, who had been hired as coach and general manager after being fired by the Leafs, suffered a heart attack in January 1972; Joe Crozier, who had coached the Leafs' Rochester Americans farm team in the 1960s (winning three Calder Cups in five seasons), was brought in behind the bench (and stayed there for the next two seasons), but the Sabres fumbled through the rest of the 71/72 season, winning only sixteen games, the third-worst record in the fourteen-team league.

As an expansion franchise, Buffalo was saddled with raw recruits and assorted castoffs, and Imlach did what he could to give the team some leadership through available veterans. He brought in Roger Crozier (no relation to Joe) from Detroit as his main goaltender the very first season; that season he also cut deals with Los Angeles (where former Leaf Larry Regan was general manager) to bring in former Leafs Eddie Shack and Dick Duff. Duff stayed for Buffalo's second season before retiring; Shack was dealt to Pittsburgh that second season, where Red Kelly was coaching and Tim Horton was playing. And on December 16, 1971, Imlach sent Mike Keeler and Doug Barrie to L.A. in exchange for Mike Byers and Larry Hillman. Imlach had not forgotten the $500 that had stood between him and Hillman after the 1967 Stanley Cup season, which ended up getting Hillman suspended and finally traded away. Imlach phoned Hillman and declared, "I guess you never expected to hear from me."

Says Hillman, "Imlach said to me, 'We're having problems with younger players. We need an older influence. I can't afford to have some of these players having a go-buy-a-six-pack drinking problem.'"

When the NHL's intraleague draft was held in Montreal on June 5, 1972, Imlach was looking for the right talent to help hoist his Sabres out of the cellar. It was an especially difficult time to be building a team. The talent pool, already thinned out by having been stretched from six to fourteen NHL teams over the past five seasons, was about to become thinner still through the addition of two more NHL teams, in Atlanta and Long Island. The NHL had hurriedly added them to help block the market incursions of the new World Hockey Association, which would launch its inaugural season that fall with twelve teams of its own. As an outlaw league, the WHA was free to poach away at players on NHL rosters whose contracts were up for renewal, and it needed more than three hundred players for its debut. WHA owners were paying big money, even for journeymen, and the NHL general managers gathered in Montreal that June were learning how much of a headache this rival league could prove to be. The new New York Islanders franchise, for example, drafted twenty players for its first NHL season but saw seven of them report to

WHA teams instead. In all, about seventy NHL players made the switch that first season. Three weeks after the NHL intraleague draft was held, Bobby Hull rocked the status quo by signing with the Winnipeg Jets of the WHA for $1 million up front and $2.75 million over ten years to serve as player-coach. Among the players who followed him to the WHA that summer was Gerry Cheevers, whose work in the net for Boston had been critical in their Stanley Cup victory the previous spring.

Imlach was frantic about the competition. Hillman remembers Imlach asking him at the end of the 71/72 season if he had been approached by the WHA, and as far as Hillman knew, he hadn't. Unbeknown to him, though, a draft notice from the WHA's Cleveland Barons franchise had arrived in the mailbox he kept at the Sabres office the day after the season ended, and sat there over the summer. When he finally discovered it at the start of the 72/73 season, having by then signed with Buffalo for another year, he learned—too late—that Cleveland had been prepared to pay him $25,000 more than Imlach had.

Going into the intraleague draft, Imlach had his eye on Bruins defenceman Ted Green, who had garnered such praise from Tim Horton only a few seasons earlier. But Imlach found his hands tied when the Vancouver Canucks (who had entered the league with Buffalo in 1970) drafted from Boston Don Tannahill, a twenty-three-year-old left-winger who had yet to play an NHL game. Both Tannahill and Green were on the Bruins' reserve list, and a club was only able to lose one player from its list through the intraleague draft.

With Green unavailable, Imlach fell back on his

stability-through-veterans strategy. Tim Horton was
up for grabs, though he was making his usual noises
about being through with hockey. At forty-two years
of age, he was firmly ensconced as one of the game's
elder statesmen. At the end of the 71/72 season, he
had played 1,322 NHL games, and was the only
active defenceman other than Bobby Orr to have
played in six All Star games. A few days before the
draft, the *Globe and Mail* had reported that Tim
"needs more time to look after the chain of doughnut shops he operates." Imlach wasn't buying that
for a minute. He drafted him.

When asked about Tim's alleged determination
to stick to donuts, he shot back, "What about it? Ten
years ago [actually six], when I tried to sign him in
Peterborough, he gave me all that baloney about his
doughnuts. Hell, at the end of the season he even
sent me a stale package of 'em... He was great when
there were six teams and 24 defencemen, and now
there's fifty defencemen. It's like wine. Some of
them get better with age. And look at Beliveau, look
at how he played last season. I'll tell you, if I was
sure he'd play I would have drafted him today.

"I've got the perfect rink for him," Imlach
declared. "It's a small rink, and that would give him
that much more time to get a hold of the other
guy." (Buffalo's Memorial Auditorium ice is one
foot narrower and seven feet shorter than a standard NHL rink.) While conceding that picking
Horton was "a gamble," he avowed that "we just
couldn't pass up a player of his calibre. He's a winner and he's also the type who sets an example by
what he does, not what he says. He can't be pushed
around, either. That's important." But wouldn't he
really rather have had Ted Green? "I'm not saying

that Green's better," Imlach cautioned, "it's just that he's 10 years younger."

Even though Imlach had called the drafting of Horton a gamble, there was a suspicion that perhaps the fix had been in, that Punch and his General from the Leaf glory days had already come to an understanding before the draft that Tim would come out of retirement if it meant playing for Imlach again. Certainly they had not lost touch. When Imlach had been hospitalised with his heart attack that January, Tim showed up at his bedside with Lori, Punch's nemesis from the 1960s, in tow. Says Lori, "Tim pushed me in the room and said, 'Here's the reason you had a heart attack, Punch!'"

Imlach sported a mischievous smile when asked at the draft if he had already spoken with Tim. "Now, you don't think I'd tamper, do you?" he posed. Later, he gibed, "Sure I talked to him—maybe five or ten years ago."

Negotiations between Imlach and Horton continued for the rest of the summer. On September 7, Tim came down to St. Catharines, as the rookie portion of the Sabres' training camp was being held. He signed his contract, had a short skate, then went back to the Tim Donut office in Oakville.

Tim maintained the over-the-hill-gang tone that had crept into his public statements since winning the Stanley Cup in 1967. Commenting on his one-year contract, he noted: "At my age and in my condition, I'm lucky they didn't give me a month-to-month contract." He kept mum on his salary, believed to be in the $125,000 range, saying only, "It was bigger than a bread box but smaller than a Volkswagen." As to why he was now a Sabre, he declared, "There's not many better to play for than Punch."

"My health improved a helluva lot when he agreed to play for us," Imlach said. "I'm happy to have a guy of his stature on my team. You wait and see, he'll help us. The hell with his age. He's got a young body, like Johnny Bower. I don't think he's a pound over his playing weight. Our rink is a little smaller than some and that will help him, too. If he's gone back a step, and I'm not saying he has, he'll get it back in our rink. He's been an All Star six times. We've never had anyone like that around here. The kids know what he has done. They'll look up to him and respect him."

"Imlach needed me for the fatherly instinct," says Hillman, "and then he reinforced that by bringing Tim in, and got an experienced player to boot. Imlach was scared of having too many young guys, too many followers. You can't run a hockey club without some examples to filter down and for them to relate to."

"Maybe he'd like to come back and get even for all the things I did to him when I had him in Toronto," Imlach cracked the day he drafted Tim. There might have been more than a hint of apprehension in that statement. Says Dave Keon, "Tim told me one time when he was playing in Buffalo, 'You know, Punch offered me so much money, he must feel guilty for all the times he's beaten me up in Toronto. So he's paying me now.'"

"I think Tim had wanted to retire the last three years or so, but Punch kept stuffing his pockets with money," says Allan Stanley. "I was talking on the phone one time with him. I had heard about the money he was getting, and I said, 'How is it down there at contract time?' He said, 'Allan, you wouldn't believe it. Money doesn't mean anything to them. Do you remember how we used to leave camp over two hundred bucks? That's all changed.' The money I think was the thing that kept him there. They were a new business [Tim Donut] and they needed the money. I know Tim told me his cheque went straight to the business, and he'd draw from the business."

Dave Dryden had first met Tim when Dryden was playing for the Junior Marlies at the start of the Maple Leafs' Imlach era. The league was still a few seasons away from making it mandatory for every team to have two dressed goaltenders on hand for a game. Dryden—who like his younger brother Ken was a goaltender—had signed a C-form with the Leafs. ("I was just sort of at the end of it," he says. "Oh, you were being manipulated so much, and we didn't know half of what was going on.") For home games the Leafs would install him in the press box as their backup. In 60/61, when Tim missed about a dozen games because of a back injury, he, too, passed his time in the press box. "It was the very first time I met him," says Dryden. "It was great. He was an amazingly terrific guy from my standpoint. I was in awe of him."

Dryden's professional career was not to happen with Toronto. The Leafs were winning Stanley Cups with Johnny Bower and Terry Sawchuk, and off loaded two young netminding prospects, Dryden and Gerry Cheevers. Cheevers went to Boston, and Dryden went to Chicago. When the Buffalo Sabres entered the league in 1970, Imlach drafted Dryden as his backup to Roger Crozier. Over the next few seasons, Dryden would steadily emerge as Buffalo's main netminder.

Finding himself, at last, teammates with Tim in 1972, Dryden's opinion of him had a chance to modify. While Imlach intended the players to look up to Tim and respect him, Tim's reputation preceded him, and it was not good. The word, after his season in Pittsburgh, was that he was over the hill, and a reckless carouser. "Within the culture of hockey at that time," says Dryden, "when Timmy came to us, we had a lot of questions in our minds, because we'd heard a lot about Tim. I guess that's why I admired him as much as I did, because in the time I saw him in Buffalo he was nothing but an admirable person. Even the way he dealt with the Lori situation. His daughters were causing him some hassles too, but he was always so gracious about things. You'd think, 'This can't be the guy I've heard so many stories about.' I guess it's important that in his Buffalo years he was right back on track with everything."

"The period of time that I really knew Tim, which was to 1967," says Bob Baun, "he was a very straight guy, a fun guy to be with, but then there were some changes that started to take place in '67. I didn't stay as close to Tim, because I went to California. I helped him with his contracts, stuff like that. That was mostly over the phone. Then we'd see each other over the season a couple times, and that would be it. There was a definite change from the time I left Toronto. I knew as early as the fall of '68 that there was a change, just from the behaviour of the Maple Leaf hockey club. The players were doing things that we would never do before. That's when the demise of the Leafs started. Punch started trading everybody off. In the end this just took the heart right out of the club. I know they started doing more drinking, that sort of thing."

Alcohol is a depressing constant in the lives of hockey players. Some careers never got off the ground because players were alcoholics by the time they were in their early twenties. The single greatest contributing factor was not the stress of the profession, but boredom. Players who were on the ice for no more than a few hours a day, who were on the road in hotels away from friends and family, sank into the debilitating routine of killing time in bars with teammates. Lori Horton came to feel that drinking together as a team was something encouraged by management, although in Buffalo Punch Imlach raised hackles by marching into bars and ordering the players back to their rooms well before curfew. While Tim, with his burgeoning restaurant business, had more off-ice distractions to occupy him than most other players, he still could not avoid the intrusion of alcohol late in his career. In Lawrence Martin's profile, published in *Canadian* magazine in 1973, the narrative is sprinkled with references to drinking, which in hindsight read like red flags. Tim sips a rum while surveying the Tim Donut office and remarks, "We've had quite a few good bashes in here"; makes a joke about perfecting a rum-flavoured donut with a limit of six per customer; notes that he prefers the crowds at Buffalo's "Aud" to the Maple Leaf Gardens audience because the availability of beer makes them livelier; and announces that this will be his last hockey season because he wants to "take up drinking a little more seriously."

"I always found Tim to be the same person," says Lori, "But I found that alcohol began changing him. I don't know if Tim was an alcoholic, but he

definitely suffered a personality change when he
was drinking. Most of the time he was happy, but
sometimes he got very violent. He was frightening
at times. It was not a good situation. Alcoholism is a
progressive disease, and at first it was fun, but after
a while it wasn't funny any more. He made a conscious effort to stop drinking when he reached
Buffalo. It was a marriage pact. We had a lot of bad
things in the summertime. I wasn't going to go to
Buffalo unless he stopped drinking. And he did it.
He was pretty good."

It was around this time that Tim and Lori were
driving to Cambridge twice a week for counselling
sessions with Gordon Griggs to deal with their marriage problems and Tim's drinking. Reverend
Griggs was (and is) of the "muscular Christian"
school of theology, unafraid of issuing profanities
and not averse to having a drink himself. He
remembers Tim calling him while he was at a training camp in Kitchener, asking him to fetch a six-
pack of beer for him. Griggs couldn't get it, so
instead the two retired to a local hotel, and talked
and drank for four hours. "He drank a bottle of rye
and I drank a bottle of scotch." Lori appreciated
Griggs's counselling, but at the same time found it
amusing that Griggs would come over to the house
to help Tim with his drinking…and sit there drinking with him.

Tim's problem with drinking, says Griggs,
stemmed from the fact that "his body just would not
succumb to alcohol. The bad news was that he
could drink three bottles. He didn't pass out and go
to sleep." Having been a beer drinker for most of
his life, in his later years he had switched to hard
liquor. Tim would become what he calls "blind

drunk. You've had so much to drink that you're not
functioning as a person. You want to die. His body
could take it all in, but his nervous system would
not accept it." Griggs says Tim got in this state "on
two or three occasions."

Lori says those final years in Buffalo were among
the best she and Tim had together. "It was wonderful. We were there with no kids. The kids stayed
home with the housekeeper. Not that I didn't miss
my children; I called them every weekend. We
drove to Niagara Falls together in the middle of the
winter. It was great. And Tim was making an honest
effort to stop drinking."

Lori would never completely shake her dependence on Dexamyl while Tim was alive—she was still
flying to New York every three weeks to get pills.
"You couldn't separate Timmy from the situation
with Lori," says Dave Dryden. "As a guy on the
team, you knew there were times when something
was wrong, and you figured it probably had to do
with the family situation."

Tim never did completely abstain from drinking.
A few hotel doors were knocked down while he was
with the Sabres. "He still did it," says Dryden, "but it
was very rare. I can't remember the place, but I
remember the guys saying, 'Holy jeez, Timmy really
did it last night,' and it was the whole door routine
again. But he seemed awfully sheepish about it."

Unlike Tim Horton, Jim Schoenfeld had grown up
in the sixties, in the age of television and "Hockey
Night and Canada," where the Leafs provided entertainment for millions on Wednesday and Saturday
nights as they assembled their four Stanley Cup victories. As a kid in Galt, Ontario, says Schoenfeld, "I

was a big Maple Leaf fan. You've got Baun and Brewer and Horton and Stanley, and Duff and Nevin, and Johnny Bower. They're winning Stanley Cups and I'm sitting there with my dad watching them on television. Then, as a twenty-year-old, Tim Horton is my partner, my mentor, and for me as a player, it was a real blessing."

Schoenfeld had played Junior hockey in London, Hamilton and Niagara Falls before being drafted by the Sabres in 1972. His first training camp was also Tim's first as a Sabre. Tim was old enough to be Schoenfeld's father. As a rookie, Schoenfeld hadn't been privy to the rumours about Horton, and so approached his teammate without doubts or apprehensions. With Schoenfeld, and many other welcoming young players, Tim fell easily into the mentoring role Imlach had cut out for him.

"When Punch brought him in," says Dryden, "he put that role on him, and I think that was a natural for Tim. He was a mentor by leading and by encouragement. He was not too directive. I think also that Imlach had him as a strong man, knowing that that was needed on the team too."

"Schoenfeld would have seen a guy at the end of his career who was quite willing to pass things on," says Dick Duff, "and Schoenfeld was wise enough to know what price Tim had already paid to be where he was. I would think he'd be affected by him. That's part of the obligation of being a veteran player. He takes great satisfaction in seeing a guy come along and get better. Timmy would have loved it if those Buffalo guys could ever have gotten their hands on the Cup, and they almost did."

"He was without a doubt the best player we had, and an experienced defenceman," says Joe Crozier.

"All the rest were kids. Paul Terbenche, Larry Carriere, Billy Hajt, Jimmy Schoenfeld, Tracy Pratt. He helped the kids. He helped them progress."

"Coaches can only teach you so much," says Schoenfeld, who went on to become a captain of the Sabres and an NHL coach himself. "But when you have a teammate you admire the way I admired Timmy, and they tell you things and you see them do it on the ice, it has a real impact and a lasting effect. If I had been shown by a lesser man, who knows if it would have stayed with me? Who knows if I would have paid attention to it, if I would have given an honest effort to find out how helpful it can be? But when it was someone with quiet strength and, in my eyes, greatness, it meant something.

"He brought an awful lot to the Sabres, but specifically to me, and helped me immensely in my early development. But what I think Timmy brought to the team and to individual players goes well beyond the hockey. He was a good example of a guy that did everything to the max. He worked hard, partied hard, played hard. It was kind of like the expression 'seize the day—carpe diem.' He epitomised that. When Hortie was having fun, he was having a great time and everybody around him was having a great time. When it was serious business, it was all business and everyone around him was down to serious business. He had that quiet way of making people fall into line without ever saying anything. He had that inner strength, and for the lack of a better word, magnetism. If you were clowning around and he gave you a serious look, you quit clowning around and got down to business.

"He was a man of few words. He wasn't a rah-rah guy. He didn't stand up and scream and yell, but that made him more effective when he did speak, because when he spoke, people paid attention. For myself, you quickly got past the idol, the guy you watched, and then you were on a different level as a friend. Although it was a short friendship, it was something that I will always cherish. He had a real positive influence on my career and on my life as a young guy growing up."

Tim was a nonstop tutor for Schoenfeld, his lessons carrying over from practices right into the games. "I would come off the ice when we were partners and he would say something right then. It was on-the-job training. He never said, 'Do this, do that.' He knew I was a hard-head. He knew how to talk to me in a way that I would listen. It wasn't like every shift, but when there was something that needed to be said, he'd say it. It would be, 'You know what? I wonder if…' or 'Why don't we try that?'"

As coached by Crozier and tutored by Tim, Schoenfeld was indoctrinated in a classic mind-your-own-end defensive style. "There was more emphasis on keeping the puck out of the net than going coast-to-coast with it," says Schoenfeld. "That was Bobby Orr's era and everybody wanted to be Bobby Orr, so nobody had to be told to carry the puck. More often than not you had to be told to pass it, because while you're carrying it four guys are standing still and you've got five opponents waiting for you." As a Junior player, and well into his NHL career, Tim had indulged himself in the electrifying end-to-end rushes that would make Orr famous. Now he was determined to purge that impulse from the young men who looked up to him. "The lesson was, the puck is the thing that saves you a lot of steps," says Schoenfeld. "You don't have to do it yourself. Pass it to this guy and you get it back. It's the old give-and-go. Trying to deke, you get yourself into all sorts of trouble."

Tim did his utmost to pass on more than two decades of hands-on defensive experience. He showed Schoenfeld how backing up into your own end might stop a puck carrier from being able to skate around you, but it also let the puck into your defensive zone and the opposing team with it. "Letting them into your zone, you're screwed, because now you've got to chase them all over the place," says Schoenfeld. "Stop them outside your blueline, you turn it over and your team counters." He showed him how to take a man into the boards and take the fight out of him—not by directing an elbow at his head, but by hitting him upwards, raising his skates away from the ice and denying him the traction to fight back. "There were hundreds of little things, and each one of them eliminated a lot of work. They were all ways to get the job done with less effort, and that's what a good veteran will teach you." No fuss, no problem: there was more than a bit of Allan Stanley in the lessons Tim delivered to the young Sabres.

"I always felt that Timmy was close to the Knoxes," says Dryden. "They were so proud to have him. We'd had Eddie Shack, and that was fine, but Timmy Horton, that was even more than Shack. We were a team of sort-of leftovers, and there was Timmy, and he was different."

"As a longtime hockey fan," says franchise chairman Seymour Knox III, "I knew exactly who Tim Horton was and why he would help us and how he would help us. He was strong and aggressive, and a real gentleman all the way through, and we always liked him very much. He had a great sense of humour. Tim was very friendly with those of us in management and ownership, too, because he was in his declining years in his career. I remember him talking about different things, subjects other than hockey, that the other players didn't or couldn't talk about, because they didn't have the experience or the reputation. He came to me when the first Tim Donut franchise was about to be opened in western New York. He wanted to talk about it, how he could get help financially from American investors or from friendly Buffalo banks."

"He was more than a star," says Schoenfeld. "You have to remember he was forty-three years old. It wasn't like he was a thirty-five-year-old veteran. When you're forty-three, there's something special about the athlete, to be able to compete at the National league level and be one of the better players on the team."

"I don't know how he did it," says Jeri-Lynn. "I don't have half the energy he had, and he was three years older than I am now. I couldn't do it, work the schedule that he did."

By the standards of the expansion-era game, Tim was not a large man. Players overall were getting bigger, especially defencemen. Schoenfeld, who stood six-two in bare feet and weighed 210 pounds, dwarfed Horton, at five-nine, and (in his final playing days) 195 pounds. But his physical presence had in no way diminished. "When I played with the Blackhawks, it used to be a joke with us that Bobby Hull would get off the scales every morning and he would be 192," says Dryden. "He was always the same. When I saw Timmy, I just equated them. They were the same height, the same build, with both of them the type that weren't vicious, just so frigging powerful.

"The thing he used to do to me all the time—it was silly and stupid, but I just can't forget it—is Tim used to talk about 'owe-me's.' I still do it to this day," says Dryden, who is now a high-school principal. "If I get someone in a position where I could just nail them, verbally or whatever, then it's, 'Well, that's an owe-me. Don't forget that.' Timmy used to do that in the skating drills with me. Joe Crozier and Punch used to have those brutal practices, and they skated the hell out of us. We'd be skating around, and Tim was so powerful, he'd get me between himself and the boards, and he'd lift me. Well, in equipment I'm 210 pounds. I'd be in a position where if he didn't let me back down again, I'm going to go crashing into the boards. But he's got me in this unbalanced position, and he just looks across at me and smirks and says, 'Huh-huh, that's an owe-me,' and lets me back down. And he used to do that continually. I got the biggest kick out of this big, powerful guy playing this kid's game of owe-me."

Schoenfeld remembers a practice at which Peter MacNab, a centre who was six-three and over 200 pounds, "came motoring down the wing and tried to jump to get by Horton. Tim put his arm out, and not only stopped him, but held him in the air. To see the guy, he was built like these musclemen, and he worked at it."

"He was like a bull in a china shop," says Joe Crozier. "He cleared the front of the net. You couldn't take the puck out of the corner away from him. He was strong, besides being a leader. He was a guy everybody wanted to have on their team. Punch was lucky when he coached the Leafs. He had him for years. That would have been a dream of anybody."

When Tim was reporting to Buffalo for his first training camp in 1972, the best Canadians in the National league (those in the new WHA had been blacklisted) were convening as Team Canada to meet the Soviet Red Machine in the 1972 summit series. (Jeri-Lynn says Tim turned down the opportunity to play for Team Canada because he so loathed Alan Eagleson, the series organizer.) Canada squeaked through with a heroic victory, but hockey in North America was immediately transformed by the lessons of off-ice conditioning drummed in by the exquisitely prepared Russians. In short order the Sabres had their own off-ice programs, both at training camps and during the regular season. "Hortie was right up there with everybody," says Schoenfeld, "and past most of them. No matter what the exercise, how many repetitions or how much weight, he'd add some, no trouble."

"Whatever we did, whether it was running or callisthenics, Horton was always first," says Joe Crozier. Tim had developed a reputation as being a bit lazy in the off-season, and for hating training camp, but he had always been careful to maintain his muscle tone. Lori bought him barbells around 1966, and visitors to the house would find him curling weights as he watched TV. Tim couldn't walk by a set of barbells lying on the floor without giving them a hoist.

"I can see where Tim might think that nothing could kill him," says Schoenfeld. "He *was* strong. He wasn't mean, and if he was he probably would have killed some people on the ice, in the era of the seventies."

Tim's conditioning may have been the most impressive lesson he could deliver to the younger players. "That amazes me, that Timmy was still playing at forty-four," says Dryden. "I remember him in Toronto as being the booming slapshot from the point and scoring and getting lots of assists off it. In Buffalo we had guys like Jerry Korab who could shoot the puck twice as hard as Timmy could by that time. To me that's where his age showed more than anything else, in the quickness of his shot. All of the other things, his mannerisms, were exactly the same as when he played in Toronto."

Tim's conditioning told Schoenfeld: "If I really want to be the best I can be, it takes no intelligence. All it takes is hard work. You don't have to be smart or take lessons, you just have to work hard. The other part of the game, you have to have some intelligence, that's a whole different learning process, but this was one thing that I thought was the easiest thing in the world. All it took was some hard work and dedication. Tim was a great example of that.

"Larry Hillman was more of an offensive player, and he was a great help, too," says Schoenfeld. "I would sit in the corner in the dressing room, Timmy to my left, Larry to my right. Sometimes between periods they would tell me old Maple Leaf stories. It was great—it would relax me."

The three men—the two Original Sixers and the Expansion Kid—regularly got together off the ice. "Schoenie would play a few tunes on his guitar, and we'd have a few beers," says Hillman. "I had my brother's place in Fort Erie, and Tim had rented a huge place in Crystal Beach. On stormy nights, many times we'd stay over at Tim's."

Like numerous players, Tim kept up his

Canadian residency while playing for Buffalo by living across the Niagara River. Players lived in Fort Erie or, in the case of Tim and a few others, in Crystal Beach on the shore of Lake Erie. The north shore of the lake was choc-a-bloc with summer homes of Americans, who all scampered back across the border when fall came. Players rented their summer homes while playing for the Sabres, vacating them just in time for their owners to take back possession for another summer.

Lori came down to live with Tim in the Crystal Beach home while their children remained on Bannatyne Drive, attending school while being watched over by the housekeeper. After the fiasco of Pittsburgh, they never again tried to make their kids move from Toronto. Lori was not taken with the Crystal Beach rental. "It was a pretty lonely, desolate place. We were the only people living on the street. And I never really got to know the wives that well in Buffalo, because I was commuting. I never got to go out after Sunday night games [Sabres home games were on Sunday and Thursday nights]. I was there through the week and then I was home when Tim left town on Friday. We had quite a few of the guys over for dinner every once in a while. I never really got that friendly—not by choice, but they were all so much younger than me by that time. Jeri-Lynn was friends with the wives. She was coming to the games and they were all her age. They were more her crowd than mine."

In Buffalo, Tim had revitalised his career, doing exactly what Red Kelly had hoped he would do for Pittsburgh before his ankle injury derailed his season. He wasn't singlehandedly responsible for the turnaround in Sabres fortunes, but he received a large part of the credit. Goaltender Roger Crozier noted that, since Tim joined the team, its goals-against had dropped a full goal per game. Dave Dryden's average fell from 3.98 to 2.65, the best of his professional career. "Tim has had a tremendous stabilising influence on the club," said Roger Crozier. "He slows the play right down, and doesn't panic with the puck. His experience is what we've been lacking."

In one season, Buffalo went from winning only sixteen games to winning thirty-seven and making the playoffs. They had a hard-fought quarter-final series with Montreal, which they lost in six games; Montreal went on to win the cup. Frank Mahovlich had moved on from Detroit to Montreal, where he'd become a superstar of the game playing with his brother Peter. In the midst of the playoff series against Buffalo, Frank was impressed by his old teammate's play. "Tim has trumped just about every fake and shift that Pete and I have used to try and deke him. I have never seen him play better defensively. And he's feeding their young forwards, giving them the jump on our defence."

Tim turned away this praise with a self-effacing return to his "old man" theme. "As you get older, you get lazier," he said. "You stay back more. I don't think I've passed the red line a dozen times all season."

When Tim's season was over, his fellow Sabres voted him the team's most valuable player. They presented him with a cheesy trophy, a glittery thing you'd see at a minor hockey banquet, but it was the thought that counted. Lori says the honour touched Tim deeply, harkening back to the same recognition he'd received from his St. Mike's teammates.

Tim again announced his retirement. The business, as always, demanded his attention. When he was playing in New York and Pittsburgh, he wasn't physically available during the regular season. In Buffalo, though, he was only a short drive from Tim Donut's head office in Oakville, and according to Larry Hillman, the business "took up a good part of his time when he wasn't on the ice. We trained in St. Catharines, and after a workout he'd jump in his big Cadillac and drive to Toronto to have dinner with Ron Joyce—have supper and a business meeting at the same time. But Tim Horton was the type that when he stepped on the ice, there was nothing about donuts in his mind. There was only winning that game and maintaining the respect of the players. That's what he was getting paid for."

Ron Joyce, who was still waiting for Tim to put hockey firmly behind him, sensed Tim's enthusiasm for the business waning. "In the last three years," he says, "the business was getting to a level where it was getting harder to grasp. I started losing Tim more. In the summer he only came in for a day or so. I felt that he had lost interest in running the company. He was sort of: I'll play hockey, I'll let you do that, and we'll share equally. I think that was part of it, but it was also that he wanted to live a life that other people had, like having the summer off, doing things, which he had never done. Because he had never had any money. It was probably only in the last three to four years of his life that he did have some money, and it gave him the time to have some leisure."

The main focus of his leisure was his cottage on Peninsula (Pen) Lake near Huntsville, close by the Hidden Valley ski resort. Tim bought the cottage when he came to the Sabres. A former fishing camp, it had five guest cottages and four acres on the water. "Tim just loved that spot," says Lori. "I'm not a cottage person. I love the city. We had a swimming pool in the backyard on Bannatyne, and every time Tim went outside there would be twenty kids around him. He loved kids, but he wanted a bit of privacy, so he bought the cottage. It was beautiful. We had some nice times up there."

Over the winter of 72/73, the main building was renovated and expanded by a contractor. It was an all-season facility, with snowmobiling and skiing in the winter, waterskiing and fishing in the summer. Tim's first—and only—summer with the cottage was 1973, and he was smitten with it. While the rest of the family (with the exception of Jeri-Lynn, who was working full-time for Air Canada at Pearson International Airport) spent virtually the entire summer there, Tim came up every weekend and whenever else he could, all year round. Jeri-Lynn sensed that her father envisioned it as a retirement home, although there had been talk of relocating to Burlington or Oakville to be closer to the donut business. Lori admits that she probably nixed the possibility of moving closer to Tim Donut, being too attached to the Bannatyne home and the surrounding community.

"He really did get keen on his cottage when away from hockey," says Dave Dryden. "We happened to be on the same lake, and went over once to see it. He had developed quite a friendship with a lot of people up there in the cottage area. I know he had a lot of hassles in his life, but a lot of it was because he had extended himself in so many directions, and he seemed to be enjoying all those directions."

Come September, the customary mating dance
between Tim Horton and the professional hockey
world resumed, with Tim forthrightly declaring that
he was finished with the game, and the game raising
its eyebrows and the ante at the same time. "I think
what happened," says Joyce, "is once the bell rang,
he came out fighting. But at the end of the season,
that was it. Because he wasn't winning very many.
He was playing on losing teams. It was tough stuff.
He hated to lose."

On September 1, with the Sabres filing into training camp in St. Catharines, Tim assured the press of
his permanent absence. "I'm going to retire. I guess
everybody has to do it sometime, and this is the time
for me. The old body won't take it any more. And
that's the way it stands right now."

The day after training camp started, Tim was
standing along the boards at the St. Catharines
arena, watching his former teammates prepare for
the new season, dressed in dapper business clothes
and sporting his horn-rimmed glasses.

He insisted to the press that he was only in town
on business. One of Tim Donut's thirty-five franchises was in St. Catharines, which gave him the
excuse to drop by the rink. But Tim did meet with
Imlach to discuss the possibility of playing again. He
left in a doubtful mood. "I just don't know if I can
do a good job on the ice," he said.

Within the week, *Globe and Mail* columnist Dick
Beddoes expressed his profound scepticism of
Tim's latest withdrawal from the game. "The retirement of Miles Gilbert Horton has been an imper-
ishable staple on the sports pages for at least five
years," he wrote. "Horton would announce, quite
straightforward, that he was quitting the National

Hockey League to concentrate on his empire of doughnut shops, upon which the sun never sets in Ontario backwaters such as Cornwall, North Bay, Sudbury and Etobicoke. Then, feeling the pinch for dough from hockey to buy, as it were, dough for doughnuts, Horton always repealed his vow to retire."

"It's true," Tim told Beddoes. "It's finally over. Truthfully, honestly, without further ado, done, finished, absolutely, no kidding."

And what if he was offered more money?

"George has already offered me more money. But I said no to the raise. From now on I'm going to spend part of the winters learning how to ski and skidoo."

Lori says Tim's retirement decisions and reversals were no negotiating strategy. "We agonised all summer. Is he or isn't he? It was terrible. And he honestly didn't make up his mind till the last minute. I didn't know, the kids didn't know, and he didn't know—which was worse."

By September 27, Tim was beginning his familiar wavering. "I wish I knew the truth," he confessed. "I know I have retired a few times, but this time I thought it was for good. You see, I'm now a year or two older. In fact, today I feel a hundred years older. I also know that the money is good. But if I keep on playing, the only guy who'll make the money will be an undertaker."

He put the chances of his returning at only one in ten. "Sure, if I'll play another year, we'll be able to invest in more stores. But you have to realize that I'm getting on in years. One has to stop playing at some time. As I said, by tomorrow night I'll make a decision. I have to. Either I'll have to forget about hockey, or I'll have to start skating. They say I don't like training camps. This is true. But I need some skating if I want to play. There's only a little over a week left before the league opens."

Tim let his own deadline pass without making a decision. On October 4, with the start of the season looming, he still hadn't made up his mind. Imlach declared himself "certain" that Tim was coming back.

With only days to go, Tim checked into a suite at Buffalo's Statler Hilton and skated by himself at the Aud, as Buffalo's Memorial Auditorium is known. He practised for two days, then signed his contract with Buffalo the day before the Sabres' season-opener against Toronto.

One player who wouldn't be back with him was Larry Hillman. After missing out on big money with the WHA the previous season, Hillman wasn't going to make the same mistake twice. "After eighteen years, with one-year contracts, one at a time, I got a lawyer in St. Catharines to represent me. Imlach was going to give me a 10 per cent raise, from $29,500 to $32,500. The WHA said, 'We'll double whatever you're getting in the NHL.' After eighteen years, it was simple mathematics. I didn't owe anything to the NHL, so I took advantage of it, and was happy that I did." As Tim returned to the Sabres fold, Larry Hillman became a $60,000-a-year Cleveland Baron.

"It honestly wasn't the money," Tim said after signing his new contract. "Maybe it's just a bad habit I've acquired. I like to play hockey. I have a long time ahead to sit behind a desk."

It was the simplest, most honest assessment Tim could offer of his life at that moment. When all was said and done, he was a hockey player who wanted to play hockey. The challenge and excitement that the business had held out for him eighteen months before, while he was in Pittsburgh returning from his ankle injury, had evaporated. Business was now an emasculating purgatory. For five years or more, it had been there for him to embrace, but he had never been able to bring himself to make the commitment. The words "sit behind a desk" spoke volumes about how he viewed his life after hockey; it begs the question of whether Tim would ever have been truly happy in the white-collar world, and what steps he would have taken to avoid it, had life given him the time.

When asked what her father would have done when the day came that he could no longer play professional hockey, Jeri-Lynn replies that, while her father would have kept his equity in the donut business, "I think he would have gone into coaching." Lori modifies Jeri-Lynn's assessment. "He never wanted to coach," she maintains. "He was interested in managing a team, but not coaching."

"Business, his personal life and his hockey life all meshed," says Gordon Griggs. "Tim was never complex in that way. When you wanted to separate them, you couldn't do it. That became very frustrating for him."

Ultimately, Tim may have had difficulty bringing himself to embrace the business world unequivocally because what he had seen of it was fraught with compromise, ruin, misfortune and a Darwinian competitiveness that compelled people to bend the rules, sometimes just to survive, sometimes purely out of greed. He had always played the game of hockey by the book, and his experiences with business were discouragingly thin on situations where pressures or temptations did not compel the people involved to resort to some measure of rule bending. Survival had caused Jim Charade to rob Peter to pay Paul, and in the end he had had to walk away from his equity in his partnership with Tim. Survival had caused Ron Joyce to borrow and sign notes and cut corners that caused tension between them. It was a time, Joyce recalls, when they were "always financing backwards, to pay for what we'd already spent."

Late in their partnership, says Jeri-Lynn, Tim's discovery that Joyce had pledged properties they no longer owned to back loans the company badly needed made him question the trust he had unequivocally placed in his friend. "R.J. [Joyce] was doing that without dad knowing," says Jeri-Lynn. "And when he found out, dad hit the roof." Lori also says the partnership was shaky, that Tim was making trips into the office to try to clean things up. But Joyce is adamant that the bookkeeping misadventure never precipitated a confrontation between him and Tim.

Tim had watched greed, not survival, destroy Stafford Smythe and send Harold Ballard to prison (although Ballard rose Phoenix-like from the humiliation to gain control of Maple Leaf Gardens). As brutal a game as hockey was, it was nothing compared to what went on in the corners, behind the referee's back, in the world of business.

"I found he really enjoyed playing the game," says Keon of Tim's final years. "One of the reasons was that he was still really a strong man. He could still skate, and was still fearless."

"It's an extremely hard game to play professionally," says Schoenfeld. "If you don't want to play, it's got to be damned near impossible. There were times when it was hard to go and I loved the game. You need that passion to get you over the hump. If you didn't have this burning love for the game, I don't know how you would be able to play.

"He loved being around the guys. He loved everything that goes with the game. The practices, the playing, the camaraderie, the same things that most players like. If you have to quit, it's a lot easier. You blow your knee out or nobody wants you— there are a lot of ways where you'll have to say, 'Well, okay, I have to move on.' A guy like Tim, although he didn't realize it when he retired, quickly realized that he still had the passion. It draws you to the rink. If you're capable, it's very hard for people to stop, and I think it was very hard for Tim. I think he'd play today if he could."

Chapter 22

The End of the Road

In his final season, Tim's salary, as stated by Imlach in his memoirs, was $150,000, but because of the tax advantages that resulted from the deferral scheme used to pay it out, in Seymour Knox's mind it was actually worth $200,000. According to Mel Rothwell, Tim's accountant, it had been his standard salary strategy for the last few years of his career to spread out the income to reduce his taxes, although as the deferrals from each one-year contract overlapped, some of the tax advantages were lost.

But the crowning touch of Tim's second contract with the Buffalo Sabres was the car. If Punch wanted him back, Tim wanted a car on top of the new salary package, and not just any car. Tim wanted a Ford Pantera. Built by Ford's European division, it was a mid-engine coupe with power to burn.

Tim had always been wild about cars, and wild when he got in the driver's seat. His first paycheque as a Pittsburgh Hornet is said to have been spent on his first car. He drove like a fiend, and wasted little time getting into trouble behind the wheel. "He wrote a car off between North Bay and Sudbury when he was just a kid," says his brother Gerry. "A brand new Mercury, too. He reached down to adjust the air vents as he went through a rock cut and forgot to steer at the same time."

"Tim was very close with his money, but he would spend any amount on his car," says his old Pittsburgh Hornets teammate, Ray Hannigan. "He always drove a big car. But his eyesight was not good. Tim always wanted to drive, and we were coming out of the CNE one time. This traffic cop was in front of us. We were only moving about five miles an hour. Tim was gawking around and the next thing you know the policeman was jumping off the hood.

"When we were in the playoffs in Pittsburgh, we were working out in Johnstown, and went to the movies. Tim was driving, and suddenly we were going the wrong way up a divided highway. When we saw the other cars coming he went right over the curb to the other side. After that, we didn't let him be our designated driver."

"I'll never forget how he came up for Ray's wedding in 1953," says Pat Hannigan. "He had a brand new Mercury and he must have driven it up at a thousand miles an hour because there was no muffler on it when he got there. He burned it right off."

"When you're young," says Dick Duff, "everybody's interested in cars. Sometimes I think that driving the car deflects the mind from other problems. You just take the car and go for a drive. It gets you away from the rink, from different things. And of course we were back and forth all the time from those small towns to Toronto. It was a kid's ambition to own a car."

Tim had an array of cars while he was with the Leafs, and they tended to fall into two categories—hopped-up roadsters and high-performance land yachts. If it wasn't a Sunbeam Tiger two-seater it was a Cadillac Eldorado. Either way, he drove them with the gas pedal fully depressed.

Russ Gioffrey recalls switching cars with Tim when they both came down for a donut store opening in Burlington. Tim had Lori's station wagon, while Gioffrey was driving a convertible. Behind the wheel of Gioffrey's convertible, Tim made short work of the Queen Elizabeth Way. "Tim gets picked up on the QEW doing about 120," says Gioffrey. "All he's got on him is a BP credit card. But the cop is so infatuated with meeting Tim Horton that he doesn't give him a ticket."

People who drove with him were almost uniformly terrified. Ed Siekierko joined Tim on a trip to Galt to help him clear some bureaucratic impediments to a new franchise. They drove together in Tim's Sunbeam Tiger. "We started home," says Siekierko. "We were doing 135, 140 miles an hour. I said, 'You've gotta slow down. I'm going to go through the roof here. If you don't, I'm going to walk home.' So he slowed down to eighty or ninety. That Tiger could really move. Tim was a good driver, but he was fast. When he had a chance to open the car up, he opened the car up."

Ron Joyce well remembers a trip from Sudbury with Tim and a Tim Donuts employee, George Chadwick. "We came down in a white Cadillac," says Joyce. "Tim terrified us. We caught air. When we went in the air, I said, 'Stop the car, I want out.'" Tim was assigned to the back seat for the rest of the trip.

"He always drove fast, and it was scary," says Jim Charade. "Going to Hamilton with him, I said, 'I don't want to go with you any more.' He would just laugh and say, 'I won't do it any more.' If you said you didn't like it, he'd stop. I remember going to North Bay in no time."

"He drove like an idiot," says Lori. "I was just as bad. He used to buy me a car, a Pontiac GTO, a Trans Am. He would have his, and I would have mine. We'd watch "Laugh-In" every Monday night with the kids, and then we'd race all the way back to Buffalo, him in his Pantera, me in my Trans Am. And he'd be caught many times, and nobody would do anything about it. The police would let him go. We were in a few accidents, though. We were visiting Pittsburgh when Tim was with the Leafs, and he rolled the car coming back. The car rolled and rolled, back onto its wheels, and the only things wrong with the car were two little dings."

In his first season in Buffalo, Tim regularly took Larry Hillman with him as he raced between the Sabres and Tim Donut, and the pace did attract speeding tickets. "It was business, business, back and forth," says Hillman, "driving with him in his Triumph or Cadillac. He was always leaving things to the last minute and trying to make up time. You can't keep doing that and not get caught."

Among the people who knew Tim well, Hughie Phillips was a rarity: he loved driving with Tim. "Tim was a fast driver, but he was very smart, and he was cautious. You can drive fast and stupid. Tim wasn't stupid. It never bothered me. Go to it! We used to go up Mount Pleasant to the home on Wedgewood Drive. We were smoking. You can't go that fast on that thing, because there are only two lanes, and there are lights. He seemed to know when the lights were green. He had it timed, and knew when to slow down because there was a light, because he never had to stop. He went straight through."

Jeri-Lynn drove regularly with her father. "I've been with him when he drove that Pantera at 150. He liked the speed, but he was a good driver. Driving back from Buffalo one night, it took us one hour to get from the parking lot at the Aud to our driveway."

At the beginning of Tim's second season in Buffalo, Jim Schoenfeld and his wife Teresa came to the Statler-Hilton to pick up Tim and Lori to go out for dinner. Tim had decided to take an apartment in the hotel in downtown Buffalo rather than spend another winter in the ghost town of Crystal Beach. The defence partners hadn't seen much of each other in this new season, since Tim had missed the entire training camp while hammering out a new contract with Punch. "We went up to the suite for a while," says Schoenfeld. "He brought out this brochure. It was the Pantera, and he couldn't wait. It had been ordered, I guess. For a guy like Hortie, who liked to drive fast…he had the big white Eldorado before that. You look back on that night and you think: If only I had been able to see into the future, I would have talked him out of getting that stupid damned car."

Tim's new lodgings were right across from Punch Imlach's suite. Imlach's health would prevent him from ever subjecting himself to the strain of coaching again: Joe Crozier was in charge of the team day-to-day as coach. But Tim provided Imlach with a vicarious view of the team. "Punch used him that way," says Seymour Knox, "not to spy on players, but to keep his eye on them. If he saw anything that should be brought to Punch's attention, he was encouraged by Punch to do this."

Players who knew him well don't remember Tim snitching so much as playing den mother. In considering the description of Tim in Buffalo as a stay-at-home defenceman, Paul Terbenche readily agrees. "He was staying at home looking after us young fellows." Terbenche wasn't quite as young as Jim Schoenfeld. He'd played his first NHL hockey in Chicago in 67/68, and while he had been part of the Sabres organization since the franchise began playing in 70/71, he didn't find a regular starting position until 72/73, when Tim arrived. Thus, although he was several years older than Schoenfeld, turning twenty-seven at the start of that season, he was still young enough and new enough to the NHL grind to accept Tim as a mentor. Two decades after meeting and getting to know Tim Horton, he remains deeply affected by the short relationship. He grasps in vain at a firm definition of what made Tim such a resilient force in his life. "His personality, his being, his self," he ventures, the loss catching at the back of his throat. "Tim was a rock for us young guys. Everybody had nothing but admiration and respect for the man, that's for sure. He was very quiet. A very genuine man. He was a very private person. I think he remembered where he came from."

Terbenche was often paired with Tim on the ice, particularly in Tim's second Buffalo season, most of which Jim Schoenfeld missed through back problems. "We used to room together," Terbenche remembers. "Mr. Imlach thought he'd keep me in line, I guess." Tim, though, was still capable of having a hell of a good time. "There was no part of the word 'no' he could understand. We had our moments with one another. I can remember being carried out of a few places—not that I was intoxicated, it was just that he had decided it was time to leave. Lots of times I got carried into the hotel by Tim."

Before the start of the season, Tim had made a firm decision to stop drinking. While he had been working at controlling his drinking since he became a Buffalo Sabre, he'd had a dreadful relapse while up at the cottage that summer. He went into a hotel in Huntsville, knocked back more than a few, and started to trash the place. "At that point I called his brother and his father in North Bay, and they came down," says Lori.

"Tim was one of the most beautiful people in the world when he was sober," she says. "He should have never drunk. That whole episode ended at a party in another cottage. Tim created another big scene, tried to get in his car to drive away, and he kept turning the car around and banging into tree stumps. Some brave soul, one of the cottagers up there, reached in and took the keys away, and Tim walked home. When we got back to the cottage he was very angry with me. The next day he was ready to see a psychiatrist. I called the [Leafs] team doctor, Dr. Murray, we got an appointment with the psychiatrist, and I never saw Tim drink again. I know he did with the guys, but he never *drank*."

By all indications, he was as close to a model of sobriety as a hockey player could be throughout his final season. "Tim was a pretty good drinker at times," says Dave Dryden. But in that final season leading up to his death, "he had been on the wagon for a fair length of time." Gordon Griggs visited with Tim over Christmas, and was told by Tim that he hadn't had a drink since September.

On the ice, Tim was again an impressive presence. "He played so well, and so methodically," says Terbenche. "He totally enjoyed it. I laugh, because he really couldn't see very well." Sometimes Tim completely lost track of the puck. "He used to holler at me, 'Where is it?' I'd say, 'It's in your corner, fool! Go get it!'"

"I didn't have a sense of Timmy losing the puck a lot," says Dave Dryden. "It almost was more the way he kept his head all the time. It was if he was groping around in the dark for the bloody thing. He always knew where it was because his chin was so far forward, like he was looking down through bifocals."

In his second Sabres campaign, the team's management was particularly careful not to burn Tim out before the playoffs. He was not expected to put in the workouts demanded of other players. "They'd rest him properly, as far as practices go," says Terbenche. "I remember Joe—Mr. Crozier—would say, 'You're not here today, Mr. Horton.'"

"Some guys you're playing with, when they're given the day off," says Dryden, "you feel, aw, screw it, the guy should be out here anyway. With Timmy, it was always: If and when he wasn't there, you knew he wanted to be there. Punch or Joe had said no, and that was it. I think there was a sense of saving him. My recollection is that Timmy certainly was there most of the time."

While players praise Tim as being their lone star in a team of nobodies when he arrived in Buffalo, Imlach had already begun to assemble a nucleus of brilliant young talent. The components of his "French Connection" line of René Robert, Richard Martin and Gilbert Perrault were in place at Tim's first Sabres training camp. They would provide the

bulk of the offence that made the Sabres a Stanley
Cup contender, while Tim's experience behind the
blueline, and his overall leadership, gave the team
the tactical and emotional stability needed to
become a championship club. His offensive role now
bordered on negligible, as he recorded only six
points, all on assists, in this season.

But there was no great leap forward for the Sabres
in Tim's second season. Schoenfeld had been out of
the lineup since surgery on October 21 to remove a
ruptured spinal disc. A week after Schoenfeld's
surgery, Gilbert Perrault broke his leg and was lost
until January. The goaltending was in disarray. Roger
Crozier was lost to recurring bouts of pancreatitis,
which left Dryden and Rocky Farr to share the netminding, but then Dryden was plagued by back
problems and Gary Bromley had to be brought in to
help out Farr. As the second half of the season
began, the Sabres were in fifth, ten points behind the
Leafs, now being coached by Red Kelly, who held the
fourth and final playoff spot in the East division.

On January 12, Tim turned forty-four. The only
player in the NHL older than him was Gump
Worsley, who was in the net for Minnesota for twenty-nine games that season, which proved to be his
last. The only other active player older than Tim
was Gordie Howe. Having retired as a Red Wing
after twenty-five seasons at the end of the 70/71 season, Howe had returned to the game in 73/74 with
the Houston Aeros of the WHA at the age of forty-
five so he could play with his sons Marty and Mark.

Eleven days after his birthday, on January 23,
Tim was rocked by the loss of his father. Late in
Oakley Horton's life Tim had persuaded Ron Joyce
to put Oak on the Tim Donut payroll. He was given

the grand title of superintendent of northern Ontario operations, and with it the nominal task of inspecting what few franchises there were up there. But Oak, who was a no-nonsense fellow with a caustic streak, took his work for his son seriously. He would call on a franchisee, inspect the premises and then give the owner a dressing-down on behalf of Tim Donut. Tim was forced to take his father aside and explain to him that if he found problems with a restaurant, he was to report on them back to Tim Donut, and not to do the franchisee disciplining himself.

"Tim and his dad would not be what we would call close in the sense of my three sons and myself, but rather in the sense of the closeness that I think of with my dad," says Gordon Griggs. "We didn't hug, we didn't display our emotions—to our mothers we did, but not to our fathers. And our fathers didn't to us. The closeness was this inbuilt thing. Tim's respect and love for his dad were tremendous, but when he wanted to talk to somebody, he'd drive up to North Bay at two o'clock in the morning, have tea with his mom, and then come down and be on the ice for a ten o'clock practice.

"Tim took the loss of his dad very hard. If Tim were alive today, and you'd say, Tim, your dad would really appreciate it if you went out and played for Buffalo, he'd be out there."

It is an indication of the importance of Oak to Tim that Ron Joyce, King Clancy, Harold Ballard and Punch Imlach came to North Bay for the funeral.

Eight days after the death of his father, Tim and the rest of the Sabres were in Philadelphia to take on

the Broad Street Bullies, who were at the height of
their notoriety. The Flyers were scrapping their way
to their first Stanley Cup, collecting a total of 1,750
penalty minutes on the season, 600 minutes ahead
of any other team in the league. Chief miscreant on
the Flyers roster was Dave "The Hammer" Schultz,
who singlehandedly contributed 348 of the Flyers'
penalty minutes. In his second full season, Schultz
was still busy brawling away at establishing his reputation as the league's toughest tough guy. That
meant seeking out and challenging every other
player deemed to be a strongman. On this night at
the Spectrum, Dave Schultz, aged twenty-five,
picked out Tim Horton, aged forty-four.

It was the new game of hockey at its most vulgar.
Schultz was a goon. Tim was a six-time All Star, a winner of four Stanley Cups and one of the most
respected players in the league. That didn't matter.
Schultz wanted to beat him up and make a point
that he could never make by trying to skate around
Tim and score in his nominal position on left wing.

"The game was really a rough one," says Dave
Dryden, who was on the bench that game. "Right in
front of the bench, Schultz challenged Timmy. It
was like Timmy just stood there. My recollection is
of Tim with that look of, not disdain, but, Aw, let's
just forget it. And Schultz persisted."

It might have helped for Schultz to know that
one of Tim's favourite television shows at this time
was "Kung Fu," in which David Carradine played
the quiet, spiritual loner who eschewed violence
and confrontations, but when forced to act (strictly
in self-defence) was all-powerfully decisive. The
character must have touched and amused Tim at a
basic level. In any event, the show inspired spirited

rough-housing with his daughters, with Tim ad-libbing his way through the martial arts.

Tim's response to Schultz's insolence was not martial arts but the old reliable Greco-Roman full-frontal assault. "Timmy just grabbed him in a bearhug, threw him down on his back and sat on him," says Dryden. "Everybody on the bench is yelling, 'Pound the hell out of the guy!' He didn't take one punch at him. Talk about putting a guy down. That was my sense of Tim always. It was: If I've got to do it, I'll do it, but I'll do it without being mean. If anything, I'll embarrass the hell out of the guy."

The Sabres struggled through a six-game winless streak that ended on February 8 when they beat the California Seals 7-2. The win pulled them within seven points of the Leafs, but they were unable to close the gap further over their next few games. A win over Detroit at home on Sunday, February 17, kept them within seven.

That upcoming Wednesday—February 20—the Sabres would come to Maple Leaf Gardens for the first of two matches left in the season between the clubs, both of which would be played in Toronto. It was a critical game for Buffalo: win it, and they would pull within five points of the Leafs; lose it, and they would sink nine discouraging points back.

The goaltending was still uncertain. Gary Bromley was expected to get the assignment while Dryden served as backup, but Joe Crozier surprised the pundits by choosing to start Rocky Farr. In the defensive corps, there was good news. Jim Schoenfeld was at last returning to the lineup. He had been healthy enough to play two games with the Sabres' American league affiliate, the

Cincinnati Swords, over the weekend, and was pencilled back into a starting position with the Sabres for the game on Wednesday night.

On the Monday, Hughie Phillips got a call from Tim, who was lining up tickets for the game and wanted to know if Hughie was going to be there. Hughie had just come off a serious bout of pleurisy that had landed him in East General. Tim had sent him a get-well card and then had followed up with the call. Although Hughie had made a point of taking in a few games in Buffalo, he wasn't able to go to this Gardens game because he'd already made other plans. For Tim, the game might have been one of his last chances to play before his old friends, family and fans in the rink in which he had made his reputation as a St. Mike's Major and a Toronto Maple Leaf. "I think he was disappointed I wasn't going to the game," says Hughie. "I think he knew it was going to be his last year, and he wanted me to go."

Tim had retired and unretired so many times that it is difficult to decide whether 73/74 would in fact have been his last season. "I think that was the understanding," says Seymour Knox. The Sabres had coaxed him back for one last run at the Stanley Cup. But Tim was certainly capable of playing another season, or more, in the minds of teammates and his coach Joe Crozier. "The shape he was in, he could have gone another two or three years," says Crozier, who notes that Tim never said anything to him about his career plans. Gordon Griggs says Tim was determined to stay on the ice so long as Gordie Howe was still out there—and Howe would still be out there in 79/80, at the age of fifty-two.

But the end began that Tuesday, at a practice in

Buffalo. His career came full circle on the ice that day. A slapshot from the point that blinded Baz Bastien in 1949 had begun the chain reaction of trades and acquisitions that had helped lead to Tim's call-up to the Leafs from the Hornets in 1952. On this day in February 1974, another slapshot came into play. A blast by René Robert was deflected and caught Tim unawares, striking him on the jaw.

Though badly bruised and swollen, he was determined to play the game in Toronto on the following night. Later that day, Tim drove himself to Toronto in the Pantera. Normally for a game like this the team travelled together by bus from Buffalo and returned right after the game, since they had a regular home game on Thursday, and the team would have to be back and prepared to meet the Atlanta Flames. But Punch allowed Tim more leeway than he would most other players. "Tim had paid me enough dues that I could afford him a few favours, like letting him drive his own car if he didn't want to ride the bus," Imlach said the day after the game.

As usual, Tim had a host of responsibilities to attend to besides preparing himself for a critical hockey game. He stopped in at the Tim Donut office in Oakville after the Tuesday practice to sign some papers for a new franchise—Ron Joyce's brother Bill was opening the first outlet in Nova Scotia, in Dartmouth. Then he proceeded on to the family home on Bannatyne. After the death of Oak, Ethel Horton had come down to stay, and she and Lori had returned from a Florida vacation together the week before the game. Tim's brother Gerry had come down as well. Tim spent the night at the house, headed to the Gardens for a morning workout with the Sabres, and then returned home to visit with family before going back to the Gardens for the game.

He showed up early at the Gardens, and on the way in he ran into Dave Keon. The Leaf captain was alarmed by Tim's condition. "His face was all blown up. He said 'They think it's a bad bruise,' and he was taking some painkillers. And I said, 'Well, I don't know, but I bet you it's broken and they're just telling you it's bruised. When you go back to Buffalo, you'd better have that X-rayed.' "

In the second instalment of his memoirs, *Heaven and Hell in the NHL*, Imlach would state that Tim went to the Leaf doctors to have his jaw examined. "They did," he wrote, "and they thought it was cracked. He asked if they would inject it to freeze that side. Remember, he was past forty-four then." Imlach didn't say whether the Leaf doctors actually administered the injection, but it seems unlikely. Tim was taking painkillers but was still in considerable pain. He suited up anyway and went onto the ice.

The Gardens was a kaleidoscope of people from different facets of his life, gathered up by him in different places at different times. They had come to the arena that was most closely associated with his long career to watch him play what might well be one of his last games in that building. Russ Gioffrey had come out, and spoke with Tim during the Sabres' warmup. Jeri-Lynn and Traci were in the seats that had been in the family since Jeri-Lynn was five: section 21, reds, row A, seats 7 and 8, right behind the Leaf goal. For two periods out of three, they were the perfect vantage point for watching their dad at work. (When Tim was traded to New

York, Stafford Smythe had vowed that the family
would be allowed to keep their complimentary seats,
and he had been true to his word.) Tim's other
daughters, Kim and Kelly, were sitting with their
Uncle Gerry and their cousin Kerry. Ron Joyce had
come to the game with his wife Teri, Tim Donut's
construction supervisor Layton Coulter, Ed
Siekierko and two real estate associates of Siekierko,
Bob Way and Red Robertson. Ray Hannigan, his old
Hornets teammate who had helped inspire him to
go into the restaurant business, had come to the
game with his son Matt. His late wife's brother, John
McLellan, who had been coaching Tim when he
was traded to New York, was now the Leafs' assistant
general manager, and he provided Hannigan with
the game tickets.[1]

Bob Goldham, one of the Leaf defensive greats
of the 1940s and the colour commentator for the
"Hockey Night in Canada" broadcast, told his audience, "Watch Horton if you want a good idea of
how defence should be played."

The Sabres' game plan was based on the notion
that the Leafs could be intimidated into losing—a
strategy encouraged by Toronto's recent loss to the
combative Philadelphia Flyers. It backfired. The
Sabres were serving penalties on the first two Leaf
goals as Toronto raced to a 3-0 lead. Tim contributed to the hard hitting, going off with a boarding penalty at 18:37 of the first period. The Sabres
went into the intermission trailing 3-1. Both teams
were scoreless in the second period.

Tim played for the two periods harassed by pain.
Paul Terbenche remembers him coming to the
bench after a shift and saying to him: "I think I
broke my bloody jaw."

He played less than one shift—thirty-five seconds—of the third period. It would be reported that he asked the Sabres' team doctor, John Butsch, to freeze the jaw for him and that Butsch had refused. But Butsch says this is impossible, since he wasn't even at the Gardens. Tim disappeared for the rest of the game. The player who had developed a reputation as an iron man in the 1960s, who could play through injuries, who had an unusually high pain threshold, had come up against an injury whose pain was intolerable.

After Tim removed himself from the game, the Sabres went on to lose 4-2. Although he had only played two periods of hockey, his play had been impressive enough for him to be picked as the game's third star. Ted Blackman, writing in the *Montreal Gazette,* would state that the crowd booed when Tim failed to appear for the obligatory skate after being selected. If this happened, it was a churlish salute from the last Gardens audience to see him play.

After the game, Tim was spotted in more places than the Scarlet Pimpernel. Bob Baun says he caught up with him in the hallway by the visiting team's dressing room, where the Zamboni enters the Gardens ice surface. They chatted, he says, for ten or fifteen minutes, two old teammates who hardly saw each other any more. That one meeting spun back and forth between two decades of friendship. It had been almost nineteen years since Baun had been plucked out of the Junior Marlies lineup to help Tim recover from the leg and jaw fractures he sustained in the Gadsby collision on this very ice surface. Now Tim's jaw was again cracked, if not broken, and the young amateur of '55 had been retired for more than a season, running his own beef cattle spread in Pickering while Tim, whose career he had helped resuscitate over that summer, was still playing on.

The Horton family cheering section went looking for Tim. "We were right by the ice, where the officials come out on the ice now," says Jeri-Lynn. "We were waiting for him at that entrance. He came out of the first aid room. There was a hallway that went underneath the seats and he stepped in there. He didn't see us. By the time we got through to yell he was gone."

"We all yelled," Traci recalls. "He was talking to somebody and didn't hear us." Having lost track of Tim, they went home.

Tim didn't seem to know what to do with himself after the game. Ron Joyce says he had arranged with Tim to go to dinner at George's Spaghetti House, where they could discuss an opportunity that Siekierko's commercial real estate business was presenting them. "We were supposed to meet them, Tim and I, to talk about developing Tim Hortons stores in Atlantic Canada on the same pad as Consumer's Distributing, because they were doing a lot of Consumer's work." Tim Donut had just signed up its first franchisee east of Ontario (there were no outlets in Quebec); Gary O'Neill, who had met Tim for the first time at Tim Donut in January, would open the outlet in Moncton, New Brunswick, that summer. (Bill Joyce's franchise in Dartmouth would open shortly thereafter.) Using the Siekierko connection could fast-track the Tim Donut expansion.

Ed Siekierko headed home rather than convene at George's, but first he went down to the Sabres dressing room to see if he could say hello to Tim. He says he spotted Tim on the other side of the customary security guard. "Tim kind of waved at me. I said 'Hi, I'll see you in a day or two,' or something like that. That was the last time I said anything to him."

"We were supposed to meet Tim outside the Gardens," says Joyce. "We waited for him there and he wasn't there. We were supposed to go to George's and we thought he might have gone there, so we drove on down and waited there."

Tim wasn't at George's. He was outside the Gardens, where the Sabres team bus was boarding. Ray Hannigan, who had become concerned when Tim disappeared in the third period, and who knew the routine and layout of the Gardens from way back, left his seat early, went to where the Sabres would board their bus, and waited for Tim to appear. Sure enough, he did.

Tim had been vacillating over whether to go to his car or call it a night and ride the bus back to Buffalo with his teammates. Paul Terbenche remembers Tim asking him if he would ride with him on the bus, but Paul had to turn him down— his parents had come to Toronto for the game and he wouldn't be making the trip back that night.

"The issue with a lot of us was, are we going to stay overnight in Toronto and go down the next morning, or are we going to go back," says Dave Dryden, "because we would have had a game in Buffalo the next night. Timmy had been talking about driving back, and it had just been: Did anyone want to go along with Timmy? Whatever my rationale was, there was a thought of checking with Timmy and seeing if I could get a ride with him. It was such a mob scene after the game, and I decided, no, I won't, and I can't even remember whether I stayed home [in Toronto] that night or went down to Buffalo."

By the time Ray and Matt Hannigan caught up with him, Tim had apparently made up his mind to drive himself back. "He said he was having a meeting on the way back with his partner. He was in pain. I'm sure he was on some painkillers." Tim had not known Ray was going to be at the game, and so the encounter at the bus came as a pleasant surprise to him. They had seen each other infrequently over the past twenty years, although since moving back to Toronto Ray had been able to see Tim when he took in the odd Sabres game in Buffalo—his younger brother Pat, living in Fort Erie, did Sabres play-by-play for a spell. "I had so much admiration for the man," says Hannigan. "He was a good, loyal friend. When he saw me at the bus that night, it was as if we'd just seen each other the day before. He was hurting, but he still visited with us for twenty minutes."

Tim then set off to collect his car. He ran into Dave Keon and his sister, and together they walked up Church Street to the lot in which Tim had parked the Pantera. Although Ray Hannigan's recollection was that Tim was intent on making a business meeting with Ron Joyce, Keon doesn't remember Tim saying anything about a meeting. He was mainly concerned with finding "Lori and the kids."[2]

According to Keon, Tim, Keon and his sister then came across Punch Imlach and his wife. Imlach would remember the sequence of encounters slightly differently: "I was staying home in Toronto that night, so my car was parked in a lot off Church Street. When I came to the Gardens'

Church Street exit, Tim was talking to my wife Dodo. [Tim may have come to the exit after his long, indecisive spell at the bus, but arrived too late to meet up with the Joyce group.] He'd told her that the reason he finally had to stay off the ice in the third period was that every time anybody hit him it was like a shot going through the top of his head. Normally, Tim never talked about when he was hurt. The three of us walked up Church Street together. At the parking lot, along came Tim's old friend Davey Keon of the Leafs. I laughed. 'There's your pal—the one you used to break down doors to say goodnight to.' Tim went over, and when Dodo and I drove away they were still standing there talking. That was the last time I saw Tim alive."

"Punch and Dodo came by," says Keon. "We just chatted, told Tim, as I recall, to make sure he went to the doctor's appointment and got his face X-rayed, because he was in a great deal of pain. They had given him some painkillers, but I don't think they were working." An appointment had, in fact, been made for Tim to see Dr. Butsch at 10 a.m. the next morning. "Tim said he was going to take a swing by the Gardens to see if he could see Lori and the girls, and that if he didn't see them he was going to head back."

Over at George's, the Ron Joyce group waited in vain for Tim to arrive. "I guess we had one drink, waited there, he didn't show up. Then we decided, 'I guess he's not coming,' and we all decided we weren't going to have anything to eat."

Instead, Joyce, his wife Teri,[3] and Layton Coulter headed back to Oakville, and stopped in at the Tim Donut office. When they pulled in, they saw the Pantera. It was a complete coincidence that they should all meet here. "All he did was drive in here on the way home and decide to stop and have a drink, with no plan to meet anybody whatsoever," says Joyce. "He didn't even know where I was. The three of us came in, and Tim was sitting in our office, his coat on, an ice pack wrapped around his jaw, his driver's gloves on. He was sitting in the dark with his feet up on the table, with a vodka and soda in his hand. And I laughed like hell. It was funny to see him with the ice pack and all that. He said, 'Laugh. I can't.'

"Layton left very shortly after we got there. Teri might have stayed for an hour. I can remember Layton and I were in one conversation, Teri and Tim were in another. It started to get very late—1:30 or 2:00. They left, and I know I was trying to get Tim to go to my house. I had to be up at eight to be in Sarnia the next morning. But he didn't want to leave. He just wanted to talk.

"We were talking about the whole spectrum. We got into everything, about where we were going. I'd been trying to get him out of hockey and devote himself to the business we were in, but every fall he wanted to go back with it. He fully intended not to go back every spring, but every September..."

Finally, about four in the morning, Tim was talked out. The two partners made their way to the front door, with Tim agreeing to stay with Joyce at his home on Burlington's North Shore Boulevard and head to Buffalo for his doctor's appointment once he'd had some rest. Tim tossed back a handful of painkillers and prepared to leave. "He always called me Blub," says Joyce. "He said, 'I love ya, Blub,' and kissed me on the cheek, and I left the office. He said he'd lock up.

"I was driving a Lincoln Town Car. He had the Pantera. I left first. There was no traffic on the highway. I was going maybe 110. I saw him coming. I thought he'd be going pretty good. He went by me, and that's the last I saw of him."

It was February 21, nine years to the day since Ron Joyce had signed his franchise agreement for the first Tim Hortons franchise on Ottawa Street in Hamilton.

The sense that people around Tim developed of his fearlessness, the aura of indestructibility that he himself may have believed in, surprises Bob Baun, who knew Tim when he was a young man demoralised by his leg and jaw fractures in the summer of 1955, not at all sure that he had a future in the game.

Larry Hillman had never thought of Tim as unstoppable. "They put him on that pedestal, as Superman," he says. "He was like the bull in the china shop. The bull can't get hurt. When he took players out, he came out better than he went into it. It was probably a false impulse he had all his life."

Responding to the idea that her father may have had instilled in him this false notion of indestructibility, Jeri-Lynn agrees. "I think deep down, I guess it's human nature, if you get built up so much, you start believing it. Everybody said he was superstrong—the Superman/Clark Kent bit. He had his old ratty shirt with the Superman logo on it that he wore around the house. That was his favourite T-shirt. You could hurt him pretty good emotionally, and the four of us [daughters] did, and mom, too. But I don't think you could hurt him physically."

He both acknowledged his advancing age—the "old man" theme of his comments in the press—

and defied it through his continued play and devotion to fitness. There was no consistent sign from him of a willingness or capability to make the transition from hockey player to businessman, from a dynamic physical presence to a more retiring, though no less challenging, role.

"When you look at Tim, doing everything to the max," says Schoenfeld, "you wonder how a guy like him would have coped with growing old. I know he loved his daughters and his family and all that, and we all get used to where we are in life, but, not that it seems fitting that he go out in a car accident, but it does seem fitting that he go out doing something all-out. It really does. Whether it was playing in an old-timers' hockey game or whatever it might have been, I don't think I could see Tim as someone who was going to sit on the porch and rock away his golden years. He was going to be a doer until he was unable to do. Unfortunately it came too soon for all of us."

His driving, his essential demeanour of everything-to-the-hilt, was more a defiance of the inevitable than an embrace of it. Tim's own brother Gerry demonstrated that same defiance and determination. Despite years of heart trouble and surgery, he insisted on continuing to play the game he loved. A few weeks after Jim Schoenfeld made his observations about Tim, in December '93, Gerry made an end-to-end rush in an old-timers' game in North Bay, returned to the bench and died of a heart attack.

As a defenceman, you carry the puck out of your own end, stepping across the blueline into the neutral zone. Your forwards wheel and align, their checkers picking them up. The spaces between the

players are elastic and disjointed until the momentum of the anticipated play, sweeping away from
you, makes those many spaces one, uninterrupted
and inviting. To step into open ice is to defy the
conventions of the game and your role. The crowd
picks up on this, as you break the pattern of the
game, and their voices join in a crescendo of
approval as you make a play that is at once selfish
and selfless. As you move through your own forwards, the play that was to be falls away behind you.
The play that is now your own is also more than
likely doomed—it is a difficult thing to dash from
one end of the rink to the other, to go coast to coast
and pot a goal without being brought down by the
opposing defence, like a knight who has galloped
brazenly into the ranks of the enemy's pikemen,
only to have them haul him down off his horse.

The road is different. Its emptiness, too, draws
you in, but there is no real beginning or end, no
responsibilities at your back. You are abandoning
no one and no duty as you race across the asphalt
toward the elusive vanishing point. The engine is
the roar in your ears, and the sense of liberation is
something that no sheet of ice two hundred feet
long and eighty-five feet wide can ever hope to
deliver. There is no goal at the end to justify the
thrill, or to taint it through failure.

Yet open ice and open road are precisely the
same in that they are as much a challenge accepted
as a challenge extended: Just try to stop me. Try to
make me understand the word 'No.'

Perhaps that is the greatest temptation to the
defenceman: to step to the other side of the game,
to feel what it is like to be the one who is unstoppable, rather than always to be the one who must do

the stopping. To be, in effect, better than yourself, because you know that if it were *you* facing you across that other blueline, the dash would end ignominiously in a corner of the rink, you on your backside, stripped of the puck, the play moving back down ice, where you no longer stand guard. You would shake your head as you said to yourself, "How perfect did you think you could be? How far across that line did you think you could wander, and still get back?"

Fate is a creature of opportunity, responding to invitations extended willingly, inadvertently, defiantly. Whether on open ice or open road, it sweeps in to claim what it always promised it would. Sometimes you can even hear the moment of its arrival.

Boop-boop.

Chapter 23

After Life

'I was playing golf with Mr. Smythe and two of his friends, Bob Hamill and Dr. Gordon Murray—lifetime friends of Smythe—at Rosedale Golf Course," says Ted Kennedy. "We came in from our game, three or four in the afternoon, and went into the locker room. We were sitting down, and the locker room steward came into the locker room and said, 'That's terrible about Bill Barilko, Mr. Smythe.' And Smythe said, 'What are you talking about?' The steward said, 'Haven't you seen the paper?' Smythe said, 'No.' He went and got him the paper, and there was the story.

"Smythe sat down after reading the article, put his head down between his knees, looking toward the ground. He said, 'Connie Smythe, eh. Another one of your publicity stunts.'

"Dr. Murray said, 'What do you mean by that, Connie?'

" 'That's what the press will be saying. That's what the public will think.'

"Dr. Murray said, 'No, they won't. They'll never think that.'

"Smythe said, 'Oh, no? Just wait and see.'

"Sure enough, there's a lot of talk. Connie was known for doing something strange or noticeable to get publicity, especially in the off-season, when the Argos were getting all the publicity.

"He was really shaken. He really was."

The deaths of Bill Barilko and Tim Horton have undeniable parallels. Barilko, a defenceman from Timmins, won four Stanley Cups—three in a row, then a fourth after a one-season dry spot—before dying in an airplane crash. Horton, a defenceman from just up the TNO line in Cochrane, was expected to replace him. He, too, won four Stanley Cups as a Maple Leaf—three in a row, then a fourth after a two-season dry spot—before dying in a car crash. Both also had ambitions beyond the rink. Bill Barilko went into the appliance business. Tim went into the fast-food business.

But at that point their parallel circumstances diverge. Barilko's NHL career lasted five seasons. Horton's career lasted nearly twenty-four. Barilko was single. Horton had been married for almost twenty-two years and had four daughters. Barilko had two appliance stores. Tim Horton's name was on thirty-five restaurants. It was understandable that, leaving the qualities of the two men aside, the loss of Tim Horton would reverberate through a far greater community, and be felt viscerally by countless people long after the tragedy had passed.

The first person in Tim Horton's circle of friends, family and associates to learn that he had died in a high-speed crash on the Queen Elizabeth Way near St. Catharines' Lake Street exit at approximately 4:30 a.m. on February 21 was Dick Trainor, far from the scene in Sudbury. A Sudbury policeman had picked up news of the accident through police communications; the news greatly upset him, and because he knew Trainor and also knew Trainor was a longstanding friend of Tim's, he felt it important to call him about 5 a.m. and tell him what had happened.

The news stunned Trainor, in the way Tim's dispatch to hospital after the Gadsby collision had. "I always thought of Tim as Superman. He was so strong. He was beyond mere mortals. But he wasn't."

At about the same time that the news reached Trainor, the phone was ringing at the home of the Buffalo Sabres' coach, Joe Crozier. It is believed that the Ontario Provincial Police telephoned Crozier because Tim happened to be carrying a scrap of paper with Crozier's home telephone number on it. The police had apparently given little or no thought to contacting Tim's family instead.

"I received a call around 5 a.m. from the police telling me they had one of my players," says Crozier. "And they didn't tell me…" He pauses, and then rushes on. "They were slowly coming up to this whole thing. And I said, 'Can it not wait?' I thought possibly Tim had had a couple beers too much and been picked up for speeding. He went quite fast. 'No,' they said, 'you'd better come over and identify the body.'

"I was in absolute shock. That was the worst experience. I've had a DC-3 go down in a field, or, say, a hockey player of the stature of Perrault breaking his leg, but this was the most difficult thing to digest. It was unbelievable, because everybody worshipped this guy. I took the address down and called Dr. Butsch. He picked me up and we took off to identify the body."

Once Crozier and Butsch knew, the Sabres organization as a whole began to pick up the news. But as word spread that Tim was dead, it moved in every direction except one that would reach his family in a timely manner.

Punch Imlach was the next key person to learn of Tim's death. Actually, his wife Dodo was next, because she answered the phone when David Forman, the Sabres' administrative vice-president, called the Imlachs at their Toronto home.

Imlach has been perplexingly inconsistent on the details of Tim's death. On the very day Imlach learned of his death, he told the press that he had been contacted by the OPP at 5:30 a.m. In his memoirs, he makes no mention of this call. Instead, he moves the role of bad-news bearer inside the Sabres organization, to Forman, whom Seymour Knox remembers getting his call from as well.

Forman never spoke to Imlach. The news was related to Dodo, who passed it to Punch. Punch then moved to spread the word. Still no one from the police or the Sabres organization had telephoned the Horton household on Bannatyne. Punch wasn't going to change the appalling pattern. He must not have been able to stomach the thought of telling Lori Horton, the woman who had badgered Punch relentlessly during Tim's Leaf days with angry letters castigating him for putting hockey ahead of family concerns. Although Lori says she and Punch came to know each other on better terms in Buffalo, he could not face telling Lori her husband had just died driving the car Punch had thrown in as an incentive to get him to play another season of hockey. Instead of calling Lori, he called Ron Joyce.

Joyce said he got the call from Imlach about 6:30. "He said, 'Ron, I want you to call Lori and the girls. Tim's been in an accident.' I said, 'Well, how bad is it?' He said, 'He's dead. I know I shouldn't have bought him that fuckin' car.' He hung up."

Joyce, like Imlach, could not bring himself to make the call to Lori. "You come out of a sound sleep and hear that kind of news. I was pretty emotional for a while, trying to get it together and phone Lori. By the time I got on the phone, the line was busy." (According to Imlach, "Ron was so upset, he forgot.") At that point, Joyce decided to get in his car and drive to the Horton house to tell them in person, in case the busy telephone line didn't mean they knew already. Lori says Joyce went to the office first to figure out whether the business should close.

"Nobody told us," says Jeri-Lynn. "Nobody wanted to tell us."

Normally when she got up to go to work at the airport, she turned on the kitchen radio to listen to the news. For some reason, that morning she didn't, and drove to work in silence while countless other people pondered the news of her father's death. Gord Hannigan's widow Anne heard the news at 6:30 in Edmonton (8:30 in Toronto) while getting her kids ready for a school ski trip.

"Sometime around eight," Punch Imlach would recall, "my wife thought she'd better phone Tim's wife to see if there was anything we could do. When my wife called, it turned out that was the first Mrs. Horton heard about it."

Lori remembers the call coming not long after seven. "Dodo asked how I was doing and I caught the tone of her voice and said, 'What's the matter?' She said, 'You didn't hear?' and then asked if there was anybody else there." The Pelletiers were staying with the Hortons at the time, and Lori put Renate's daughter Carol on the line. As Dodo broke the news to Carol, the upstairs phone began ringing. Friends of the children had just heard the news and were calling as well.

The house began to fill up with friends, who instinctively headed for the Horton home as soon as they knew what had happened. Ron Joyce showed up; so did Ed Siekierko, and Bob Baun, and Eddie Shack, and many others. Gordon Griggs got there from Cambridge about ten o'clock. When Ed Siekierko arrived, he found Lori shut in her bedroom, sobbing, inconsolable. Gerry and Ethel Horton, already there because of Oak Horton's death, were now together with the rest of the family to grieve the loss of Tim.

"In four months," says Gordon Griggs, "Gerry's hair went from the colour of yours [dark blond] to mine [silvery]. First his dad died, and then his brother."

While the mourning began at the Horton household, still Jeri-Lynn did not know. "I can't believe I didn't hear anything that morning. I worked in transborder flights, working the gate, and all these passengers were going by. I could have heard anything." The news then reached her co-workers, who huddled when the awful realisation struck that Jeri-Lynn had no idea of what had happened to her father. "Nobody wanted to tell me," she says. "They finally elected my supervisor to tell me." And Jeri-Lynn finally knew.

"I think that Tim fully intended to go to my house," says Ron Joyce. In 1974 the Plains Road exit that would take Tim to Joyce's house in Burlington was an unusual configuration—the exit was to the left, while the highway curved away to the right. (With the construction of a new cloverleaf, the exit has since disappeared entirely.) "He was seen leaving the road, heading into the exit, and he touched the shoulder. There was a large cloud of dust. I've heard this report. My gut feel is that he made the decision to go there but was going too fast to make the exit. He tried to, but then decided, 'Oh, hell…'" Having missed the exit, Tim tore over the Skyway Bridge in Hamilton and headed down the straightaway to St. Catharines.

The family has long blamed the police for causing Tim's death by bungling its attempt to apprehend a garden-variety speeder. Jeri-Lynn does not mince words: she calls her father's death "murder."

Over the years, family and friends have gathered circumstantial evidence of a large police presence near the crash site just before Tim died. Larry Hillman spoke with the proprietor of a Texaco beside the crash site who recalled police cars streaming onto the highway shortly before the crash.

The day of the crash, Canadian Press carried a wire story noting that Constable Mike Gula of the St. Catharines OPP detachment had been passed at about 4:30 a.m. near the Lake Street exit by "a German sports car, a Porsche"—an erroneous description of the Pantera. Gula, said the story, gave chase and clocked the car at over 100 m.p.h. The story noted that officers had been advised by police radio to be on the lookout for a speeding car after a motorist told the OPP at Burlington that a car had passed him at high speed. Gula noted that Tim's car somersaulted and he was thrown from the car, landing 123 feet from the vehicle. Gula detected a faint

pulse, and called an ambulance. Tim was pronounced dead on arrival at the hospital.

There was a basic inconsistency in this report.
The accident had taken place at the Lake Street
exit. If Tim had passed Gula's cruiser near the exit,
he would have been past him in a blur. There would
have been no time for Gula to give chase. The time
between his first encounter with Tim and the accident would have been a matter of seconds. It sounded very much like Tim had been intercepted by
police given advance warning from Burlington, and
that the accident had immediately followed.

"He was braking when he left the road, which
made me think it was a roadblock," says Lori. She
also says a Niagara Regional policeman told her of
having just dropped his girlfriend off on Lake
Street when he saw "police cars everywhere" just
minutes before the crash.

As a former cop, Joyce did what he could to
understand the circumstances of Tim's death. "The
only thing that bothered me was that he went off
on a straightaway, when there had been all those
curves," he says. Indeed, the QEW at that point is a
die-straight run toward the skyway spanning the
Welland Canal. "The story has it that there was a
roadblock. The OPP deny that. But I think what
they did was they had cars on the side of the road
with lights flashing. I don't know if that's true. That
was the story. He came around the corner at
Ontario Street and he's on a straightaway. It makes
sense that there were cars there. Probably the police
were trying to slow him down. There's some
thought he tried to run off and the front left end
hit the storm sewer. There was no other vehicle
involved."

At the heart of the controversy is the accident report, which no one has ever seen.[1] Lori fuels the controversy further by declaring that Tim was drunk when he died. "The night he died," she avows, "he was drinking. A lot."

Street-level wisdom would emerge that the crash had been the result of the usual combination of a fast car, a careless celebrity and alcohol or drugs. A well-circulated joke held that the police had found LSD in the car—last Saturday's donuts.

Ron Joyce does not refute the fact that Tim had been drinking, but rejects the idea that alcohol was a factor in the crash. The coincidence of Tim's death and the anniversary of Joyce's first franchise, combined with the fact that the office often did serve as an impromptu party room, all make it possible that Tim had fallen off the wagon that night. But as everyone who encountered him before and after the game has remarked, he was in considerable pain and feeling under the weather. Although he might have had a few drinks to kill the pain, he probably wasn't having a grand old time.

The argument that Tim was legally sober was supported by a leak from the office of coroner Peter O'Halleran, in which a nurse said the autopsy showed no evidence of alcohol; Dr. O'Halleran declared there would be no inquest. One family friend who claims to have seen an accident report says the report indicated that the only substance in Tim's blood was codeine from the painkillers. But Tim clearly had been drinking that night, and the official position that he was clean as a whistle speaks of a decision to turn a benevolent blind eye on the end of an otherwise exemplary life. Far from having settled the issue of Tim's death, the evidentiary contradictions and the absence of such basic documentation as autopsy and accident reports have allowed the rumour mill surrounding his death to continue to churn.

The essential factors in his death are these: he was forty-four years old and had played two debilitating hours of professional hockey; he had been up all night; he had been drinking, probably not enough to impair someone like Tim, but enough to make him less than fully alert; and perhaps most important, he was in tremendous pain and indiscriminately taking painkillers to find some relief. The critical event of that night might well have been when he tossed back a handful of painkillers as he left Tim Donut. Alcohol and the medication would have compounded the drowsiness each would have separately engendered. Lori notes that a 222 was enough to put Tim to sleep. When he took to the road, he would have been fighting to keep his head clear.

There is one other possible explanation for the accident: Tim may have lost consciousness through an embolism. Serious facial bruises like the one to his jaw carry the risk of a blood clot moving to the brain, and he may have passed out at the wheel as a result. But Lori's contention that Tim was braking would rule out the possibility that he was unconscious when the accident occurred.

"I went down to see the vehicle the next day," says Joyce. "He went out of the car through the passenger door. You could see the imprint of where his body struck the door. If he had been wearing his seat belt... The car was damaged, but not that badly. There was no alcohol in the car."

The long-simmering controversy over how Tim died has not been embraced by everyone who knew and loved Tim. "I don't think there was anything in that accident other than speed," says Allan Stanley. "The time of the morning he was driving, no traffic, he's got a fast car and no place to give it a little blowout except in that stretch. An accident is hardly an inch away. At that speed, you move over a little to the left...apparently, he got caught in the median. The tracks there showed him trying to get out of it. He'd be holding on for dear life and be just starting to come out of it and then hit one of those drainage culverts, which is like a hole, it goes down and up. It tore the back wheel of the car right off, and it flipped over. If he'd had his seat belt on he'd be here today. The driver's side door opened and closed like a new car, but the other side was all bashed in."

Punch Imlach also inspected the car at the police garage, and was satisified with the police explanation. "It was a mess," he recalled. "Tim must have been going very fast. I knew he had been taking painkilling pills because of his jaw. Right where the incident happened there is the slightest little bend in the road. Tim had driven by it a thousand times. The way the police figured it, one wheel just got off the road a few inches. When he tried to get it back, with all that power and the car's quick responses, it rolled out of control through the median and into the lanes on the other side. I stood looking at the wreck of that damned car that I had handed to him less than five months before so he would play for me."

"We lived in Crystal Beach then," says Jim Schoenfeld. "I got the news that morning, around 8:30 or 9:00. I forget who called me. I went for a long walk on the beach. It was winter and there was ice out there on the lake. It looked kind of eerie. And then I shovelled all the snow off the patio. There was no need to shovel it. I just wanted something physical to do. Trying to come to grips with it, trying to emotionally handle it, I felt that I had. I didn't break down. You know, you ask all the questions why, and I went through the whole mental process of trying to understand why a good friend could be taken like that, and how to deal with it, the void, the loss, and then I thought, I'm all right. I've made it through this, and...ah..." Nearly twenty years after the loss, Jim Schoenfeld's eyes suddenly brim with tears and his expression compresses to hold them in check. He is reclining on his living-room couch, and he brings his hand to his brow, as if to shield his eyes from a harsh glare. Collecting himself, he wipes the tears away and, almost laughing at their arrival, remarks, "Strange!"

The show goes on. The Sabres had a home game that very night, against the Atlanta Flames, and, Tim's death or no, it had to be played. "I was slated to play the game that night," says Dave Dryden. "I couldn't. That was it. I couldn't believe they were going to play the game. I was really, really upset. I was the player rep [for the players' association] at the time. I went to a Catholic church in Buffalo that morning. I just didn't know what was going on." Walking back to the Aud, Dryden saw Bernie "Boom-Boom" Geoffrion coming up the other side of the street. The man who had introduced the slapshot to the NHL just ahead of Tim was now coaching the Flames. "Atlanta had practised before we had. Boomer called across and gave his condolences. I

went down and put my stuff on, and I guess Joe
Crozier knew me pretty well. Joe just said, 'Forget it
Dave, we won't dress you tonight.' I didn't, and I
spent the evening driving around Niagara Falls,
totally bewildered by the whole thing. It was just
awful."

The Sabres actually managed to tie the game 4-4,
and people like to say that after Tim's death the season fell apart. On paper, his loss seemed to make no
difference. The Sabres were nine points behind
Toronto when Tim died, and finished the season
ten points behind the Leafs. But there is no question that the late season surge hoped for, with
Schoenfeld and Perreault back in the lineup, failed
to gel once Tim was lost. It was Dave Dryden's last
season in the NHL. He switched to the WHA the
next season. So did Paul Terbenche, who would be
nagged by one of those terribly unfair "if onlys": if
only he had said yes when Tim asked him to ride on
the bus with him that night.

The guilt was shared by others. Tim's youngest
daughter also came to blame herself. After coming
home from the game, Traci had retired to her room
with her cousin Kerry to listen to the soundtrack to
"Jesus Christ Superstar." They had the Bible out
along with the album, and when Traci climbed into
bed she stepped on it. When she learned the next
morning that her father was dead, she decided that
it was because she had stepped on the Bible. She
had offended God, and God had exacted his punishment by taking her father away.

Even though the game had to be played, it would
have been grotesque had some acknowledgment
not been made of Tim's death. The Sabres made

his loss emphatically clear, issuing black armbands to the players and observing a minute of silence after the national anthem was played.

Up until that moment, Jim Schoenfeld thought he had it all together, the questions answered, the loss neatly packaged and in its place. And then, he says, "I was overwhelmed." As the crowd marked the silence, Schoenfeld wept openly as he stood on the ice with the rest of the team. "Jim Schoenfeld was more moved than any player on the ice, when it was announced what had happened, and in the moment of silence," says Seymour Knox. "He was crying, and visibly so to most of us down lower in the bowl."

The game was a nightmare for him. "I'm playing and I'm crying. The puck is on my stick! I went to the bench and Joe Crozier came down and hugged me and tried to comfort me. That's how much he could mean to you in such a short time. That's how rich the guy was, that he would be able to affect your life in a year. For me, it was virtually a year because I missed most of the second year.

"When you look at the year Tim died, we didn't make the playoffs. The first year he came was the first time the team ever made the playoffs. The year after he died, we went to the finals. I think his death did a lot in bringing the team closer together. We had a young team with different types of players. We had our fancy high-scoring guys, we had our tough guys, we had our hard-working guys. Sometimes I think there was a lack of appreciation of one ability over another. Losing Timmy united us. We appreciated each other more. We appreciated each others' contribution more, and we saw each other on a different level for the first time, where it was more than hockey. You quickly realized hockey is one piece—it's not the whole picture. We saw each other more deeply as people, rather than just as teammates. We all showed it differently, we all felt it differently, but we all felt the loss. It may have been strange, but I think it was something that helped that team to excel."

Up in Bobcaygeon, Allan Stanley had watched Tim's last game on television. Nearly five years after Stanley's last season, the two had not lost touch; Stanley had visited with Tim and Lori that Christmas. "I watched that game Wednesday night and Tim was the best defenceman on the ice," he said. "He didn't carry the puck as much, of course, but in his own end, he was the boss. My memories of Tim? I guess it would be a Leaf player down on the ice, losing a fight, and Tim rushing in, lifting the guy off and pitching him away. And I'm not kidding. Just like that. Or some so-called tough guy being put on his back by Tim. Or a man who had total respect in his profession, yet never hurt anybody in his life. Could you say anything better about a guy? I hope not, because Tim was the finest person I ever knew."

Dennis Griggs called Jim Charade early on the morning of February 21 to tell him Tim was dead. Jim had seen Tim a few months earlier. The night of Tim's last game, Charade had been at the Inn-on-the-Park for his son André's high-school senior prom; the significance of the date to the donut business had been on his mind.

"I heard rumours that Tim killed himself," he says. "But he was too religious. He cared about his children too much.

"Tim," he says, "was my best friend. I look at the picture of him sometimes in the donut shop that says 'The Legend,' and I think: I don't know. He was just real people."

When Tim died, Hughie Phillips was at a low point in his life. The recent bout of pleurisy had almost killed him, and now it seemed that he was going to lose the little house he had only recently bought. He had a modest job tending to landscaping at Bloorview hospital. The plumbing was backing up in the basement—tree roots were blocking it. Tim had always offered him money, and Hughie had always refused it. Now he had none to his own name, his world was crumbling, and he thought, *Oh Tim, I need you now.*

The night of the game, "I went some place with a friend of mine. I got home, a buddy was watching the game upstairs and I started to watch it with him. Tim was one of the stars. I didn't know there was anything wrong. I had no idea. I'm so mad, because I like to think that if I went, that would have never happened. Maybe if I had been there, I would have gone with him—who knows. I feel a little bit responsible. I know that's stupid, but that's me, because I miss him so bloody much. And it still really bothers me, and it's a long, long time ago. And it hurts. It really does.

"And there are so many things I would have liked him to see. Like me paying for this house. I know he would have been so bloody proud. And I wish he could have seen me drive. I started driving that next summer. I would have loved to have gone up to his house in my car. Just gone in, and Tim would say, 'How did you get here?'" Hughie grins irresistibly at the line he can never deliver. "And I would say, 'Well, come on and I'll show you.'"

Tim lay in state for several days at Jerrett Funeral Home in Willowdale (the funeral home's owners were cottage neighbours of the Hortons on Pen Lake), as Lori postponed the funeral until the Monday after Tim's death so that the Sabres players and personnel would be able to attend. A steady stream of people filed into the funeral home to pay their respects.

"One of the most vivid memories I have is of Frank Mahovlich flying in from Montreal on Saturday," says Gordon Griggs. "He spent a good hour with Lori and then flew back to Montreal and played hockey that night. There's an awful lot of love when he did that, because he could easily have said, 'Well, I'll go down for the funeral on Monday, because I'm not playing on Monday.' A guy and his wife drove all the way down from Sudbury on a motorcycle, stayed at the casket for thirteen, fourteen seconds—there was a lineup——then drove all the way back."

The Sabres and their wives arrived together in a chartered bus for the funeral. No one was going to be driving that stretch of road alone. Some were wearing their black armbands.

The crowd at Oriole-York Mills United Church was estimated at twelve hundred. TV monitors were set up in an auditorium to handle the overflow of mourners and curiosity-seekers who could not make it into the actual church. Every NHL team sent a representative. Among the hockey figures attending were league president Clarence Campbell, Maple Leaf Gardens president Harold Ballard, former Leaf greats Bob Goldham, Hal Cotton and Gus Bodnar, and his old coach Gentleman Joe Primeau. Eight uniformed Buffalo police officers who served on traffic patrol at the Aud brought two squad cars to serve as an honour guard. Gordon Griggs delivered the eulogy.

"To Tim," he said, "life was a gift from God. He gave of himself in the game of hockey more than was required of any athlete. He shared the glory of a Stanley Cup with his family and friends. He accepted his gift of life, this brimming love that he possessed and shared with all those who could celebrate with him."

The pallbearers were six of his close friends from the great Leaf teams of the Imlach years: Allan Stanley, George Armstrong, Dave Keon, Dick Duff, Billy Harris and Bob Baun. The honorary pallbearers were Punch Imlach, Dickie Moore, Red Kelly, Jim Schoenfeld, Paul Terbenche, Joe Crozier, Bryan Watson, Eddie Shack, King Clancy, Bill Landon, Ken Gariepy, Sid Quarapell and Larry Mann.

In Allan Stanley, the line of experience passing through Bill Barilko and Tim Horton was drawn closed. When Barilko's remains were found in the bush north of Cochrane after Tim set up the goal that won the Leafs the 1962 Stanley Cup, Stanley, as a fellow Leaf defenceman and Timmins native, was one of the pallbearers called upon to deliver Barilko to the grave. Twelve years later, Stanley was again called upon to serve as a pallbearer, this time for his own defence partner, the man the Leafs had envisioned as Barilko's replacement.

At York Cemetery, Lori Horton placed a bouquet of yellow and white daisies on the casket. Tim and Lori's four daughters knelt to kiss the wood of the casket before it was lowered into the ground.

"When I saw him in the casket," says Schoenfeld, "it seemed like such a wrong place for him. There was no way that man should ever have been confined in a box. I know it's the way it's always done, but, goddamn, when I saw it, it was not Hortie. I've seen other people in caskets and it seemed appropriate. It didn't seem right for him, not because he was young and he was killed—it didn't seem right for *him*." Schoenfeld pantomimes Tim Horton thrusting his arms through the sides of the coffin. "It seemed too confining for a guy like Timmy. That was my perception of him. He was almost a guy who couldn't be confined.

"It didn't seem right for him to have been killed in an impact with something. Not Hortie. But when you look back, it wasn't a shock that he died in some sort of accident, whether it was driving an automobile or parasailing or whatever. It was like: Yeah, I'm going to do it, and I'm going to do it as hard as it can be done."

Schoenfeld finds some gentle relief in the idea of Tim's taking charge of his own funeral, a man of action to the end, not a body inert and hemmed in. "That's what you're expecting: Let me dig my own hole and dive in." Perhaps, without realising it, that is precisely what Tim Horton did.

"He left his mark," says Dick Duff. "Everybody would have loved to see the guy around for a long, long time, just to enjoy his company. I don't know what more he could have done in the time he was around. He touched lots of people in different avenues of life, and stayed the same through it all. I see a lot of value in his life experience. From down through the years there are probably a lot of people, unbeknown to us, hanging on to things he said or suggested they try to do—to restart the engines and see what you can do."

The *Buffalo Evening News* received an anonymous letter. It read: "I'm a 15-year-old girl and I don't have no father. He died a few years ago… Anyway, I've never had no respect for anyone cept Tim Horton." She explained how she had met him after a Sabres practice. "First I was scared cuz he looked really strong and mean. But we got to talking and I told him I didn't have no father and he told me something I'll never forget. He said: Just becuz someone's left the earth doesn't mean they're dead. You're only dead if you're forgotten and not loved. If you still have a place for that person in your heart they're still with you and will never be dead. They've only taken a trip, a long trip… I guess I've learned a lot from that. But I never cried as hard as when I heard Horton went on that trip."

Whenever Larry Hillman drives past the spot where Tim Horton was killed, he turns off his car stereo and observes a moment of silence.

Afterword

The legacy of Tim Horton is as varied as the life he lived and the people he knew.

After Tim's death, his youngest daughter Traci named a son after her father. He had already been so honoured by his brother Gerry.

In his birthplace of Cochrane, Ontario, the local arena carries his name.

At Tim's funeral, Gordon Griggs announced that the Tim Horton Memorial Camp for underprivileged children would be established on a 150-acre site in Orangeville, the land owned by Tim, Ron Joyce and Ken Gariepy. As events proved, Gariepy backed out of donating his share of the land at the eleventh hour, unable to afford the gesture. An alternate site was found near Parry Sound, which became the first of what are now four Tim Horton camps in Canada.

They are sparkling, first-class facilities, a long way from the original when it opened, which was a reclaimed fishing camp. Joyce remembers it as the "underprivileged camp for underprivileged children." Lori Horton, who is no longer on the board of the Tim Horton Children's Foundation, the non-profit enterprise that runs the camps, holds that the first camp is the true memorial: the rest just promote the donut chain. Ron Joyce says that he has considered changing the name of the camps, but that the franchisees, who are the camps' greatest supporters, would never tolerate it. He says the camp program is considering a shift in focus, providing follow-through assistance for children rather than simply a two-week retreat.

Jim Schoenfeld appeared at every camp for the first seven years.

Patrons of the more than 1,000 Tim Hortons franchises buy mini-donuts called Tim Bits and drink coffee from dashboard cups called Tim Mugs. Recent advertisements for Tim Hortons show a father wearing a hockey jacket with the crest of a Wexford team. Wexford, Quebec, may be home to a team in the Quebec Major Junior A, but Wexford coincidentally also happens to have been the Toronto neighbourhood where Jim Charade opened the first Tim Horton Do-Nuts.

Tim Hortons remains one of the most highly regarded franchising operations around. In 1991, the *Financial Times of Canada* identified it as one of five "solid, second-level franchises"—the first level being occupied by such juggernauts as McDonald's and Kentucky Fried Chicken.

In 1989 the business had sufficient financial heft to become the principal backer of a $50-million bid for an NHL franchise for the city of Hamilton, Ontario, where the first Tim Hortons franchise opened in 1964. Although the bid was turned aside by the league, in 1994 Joyce became a minority shareholder of the Calgary Flames, and established a new vacation home near the city. The corporate Piper Cherokee 235 is now a corporate jet, and Ron Joyce is still the pilot. While from time to time rumours surface that Joyce is considering selling the business, he has yet to do so. It has made this ex-cop with relentless ambition and an attention to detail a very wealthy man.

After leaving Tim Donut in 1970, Jim Charade spent twenty-three years—nearly the equivalent of Tim's NHL career—in the franchise business, most of those years in the United States. Jim's wife Claudette died in 1988, and in 1990 he came to Mississauga to open an office for Amco. He was playing drums in his spare time at Hy's on Richmond in Toronto when Ron Joyce came in one night. "Maybe you should come back with us," Joyce said to Charade. On March 1, 1993, with Lori Horton's suit having been found in the defendants' favour, Jim Charade took a job with Tim Donut in real estate.

Jim Charade was never called to testify in Lori Horton's lawsuit. He was a mere aside in the proceedings, a name spelled wrong in the judgment. Others who were called felt the harsh consequences of becoming involved in a case where half of a national business phenomenon, or $10 million, was at stake. In particular the lives of the four Horton daughters, the role their own behaviour might have played in their mother's conduct, were subjected to probing. The emotional upheaval of the case reached its apex in the circumstances of Jeri-Lynn Horton, eldest daughter of Tim and Lori, who testified on her mother's behalf, happened to be married to Ron Joyce's son, Ron Jr., happened to be a Tim Donut franchisee herself, and happened to be the mother of a grandson shared by Lori and Ron Joyce.

The case deeply divided the large circle of friends, former teammates and associates of Tim

Horton. Some stood by Lori unequivocally. Some supported Lori's contention that she had been unfairly treated, but did not support her decision to subject herself (and her family) to a public trial which could prove so corrosive for all involved. Some determined to maintain their friendship with her while staying clear of the fray altogether.

And some simply did not believe that the suit had any merit, and were outraged by the public flaying of reputations that resulted. "The sad thing about it is that all of this came out at trial," one former friend and teammate of Tim (who has no connection to the donut business) said to this writer. "I personally think the suit is baseless. I don't know where it started, but I have an idea where it started, and it was badly thought out. It did nothing but harm her and harm their family, and it dragged Tim's name through all kinds of crap that needn't be."

Eddie Shack, whose wife Norma remains a good friend of Lori, who does not like Ron Joyce, and who is credited with helping convince Lori to launch her suit, launched his own chain of donut stores after Judge German handed down her decision. A flying squad of Leafs from the great 1960s teams, including Johnny Bower, Frank Mahovlich, Billy Harris and Dick Duff, came out for the grand opening, the way they always have when a teammate has gone into business. (Not everyone was there. Bob Baun is a Tim Hortons franchisee.) Lori Horton also made an appearance. She agreed to show up only when Shack promised not to open any outlet that would compete directly with her daughter Jeri-Lynn's Tim Hortons franchises. Jim McKenny, the former Leaf defenceman who is now a Toronto sportscaster, put her before the television

camera at the grand opening and asked her how
Eddie's product compared with Tim Hortons. She
was diplomatic. "Very favourably," she said.

In the American Hockey League, since 1978 the
Tim Horton Trophy has been presented annually to
the top two players on the rosters of the Canadian
teams, based on their accumulation of Three Star
Selections at regular-season home games.

Tim Horton's number was never assigned to a
player by the Buffalo Sabres in the twenty seasons
following his death. In the spring of 1995, its retirement was made official, a remarkable accolade for a
player who had been with the team less than two
seasons.

In the NHL record book, Tim Horton is tied
(with Larry Robinson) for thirtieth (twelfth among
defencemen) in lifetime All Star selections, with
three nominations to the first team and three to the
second team.

He ranks forty-first in all-time penalty minutes,
more through the length of his career than brutish-
ness. He averaged 1.11 minutes per game, compared
to 4.12 minutes for list-leader Dave "Tiger" Williams.
(Bobby Orr averaged 1.45 minutes per game.)

He ranks fourth in all-time games played, with
1,446, behind Gordie Howe (1,767), Alex
Delvecchio (1,549) and John Bucyk (1,540). No
defenceman has played more games. His total games
as a Maple Leaf (1,185) is two less than the record
held by George Armstrong. Tim's Leaf record for
most consecutive games played—486—still stands.

Tim Horton was inducted into the Hockey Hall of
Fame posthumously in 1977. Already in the Hall
from the great Leaf teams of the 1960s were Red

Kelly (1969), Terry Sawchuk (posthumously, in 1971), George Armstrong (1975) and Johnny Bower (1976). They have been joined by Frank Mahovlich and Allan Stanley (1981), Bert Olmstead (1985), Dave Keon (1986), and Bob Pulford (1991). Very few of Tim's Leaf teammates from the 1950s have made it. The exceptions are Ted Kennedy (1966), Harry Lumley (1980) and Harry Watson (1995).

There is no category for coaches. King Clancy was inducted as a player in 1958, Hap Day in 1961, Joe Primeau in 1963.

Tim is one of seven St. Michael's College students to have been inducted. The others are Kelly, Mahovlich, Primeau and Keon, as well as Gerry Cheevers and Ted Lindsay.

Bill Gadsby, whose body check broke Tim's leg and jaw, was inducted in 1970. Referee Bill Chadwick, who saw no reason to call a penalty, was inducted in 1964.

Punch Imlach was inducted posthumously in the "Builders" category in 1984. Conn Smythe made it right after he gave up control of the Maple Leafs, in 1958. Foster Hewitt followed him in 1965. Harold Ballard came out of jail, wrested control of Maple Leaf Gardens, and was inducted in 1977. The late Stafford Smythe has never been so honoured. Alan Eagleson was inducted in 1989.

Lori Horton still has the most-valuable-player awards presented to Tim by his teammates on the St. Mike's Majors and the Buffalo Sabres. They were among his most treasured honours, having been voted upon by his peers, not by fickle sportswriters or team owners. They're lined up on a shelf in the home Lori shares with her daughter Traci, every one of them a little man of steel.

SEASON	CLUB	LEAGUE	REGULAR SCHEDULE					PLAYOFFS				
			GP	G	A	TP	PIM	GP	G	A	TP	PIM
1949-50	Pittsburgh	AHL	60	5	18	23	83	–	–	–	0	–
1949-50	Toronto	NHL	1	0	0	0	2	1	0	0	0	2
1950-51 CF	Pittsburgh	AHL	68	8	26	34	129	13	0	9	9	16
1951-52 C,a	Pittsburgh	AHL	64	12	19	31	146	11	1	3	4	16
Career: American Hockey League			192	25	63	88	358	24	1	12	13	32
1951-52	Toronto	NHL	4	0	0	0	8	–	–	–	–	–
1952-53	Toronto	NHL	70	2	14	16	85	–	–	–	–	–
1953-54 b	Toronto	NHL	70	7	24	31	94	5	1	1	2	4
1954-55 I	Toronto	NHL	67	5	9	14	84	–	–	–	–	–
1955-56	Toronto	NHL	35	0	5	5	36	2	0	0	0	4
1956-57	Toronto	NHL	66	6	19	25	72	–	–	–	–	–
1957-58	Toronto	NHL	53	6	20	26	39	–	–	–	–	–
1958-59 SF	Toronto	NHL	70	5	21	26	76	12	0	3	3	16
1959-60 SF	Toronto	NHL	70	3	29	32	69	10	0	1	1	6
1960-61	Toronto	NHL	57	6	15	21	75	5	0	0	0	0
1961-62 S	Toronto	NHL	70	10	28	38	88	12	3	13	16R	16
1962-63 S,c	Toronto	NHL	70	6	19	25	69	10	1	3	4	10
1963-64 S,d	Toronto	NHL	70	9	20	29	71	14	0	4	4	20
1964-65	Toronto	NHL	70	12	16	28	95	6	0	2	2	13
1965-66	Toronto	NHL	70	6	22	28	76	4	1	0	1	12
1966-67 S,e	Toronto	NHL	70	8	17	25	70	12	3	5	8	25

CF Pittsburgh reached Calder Cup finals
C   Pittsburgh won Calder Cup
SF Toronto reached Stanley Cup finals
S   Toronto won Stanley Cup

SEASON	CLUB	LEAGUE	REGULAR SCHEDULE					PLAYOFFS				
			GP	G	A	TP	PIM	GP	G	A	TP	PIM
1967-68 G,f	Toronto	NHL	69	4	23	27	82	–	–	–	–	–
1968-69 g	Toronto	NHL	74	11	29	40	107	4	0	0	0	7
1969-70 B	Toronto	NHL	59	3	19	22	91	–	–	–	–	–
1969-70*	NY Rangers	NHL	15	1	5	6	16	6	1	1	2	28
1969-70	two-team total		74	4	24	28	107	6	1	1	2	28
1970-71	NY Rangers	NHL	78	2	18	20	57	13	1	4	5	14
1971-72**	Pittsburgh	NHL	44	2	9	11	40	4	0	1	1	2
1972-73***V	Buffalo	NHL	69	1	16	17	56	6	0	1	1	4
1973-74****	Buffalo	NHL	55	0	6	6	53	–	–	–	–	–
Career: National Hockey League			1446	115	403	518	1611	126	11	39	50	183

I Injured in collision with Bill Gadsby on March 12, 1955, with fractures of leg and jaw.

R Established league play-off scoring record for defencemen

G Established team record for most consecutive regular-season games (486) from February 11, 1961, to February 4, 1968

B Voted recipient of J.P. Bickell Memorial Trophy, awarded to the team's most valuable player, by the Maple Leaf Gardens board of directors before start of 1969/70 season.

V Voted most valuable player by his Buffalo teammates at end of 72/73 season

* Traded by Toronto to New York Rangers on March 3, 1970 for future considerations. Toronto received in return Denis Dupere and Guy Trottier via 1970 intraleague draft.
** Drafted by Pittsburgh in intraleague draft, June 8, 1971.
*** Drafted by Buffalo in intraleague draft, June 5, 1972.
**** Died February 21, 1974

a first-team All Star (AHL)
b second-team All Star
c second-team All Star
d first-team All Star

e second-team All Star
f first-team All Star
g first-team All Star

MILES GILBERT (TIM) HORTON

Born: January 12, 1930, Cochrane, Ont.
Position: right defence
Height: 5 feet 9 inches
Weight: 165 pounds (amateur), 175 pounds (AHL),
180–185 pounds (ideal NHL), 195 pounds (final
season)

Junior amateur teams:
Copper Cliff Redmen, Northern Ontario Hockey
    Association, 1946/47
St. Michael's College Majors, Ontario Hockey
    Association, 1947/48, 48/49
Voted Most Valuable Player by St. Michael's
    teammates in 47/48 and 48/49
Named to OHA Junior 'A' All Star Team in 1949.
Placed on Toronto Maple Leafs reserve list
    (via C-form) in 1947. Called up to play
    professionally in September, 1949.
    Assigned to Amercian Hockey League farm
    club, Pittsburgh Hornets, on a three-year
    contract.

Endnotes

Chapter 1—Natural Resources

1. Written accounts of the railway usually refer to it as the T&NO, but in its own advertising the railway billed itself as the TNO.

2. While shorthand biographies of Baun will note that he is from Lanigan, Sask., he moved to Toronto's east end before he started kindergarten.

3. Cobalt and Haileybury teams were part of the National Hockey Association, a league boiled down from fierce, ultimately self-destructive competition for players between the Eastern Canadian Hockey Association and the Federal League. But the Temiskaming teams did not survive the parsimony of the First World War, and it was left to the surviving NHA teams in Toronto, Ottawa and Montreal to form the National Hockey League in 1917.

4. Gerry Horton died within a few weeks of being interviewed by the author.

5. Smythe was one of a number of University of Toronto students who enlisted in the Canadian army in 1915. Harvey Aggett joined him. Before enlisting, the pair helped the Varsity hockey team win the 1914/15 OHA Junior title. Aggett was killed at Passchendaele on November 6, 1917. Two weeks later, Smythe was captured by the Germans and spent the rest of the war in a POW camp.

6. Gerry Horton played left wing in the OHA Junior A for the Barrie Flyers and the Oshawa Generals.

Chapter 2—Copper Cliff

1. Yacker Flynn was the son of Bert "The Mighty Atom" Flynn.

In 1914 a baseball team from Cobalt had come to town to play against the Canadian Copper Co. (Inco's forerunner) team. Bert Flynn was a five-foot, two-inch shortstop for Cobalt, and he was immediately recruited to play ball for Inco.

2. Local semi-pro baseball during the First World War had featured future NHLers Red Green and Sam Rothschild. No one could mention Nickel Belt baseball without mentioning Phil "Babe" Marchildon, a former all-star with the Creighton Mines team who would record a nineteen-win season with the Philadelphia Phillies of the American League. In September 1946, Ralph "High Pockets" McCabe, a former Copper Cliff Redmen pitcher, was called up from Oklahoma City by the Cleveland Indians.

Chapter 3—"Just Sign Here"

1. An article in the 1966/67 Maple Leaf program by Henry Roxborough offered a confused defence of the C-form— albeit after the league had finally abandoned it. "Its terms did seem restrictive and yet it also had some commendable features," Roxborough persuaded Leaf fans. "Under its arrangement some hundreds of boys were equipped and coached by experts; they were provided with scholastic education including fees, tuition and books; they were given spending money to enable them to enjoy social advantages and to be neatly dressed. Some of the lads who might have become drop-outs or loafers developed into very fine citizens. To provide all those advantages cost, in some individual instances, through the teenage years, as much as $20,000[!]. Any reasonable person would agree that after expending so much, the recipient did have an obligation to repay his sponsor by making his services available. Still, if the youth didn't make good or if he preferred another profession, he was not expected to repay a plugged nickel of the funds involved in his development. However, in such circumstances it would be unrealistic to permit some rival professional club who had not spent a cent on the individual player to come along and snatch his services. It should also be noted that no contract with a young prospect was binding unless it had been approved and signed by the par-

ents or guardian of the lad." Such writers never seemed to stop and try the shoe on their own foot, to consider what it would have been like, at the age of sixteen, to find that you were destined to earn your living reporting for the *Toronto Telegram*, and that you had little say in the matter.

2. Recollections of how many spots a team had on its reserve list vary widely, in part because the total reserve list was sometimes considered to include the negotiating list as well. Sam Pollock, general manager of the Montreal Canadiens from 64/65 to 77/78, remembers a figure of "33 and 4"—thirty-three players on the reserve list, four on the negotiating list. A Canadian Press article from the late 1940s placed the size of the reserve list at forty four: forty skaters and four goaltenders. The size of the list may simply have changed through time.

3. The mining analogy is well nigh irresistible. Foster Hewitt, in his book *Hockey Night in Canada*, compared Leaf scout Squib Walker to a mining prospector, and referred to the minor leagues as "hockey's salt mines."

Chapter 4—The Redmen

1. Weiland, who is no longer alive, was inducted into the Hockey Hall of Fame as a player in 1971.

2. Team owners were as suspicious of the impact television broadcasting would have on ticket sales as they had been of radio broadcasts. Detroit's Channel 4 was only permitted to broadcast the latter half of the game because Red Wings management believed a partial broadcast would force anyone who wanted to see the entire game to buy a ticket. Conn Smythe was of the same mind: "Hockey Night in Canada" broadcasts right through the 1960s only began after the first period.

3. Tim Horton's future defence partner, Allan Stanley, underwent a similar ordeal when caught between the Bruins organization and the Oshawa Generals. Bep Guidolin, who like Stanley was from Timmins, had just begun his NHL career with Boston in 42/43, and took the seventeen-year-old prospect to the Bruins training camp with him in Quebec City in the fall of 1943. Guidolin had played with

the Generals, and made the connection with Oshawa for Stanley as well. While in Quebec at the Bruins camp, Stanley decided he wanted to play for the Generals, and went to see Art Ross and Dit Clapper of the Bruins in their hotel suite to tell them. "Holy jeez, Art Ross hit the ceiling," says Stanley. "He cursed and swore. 'Those bastards, they've been screwing me for years. You're going to talk to Frank Sargent.' Ross telephoned Sargent, president of the CAHA, that minute. Frank said, 'Allan, I hear you have a problem. What's going on?' So I told him briefly. Boston wanted me to go to extended training camp, and I've been offered to go to Oshawa. Sargent said, 'Look, why don't you just go down to training camp for two weeks? If you don't like it, you can go anyplace you want. But if you don't go, I'm going to have to suspend you while I look into it.' That sounded reasonable enough. At that time the Boston Olympics were the direct farm team of the Bruins. I went down to the Olympics, and liked it enough, so I stayed. Oshawa won the Memorial Cup that year. Boston Olympics, we won the U.S. amateur championship."

Chapter 5—St. Mike's

1. At a Maple Leaf Gardens tribute to King Clancy in 1934, a series of floats traversed the ice surface. Joe Primeau was ensconced in one, brandishing a harp. The float bearing a handful of St. Mike's players was shaped like a potato.

2. The Leafs' chief scout and Conn Smythe had known each other a long time. The pair had played together on the University of Toronto Varsity squad when it won the Ontario Junior championship in 1915. Opposing them on the Berlin Union Jacks had been Frank Selke, who went on to become Smythe's right-hand man at Maple Leaf Gardens. Walker and Smythe had enlisted together following the championship, but Walker's poor eyesight got him washed out of training. He finally made it to France with an anti-aircraft unit, and Smythe and Walker were reunited on the battlefield. During the Second World War, when Smythe headed overseas as a major and commanding officer of the 30th Battery, 7th Toronto Regiment, he left behind a "Big Three" to run the Leafs in his absence: Hap

Day (whom Smythe had coached at the U of T in the 1920s), Frank Selke and Squib Walker. Walker wrote Smythe faithfully overseas and sent him packages.

3. Smythe may have been making a convenient scapegoat of his father, a man who seemed in many ways the antithesis of his narrow, hard-driving son. In addition to being a poet and a newspaper editor (first of the *Toronto World,* then of the *Hamilton Herald*), Albert E.S. Smythe was a charter member of the Canadian Theosophical Society and the editor of its journal. Theosophy was devoted to a broad-minded spiritual searching for enlightenment that embraced Buddhism and Hindu's Brahmanism, and sought to bring about a universal brotherhood. A list of reading Conn Smythe included in his diary during the First World War included pamphlets devoted to eastern mysticism, but it's doubtful father and son ever shared the same philosophical ground. The two had become estranged after Albert remarried in 1913. Conn's mother Mary had died in 1906, when he was eleven years old.

4. Smythe's west-end sand and gravel operation was incorporated as C. Smythe Ltd. in 1927. At that time Hap Day became a minority partner. In Smythe's recollection, Day's share was about 16 per cent. Part of the operation survives today as Smythe Park, on the east side of Lambton Golf and Country Club near Jane and Dundas. Joe Primeau's block company was located at what is now the club's north side. The Primeau home was a few bends along the Humber River south of both operations.

5. Future Leaf coach and general manager Punch Imlach also participated in this controversial wartime hockey phenomenon. As he described it in the second instalment of his memoirs, *Heaven and Hell in the NHL,* "There were some very strong hockey teams in the services about that time, seen as a way to keep men busy and interested while they were training. I wound up playing for Cornwall Army [the base in Cornwall, Ont.]. I was commissioned a lieutenant in 1942 and spent the rest of the war as an instructor." Also at Cornwall, as a sergeant giving instruction in chemical warfare and platoon weapons, was Tommy Ivan. Before arriving at Cornwall he had coached Junior hockey for five

years, in Barrie and Galt. After the war he served as coach and general manager of the Detroit Red Wings and Chicago Blackhawks.

6. It's not always easy to establish exactly who said what and when, based on the printed record. Writer George Gross, in Maple Leaf program profiles in 1966/67 and 68/69, shifted several key quotes between Tim Horton and George Armstrong. This quote, for example, attributed to Horton in 68/69, is originally split between Horton and Armstrong in 66/67. "He knew the game inside and out and never raised his voice," Gross has Armstrong saying. "He got a great deal out of his players because of his attitude. Actually it would have been useless for him to scream, because we would have thought he was sick." Gross then has Horton add: "It would just be the opposite with Punch. If he stopped yelling, we'd go looking for a doctor."

7. Campbell cannot be held solely responsible for the changing mood of the game. He was there to do the league owners' bidding. As Conn Smythe would reflect, Campbell as NHL president "was doing well—because he would do what he was told."

8. The relative quality of the NHL over the years is a constant source of debate. Most people would probably be willing to agree that the NHL during the Second World War was a makeshift product, were it not for the fact that doing so immediately casts aspersion on the Leaf Stanley Cup victories and Maurice Richard's fifty-goals-in-fifty-games record of 44/45. But given the number of existing and potential new stars who enlisted in the armed forces, the NHL was clearly weakened by war, and the startling increase in total goals per game is good evidence. Conn Smythe, away at war (as was his star goaltender, Turk Broda), believed the game was suffering. In a letter to his head scout Squib Walker on April 2, 1944, he wrote: "You have to admit that one NHL player is worth two wartime NHL'ers."

Chapter 6—Looting the Ranks

1. Pratt, who had been the league MVP in 42/43, was suspended, and then reinstated, by NHL president Red Dutton in January 1946 for gambling on league games. In

the wake of the scandal, Conn Smythe decided to cut his star loose, selling him to the Bruins on June 19. They assigned him to Hershey, and he never made it back to the NHL. Two years later, under the new league president, Clarence Campbell, such gambling would result in a lifetime ban for Billy Taylor and Don Gallinger. It's worth speculating whether Smythe would have put up with a lifetime ban of one of his players—he wouldn't have been able to recoup his investment. With Pratt, he was at least able to sell him. The two players suspended for life in 1948 were with weaker American franchises, the Bruins and the Rangers. It may not be a coincidence that Smythe dealt away Billy Taylor after the 45/46 season, when he also sold Pratt. The Major may well have had more than an inkling that Taylor was trouble.

Pratt, Taylor and Gallinger were not the only NHL players wagering on games—just the only ones caught and punished. The author is aware of at least one other player (who is still alive), traded away at the time of the scandals, who was known by teammates to bet on his team's games.

2. Conn Smythe's largest player purchase to date was the $35,000, plus the rights to Art Smith and Eric Pettinger, that he handed over to the Ottawa Senators in 1930 for star defenceman King Clancy. By Smythe's own reckoning, the total deal was worth $50,000, as he placed a value of $10,000 on Smith and $5,000 on Pettinger. Had he got his way, the Lewicki purchase wouldn't have been his biggest outlay after returning to the Leafs from the Second World War. In his memoirs Smythe says he offered Boston $30,000 for Milt Schmidt, the same amount to New York for Neil Colville, and $25,000 to Montreal for Maurice Richard. According to Foster Hewitt, who was a good friend of Smythe's, during the 1930s Smythe tried to buy the entire "Kraut" line of Woody Dumart, Milt Schmidt and Bobby Bauer from the Bruins for $30,000, and also offered $20,000 to New York general manager Lester Patrick for Patrick's own son, Lynn.

3. The Aces were operated by the Anglo-Canadian Pulp and Paper Company of Quebec City, and took their name from the initials of the company's employee group; Imlach was

paid $135 a week to work in the company office, plus "something on the side," as Imlach recalled, for his efforts with the Aces.

4. Conn Smythe's recruitment of Mathers bears a striking resemblance to the tale of Hap Day's recruitment by Charlie Querrie, as told by Foster Hewitt in his book *Hockey Night in Canada*. According to Hewitt, Querrie, who was managing the NHL's St. Patricks, approached Day while he was still a pharmacy student at the University of Toronto and persuaded him to turn pro. Hewitt has Day turning to his friend Conn Smythe, who was coaching collegiate hockey, for his advice, and Smythe advising him to jump to the professional ranks. Hewitt's story may well have been modelled on Smythe's well-publicized recruitment of Mathers, particularly in the details of Querrie telling Day he would make $50,000 in ten years—Smythe would tell Mathers he could make $100,000 in ten years. Smythe signed up Mathers in 1948; *Hockey Night in Canada* was first published in 1953. In his memoirs, Smythe gave this account of Day's recruitment: "Hap Day was taking pharmacy then. I wanted him badly to sign with the Varsity team [which Smythe was coaching]. He played a couple of games with us and was a standout, head and shoulders above some pretty good guys. I went one night to a place on McCaul Street where he was living at the time with about six other fellows from the university, and almost got him to agree, but he needed money badly right then and would have had to leave school if he didn't make some somewhere. Toronto St. Patricks of the NHL made him a good offer, which he accepted."

5. In the deciding game of the 1951 Stanley Cup, with Joe Primeau behind the Leaf bench, Cal Gardner and Harry Watson, playing on a line with Howie Meeker, produced the offensive press that led to Bill Barilko's series-winning overtime goal.

6. Ray Hannigan played three games as a Leaf, all of them on this call-up. John McLellan didn't actually get on the ice as a Leaf until two games in 51/52, when he was used as a centre. Ray married John's twin sister. McLellan would become a Leaf coach and assistant general manager.

Chapter 7—School's Out

1. Smythe's comparison of Armstrong and Lewicki to Conacher and Jackson was, in hindsight, an odd one. If he truly thought the pair were spectacular, he could have picked a better precedent for them, since Smythe privately actually disliked Conacher and Jackson, although the public would not question the analogy. "I must say that for all the goals they got and all-star teams they were on," Smythe wrote in his memoirs, "Conacher and Jackson were never half as good players as they were thought to be. They wanted Joe [Primeau, their centre] to do all the work, and they'd score the goals, which they were pretty good at...I fought for years to keep Busher Jackson out of the Hall of Fame."

2. McCarthy attended four successive Flyers training camps, but in the end wound out his career playing Senior hockey in Boston and Nelson, B.C., before becoming the recreation director of Espanola, Ont. (a job he's held for forty years) and coaching amateur hockey.

3. Yet another version of this alleged recruitment of Tim Horton was offered a few years later by the *Toronto Star*'s Milt Dunnell, but in Dunnell's version the role played by Squib Walker, who by then was dead, was taken over personally by Conn Smythe.

Chapter 8—Missing in Action

1. Since 1982, NHL teams have been permitted to dress eighteen skaters and two goaltenders.

2. The Maple Leafs were shot through with mining fever. Mortson and Thomson were known as the "Gold Dust Twins," Barilko had his gold investments as well, as did Joe Primeau. Conn Smythe was ahead of everyone, having put money into gold in the mid-1920s with shares in Gold Hill Mining Co., and in the 1930s was a partner in Crossroads Gold Mines.

3. Although Tim Horton's former St. Mike's teammate Willie Marshall set one American league scoring record after another (records that still stand today), he could never quite break loose from the American league: his quest to

become a Leaf ended in 58/59 when the newly arrived
Punch Imlach dealt him away to get Gerry Ehman.

4. As noted in Chapter 5, quotes in articles by George Gross
appearing in Maple Leaf programs in 66/67 and 68/69
drifted between Tim Horton and George Armstrong. This
observation is made almost verbatim (with the exception of
the word "usually") by Armstrong in the 66/67 program.

Chapter 9—Life After Bill

1. Tim Horton was a teammate of Bill Ezinicki's in Pittsburgh
at the start of the 50/51 season when Toronto parked
Ezinicki and defenceman Vic Lynn with the Hornets for
thirteen and sixteen games respectively before trading
them to Boston. They also played together at the end of
Pittsburgh's championship 51/52 season, when Toronto
bought Ezinicki back from the Bruins to fill in for George
Armstrong, who had been called up by the Leafs.

2. Bastien immediately became the Hornets' business manager. He won the Calder Cup as coach of the Hornets in
1967, and served as general manager of the Pittsburgh
Penguins from 1977 until his death in 1983.

Chapter 10—Setback

1. Officially, Conn Smythe held the title of general manager.
King Clancy called Day Smythe's "aide-de-camp."

2. Actually, Tim only had Hap Day as his coach when he
played one regular season and one playoff game for the
Leafs in 49/50. Joe Primeau was his first true Leaf coach.
Day's influence on Tim was exerted as a manager.

3. Kennedy did make a thirty-game comeback in 56/57.

Chapter 11—Recovery

1. It's possible these particular shares actually belonged to
another George Armstrong, a business associate of
Smythe's.

2. When Tim was asked to pick an All Star team in 1969, he
stuck to this etiquette of eschewing players on his own
team. He put Sawchuk—from his Detroit days, he insisted—in goal, Bobby Orr and Doug Harvey on defence, Jean

Beliveau at centre, Gordie Howe on right wing and Bobby
Hull on left wing.

Chapter 12—Hustling

1. Until informed by this author, Mahovlich had no idea of
   the bonus arrangement St. Michael's College had struck
   with the Leafs based on his rookie season performance.

2. The *Telegram* was owned by John F. Bassett, one of the
   members of the "Silver Seven" hockey committee established by Conn Smythe when he retired as general manager in 1957. Bassett, hockey committee chairman Stafford
   Smythe and fellow committee member Harold Ballard
   acquired control of Maple Leaf Gardens Ltd. in 1961.
   Stafford became president, Ballard vice-president and
   Bassett chairman of the board.

3. The Hannigan Burger King had no connection with the
   Burger King franchise chain, which was founded in Florida
   in 1953.

Chapter 14—Turnaround

1. One of Clarence Campbell's first acts as league president
   was to introduce a no-fraternising rule. He didn't want the
   fans having any doubts that opponents were genuine enemies. Merely exchanging pleasantries with an opponent
   during a pregame warm-up could result in fines.

2. Tim Horton was merely upholding an old Maple Leaf tradition. Back in the 1930s, Charlie Conacher hung Ace
   Bailey by his feet out of a hotel window.

3. After retiring from the game in 1969, one of the business
   ventures Pilote eventually pursued was a Tim Horton's
   franchise.

Chapter 15—Wexford

1. The store was on the north side of Kingston Road, at
   Manderley. There's a small strip mall there now, anchored
   by a Becker's.

2. In 1990 Mister Donut was purchased by Dunkin' Donuts
   after a Canadian partnership of Kingsbridge Capital Group
   and Cara Operations (which owns Harvey's and Swiss

Chalet) failed to execute a hostile takeover of Dunkin' Donuts.

3. Charade may be mistaken about the specific date. February 21, 1965, is the day Ron Joyce purchased a Tim Hortons franchise in Hamilton, which is verified by papers in Joyce's possession. Either the two events shared the same date, or Charade is confusing the date of his first store opening with that of Joyce's beginning as a franchisee.

4. There was no one named Bruce MacDonald. One investor's last name was Bruce, the other's was MacDonald. An Ottawa businessman the author contacted named Bruce MacDonald and operating as Bruce MacDonald Ltd. noted that he had once received a notice of tax arrears intended for the soundalike partnership, and that the properties still carrying the Bruce MacDonald name today have gone through "at least three transmogrifications of ownership" and have nothing to do with the original partners. He has nothing to do with them, either.

5. When being interviewed for this book nearly twenty years after Tim Horton's death, Ed Siekierko paused in mid-reminiscence to ask his daughter Cathy, "Which player was that, the one with number 14?" Without missing a beat, she said, "Keon."

6. The Lawrence Avenue building no longer stands: the lot is the site of a new retail development called Wexford Centre. Colony Plaza carries on, with a realtor occupying the site of the world's first Tim Horton donut shop. It's only fitting that a few doors down from where the Tim Horton Drive-In once stood is the restaurant of John Anderson, the right-winger who played with the Leafs from 77/78 to 84/85, complete with a facsimile of the Leaf logo in the signage.

Chapter 16—A New Trick

1. Several hockey associates of Tim's became involved with the Tim Hortons chain, but only after his death. Dave Keon owned a Tim Hortons franchise in Nova Scotia from 1977 to 1982. Dick Trainor's son and daughter-in-law own a franchise in the Maritimes. Bob Baun operates franchises in the Toronto dormitory communities of Pickering and

Ajax. For a time, Tim's old St. Mike's teammate, Joe Primeau, Jr., was a member of an investment partnership that owned a Toronto franchise.

2. The donut venture's ownership wasn't actually incorporated as Tim Donut Ltd. until the following year. Confusion about the name of the chain persists. In the early years of Tim Donut Ltd., the franchises were called Tim Horton Donuts. The modern signage reads Tim Hortons, although a few new signs say Tim Horton's, and there are still franchises with the old Tim Horton Donuts signage. For consistency, this book employs Tim Hortons when discussing the chain, regardless of the era.

3. At the time Spencer Brown met him, George Sukornyk was actually secretary-treasurer of Harvey's Foods Ltd.—he became president in 1966. Sukornyk, a former oil company attorney, was a key figure, along with Richard Mauran, in both Harvey's and Swiss Chalet. Harvey's had just gone public in April, 1964, and Sukornyk was serving as the point man in its expansion efforts. The fact that a restaurant chain's product and service was more important than its name was emphasized by the Harvey's phenomenon. Rather than attempting to attract customers through affiliation with a celebrity, its founders had pulled a name out of thin air that they felt would sound friendly and inviting. After first trying "Humphrey's," they had settled on Harvey's.

Chapter 17—Tim and Ron

1. At some point early in the business's history, Tim Horton borrowed $10,000 from Bob Baun. This may have been that point.

2. As stated in the Introduction, Lori Horton's suit alleged that she had been taken advantage of by Joyce and improperly counselled by her lawyer, Jim Blaney, when she sold to Joyce, in December 1975, the half of Tim Donut she inherited from Tim upon his death in February 1974.

Chapter 18—Chain Reaction

1. Alan Eagleson was a lawyer in the office of Blaney Pasternak Smela and Watson when a group of Leaf players

who came to the team from the Marlies, including Bob
Baun, Carl Brewer and Bob Pulford, formed the Blue and
White investment venture with Jim Blaney and Eagleson.
(Herb Kearney of Hearn Pontiac, where Baun and Pulford
got into the leasing business, was also a member.) The
investment vehicle was an important ice-breaker for
Eagleson with the Leaf organisers of the players' association in 1967—he already knew some of them from his
school days. After Tim's death, Blaney Pasternak handled
the probate of his will, and Jim Blaney was recruited to give
Lori investment advice. He served as her lawyer when she
sold her half of the company to Ron Joyce in December
1975, and was a codefendant of Joyce in Lori's lawsuit.

2. The franchising industry as a whole was under siege in
   1969 and 1970, attracting the concerned attentions of leg-
   islators in the U.S. over the explosion of new ventures with
   few regulations to govern them. Among the celebrities
   being recruited to front franchise ventures that were floating public offerings were football greats Johnny Unitas and
   Joe Namath, ex-jockie Eddie Arcaro, boxing legend Rocky
   Graziano, and, from the show biz world, Tony Bennett,
   Johnny Carson and Minnie Pearl.

Chapter 19—The Future Considered

1. Pat Quinn would hang on for fifty-nine games before being
   picked up by Vancouver's new expansion club, the
   Canucks. Rick Ley would stay for another three seasons
   before jumping to the WHA. Jim Dorey would remain for
   another two and a half seasons before being traded to New
   York, where he decided to follow Ley to the WHA's New
   England Whalers. Mike Pelyk would remain a Leaf until
   1974, when he, too, switched to the WHA.

Chapter 20—"I'm a Tired Old Man"

1. Emile Francis's lattermost NHL seasons as a goaltender
   were with New York, although he spent far more time in
   the American league than in the National league in those
   years. Tim had played against Francis during his own
   American league years. In 50/51, for example, Francis produced the third-best goaltending average of the American

league (after Gil Mayer of Pittsburgh and Johnny Bower of Cleveland) while playing for the Cincinnati Mohawks, the short-lived franchise being coached by King Clancy. It's a coincidence that suggests Clancy, who had wanted Tim benched during his last season in Toronto, may have played a front-line role in dealing Tim to Francis.

2. Arnie Brown, Larry Brown and Mike Robitaille were traded to Detroit. DeMarco had to wait another year to crack the starting lineup. André Dupont played a handful of games and then went to St. Louis the following season before finding his way to the Broad Street Bullies of Philadelphia.

3. The share trust agreement was not activated by Ron Joyce after Tim Horton's death, although he was prepared to do so if Lori Horton did not agree to sell him her shares.

4. Like Gord Hannigan, Sawchuk had suffered through a bout of mononucleosis, enduring similar charges that he was simply lazy when he dropped out of the Bruins lineup in 56/57. Traded back to Detroit, who had shipped him to Boston in 1955, he rebuilt his career.

5. The inventory and valuation of Tim Horton's estate confirms that he carried no life insurance when he died, and that none of the family real estate was included, having been placed in Lori's name. Total valuation of the estate was $675,426.45. This included the $9,750 salvage value of the car in which he was killed, and $464,552 in "bonds, debentures, stocks and other securities," which represented his share of Tim Donut and Tim Horton Holdings.

Chapter 22—The End of the Road

1. Twenty years after the death of his wife, Ray Hannigan was ordained as a diocesan priest and moved to Montana.

2. There is still some confusion over who was or wasn't at the game that night. If Keon's memory is precise, then Tim had been expecting his wife to be there. Lori says Tim couldn't have been looking for her. "I wasn't at the game, and I hadn't planned to be. Tim's mother didn't want to go, and I didn't want to leave her alone." But Traci Horton, who was fourteen at the time, thinks her mother

did go to the game, and believes that Ethel Horton was no longer staying at the house. She remembers her mother and Gerry Horton making the telephone call to tell Ethel that Tim was dead.

3. Teri was Joyce's second wife. They later divorced.

Chapter 23—After Life

1. The author was unable to secure an accident report. Five years after an accident, a report is transferred by the Ontario Provincial Police to the provincial Ministry of Transport. The ministry's data-base on accident reports only reaches back ten years.

Index

There is no other position in sports quite like it: one that combines agility with aggression, nerves with knowledge.

A Breed Apart

Douglas Hunter

A Breed Apart explores the fascinating history of goaltending from the late nineteenth century, when players stopped pucks with minimal equipment and without ever dropping to the ice, to the modern era of goalie-as-gladiator. Along the way readers are introduced to the many changes in the game that have affected the goaltender's lot in life.

Goalies have always been truly a breed apart, and their demeanor and determination have created a bond that stretches across time. Breathtakingly illustrated with hundreds of photos, charts, drawings, illustrations, and memorabilia — this is truly a one-of-a-kind volume, celebrating a rare breed of athlete: the guardian of the gates in the world's fastest team sport.

Look for
A Breed Apart
in bookstores everywhere

**For more than a century, the goaltender
has been a focal point of hockey...**

"In giving Canadians Felix Batterinski, Roy MacGregor has shown them a part of themselves." — *Maclean's*

THE LAST SEASON

ROY MACGREGOR

Felix Batterinski enjoyed brief fame as a hockey "enforcer" with the Philadelphia Flyers. When he's cut from the team he tries for a second career as a playing coach with a Finnish club, but a controversial play spells the end of his come-back bid. Faced with his own obsolescence, Felix begins his personal descent into disillusion, despair, and ultimately a bizarre death.

"MacGregor's description of this rural Ontario family is reminiscent of William Faulkner's descriptions of rural Mississippi families — the sense of foreboding, the family members bound together by dark secrets, the mentally retarded relative, the clash of organized religion and the occult....Clearly then, *The Last Season* is much more than a sports book." — *The Globe and Mail*

Look for
The Last Season
in bookstores everywhere

"A compelling fable about violence, superstition, love and the shallowness of modern life." — *Maclean's*